Albert Z. Conner, Jr., with Chris Mackowski

SEIZING DESTINY

The Army of the Potomac's "Valley Forge"
and the Civil War Winter that Saved the Union

Savas Beatie
California

Library of Congress Cataloging-in-Publication Data

Conner Jr., Albert Z., 1943-
Seizing destiny : the Army of the Potomac's "Valley Forge" and the Civil War Winter that Saved the Union / Albert Z. Conner Jr. with Chris Mackowski.
pages cm
Includes bibliographical references and index.
ISBN 978-1-61121-156-6
1. United States. Army of the Potomac--History. 2. United States. Army of the Potomac—Military life. 3. Military morale—United States—History—19th century. 4. Desertion, Military—United States—History—19th century. 5. United States—History—Civil War, 1861-1865—Desertions. 6. Virginia—History—Civil War, 1861-1865—Campaigns. I. Mackowski, Chris. II. Title. III. Title: Army of the Potomac's "Valley Forge" and the Civil War Winter that Saved the Union.
E470.2.C715 2015
973.7'3—dc23
2013046363

First edition, first printing

SB

Published by
Savas Beatie LLC
989 Governor Drive, Suite 102
El Dorado Hills, CA 95762

Phone: 916-941-6896
(E-mail) sales@savasbeatie.com

Savas Beatie titles are available at special discounts for bulk purchases in the United States by corporations, institutions, and other organizations. For more details, please contact Special Sales, P.O. Box 4527, El Dorado Hills, CA 95762, or you may e-mail us at sales@savasbeatie.com, or visit our website at www.savasbeatie.com for additional information.

Proudly published, printed, and warehoused in the United States of America.

Dedications

To my wife, Jane—fully equal to the best of the women of the "Valley Forge"
— Al

In memory of my grandfathers, Capt. William D. Mackowski, Sr., and Cpl. James "Swingin' Jim" Cawley—citizen-soldiers, both, and the finest men I have ever known
— Chris

Jointly, we dedicate this book to

Rufus Robinson Dawes, Brevet Brigadier General, U. S. Volunteers.

Dawes correlated the 1778 Valley Forge in the Revolution with the 1863 "Valley Forge" the Union Army of the Potomac faced in Stafford County, Virginia when he wrote, "This winter is, indeed, the Valley Forge of the war." At least 1,000 other Federal soldiers made the same connection, but Dawes, more than any single individual, was the most perceptive. In retrospect, his 1890 memoirs, *Service with the Sixth Wisconsin Volunteers*, could stand as "Exhibit A" for this work's central thesis.

Rufus Dawes personified the extraordinarily difficult, but ultimately successful struggle to save the Union. He entered the war as a captain and company commander, rose to lieutenant colonel and regimental commander, and was breveted brigadier general. A postwar businessman and congressman, Dawes also fathered a future vice- president of the United States. On the shoulders of such citizen-soldiers in citizen- armies, the fate of the republic has always been secure.

May it always be so: E Pluribus Unum.

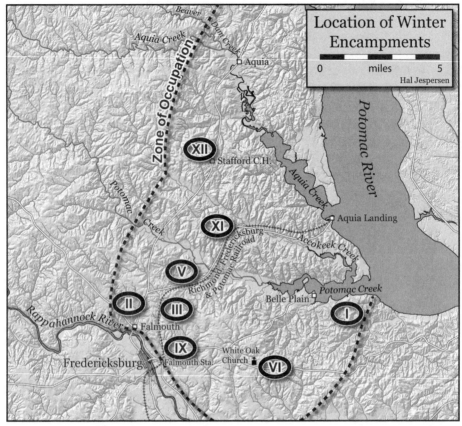

Location of Winter Encampments. With more than 100,000 men occupying the north bank of the river, the Federal presence took a strong toll on the area's resources. Most of the Army of the Potomac concentrated along the spur of the Richmond, Fredericksburg, and Potomac Railroad that ran from Falmouth to Aquia Creek. This facilitated the distribution of supplies. The I and VI Corps shifted eastward and the IX Corps was transferred out of the army, freeing up some physical space even as winter hardened.

Table of Contents

Table of Contents (continued)

~~

List of Maps

Acknowledgments

This book has three direct inspirations: Thomas Fleming's *Washington's Secret War: The Hidden History of Valley Forge*; Jane Hollenbeck Conner's *Lincoln in Stafford*; and the realization of the powerful and positive attraction of nationally significant "local" history. The first, Fleming's magnificent study, revealed the Revolutionary Valley Forge in deeper and broader contexts. The second revealing book uncovered fascinating political-military dimensions of President Lincoln's six wartime visits to Stafford County, and especially his interactions with the Army of the Potomac in April 1863. The third brought the realization that "this all happened right here!"[1] Additionally, Jane read and discussed every word of this study, while nursing a sick husband back to health.

Both authors have been connected in various capacities to the Fredericksburg and Spotsylvania National Military Park. This connection produced a better understanding of the linkage between America's Revolutionary War, Civil War, and modern times. Chief Historian John Hennessy inspires all connected with the park to learn more and gain new interpretive insights. John was particularly helpful in assisting this project by sharing his research materials and initial skepticism. Cultural resources manager and historian Eric Mink and historian Don Pfanz unfailingly helped with facts, sources, and access to the park's vast research collection—a true national treasure. Volunteers Jim Padgett, Jane Hollenbeck Conner, and the late George Wyant all assisted: Jane's contributions have been mentioned; Jim provided invaluable technical assistance and substantive information access without which this research simply couldn't have been finished in less than a decade; George proved an excellent sounding board on research revelations.

1   Thomas Fleming, *Washington's Secret War: The Hidden History of Valley Forge* (New York, NY, 2005), and Jane Hollenbeck Conner, *Lincoln in Stafford* (Stafford, VA, 2006).

Military historian Bob Poirier provided invaluable insights on the Army of the Potomac. Others also substantially aided this project. Charles Siegel of the Rappahannock Valley and Bull Run Civil War Round Tables made a pioneering driving tour brochure, *The Army of the Potomac in Stafford County*, featuring 39 Union Army historic sites. Stafford historian Jerrilynn Eby MacGregor generously provided information on horses and their care, and insights on Stafford's people. Lee Woolf, retired reporter for Fredericksburg's *The Free Lance-Star*, provided valuable communications insights. Erik F. Nelson, former president of the Central Virginia Battlefields Trust, supplied thoughtful suggestions and analytical comments.

We would also like to highlight a related public-private partnership of Stafford County Government and the Friends of Stafford Civil War Sites (FSCWS). They developed a Civil War Park that honors the "Valley Forge." FSCWS's leaders—Colonel Glenn Trimmer, USAF (retired), and D. P. Newton, director of the increasingly renowned White Oak Civil War Museum and Research Center—have documented many surviving Union and Confederate sites in eastern Stafford County. The park is located on a 40-plus acre site and contains pristine artifact fortifications; entrenchments; sections of "corduroyed" road; logistical positions; and campsites. FSCWS worked with Stafford County's Board of Supervisors and governmental staff. Stafford County supervisors Paul Milde and Harry Crisp and economic development and tourism officials Tim Baroody and Margaret Clay Moncure assisted the project. Virginia Army and Air National Guard engineer units—at once a personification of a citizen-army and a reconciled America—provided the critical clearing and construction of the park. Vulcan Materials, Inc., donated the basic road materials. All of the principal author's proceeds will be contributed to the Stafford Civil War Park, opened on April 27, 2013, the 150th anniversary of the army's departure for Chancellorsville.

Several other private acts of "Valley Forge" 1863 preservation and commemoration are noteworthy: Dr. Thomas Mountz purchased, preserved, and restored one of Stafford's few surviving Civil War redoubts. He generously shares it with historical groups and scholars. Norman and Lenetta Schools initiated the annual "'Yankees in Falmouth!' (and Confederates too!)," living-history event honoring all who served in Stafford. Union reenactors from the 2nd United States Sharpshooters, 7th Michigan Infantry and the United States Christian Commission; and Confederate reenactors from the 47th Virginia Infantry Regiment and Fluvanna Artillery pioneered this event. We also thank the Stafford County Historical Society, the Fredericksburg Civil War Round Table, and many other community groups for their enthusiastic support.

On a personal note, Chris would like to extend his thanks to historians Kristopher D. White and Daniel T. Davis; Dr. Pauline Hoffmann, dean of the

School of Journalism and Mass Communication at St. Bonaventure University; his colleagues at Emerging Civil War; Stevenson Ridge in Spotsylvania County; and most of all, his family, especially his children, Stephanie and Jackson, and his wife, Jennifer.

Hal Jespersen's maps enhanced the tale in a way that made the winter-bound events recounted here much clearer.

Finally, we extend our thanks to Theodore P. Savas, managing director of Savas Beatie LLC, who recognized the inherent value of this untold story and his unflagging passion for helping us share it. Thanks, too, to marketing director Sarah Keeney, Yvette Lewis, who keeps Ted in line, and the rest of the staff whose behind-the-scenes work in support our book has been invaluable.

Albert Z. Conner, Jr.
Stafford, Virginia

Chris Mackowski, Ph.D.
Spotsylvania, Virginia

Introduction

The Strategic Pause that Saved the Union

Gettysburg (July 1-3, 1863) is widely recognized by the public, and by many historians, as the turning point of America's Civil War in the Eastern Theater. Certainly it was the Union's first comprehensive victory after 27 months of fighting in that troubled theater. After Gettysburg, the Army of the Potomac would permanently seize—and the Confederates would lose—the strategic initiative for the remainder of the war, and General Lee's Confederate Army of Northern Virginia would never again mount a major offensive.

Equal in universal acceptance among historians, the Army of the Potomac reached its lowest point in morale and efficiency after January 24, 1863. Twenty months of defeat, beginning at First Manassas, including a "strategic draw" at Antietam, and capped by a brutal defeat at Fredericksburg and the humiliation of the "Mud March" had brought the Union's premier army—in terms of numbers, resources, and expectations—to the precipice of disintegration.[2]

This incongruity begs several critical questions. Precisely what happened to turn around the fortunes of the army in the six months between January and July? What happened to them and when, where, and how did such a dramatic turnaround take place? Why has history thus far neglected to comprehensively examine or explain this process?

We can be certain that it didn't turn around on the battlefield of Fredericksburg or the abortive effort to flank Lee's army through an impenetrable sea of Virginia mud in Stafford County. And it didn't happen on the mid- to late-June march from Stafford to Gettysburg. It surely didn't take place in the skirmishes and oppressive summer heat on the grueling 125-mile march with its accompanying major command change en route to Pennsylvania.

2   Here, "army" means Army of the Potomac, while "Army" refers to the entire Union Army.

That brings on additional questions. Was Major General George Gordon Meade, appointed on the march and arriving in Gettysburg in darkness after the first day's fighting, such a great field commander as to bring on instant victory? Where had the cavalry division, that had bought the army precious time and space on July 1, come from? Why did the army's infantry, cavalry, and artillery fight better—and without a master plan—than it had on previous fields? If something had been so lacking in the Army of the Potomac during the early part of the war, why was success now, suddenly, to be found in Adams County, Pennsylvania? Can an under-performing field army "fix itself" in battle?

Our goal study answers these questions in the largely untold story of an American field army's non-battle resurgence. We rely upon an in-depth and fresh analysis of primary official records, diaries, letters, newspaper accounts, and editorial letters. We also seek to balance these findings with existing secondary-source findings and analyses of war fighting, while interweaving important aspects of political, social, and cultural history.

Seizing Destiny tells that story of systematic and, frankly, inspired military leadership by the generals, other officers, and enlisted men of the Army of the Potomac that produced a non-battle turning point during a vital strategic pause in the war. By one estimate, that army spent only 45 days during its roughly 1,500-day existence in battle. Any reorganizations or revivals of spirit and military efficiency had to occur during a non-battle period.

This is a story that has only been summarized—where it has been examined at all—in broad-brush descriptive references to a "winter encampment." That term conjures images of a mature Boy Scout jamboree, with soldiers languishing about and waiting out the winter, pining for occasional mail from home. Some specialized and out-of-print histories have pointed in the direction of a more decisive and massive-scale event, but to date no historian has declared this to have been "the" or "a" major turning point in the war in the East. Instead, it is typically dismissed as having no greater significance than a glib, "Hooker improved the army's administration and morale" sort of statement.

Lost in such reveries are many and varied military activities that turned 200 square miles of Virginia's "sacred soil" into a virtual human ant-hill, alive with military operations and activities, soldiers and civilians, horses and mules, and machines of all types—all in perpetual motion. The army prepared to defend itself on a huge scale, and then take the offensive and achieve the final defeat of their thus-far victorious enemy. Amid vast spatial expanses, swirling events, and myriad activities in a harsh environment of frequently changing weather and minimal infrastructure, this complex story unfurled.

Although the battle histories of the Army of the Potomac and Army of Northern Virginia have been thoroughly studied and rightly told and retold, this work concentrates on the former's experiences in Stafford County and surrounding jurisdictions between the battles of Fredericksburg and Chancellorsville. Our focus is on the Army of the Potomac's citizen-soldiers during their darkest hour and describe their non-battle resurgence in morale and combat effectiveness. Overcoming bad leadership, rampant desertion, poor troop care, and devastating illness and disease, every aspect of the army's command and administration was challenged. During those months, through an extraordinary mass exercise of military leadership and unit and individual accountability, an amazing turnaround took place that carried the army to operational readiness and set it on the rugged road to ultimate victory. It is one of the greatest reversals of fortune witnessed by an American field army in our country's history. *Seizing Destiny* is a full account of that army's "Valley Forge" winter—experienced on a scale ten times the magnitude of its Revolutionary War predecessor. It documents the beginnings of America's ability to organize and fight in a complex and integrated, but still pre-modern, war.

It is appropriate at this juncture for us to further explain a couple key terms we use about this non-battle turning point during the Civil War's middle-years: strategic pause, and non-battle turning point.

The former, "strategic pause," is a term regrettably (but revealingly) missing from U. S. military historical terminology. A "strategic pause" is a vital concept that precisely describes the events in this study. A strategic pause is a protracted halt to fighting in a theater of operations (a geographic section of a theater of war) that is caused by changes in the political situation and/or attrition of the warring forces. It includes concurrent needs to rest, restore, resupply, and regroup forces in preparation for continued campaigns. It further includes limited combat operations with limited objectives. Operations generally feature a defense, active reconnaissance, security operations, raids, and flank naval patrolling, etc. A strategic pause provides opportunities to develop plans; revise tactics, procedures, and techniques; and make necessary personnel and organizational changes.[3]

A "non-battle turning point" is a time in a war during which fundamental changes take place and people and events begin to move in new and more successful directions not caused by or involving a specific battle or campaign.

The general historic period of this study is the seven-month period from November 1862 to June 1863—from the army's advance on Falmouth and Fredericksburg to its departure for Gettysburg. It includes the Fredericksburg battle

---

3 Ministry of Defense, Moscow, USSR, *Dictionary of Basic Military Terms*: "Strategic Pause (strategicheskaya pauza), (historical term): A more or less protracted halt to fighting in a theater of operations, arising as a result of political reasons, and due to attrition of the warring parties, and usually associated with the need to restore and regroup forces. A strategic pause did not mean complete cessation of troop reconnaissance and operational activity, and not infrequently included hostilities with a limited goal."

and "Mud March" in December 1862 and January 1863, respectively; and the Chancellorsville/Second Fredericksburg battles in May 1863 and their aftermath. Although these battles and maneuvers will not be discussed in detail, they are vitally important to a full understanding, and supplemental reading in the general study period is highly recommended.

The study's specific historic focal period spans January 25 to April 27, 1863—a 93-day period during which the primary, significant events and actions occurred. This period provides the direct evidence to make conclusions and the case for this work's thesis.

The more detailed thesis of *Seizing Destiny* is that the Army of the Potomac saved itself in a non-battle turning point during a strategic pause in the winter of 1863 in Stafford County and surrounding jurisdictions in Virginia. Operations included a large-scale area defense, reconnaissance and security actions, and combined-arms raids and skirmishes. Morale and fighting qualities were restored, first through dramatically improved troop care. Infantry, cavalry, artillery, and military intelligence were reorganized. Tactical logistics and ordnance systems were refined and improved. Operational plans, medical and veterinary systems, signal communications, and operational logistics techniques matured. The army reoriented its goal from "not losing" to achieving decisive battlefield and total victory. The army's units and soldiers improved teamwork, developed esprit, and bonded politically with the Lincoln administration in common purpose. They played the key political role in defeating the "Copperhead" antiwar movement in the North.

This period also set the conditions for dramatically improved battle performance at Chancellorsville and led directly to victory at Gettysburg. By building on this resurgence, the Army of the Potomac would achieve military victory in the Eastern Theater, and thus help achieve President Lincoln's strategic objectives to defeat the South militarily, restore the Union, and free the largest concentration of the South's slaves.

By saving itself the army rescued America's future. Because it is speculative, we do not discuss that future in detail. Nevertheless, its conceptualization is critical to understanding the "Valley Forge's" importance. It eliminated a short-term future during which an ineffective Army of the Potomac would not have defeated Lee's next invasion at Gettysburg. The long-term future envisions a postwar America that was severed, unreconciled, condemned to perpetual internal strife and territorial grabs, and unable to realize its twentieth-century potential on the world stage. The "Valley Forge" led to victory in the Civil War, which led at least indirectly to the twentieth or the "American Century."

The "Valley Forge" allusion deserves some passing comment. We assert the Army of the Potomac accomplished a "Valley Forge" of its own, analogous to what transpired at Valley Forge, Pennsylvania, in 1777-1778 during the American Revolution. Some may think that comparison a reach historically, and it would probably require another book to completely convince them. (We try to explain the Revolutionary linkage in Appendix B). More importantly, as described in the text, nearly 1,000 perceptive Union soldiers in 1863 Stafford, as well as a chronicler of the war, made that specific contemporary connection. If it is a reach, then, tell that to the soldiers who lived it. Although no historian has similarly concluded or studied in-depth these specific intra-battle periods, a number of historians have made reference to the linkage (see Chapter Thirteen). *Seizing Destiny*, then, is a new interpretation of these events.

But, beyond all else, it is a great American military-political story worthy of greater study in its own right because it illuminates a critical strategic period of the war. Although not precisely about government officials, generals, officers, or soldiers, they are its principal actors. Because it addresses generalship, leadership, organizational and operational effectiveness, and military character during the darkest of times, and how they all harnessed political and military will and national energies to produce decisive results, it has significant lessons for the ages.

We further argue that no subsequent event in American military history has been more significant or transpired at greater risk for more important stakes. Yet no story of such magnitude has been less understood, less discussed, or less remembered. The first of these three, as will be shown, is plainly attributable to the first person to write a history of the Army of the Potomac, which naturally influenced subsequent historians. The last of these is attributable to the fact that these events took place in a hostile space amid people with little motivation to embrace its history or memory. Hopefully, that can now be rectified with new understanding and more enlightened perspectives. As much as possible, the army's soldiers (through their official records, letters, and diaries) will tell you the story themselves. Much of what they say has not been previously published.

We believe in a concept of historical justice, in which particular events and participants are thoroughly analyzed, reported, discussed, remembered, and recognized. That most surely has not happened for the Army of the Potomac during the period of January 25 through April 27 in 1863 in Stafford, Virginia. Therefore, we unapologetically pronounce that this was indeed their "Valley Forge," and unequivocally assert their experiences comprised the 93 days that saved the Union. We earnestly invite others to delve into this material, state their interpretations, and to research its depth and width.

Chapter One

The Bedraggled Army

Dissatisfaction swept over the Army of the Potomac like a midwinter blizzard. Morale plummeted. Men grew bitter. Hope froze.

The chill was far worse than anything Rufus Dawes had seen back in Wisconsin, and it was only late December. The 24-year-old major of the 6th Wisconsin Infantry, born on the Fourth of July in 1838, had watched conditions worsen ever since the debacle in Fredericksburg earlier in the month. Major General Ambrose E. Burnside had led the army to its most lopsided defeat of the war thus far, and the ill winds began blustering shortly thereafter. The squall hit furiously, almost as soon as the army retreated across the Rappahannock River into Stafford County.

"The army seems to be overburdened with second rate men in high positions, from General Burnside down," Dawes wrote. "Common place and whisky are too much in power for the most hopeful future. This winter is, indeed, the Valley Forge of the war."[1]

Dawes, whose great-grandfather rode with Paul Revere on the famous midnight ride in 1775, wasn't the only Union soldier to allude to the Revolution. "As something of the spirit of '76 still continues to course through your veins, and as the heroic deeds of our ancestors still bring tinges of patriotic pride to your cheeks, whenever recounted, I will beg the liberty of giving you a short chapter clipped from this present age," wrote Nathaniel Weede Brown of the 133rd Pennsylvania Infantry in a letter from "Camp near Fredericksburg." As a "War Democrat," Brown had conflicted feelings. "This rebellion," he wrote, "concocted in iniquity

---

1   Rufus R. Dawes, *Service With the Sixth Wisconsin Volunteers* (Marietta, OH: E.R. Alderman & Sons, 1890), 115.

Major Rufus Dawes of the 6th Wisconsin Infantry may have been the first person to connect the winter of 1862-63 with the Continental Army's Valley Forge winter of 1777-78. LOC

and carried on for no other purpose than for the abolition of slavery and the aggrandizement of partisan spite, has cancelled the lives of thousands, destroyed property to the amount of millions." To Brown, "the butchery and pillage" had just begun. He praised his comrades' bravery in "fighting in a doubtful cause—for no one can tell what we are really fighting for."[2]

President Lincoln did what he could to bolster the army's flagging spirits. "Although you were not successful, the attempt was not an error, nor the failure other than an accident," he said, but his praise sounded faint. "The courage with which you, in an open field, maintained the contest against an entrenched foe, and the consummate skill and success with which you crossed and re-crossed the river, in face of the enemy, show that you possess all the qualities of a great army . . . . Condoling with the mourners for the dead, and sympathizing with the severely wounded, I congratulate you that the number of both is comparatively so small."[3] Small consolation it seemed.

Ironically, on a December 18th nearly 85 years earlier, Congress had offered praise to another bedraggled American army, calling for a national day of Thanksgiving. General George Washington, leading his ragamuffin band into Valley Forge, paused the army's march in recognition of the honor.

Now, in 1862, the Army of the Potomac headed into its own Valley Forge, although they had no way to know it. Quickly, though, it became a winter of

2   BV 74, part 11, FSNMP.

3   Abraham Lincoln, "Message to the Army of the Potomac," December 22, 1862 as collected by Don E. Fehrenbacher, ed., *Lincoln: Speeches and Writings 1859-1865* (New York, NY, 1985), 419.

discontent. Army morale plummeted precipitously in the days and weeks after Fredericksburg. Not even Christmas brightened spirits. "We are suffering very much with cold and hunger," wrote Lt. Albert P. Morrow of the 6th Pennsylvania Cavalry—known as Rush's Lancers—on December 25. "The roads are in such wretched condition that we can't transport supplies and we can't buy a single article in this miserable poverty-stricken country."[4]

Across the North, things looked just as bleak albeit for different reasons. "[The American people] have borne, silently and grimly, imbecility, treachery, failure, privation, the loss of friends and means, almost every suffering which can afflict a brave people," editorialized the venerable *Harper's Weekly*. "But they cannot be expected to suffer that such massacres as this at Fredericksburg shall be repeated."[5] Unseemly as it appeared, the Union was apparently losing.

"In fact the day that McClellan was removed from the command of this Army the death blow of our existence as the finest army that the World ever saw was struck," wrote Maj. Peter Keenan of the 8th Pennsylvania Cavalry. "What was once, under that great leader, the 'Grand Army of the Potomac' is today little better that a demoralized and disorganized mass of men."[6]

Twice offered command of the Army of the Potomac before he accepted it, Maj. Gen. Ambrose Burnside knew the job would be too much for him. He finally accepted so political rival Maj. Gen. Joseph Hooker wouldn't get it. Burnside was right, as he proved on the Fredericksburg battlefield in December and on the "Mud March" in January 1862, as well as with his inability to administratively manage the army entrusted to him. LOC

4   Eric J. Wittenberg, *Rush's Lancers: The Sixth Pennsylvania Cavalry in the Civil War* (Yardley, PA, 2007), 70.

5   *Harper's Weekly*, December 27, 1862.

6   BV 271, part 1, 204; FSNMP. Maj. Peter Keenan, letter, 1/30/63.

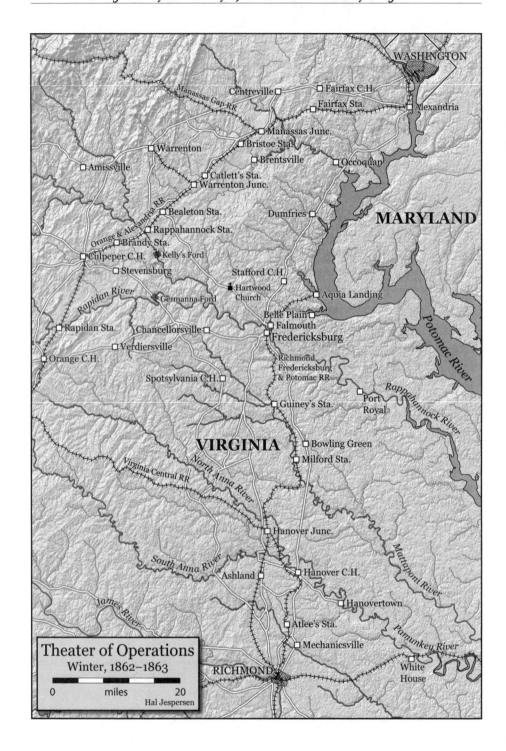

Theater of Operations
Winter, 1862–1863

0   miles   20

Hal Jespersen

Theater of Operations (Winter, 1862-1863). Fredericksburg sat midway between the opposing capitals. After the December 1862 battle there, followed by an aborted Federal maneuver known as the "Mud March," the armies went into winter quarters on opposite sides of the Rappahannock River. The Federal supply line depended on the railroad from Aquia Landing, where goods were shipped in from Washington along the Potomac River. The road network northward through Stafford Court House, Dumfries, and onward provided an extra communication and transportation link, although Federals worried about its vulnerability to Rebel raids. The Southern supply line reached up from Richmond along the Richmond, Fredericksburg, and Potomac Railroad, as well as along the Telegraph Road. Both armies stretched their influences west, although the Federal grip, in particular, became more tenuous the farther it reached beyond the main army, which concentrated along its roads and rail lines.

The army began to hemorrhage more than 200 deserters a day, which immediately sapped the army's strength and will. By month's end, the first 2,000 of at least 25,000 deserters had faded from the front. With Washington access tightly sealed at the Potomac River, most made it only as far as Alexandria, where they huddled around campfires with fellow "skedaddlers." Burnside began the unpleasant but necessary process of rounding them up. On December 24, he issued General Order No. 192. "In order to facilitate the return to duty of officers and men detained at the camp of convalescents, stragglers, &c., near Alexandria," Burnside ordered an assistant provost marshal general to "repair to Alexandria and take charge of all such officers and men in the various camps of that vicinity as are reported 'for duty in the field.'"[7] Each corps sent an officer and armed troops to round up stragglers and ship them to Stafford's Aquia Landing, where the returnees were systematically re-clothed, re-equipped and re-armed. Pointedly, Burnside used Regular Army troops to police up volunteer deserters and stragglers.

Although Burnside's provost marshal force and infantry and cavalry patrols arrested men lacking passes, substantial numbers of men still slipped through. The main desertion path flowed through Aquia-Dumfries-Occoquan. Soldiers walked or caught rides with sutlers, civilians, or fellow soldiers, some of whom brazenly stole wagons. In a common ruse, deserters posed as "telegraph repair work details."

The wounded had a far easier desertion route through the numerous Washington general hospitals. Once sufficiently recovered, a wounded soldier—frequently aided unwittingly by good-hearted U. S. Sanitary or Christian Commission workers or citizens—easily escaped.

---

7 Field-printed order, Author's Collection.

Maj. Gen. James Ewell Brown "Jeb" Stuart kept Federal occupiers on their toes by threatening supply lines and testing perimeters. LOC

For the non-wounded, desertion from the army's sector was best achieved by crossing the Potomac River into southern Maryland. Boats hired by deserters were almost certainly operated by men engaged in covert activities. The Confederate Signal Corps and Secret Service's "Secret Line" operated throughout the war with impunity from Aquia and Potomac Creeks in Stafford all the way up to Maryland. Rebel boatmen were happy to row as many Yankee deserters across the river as possible, probably demanding substantial fees.[8]

Compounding Union problems, Confederate Maj. Gen. James Ewell Brown (Jeb) Stuart, who gained lasting fame for his June and October 1862 cavalry raids around Federal armies, launched a large-scale operation to Dumfries and Fairfax Station on December 27-29, 1862. While of little direct threat to the Federal defenses, this revealed the Federal cavalry's continued haplessness. Stuart's ability to raid through and around Union defenses at will frustrated top Union commanders. It also exposed the vulnerability of Aquia Landing, the main Federal logistics center.[9]

By December 30, the army's Quartermaster General, Montgomery C. Meigs, had seen enough and let General Burnside know it. "In my position as Quartermaster-General much is seen that is seen from no other stand-point of the Army," wrote Meigs, who was bureaucratic, patriotic, strategically sound, and naive

---

8 "Secret Line" descriptions in: William A. Tidwell, James O. Hall, and David W. Gaddy, *Come Retribution: The Confederate Secret Service and the Assassination of Abraham Lincoln* (Baton Rouge, LA, 1988); William A. Tidwell, *April '65: Confederate Covert Action in the American Civil War* (Kent, OH, 1995).

9 Brigadier General Vincent J. Esposito, USA (Ret.), ed., *The West Point Atlas of the American Wars* (New York, NY, 1959), Volume I.

Quartermaster General Montgomery Meigs ascended to his position because the previous quartermaster general, Joseph E. Johnston, resigned to join the Confederate army. Meigs proved exceptionally brilliant and effective at his job, although the winter of 1862-63 would prove his greatest challenge to date. LOC

all at once. "I venture to say a few words to you which neither the newspapers nor, I fear, anybody in your army is likely to utter." Meigs warned the treasury was rapidly depleting, although prices, currency, and credit remained intact. He sensibly worried about horse feed prices: "Hay and oats, two essentials for an army, have risen," but it was "difficult to find men willing to undertake their delivery and the prices are higher than ever before." Meigs feared supplies would run short of fail altogether. "Should this happen," he noted, "your army would be obliged to retire, and the animals would be dispersed in search of food." After repeating his warning that the war's cost was leading to fiscal disaster, Meigs then turned to strategy. "General Halleck tells me that you believe your numbers are greater than the enemy's, and yet the army waits!" he wrote. "Upon the commander, to whom all the glory of success will attach, must rest the responsibility of deciding the plan of campaign."

General Meigs finally arrived at his main point: "Every day weakens your army," he wrote; "every good day lost is a golden opportunity in the career of our country—lost forever. Exhaustion steals over the country. Confidence and hope are dying."

"An Entire Army Struck with Melancholia"

That the Army of the Potomac could be so weakened spoke volumes about the spiritual gangrene that infected it. "An entire army struck with melancholy," said an officer with the 140th New York, writing to his hometown paper in Rochester.

"Enthusiasm all evaporated—the army of the Potomac never sings, never shouts, and I wish I could say, never swears."[10]

The army had been significantly bruised—and undoubtedly humiliated—by its loss at Fredericksburg in December, where the 135,000-man army suffered 12,653 casualties—1,284 killed, 9,600 wounded, 1,769 missing.[11] In the immediate aftermath, with Christmas calling soldiers home, the army was hemorrhaging another 25,000 men.

That still yielded about 97,647 after-battle effectives.[12] By the end of January 1863, army returns showed some 147,144 combat arms troops. Such a number suggests the army was able to replace and regenerate sufficient combat power drawing on the Washington defenses and on the states. It also suggests personnel accountings may have been padded, confused, or concealed.[13] At any rate, there were sufficient men on hand for an "army of quantity"—especially since that army only had to engage an enemy army roughly half its size.

Questions lingered, however, over whether the "army of quantity" was also an "army of quality." Two years of war had seen heavy attrition in most regiments, injuries, deaths and disease that had reduced them, on average, to about 400 men each out of an original 1,000. Many individual companies reported only 25-30 effectives. Units like the 110th Pennsylvania had so few effectives in early January 1863 that it consolidated its companies from eight to four. However, as most army units had fought at least five battles, the survivors at least had substantial combat experience.

The army was also well-armed. Fully 74 percent of its riflemen carried first-class rifles: .58 Caliber Springfield Model 1861 Rifle Muskets [46%]; .577/.58 Caliber

---

10 John J. Hennessy, "We Shall Make Richmond Howl: The Army of the Potomac on the Eve of Chancellorsville," in Gary W. Gallagher, ed., *Chancellorsville: The Battle and Its Aftermath* (Chapel Hill, NC, 1996), 1-35. The letter, signed "Adjutant," appeared in the February 3, 1863, Rochester *Democrat and American.*

11 Thomas L. Livermore, *Numbers and Losses,* 96.

12 An ordnance-based analysis by NPS Historian Eric J. Mink demonstrates that, as of December 31, 1862, the army reported 80,569 rifles in its line infantry inventory. Subtracting that rifle inventory number would yield a remaining 17,078 non-rifle-bearing soldiers, a reasonable number to accommodate line and staff officers, staff noncommissioned officers and military support functionaries (not including large numbers of hired and volunteer civilians).

13 A cautionary note: because of the dubious nature of some of the record-keeping, all unit/organization numbers used here or in any work are mere illustrative "snapshots" or estimates.

Enfield Rifle Muskets [25%]; or comparable weapons [3 %]. However, when cumulative losses necessitated the redistribution of soldiers within a regiment— such as the 110th Pennsylvania, mentioned earlier—it frequently led to bizarre weapons combinations because soldiers typically kept their original weapons. Such hodge-podges were an ordnance sergeant's nightmare. For example, Company A, 46th New York Infantry, had eight different weapons on hand in six different calibers.[14]

Along with their individual armaments, soldiers had the backing of a strong technical specialist infrastructure: administration; ordnance; quartermaster and commissary; signal; and railroad. The army was also backed by the North's extensive technological, economic, transportation, and industrial superiority.

However, crowing about the Union's material superiority as the end-all is woefully simplistic, just as it's equally simplistic to categorically dismiss the quantity and quality of Southern troops' weapons, equipment, and clothing. Antebellum Congresses had chronically ignored military preparedness, thereby creating institutionalized organization and mobilization issues. It wasn't that the United States was wholly unprepared for the Civil War; it was wholly unprepared to fight any war.

Historian Fred A. Shannon, writing in the 1920s, suggested that poor food and supply practices made military life unnecessarily difficult. Shannon emphasized a "shortage of supply, poor methods of distribution, inferior materials and workmanship, and [the soldier's] own improvidence—the latter being largely the result of poor army organization and worse discipline."[15]

Poor leadership and administration brought excessive desertions. Pervasive sickness, aided by indifferent camp sanitation and hygiene, brought unnecessary deaths. It took half the war —until roughly the period of this study—for supplies to reach acceptable levels, although the quality of those supplies never fully made muster. Shoes, overcoats, uniforms, and other equipment were all deficient in quality, and soldiers suffered. Understanding the men in this study depends on clearly recalling all of these dimensions.

---

14 BV 322, part 9, FSNMP. The 110th Pennsylvania consolidated its remaining companies as follows: A with K; B with D; E with F; and G with I. Additional weapons data provided by NPS/FSNMP historian Eric J. Mink, based upon returns of December 31, 1862.

15 Fred A. Shannon, "The Life of the Common Soldier in the Union Army, 1861-1865," Chapter 7 in Michael Barton and Larry M. Logue, ed., *The Civil War Soldier: A Historical Reader* (New York, NY, 2002). Original article published in *Mississippi Valley Historical Review* (March 1927), Vol. 13, No. 4, 465-482.

The Citizen-Soldiers of the United States

Despite its institutionalized deficiencies, the army possessed substantial war-fighting potential. What it most lacked was a winning combination of fighting leaders and troops who knew how to work together with their combat support and service support in the face of a formidable foe.

Naturally, the army's human element was crucial. It's surprising then, per Shannon, that the common soldier ranked "as the least-considered factor in the prosecution of the Civil War" by the government.[16]

The Army of the Potomac, like all Northern armies, consisted almost completely of citizen-soldiers. As such, the men embodied inherent contradictions: Citizens, as the nation's sovereigns, possessed the power to vote in or vote out their political leaders and vested them with authority to act in their names. They also influenced other voters (e.g., spouses, parents, relatives, friends, etc.). Paradoxically, once in service as soldiers, they became pawns of the political and military leaders to whom they had directly or indirectly granted power.

Early in its history, America had rejected large standing armies in peacetime, so the federal government maintained only a small professional, or "regular," force. Wartime armies, in contrast, consisted of citizen armies comprised of militia (standing reserve forces) and volunteers (forces assembled in emergencies). These elements, when cobbled together, became "the Armies of the United States" for that war. A remarkable aspect of U. S. mobilization was the institutionalized marginalization of professional soldiers, who generally had to resign in order to gain volunteer appointments.

Such disparate and untrained forces required time and experience to come together effectively, and leading such citizen-armies was far more art than science. A commander had to demonstrate sincere respect—even affection—for his subordinates, yet still be able to order them to risk life and limb with reasonably unquestioning attitudes. This delicate balance was best achieved when commanders of good character were trusted by their men with an implicit compact that soldiers' lives would not be unnecessarily risked or wasted. Gaining that trust required time. Until then, wartime officers typically began with comparatively little institutional respect from their subordinates. They had to earn the respect of their troops.

Unfortunately, the United States never had a reliable system for picking or training all of its officers to be those kinds of leaders, so results were uneven and

16 Ibid.

improved only gradually during war. Some historians have gone so far as to rate the process as a "little short of disastrous."[17] In the Civil War, direct or indirect political influence within a state was the surest path to selection and promotion for Union officers—hardly the best process to ensure an army of quality. "It is no less than madness to put an officer at the head of a great Army in the field because some ordinary uninstructed men call him smart," one officer groused.[18]

At their worst, citizen-officers were strutting popinjays and incompetents, appointed through political influence or nepotism, who conducted military affairs from the poorest foundations: arrogance, martinet tendencies, and insecurity. Their military skills and knowledge were suspect, and their decisions were frequently driven by expediency—to gain promotion or curry favor; avoid explanations and accountability; or dominate powerless subordinates. Officers of this ilk relished personal comforts and recreation, and ignored the well-being of their troops. Historically, these officers made military leadership in a democracy more difficult. The crucible of combat tended to clean up mistakes but, unfortunately, at substantial collateral costs. "Led on to slaughter and defeat by drunken and incompetent officers," mourned a Connecticut private, "[the 'soldier of today'] has become disheartened, discouraged, demoralized."[19] One bright spot was that these types of officers usually managed to weasel out of line duty, in a sense self-selecting themselves out.

At their best, though, citizen-officers listened and learned. They developed tactical skills and instincts and administrative abilities that grew steadily through study and practice. They led by example and with prudence, accomplishing assigned missions with minimal losses. They applied good sense and judgment to their commands, and they respected themselves and their soldiers. Their soldiers, in turn, grew to trust them.

Good officers recognized that the key to the army's effectiveness rested there, at the bottom of the military food chain, with the private soldiers—although few of those soldiers would have understood that fact, even were it explained to them.

---

17 See Shannon, for one.

18 Francis Augustín O'Reilly, *The Fredericksburg Campaign: Winter War on the Rappahannock* (Louisiana State University Press, 2003), 491. O'Reilly's original source was a December 19, 1862, letter by Gen. Erasmus Keyes, speculating on a rumored change of command.

19 Stephen Sears, *Chancellorsville* (Mariner Books, New York, 1996), 16. Author Sears quotes from a February 14, 1863, letter by Private Robert Goodyear of the 27th Connecticut Infantry to "Sarah," found in the archives of the U. S. Army Military History Institute in Carlisle, Pennsylvania.

Success ultimately depended on them. "All we want is competent leaders, men who are capable of the duties to be performed," said one Mainer, understanding the officer-infantry dynamic just fine, "and we will show the country that we are a mighty army, a conquering host."[20]

They were indeed quintessentially American soldiers. As the song goes, "they left their plows and workshops, their wives and children dear," and answered the nation's call to arms. They understood that, all questions of manhood and bravery being equal, their side would ultimately prevail because of its economic and industrial strength and its "righteous" cause, the preservation of the Union (emancipation as a cause still remained controversial within the army at the end of 1862). Confident soldiers, "knowing" their side would ultimately prevail, were correspondingly reluctant to risk, sacrifice, or waste themselves. It is universally correct that those who persevered over time did so out of loyalty to their comrades.[21]

They were also quintessentially American soldiers because they came from all over America: from Pennsylvania, New York, Massachusetts, New Jersey, Connecticut, Rhode Island, Vermont, New Hampshire, Maine, Ohio, Indiana, Illinois, Michigan, Wisconsin, Maryland, Delaware, and (West) Virginia.[22] A very small percentage had served in the antebellum Regular Army, but more than 98 percent of them were nonprofessionals.

If they did not vary greatly from general Union Army averages, the soldier of the Army of the Potomac was about five-feet, eight-inches tall and weighed about 143.5 pounds. Thirty percent had brown hair, 25% dark hair, and 24% light hair. About 45% were blue-eyed, 24% had gray eyes, and 31% were brown-eyed. Sixty percent had light complexions. Forty-eight percent were farmers; 24% mechanics (a conglomerate term for those skilled at hand work); 16% laborers; 5% businessmen; and 3% professionals (generally limited then to lawyers, physicians, clergymen and teachers). Another 4% worked in "miscellaneous occupations." Ages ranged from late-teens to late-20s, with a sprinkling of "older men" in their 30s and 40s. A few, mainly drummer boys and musicians, were as young as 11 or 12 years. A smaller

---

20 George Rable, *Fredericksburg! Fredericksburg!* (University of North Caroline Press, Chapel Hill, 2002), 400.

21 James M. McPherson, *For Cause and Comrades: Why Men Fought in the Civil War* (Oxford, UK, 1997).

22 West Virginia would not become a separate state until the summer of 1863.

number were over 50 years. A more rigorous statistical rundown puts their average enlistment age a little higher at 25.8 years, and with a median age of 23.9 years.[23]

They were, therefore, a typically American army of citizen-soldiers, predominantly "fair-haired," "blue-eyed," "20-something" farm boys caught up by history's tides in their nation's greatest trial. They toughed-out their long, brutal war because they did not want to let down their comrades, families and homefolks (at least those home folks that supported them).

Their average educational level is not known, but, from their writings it can be reasonably speculated to average about six to eight years (four months per year) of formal education. They were literate and could, with wide variation, express ideas and feelings in writing. That fluency had its downside, too. At least one surgeon , for example, lamented the "wholesale swearing among officers and men." "Why this profanity I cannot imagine," wondered Dr. Daniel M. Holt of the 121st New York. "It is like water spilt upon the ground; lost to all appearances, yet watering and vitalizing evil passions and ultimately developing a nature fraught with propensities to evil, as naturally as smoke curlingly ascends the zenith."[24]

Culturally, the soldiers were innocents set afoot in a strange land with strange sights, unprepared to face troubling realities.[25] Few had traveled more than 50 miles from their homes before the war. Most had never seen a black or "foreign" person. Their trip south was to a different world—Virginians were not the only Americans who considered their state "a country"—and these erstwhile Northern farmers, mechanics, businessmen and students carried their pride and prejudices to war. Most became more enlightened, but, in the end, it was not necessary for soldiers to love the people for whom they were fighting to free or protect; carrying out their missions with as little malice as possible was sufficient. Although some war-related hatred did naturally evolve, Union soldiers were not indoctrinated to hate. "You Yankees don't know how to hate," one Rebel blurted to a Pennsylvania cavalry officer during the post-battle truce in Fredericksburg in December of 1862. "You don't hate us near as much as we hate you."[26] For Confederates, whose home

23 Appendix in Ralph Newman and E. B. Long, *The Civil War: An American Iliad*, 2 vols. (Grosset & Dunlap, 1956), vol. 2.

24 James M. Greiner, Janet L. Coryell, and James R. Smither, eds., *A Surgeon's Civil War: The Letters & Diary of Daniel M. Holt, M.D.* (Kent, Ohio, 1994), 65.

25 Newman and Long, *The Civil War*, Vol. 2, 219, 221-222.

26 Catton, *Glory Road*, 69-70.

territory was being invaded and occupied, the war was by-and-large far more personal.

Three revealing examples demonstrate the experiential confusion faced by the average young soldier in the Army of the Potomac.

In the first instance, a Hoosier named "J. Hawk" issued a War Democrat diatribe on January 9. "This grand army is the worst demoralised it ever was," he complained. "The boys all say compromise and in fact they say they never come here to free the negroes. At best, I had thoughts of fighting for anything only the restoration of the union, which might have been done before this late hours if our Generals had not worked against each other for the sake of honor, the Generals wate for that Abolition President and War department."[27]

In the second instance, on January 12, Lt. George Breck of the 1st New York Light Artillery reported: "Small and large flocks of contrabands continue to pass our camp on their way to Washington. There is every variety of the African. Little negroes and big negroes, with all the intermediate sizes, from—we will not say how many days old, to four score years of age and upwards." Breck described a "comical sight" in ox carts, wagons and afoot. He revealed his cultural sources referring to "Uncle Toms and Aunt Dinahs, Sambos and Topsys—a complete representation of the colored population, of the 'poor slave,' passengers for Freedom—swarming northward in response, we suppose, to the emancipation edict." Alluding to those he witnessed, Breck described a second exodus to freedom, adding, "They go to Belle Plain or Aquia Creek, and are thence transported to Washington, all their traveling appurtenances being confiscated by government, through the quartermasters, at the place of landing." Somewhat sympathetically he added, "What provision is made for them on their arrival at the Federal Capital we do not know."[28]

In the third instance, a few months later, a young 8th Illinois Cavalry trooper, DeGrass L. Dean, thanked Mrs. J. F. Dickinson of King George County for her kindness to him while on picket duty at their farm (Hop Yard): "[T]hough an enemy to your Country, yet remember me as a friend." Lieutenant Henry H. Garrett, 8th Pennsylvania Cavalry, also thanked her for kindnesses during the previous (1862) Christmas period.[29]

---

27 http://www.rootsweb.com/~inhenry/letters1863.html (accessed on January 25, 2000).

28 Information on transiting slaves provided by John Hennessy from FSNMP files.

29 BV 120, FSNMP.

The Soldiers' Life

Amidst that sea of disparate experience and strange uncertainty, one thing that grounded the men and gave them context was the army's internal culture—a less quantifiable factor than the demographics that defined them. The soldiers adopted the views, language, practices, and attitudes of their units and fellow soldiers to a remarkable extent. As the war progressed, the ranks thinned, and the chances of survival declined, these internal cultural traits became even more pronounced. Individualism, far rarer than wished or believed, became rarer still in mid-war. Common ideas and attitudes ran through the camps as readily as dysentery. A Pennsylvania surgeon, in as good a position to know both as anyone, remarked on a typical example: "You have no idea how greatly the common soldiers are prejudiced against the negroes."[30] Even more universal was the contempt soldiers had for political meddlers in Washington and pessimistic naysayers on the homefront. The men circled wagons and banded together to withstand the onslaughts of the perceived uncaring outer-world, and their units became their world instead.

That homogeneity covered social views, as well. The army was insensitive and prejudiced concerning racial, ethnic, regional, denominational, class and other social issues—no doubt attitudes that carried over from the larger society. In particular, blacks and post-1840s Irish-Catholic and German immigrants were decidedly "outside the circle" of the relatively homogeneous mainstream population of Scots-Irish-Protestants and English-Protestants. With regard to race specifically, their views were awash in ignorance and flavored by minstrelsy and *Uncle Tom's Cabin*. They abounded with anti-foreign "know nothing-isms," prejudiced jokes and criticisms of "darkies," "niggers," "'ouirishmen'," "paddies," "papists," "Germans," and "Dutchmen." Despite their common sacrifice and suffering in nearly two years of war, such men were still looked down upon and referred to only by ethnic slurs. With specific regard to anti-black racial prejudice, the incessant use of "nigger—already a socially offensive term in many places in the North—was sometimes used for intentional effect, but sometimes born of complete ignorance. A simple manifestation of white societal dominance, it was a political code-word, especially among Democrats, that expressed political outrage about the Emancipation Proclamation and Lincoln's expanded war aims.

---

30 Paul Fatout, ed., *Letters of a Civil War Surgeon* (West Lafayette, Ind.: Purdue University Press, 1996), 53. The letters are those of Maj. William Watson of the 105th Pennsylvania Volunteer Infantry.

Despite other shortcomings, patriotism and faith provided the bedrock for most Northern soldiers. Patriotism remained evident even during this darkest of periods and among the most discontented men.[31] Faith, for the majority who professed it, followed suit. Biblically informed that man did not live by bread alone, faith relieved their suffering and strengthened their resolve. A substantial component of the army's morale derived from its extensive religious activities. Although no one this side of heaven could read men's hearts to discern sincerity from hypocrisy, ample evidence showed religion was alive in soldiers' lives. Ministers and religious workers flourished, and faith revivals blossomed. U. S. Christian Commission delegates and workers, American Bible and Tract Societies, and the U. S. Sanitary Commission personnel all provided substantial spiritual support.

During stable periods, with time for reflection, soldiers came to grips with their faith. Conversely, sedentary and isolated camp life also bred vices (e.g., drinking, gambling, and sexual dalliances). These realities curiously interacted: religious soldiers, repulsed by moral decay, were compelled toward church activities and religious expressions. Perceived sanctimoniousness sometimes drove secular men to drink and rebel.[32]

Naturally, there were different experiences. Soldiers from strong religious families generally maintained their faith. Others with no religious backgrounds at all, grasping for meaning in a long bloody war and hard life, found new solace in the gospels. Generational differences amongst the soldiers revealed significant traits. Those born before 1822—members of the "Transcendental Generation"—tended to be idealists, prone to deep spirituality and generally unable to compromise on principle, possessing "inner-driven passions." They almost always believed themselves "right," even when their views changed. Transcendentals were the driving forces in religion and literature of that era, and they influenced the other generations in close quarters. Those soldiers born after 1822—the "Gilded Generation," which made up most of the actual combatants— were more reactive, realistic, cynical, pragmatic, and non-idealistic. The third cohort, the "Progressive

---

31 Rable, *Fredericksburg! Fredericksburg!*, 400.

32 Recent scholarship has illuminated the war's spiritual aspects. See George Rable's *God's Almost Chosen People: A Religious History of America's Civil War* (Univ. of North Carolina Press, 2010) and Steven E. Woodworth's *While God Is Marching On: The Religious World of Civil War Soldiers* (Univ. Press of Kansas, 2003).

Generation"—those born after 1843—adapted to the carnage and became pragmatists for life.[33]

"Of one thing at least we may be confident," wrote Rev. A. M. Stewart, chaplain of the 102nd Pennsylvania Infantry: "the incoming period will be greater than its predecessor—fuller of stirring, important, and decisive events. Jesus is revolutionizing the globe, and each successive annual not only brings nearer, but with accelerated speed, His reign of peace and love."[34]

On the Hoof

There was also a significant non-human component of the army. Largely overlooked by historians were the army's 60,000-70,000 horses and mules, generically termed "animals." They provided all of the logistical "lift" and mobility for the vast force. They also represented a vast number of mouths to feed and hooves to shoe, and they produced tons of manure that needed to be disposed of. Unfortunately, unlike the men, we only have accounts about them, not by them. Nevertheless, these fellow actors in the drama were documented adequately and deserve analysis.

A 1911 study reflected that Civil War animals were the victims of general problems in organizing and training the Federal cavalry. They too paid an unpreparedness price—"a tremendous loss in horse-flesh"—especially during the war's first two years. Some 284,000 horses had been furnished to fewer than 60,000 Federal cavalrymen during the first two years of the war alone—an astounding four horses per man. The study blamed non-combat animal deaths on "ignorance of inspecting and purchasing officers, poor horsemanship by untrained men, control of tactical operations of cavalry by officers ignorant of its limit of endurance, the hardships inseparable from the great raids of the war, and . . . oftentimes gross inefficiency and ignorance on the part of responsible officers as to the care of horses in sickness and in health."[35]

33 William Strauss and Neil Howe, *Generations: The History of America's Future* (New York, NY, 1991).

34 Alexander Morrison Stewart, *Camp, March and Battlefield; or, Three and a Half with the Army of the Potomac* (Philadelphia: J.B. Rogers, 1865).

35 Captain Charles D. Rhodes, General Staff, U. S. A., "The Mounting and Remounting of the Federal Cavalry," in Francis Trevelyan Miller, ed., *The Photographic History of the Civil War*, 10 vols. (Castle Books, NY, 1957), Vol. 4, *The Cavalry*, 322-336.

Winter weather and constant use kept blacksmith shops working constantly to keep horses and mules sufficiently shod, but high demand taxed thin resources. LOC

The animal care system was incomplete during the "Valley Forge" winter, but it paid great dividends afterward.[36] Veterinary surgeons were added (on paper) beginning in March 1863, but they proved difficult to find and recruit in adequate numbers. Probably as an expedient, veterinary sergeants were added to company tables of organization about this time. The cavalry therefore depended on its own inadequate resources to maintain large numbers of animals.

The 1911 study continued: "The bane of the cavalry service of the Federal armies in the field was diseases of the feet. 'Hoof-rot,' 'grease-heal,' or the 'scratches' followed in the wake of days and nights spent in mud, rain, snow, and exposure to cold, and caused thousands of otherwise serviceable horses to become useless for the time being." Prior to these events, the army's remount replacement needs exceeded 1,000 a week.[37]

Mules, as recalled by Warren Lee Goss in 1890, had specific ties to the "Valley Forge" army. "I believe it was General Hooker who first used the mule as a pack animal in the Army of the Potomac," he wrote. The stoic creatures drew both Goss's admiration and consternation. Six normally pulled a wagon. Remarkably sturdy and hardworking in battle and on the march, their steadiness under fire was noteworthy. Alternatively, the mules' notorious "independence of thought and action" befuddled handlers and supply recipients. Goss wrote mules lacking feed

36 The crown jewel of the animal care system was a preparation, rehabilitation and remount depot at Giesboro Point, near Washington. It was completed in July 1863 at a cost of over $2 million and was capable of treating 30,000 animals.

37 Captain Charles D. Rhodes, General Staff, U. S. A., "The Mounting and Remounting of the Federal Cavalry," in Miller, ed., *The Photographic History of the Civil War*, vol. 4, *The Cavalry*, 322-336.

were known to eat "rubber blankets, rail fences, pontoon boats, shrubbery, or cow-hide boots, with a resignation worthy of praise." Despite such destructive eating habits, the mule was rated the most effective animal in dealing with Virginia's "miry clay" and mud. Goss added, "Not least among [the army's] martyrs and heroes was this unpretentious, plodding, never-flinching quadruped."[38]

Pack mules, as an innovation, initially left something to be desired. "I don't know who it was that during the war invented the pack mule system," Goss admitted. "The pack mule, when loaded with a cracker box on each side and a medley of camp kettles and intrenching tools on top, was, to express it mildly, grotesque. At times, when in an overloaded, top-heavy condition, I have known him to run his side load into a tree, and in this manner capsize with his load, and it was comical to see him lying on his back with a cracker box on each side, and his heels dangling dejectedly in the air, a picture of patience and dignity overthrown; and in his attitude looking like a huge grasshopper."[39] Other observers described mules divesting their pack loads by scraping split-rail fences until their loads tumbled. However comedic their appearance, mules suffered heavy losses: killed in battle; worked to death in interminable mud, sleet and snow; or killed by apathy, poor feeding and mishandling.

Despite their large size, equines were extremely fragile. Although they'd been long used by armies, horses were not naturally fitted for war. "In the wild, they travel in herds, moving and eating constantly," says historian Jerrilynn Eby MacGregor. "Their stomachs are quite small relative to the rest of their body size and they were 'designed' to spend most of their waking hours nibbling at grasses and other vegetation. Left on their own, they wouldn't normally have access to a large volume of food at any one time. Because they are grazers, most of their food is quite fresh. Vegetable matter that has died and molded would never be willingly consumed by a horse left to its own devices."[40]

Even in camp, horses had special risks. Confined horses in pens or stables drastically changed their eating patterns. Ideally, they received two large meals a day, along with hay to chew on, and their feed would be "fresh and free from mold spores, dust, or other contaminants." More aggressive horses, often at risk of their

---

38 Warren Lee Goss, "Carrier of Victory? The Army Mule," *Civil War Times Illustrated* (July 1962), Vol. 1, No. 4, 17-19. Derived from Warren Lee Goss, *Recollections of a Private: A Story of the Army of the Potomac* (Thomas Y. Crowell and Co., 1890).

39 Ibid.

40 Correspondence with Jerrilynn Eby MacGregor.

An army might move on its stomach, as the old saying goes, but it doesn't move at all without horses. Equines provided essential service for cavalry and artillery—not to mention basic transportation and communication services—and comprised a unique set of challenges for the quartermaster's department. LOC

own lives, would eat other animals' food. The army's animals were, like its men, highly susceptible to then-unknown bacterial and viral infections. Infections, especially among confined animals, could spread rapidly, even wildly.

Operational areas like Stafford imposed special tyrannies on animals. Mosquito-borne infections abounded in soggy, swampy areas. Fungus affected animals' skin, and such infections, often called "rain rot," were highly contagious and easily spread by shared saddles or saddle pads. Every part of the horse was susceptible, but especially backs and belly, making it impossible to put saddles on infected horses. Wet hooves were prone to fungal infections, most commonly "hoof-rot" and "thrush." Of particular concern was the "frog"—the soft, triangular-shaped wedge of tough flesh on the bottom of each hoof, which helps pump blood up from the animal's feet and legs. The deep crevice on each side of the frog, when constantly wet, was particularly vulnerable to fungal infections.

"Thrush," highly contagious, caused the frog to become so tender and inflamed that animals were immobilized.[41]

Animals had unique logistics requirements. Ensuring reliable horseshoe resupply necessitated mobile "traveling forges" traveling with company-level equestrian units in the cavalry, artillery, and quartermaster departments. Forges were amply equipped with a bellows, windpipe, air-back, sheet-iron fireplace back, fireplace, fulcrum and bellows-support pole, bellows hook, vise and coal box—all on two wheels. Accompanying limbers had tools such as chisels, hammers, tongs, approximately 200 pounds of horseshoes, and 50 pounds of nails. Well-made and well-applied horseshoes were absolutely essential, especially for animals worked on rough, stony terrain. In the wild, the hooves of unshod horses wore down naturally; at work, horses' feet experienced greater wear and tear. If worn down to nubs, the horses became unserviceable. Shoes, necessary for working horses, could further contribute to their demise. Expertise in shoeing was especially critical—a nail placed too near the hoof's quick could make an otherwise healthy animal lame. A shoe coming partially free could twist around and cause damage to an animal's other feet or legs. A lost front shoe needed to be replaced immediately or the remaining one had to be pulled, or risk lameness.[42]

Federal horse procurement should have been relatively simple given that approximately 4.7 million horses existed in 1860 in the North and West. However, as with manpower, no reliable mobilization system existed prior to the war to provide necessary animals. Initially, from April 1861 to July 1862, individual soldiers could provide horses that could be "rented" to the army at 50 cents per day (owners bore responsibility for replacements). After July 1862, the Federal government procured all animals. Unfortunately, that still involved states, mustering authorities, and individual regiments. Initial animal purchase amounted to $20,000,000 for 150,000 horses. Such volume resulted in fraudulent sales and other criminality.[43]

The months-long occupation of Stafford during the "Valley Forge" winter was especially harsh on animals. "In the months following the Union repulse at Fredericksburg," said one account, "Union cavalry horses suffered so extensively from lack of cover and forage that many animals ate each other's manes and tails

41 Ibid.

42 Captain Charles D. Rhodes, General Staff, U. S. A., "The Mounting and Remounting of the Federal Cavalry," in Miller, ed, *The Photographic History of the Civil War*, Vol. 4, *The Cavalry*, 322-336.

43 Ibid.

down to the flesh. Horses died on the picket lines by the scores."[44] Meigs had worried in December 1862 that the army might have to turn its animals loose to forage—a practice routinely exercised by cavalry units on extended picket/outpost duty and on raids and patrols. One horse-savvy witness during the winter noticed that the army's unserviceable horses were regularly turned loose to fend for themselves.

The Burden of the Wagon Train

The Army of the Potomac also had well-documented evolutions in its "man-animal-wagon" history. The army struggled for its entire existence to determine proper numbers of wagons for baggage, ammunition, and food trains. Lack of standardized loads created variances, which in turn led to logistics problems. Wagon allowance per regiment was a special concern. Meigs started with the Napoleonic standard of 12 wagons per 1,000 men—in other words, roughly a dozen wagons per regiment in 1861. Commanders, however, submitted requests ranging from 6 to 15 wagons per regiment. These basic numbers affected campaigns, tactics, and operations.[45]

Road conditions affected things even further. On good roads, four horses could pull a wagon laden with 2,800 pounds. A six-mule team on a macadamized road, meanwhile, could pull 4,000-4,500 pounds per wagon. In all cases, that included five-ten days' grain for the animals pulling the freight. Good roads, incidentally, could allow speeds of only 2 to 2½ miles per hour—the typical speed for infantry not on a forced march. Of course, good roads during the Civil War were a rarity, and in Stafford, in particular, they were seldom existent without "corduroying" (laying parallel logs across the roadbed).

Each wagon, of course, came with its own animal team. That meant every wagon train needed to carry adequate feed for those animals. Supply trains typically carried 12 pounds of grain per horse and 9-10 pounds per mule, plus 14 pounds of

---

44 John V. Barton, "The Procurement of Horses," *Civil War Times, Illustrated* (December 1967) Volume VI, No. 8, 16-24.

45 Edward Hagerman, *The American Civil War and the Origins of Modern Warfare: Ideas, Organization, and Field Command* (Indiana Univ. Press, 1992), provides important insights on mobility and sustainability. See also Chapter 2, "Tactical and Strategic Organization," and Chapter 3, "More Reorganization: The Army of the Potomac," and especially 44-46, 62-65, 70, and 73-74.

hay or fodder, or a total food weight of 26 pounds per horse and 23-24 pounds per mule. Each animal additionally required about 15 gallons of water a day.[46]

Actual reported numbers of the army's wagons and animals varied as widely as those of manpower. On the Peninsula, the army began with a standard of 45 wagons per 1,000 men and had 21,000-25,000 animals for about 5,000 wagons supporting about 110,000 men. These far exceeded Meigs' Napoleonic standards.

To alleviate the pressure, the army's chief quartermaster, Rufus Ingalls, looked to acquire more animals. By the end of October 1862—despite a severe hoof-and-mouth epidemic in the weeks after the battle of Antietam—he managed to acquire 3,911 baggage and supply wagons and 37,897 animals. Those additions brought the army to nearly 6,000 wagons—including, presumably, 1,000 ambulances—and 60,000 animals by the Fredericksburg campaign. This force was calculated capable of hauling ten days' supplies, and about half were allotted for subsistence for men and animals.

Fredericksburg and the subsequent "Mud March" operations in January took further tolls. By March 1863, the army's inventories fell to 53,000 horses and mules and 3,500 wagons. Reduction in wagons did have a positive effect, though, in that it freed more animals—as many as 22,000 mules—for use as pack animals, capable of carrying the equivalent of 1,800 wagons. This effectively raised the carrying capacity to 5,300 wagon-equivalents or 33 "wagons" per 1,000 men (regiments at this point were averaging 400 men; many were half that size).[47]

By Chancellorsville, Ingalls estimated that the army achieved a balance of some 20 wagons per 1,000 men, hauling seven days' worth of supplies. When it actually marched to Chancellorsville in April, the army had 4,300 wagons (30 per 1,000 men); 8,889 horses and 21,628 mules, and 216 pack mules (1 animal per 4 men).

To simply count beasts, however, overlooks a crucial fact: hauling an individual pack load is more difficult than hauling a wagon. In other words, the animals and their roles were not interchangeable. Readily re-supplying combat units closer to the scene of action, as appealing as that was, was trumped by difficulties managing long columns of independent-minded pack animals.[48]

Subsistence (and nourishment) requirements—whether in battle, on the march, or in camp—were equally elusive. A 1,600-pound horse drew about 70-75 percent

---

46 Ibid. Required water consumption amount from National Museum of Civil War Medicine.

47 Ibid.

48 Hennessy, "We Shall Make Richmond Howl."

of its necessary daily nourishment from the supplies carried by the train. The remainder—again per Napoleonic concepts—was to be foraged. But, again, what worked for Napoleon didn't necessarily work in America. Statistical analyses suggest that American conditions made foraging more difficult than it had been in Europe.[49] If the animals' efforts required more strenuous exertions, then they were only able to get about 60 percent of their basic nourishment. Mules drew a greater percentage of their nourishment from feed than horses—80-90 percent. As a result, a "hidden nutritional factor" resulted in high animal attrition. This nutritional deficit persisted through the Fredericksburg campaign and into the "Valley Forge" winter and led to animal losses. Subsistence improvements were enhanced by standardization—what historian Edward Hagerman terms "baggage reform," or the amount of baggage that moved with the army.

Despite its flaws, the army's logistical and transportation systems were improving by the winter of '62-'63, approaching a level where the entire army—then eight infantry corps with cavalry and artillery—could operate for ten days away from its logistics base. Much of that was due to improvements in railroad operations, which facilitated army resupply in static situations and during campaigns by advance stockpiling and managed movements. Railroad and complementary waterborne support, where operative, reduced dependence on inferior roads.[50]

Reckoning proper numbers of wagons and their effective coordination with road, rail, and steamboat resupply continued for the rest of the war. These macro-dimensions set the scene for increased army micro-focus on the individual soldier's carrying capacity for weapons, equipment, and supplies. The key was development of well-founded standard operating procedures that factored in experience and changing operational conditions. Where norms were developed, analyzed, and tested, they proved significant and set new standards.

"Interior Administration": A Concealed World of Sin

These were many of the things Meigs had fretted about when he wrote to Burnside in late December. "In my position as Quartermaster-General much is seen that is seen from no other stand-point of the Army," Meigs had written.

Ninety-six years later, writing with the benefit of hindsight, the faculty of the United States Military Academy saw many of the same things Meigs commented

49 Citing a 1960 *Military Affairs* 24 article by John G. Moore.

50 Hennessy, "We Shall Make Richmond Howl."

upon. The faculty examined the army's general military effectiveness at the end of Burnside's tenure—which would last less than a month after Meigs wrote to the congenial but befuddled commander. In an under-stated, professional, and telling historical judgment, the faculty wrote: "When Hooker had relieved Burnside after the disastrous Fredericksburg campaign, he found the Army of the Potomac in a low state of morale. Desertion was increasing, and the army's own interior administration—never too good—had deteriorated."[51]

The military-bureaucratic term "interior administration" conceals a world of sin. The army was as political a beast as anything in Washington, and the intrigue, subterfuge, and bickering that went on was at least as serious a threat to its survival as the Army of Northern Virginia. Poisonous and unproductive internal relations at every level of the army damned and delayed its progress as an effective field force.

Perhaps most significantly, the Army of the Potomac's "interior administration" was demonstrably inferior to that in Robert E. Lee's army, where mission-type orders, civil social discourse, personal interaction, common purpose and trust, and comradely feelings permeated. The Army of the Potomac, at the beginning of January 1863, had a long way to go to achieve a level of basic military teamwork and cooperation remotely worthy of the terms.

Official records, especially correspondence between generals and officers of this period, shed necessary light. Seemingly, no commander could issue an order to a subordinate without including a snide or sarcastic comment or a vacuous tutorial on performing the simplest task. Phrases like "send a good brigade" or "have it commanded by an energetic officer" belied a command in which insecurity shadowed and distrust permeated seemingly every command. Similarly, officers could not share problems with superiors without being concerned about rebuff or ridicule.

Analogous problems existed in the army's external relations with Washington authorities. The political atmosphere of the capital clouded the text of even the simplest written orders. Commanders felt second-guessed or judged by some higher authorities, politicians, or inquiry boards. The army's officer corps, infected with demonstrable careerists, political hobgoblins, opportunists, and dysfunctional factions (or perceived factions), could never presume loyalty from any quarter, above or below.

---

51 Esposito, *West Pont Atlas*, Map 84.

Fortunately, there were men of merit and conviction who negotiated these obstacles and rose to more responsible positions. They just needed the time to do it. In fact, that was the one thing this entire army required: more time.

With these aspects as background, we can now begin to unravel the chronology of the army and its men and animals in their 1863 "Valley Forge."

Chapter Two

The Old Year has Closed

President Abraham Lincoln's 1863 White House New Year's Day formally began at 11:00 a.m. Once the doors opened, the president spent three hours patiently greeting streams of visiting dignitaries, job-seekers, and strap-hangers. Midway through the afternoon, the exhausted chief executive quietly slipped away to join Secretary of State William Seward in the executive office to sign what would be the most significant—and controversial—order of his presidency: the Emancipation Proclamation. The day's hand-shaking had, not for the first time, rendered the president's writing hand weak and palsied, but he forced an "Abraham Lincoln"—his typical "A. Lincoln" apparently seemed insufficient. "I never in my life, felt more certain that I was doing right than I do in signing this paper," he said.[1]

But the signature on the proclamation would not suffice—not in and of itself, at least. For the Proclamation to do anything, military success was desperately needed. Federal armies needed to prevail and, in particular, the North's premier army, the Army of the Potomac, needed to defeat Robert E. Lee's Army of Northern Virginia. On this first afternoon in January, that goal still seemed unattainable. Not only had the Army of the Potomac suffered a humiliatingly lopsided defeat weeks earlier in Fredericksburg, but in the weeks since, conditions and morale in the army had deteriorated steadily. Dishearteningly, Lincoln had no one on hand who seemed capable of reversing the army's fortunes. The affable Burnside was in over his head. McClellan was gone—except in the minds and hearts of his loyalists—and Halleck, the alleged general-in-chief, was proving a failure. Asked to sort out Burnside's Rappahannock front problems—certainly a legitimate presidential expectation—Halleck could not

---

1 David Herbert Donald, *Lincoln* (Simon and Shuster, 1966), 402.

perform. Exasperated, Lincoln exclaimed, "Your military skill is useless to me, if you will not do this." But Halleck inexplicably lingered in office.[2]

Forty-five miles to the south, where that army was hunkered down in its Stafford camps, the new year brought wisps of hope. "The common wish of a Happy New Year, I have heard from a hundred lips to-day, wrote Capt. Frederick C. Winkler of the 26th Wisconsin Infantry, serving that day on special duty as the XI Corps' judge advocate. "If we were to regard the weather as an omen, it would promise good to Virginia, poor, war-beaten Virginia. This morning is clear and bright and genial, as if angels ruled the skies."[3]

Winkler rode to Hope Landing on Aquia Creek. On a high hill, he saw the creek as "an expansive sheet of water, smooth as a mirror in the sunshine," with a steamer and several sailing vessels upon it. He could see several miles of the Potomac River, as well, also busy with vessels. "The old year has closed, and the history of America, 1862, will form an eventful chapter," he reflected. "The chronicles of many families have their pages of sorrow, of deep and bitter grief, and the public records too will tell of subjects of regret, of occurrences that every patriot will deplore. Ah, yes, who would have thought a year ago that, at this time, things would be in the condition they are."[4]

Word of Lincoln's executive order reached the army later that afternoon. "President Abraham Lincoln issued his emancipation proclamation today!" exclaimed Sgt. John Frederic Holahan, 45th Pennsylvania Infantry. It took only a few days to pass before Holahan fathomed the greater meaning of Lincoln's actions. "The Emancipation of the negroes excites some comment throughout the army, but we are not half as wild over it as they are up North," he noted on January 4 after attending a joint church service with the 100th Pennsylvania and 36th Massachusetts Regiments. "Some think it is just what was wanted to give high moral tone to our warfare, and now that the blot of slavery has been wiped out, success must perch upon our shoulders."

Holahan predicted "rebel sympathizers" would see the edict as "the sum of iniquity and villainy, the robbery of our Southern brethren, [and] the inciting of an inferior race to rise up and murder their masters." Characterizing that as "weak logic," Holahan assessed the proclamation pragmatically: "many of us have grave doubts, not of the justice, but of the practical workings of this new feature added to our cause. We fear alienation of some staunch Union men in the South, and the moral effect on the

---

2 John F. Marszalek, *Commander of All Lincoln's Armies: A Life of General Henry W. Halleck* (Cambridge, MA, 2004), 164.

3 Letters of Frederick C. Winkler, http://www.russscott.com/~rscott/26thwis/ winklett. htm (Accessed November 20, 2009).

4 Ibid.

unanimity of the North necessary to furnish us arms and supplies to 'conquer the rebellion.'" Intra-army political divisions became more evident.[5]

By the 15th, news had begun to trickle in that suggested Holahan's fears were coming true. "The Proclamation of the President has thrown the Nation into a convulsion!" he wrote, adding, "The South is almost a unit against us, and many Copperheads [Peace Democrats] throughout the North are organizing to resist drafting, and some of the more deluded are arming to resist its enforcement . . . . No patriotic love of Union seems to live in the Copperhead heart!"[6]

Captain David Beem of the 14th Indiana wrote home from Falmouth on January 8, reflecting on the changes Lincoln's proclamation seemed to portend. "We are again fairly entering on a new year, and the time passes, oh! so rapidly," he mused. "It seems scarcely a fortnight since I left you, almost one year ago; but in a year how much has transpired of the greatest importance to the people of our country, and how much pleasure and happiness have been sacrificed by those who leave their homes to fight for their dearest rights." Beem naturally wanted peace, but "[s]till, I would not stand idly by with my hands folded in an hour of danger to my country, for the sake of any happiness short of Heaven. The greater the danger, the greater the necessity; and notwithstanding we have seen many dark clouds over our land, and met many severe reverses, yet I am not of that class who get frightened by apparent danger, and discouraged by failures." Perhaps buoyed by a new year, he asserted, "I am today disposed to believe that our cause is in a fair way to a successful termination, and believe that God looks with pleasure upon every man who is doing what he can in this great and good cause." He warned his wife to guard against the "great many around you who are enemies to the government and secretly rejoice at every failure to our arms. The consequence is, they constantly exaggerate every reverse, and say but little about our victories. They find fault with everything connected with the war, and they do all they can to discourage those who have friends in the Army. They forget that it was the South who commenced the war, and who would invade our own homes if we were not out fighting to keep them back."[7]

Patriotically, Capt. Beem spoke for many: "The question to be solved in this war is whether we shall have a great, good and free government, or one of tyranny and oppression. All who oppose this war and sympathize with the rebel cause, and there are

---

5   BV 92, part 1, FSNMP. Civil War Diary of John Frederic Holahan.

6   Ibid.

7   BV 117, part 4, FSNMP, letters of Captain David E. Beem, 14th Indiana Infantry, especially his January 8, 1863 letter, 34-37.

many at home who do so, are opposed to the best government the world ever saw, and deserve to be slaves, not free men." He offered advice to his home folks:

> Now, when you hear anyone denouncing the president & his policy, and declaring that the Emancipation proclamation will ruin the cause, and all that kind of thing, you may be assured that such a one is either disloyal, or very ignorant. No person is more opposed to war than I am; but when it becomes a necessity and is forced upon us by the enemies of Freedom, then I am for war, and as a means of putting down rebellion, I sanction everything that helps to effect it. I would burn and destroy every city in the south and emancipate every slave, if by doing so our cherished institutions could be preserved and handed to future generations.[8]

Demoralization still circled the soldiers, but their inherent patriotism was strong. They weren't just "in the service"; they were fighting for a cause.

Settling In

Despite the blush of the new year, the army had still not recovered from its bruising loss at Fredericksburg the previous December. "The old regiments have a good deal to complain of," wrote Surgeon J. Franklin Dyer of the 19th Massachusetts Infantry. "They do the greater part of the fighting and the hardest work and never have any favors shown them." As if that wasn't bad enough, Dyer noted the lingering effect of the army's McClellanites on the morale problems. "I hope we shall do something to shut their mouths," he added.[9]

Depending on their Fredericksburg battle perspectives, soldiers' morale varied widely. "It is possible that . . . I may fall a Sacrifice to my countries honour," admitted Hiram J. Snyder of the 50th Pennsylvania Infantry—a unit that hadn't seen much action. "I truly have been greatly blessed with health, since I have been in the army also shielded from harm in many a hard fought battle. I am somewhat tired of being a Soldier."

Those who might have been most apt to help the army's weariness and flagging spirits—the chaplains—seemed to be in very short supply. "We have but very few chaplains left in the army and I doubt whether those who remain are of any benefit to it," noted Col. John S. Crocker of the 93rd New York Infantry on Sunday, January 4.

---

8 Ibid.

9 Michael B. Chesson, ed., *J. Franklin Dyer, Journal of a Civil War Surgeon* (Lincoln, NE, 2003), 58-59.

"The day has been passed by the army as one of rest and recreation, scarcely of worship."[10]

Burnside tried to bolster morale on January 5 with a Grand Review. As they passed in review, members of Burnside's former command, the IX Corps, "gave him cheer after cheer that he might know that his own Corps had not lost confidence on account of our defeat," a member of the 45th Pennsylvania wrote.[11] Smiling, Burnside seemed pleased; otherwise, the effect of the review was hardly salutary. "Old Burnside wanted to see how many more men he had to kill off. He need not take so much pains as we will all die in a little while," wrote Byron Frost of the 140th New York. "They don't want to settle this war, they have not made money enough out of it yet."[12]

Otherwise, the army tried to settle into the new routine dictated by the expectation of winter encampment. "I am having my tent put up at General [O. O.] Howard's [2nd Division] headquarters today and shall move over [to Falmouth] tomorrow," wrote Dr. Dyer. "They have got a new mess kit and some supplies, and I shall get something fit to eat." Sick of bread and meat, the surgeon happily noted sutlers were being allowed back into camps.

Even that came with caveats, though. "Mention Stuart's name to one of our sutlers if you wish to see a man turn pale," wrote Lt. William Landon of the 14th Indiana. "[Stuart's] always 'wide awake' cavalry is a terror to ye military store-keepers of ye Army of ye Potomac. Our cavalry (like a colt's tail) is always in the rear, when these daring rebel horsemen make a 'raid.'"[13]

Such occupational hazards contributed to the price-gouging sutlers typically plied. "We pay big prices here for things to eat," reported Lieut. Elisha Hunt Rhodes of the 2nd Rhode Island Infantry. "Butter is 60 cents per lb. Cheese the same. Bread 25 cents per loaf. Soft crackers 30 cents per lb. Cookies (which children and soldiers love) 3 cents apiece. Today I found a small cod fish at 16 cents per lb. It tasted good."[14]

Rhodes, encamped with his regiment near Falmouth, had already climbed from private to company commander; he was about to oversee the unit's new work detail.

---

10 CHJHCF. Cites: "Letters of Col. John S. Crocker to his wife, 93rd NY, New York State Library."

11 BV 92, part 1, FSNMP; Civil War Diary of John Frederic Holahan.

12 CHJHCF. Cites: "Letters from Byron and Henry Frost, 140th NY, Private collection. Excerpts provided by Brian Bennett [from Byron Frost]."

13 Landon wrote under the pen name "Prock." His letters are quoted from *Indiana Magazine of History* (September 1937), Vol. 33, No. 3, 342.

14 Robert Hunt Rhodes, ed., *All For the Union: The Civil War Diary and Letters of Elisha Hunt Rhodes* (New York, NY, 1992), 87-88.

"But for our drills we should be unhappy in our laziness," he wrote. On January 5, the regiment marched to "Pig Point" at Pratt's Landing on Potomac Creek. The men had a fine view of the steamers and sailing vessels that constantly arrived with supplies for the army. The next day, they set to work building a road. "So the gallant Second is again shoveling Virginia," Rhodes said. It wasn't their first experience in road-building and Rhodes joked he was in training for a new occupation. "We are making what is known as a corduroy road," he explained. "That is, we lay down logs length-wise of the road and then lay other logs across. In fact it is a continuous bridge." For three days, they toiled past brooks and through mud- and water-filled holes before finally being relieved.[15]

Road building and camp building continued in an attempt to create the physical infrastructure necessary for accommodating the vast army that had settled into Stafford. An estimated 30,000 makeshift huts and tent shelters filled the interior of the army's perimeter defense. Many soldiers, lacking tents, sat up all night by fires. Others slept beneath blankets covered by falling snow.

A decade later, a veteran of the 107th New York Infantry spoke of those days "so often alluded to by our men as the Valley Forge of the 107th." Their "little isolated camp at Valley Forge" became a base for building corduroy roads and that "hard, wet, dirty work, and the exposure cost our regiment many lives . . . . But the exposure and hard work at [Camp] Valley Forge told upon the men and we buried twenty-two in a short space of time."[16]

Each evening, "Taps" was "taken up and repeated by bugle after bugle in camp after camp for miles over the country, each call being longer drawn out, fainter and sweeter than the last," said Lt. Sam Partridge of the 13th New York Infantry, who celebrated his twenty-fourth birthday on January 9 far from home and family. The bugle call, he said, echoed "a thousand times among these forests, reechoed by ravines and glens, and repeated over the hills and dales."[17] "In this dark motionless silence," he concluded, "the Great Army of the Potomac is at rest."[18]

Mud

With the defeat at Fredericksburg still fresh in his mind, and with the newly added—and incredibly intense—political pressure of the Emancipation Proclamation

---

15 Known today as Waugh's Point, located in King George County.

16 Newspaper report on the reunion (September 17, 1872) in the files of the FSNMP. George Farr, Chemung County Historical Society, provided pertinent materials on this regiment.

17 BV 146, FSNMP, Samuel Selden Partridge Papers, parts 28, 29.

18 Ibid, 29.

now weighing on him, Burnside hardly felt content to wait out the winter. "I am not disposed to go into winter quarters," an impatient Burnside announced to Washington.[19]

To add insult to injury, the rival Army of the Cumberland, commanded by Maj. Gen. William T. Rosecrans, had scored a bloody but hardly overwhelming victory in central Tennessee. "[H]ad there been a defeat instead, the nation could scarcely have lived." Lincoln later wrote to Rosecrans, inflating the victory's importance because it had been the only thing to yet give his Proclamation any bite whatsoever. Curiously at the time, though, the commander-in-chief was trying to reassure Burnside that political pressure should not force him and his army into action. "Be cautious, and do not understand that the Government is driving you," Lincoln said. Nonetheless, he kept Burnside on a short leash, and it took another week of dickering between them before Burnside settled on—and Lincoln and Halleck approved—the details of the next offensive.[20]

Finally, on January 20, Burnside set into motion a plan to cross upriver at Stafford's Bank's Ford and U. S. Ford and then strike at Lee's left flank and rear even as feints at and below Fredericksburg held the Confederate army in place. "You may depend on it that a great effort will be made to wipe out the stain of our late defeat at Fredericksburg," vowed surgeon Daniel M. Holt, reflecting the grit many Federals felt in their gut.[21]

The maneuver, a shallow envelopment, was conceptually sound, and at the outset, everything seemed fine. "The roads were in good order and the troops in fine spirits," said Elisha Hunt Rhodes. By sunset, though, everything began to unravel. General Lee had anticipated Burnside's move and placed George Pickett's and R. H. Anderson's divisions at the crossing sites, while Rebel cavalry screened upstream. And then the weather turned. Sudden warm weather and torrential rains slowed the movement of at least 120,000 men, 60,000 animals, 6,000 wagons and ambulances, and 400 guns.

The Federal army, boasting some of America's best-trained military engineers, had launched its operation with no appreciation of the soils conditions along the route of march. As the heavy rain cut through surface soils, it exposed bottomless clay and loam and created quagmires through which no nineteenth-century army could maneuver. By dawn, Rhodes reported, "the roads were impassable by reason of mud. Daylight showed a strange scene. Men, Horses, Artillery, pontoons, and wagons were stuck in the mud."

19 BV 133, FSNMP, Burnside letter, January 5, 1863.

20 Lincoln, *Collected Works*, 6: 46-48.

21 James M. Greiner, *A Surgeon's Civil War*, 65.

This sketch of the camp of the 16th Michigan Infantry depicts a typical arrangement of tents, huts, and varying makeshift chimneys. LOC

Soldiers worked to exhaustion and animals worked themselves quite literally to death in the endless, bottomless mire. "The mud was so deep that sixteen horses could not pull one gun," complained Rhodes. "The companies of men would take hold of a rope called a prolong and pull the gun out of the mire. It was hard on men and horses, but our boys did their duty as usual. Rations gave out and we became hungry," continued Rhodes, "but found after awhile some hard bread on the road. Many horses and mules were lost."

Quartermasters tried to send commissary trains to the rescue. "We loaded no wagon more than 1000 pounds, put ten mules to each load. They got part way and got set [in mud]—every wagon of them," wrote 13th New York quartermaster Sam Partridge. Though discounting the overburdened horses, he noted a new twist: "For the first time, I saw Cavalry made useful. Two thousand cavalry men each took fifty pounds of hard bread on his saddle, and that's the way we got rations over the road." Stafford's infernal mud ensnared and defeated Burnside's army more effectively than had Lee's army—and at less cost.

General Lee's veterans, quick to spot irony, taunted their Yankee foes with sneers, jeers and signs suggesting the army was too "stuck in the mud" to fight. Sarcasms and witticisms by Burnside's men also proliferated. "Stuck in mud" seemingly screamed from every diary page and letter. An unknown soldier of the 140th Pennsylvania pronounced the "Mud March's" simple epitaph: "[I]t swamped the whole army in mud."[22]

After two dispiriting days, Burnside called off the maneuver, but Mother Nature took no notice. By January 24, Robert Gould Shaw, a 2nd Massachusetts Infantry officer returned to the army from an Antietam wound, found his unit deeply dispirited by the unrelenting weather. "The corps had a very hard march down . . . . [I]t was raining hard here, and everyone was soaked through and through for three days," he wrote. "The artillery had to throw away their ammunition and the commissaries the rations, in order to get their wagons through the mud. As it was, many wagons were abandoned, and many mules were so hopelessly stuck in the mud, that they had to be left to end their days there."[23]

The Army of the Potomac had returned to the very place it had started from—geographically speaking, anyway. Mentally, it returned to a much darker place, at a much lower level of morale. Compounding the misery, Burnside had ordered units to destroy their camps and furniture, assuming that they were not returning; wiser heads prevailed in some units, and the order had been ignored. Those who complied returned to destroyed camps full of nothing.

"Before starting, Burnside issued an order in high flown terms—congratulating the army because they were about to meet the enemy again, proclaiming that now was the auspicious moment to strike the decisive blow," Sam Partridge recalled. "His will was good enough perhaps, but the sequel showed he was most woefully sucked in."

Elisha Hunt Rhodes saw it differently. "Of course Gen. Burnside is not to blame for the failure," he argued. "He could not control natural forces notwithstanding the views of certain newspapers who to seem to think he could. If the weather had continued good I think the move would have been a successful one. We can fight the Rebels but not mud."

---

22 Catton, *Glory Road*; BV 112, part 13, FSNMP, letters of an unknown soldier of the 140th Pennsylvania Infantry.

23 While the 2nd Massachusetts' "Valley Forge" was just beginning, the officer's personal destiny was being worked out in Washington and Boston, as Secretary of War Stanton and Massachusetts Governor John Andrew authorized and organized the first black volunteer regiment in the North, the new 54th Massachusetts Infantry. The captain's fate would be sealed at Stafford Court House in a few weeks. Robert Gould Shaw, scion of wealthy and privileged Bostonians, when he was offered a difficult military option. His father traveled to Stafford and, on February 3, offered Shaw the command of the new 54th Massachusetts. The younger Shaw struggled with his decision, but finally accepted by February 8. It meant leaving friends and apparent promotion opportunities behind and throwing in his lot with this new and rather risky enterprise. Russell Duncan, ed., *Blue-Eyed Child of Fortune: The Civil War Letters of Colonel Robert Gould Shaw* (Athens, GA, 1999), 279-280.

"Never in finer spirits"?

With Robert E. Lee's unmolested army still sitting on the far bank of the Rappahannock River, General Burnside had little room for any other maneuvers. Charged with defending Washington, he had to keep his army between Lee and the Northern capital. Burnside's men could do little but glower across the river at Confederates.

"The movement begun by Burnside was abandoned because of the impracticality of moving farther. What is now in store I do not know," wrote Ohio Col. J. C. Lee. "Our masters, the people, will not allow us to keep still, and, if we move forward and fail, they censure us." Lee lamented "so many difficulties in the way of winter campaigning in this or any other part of Virginia" and advocated resting the troops pending spring weather. "We can at least hold them here for the present if we cannot advance against them," he said. "The army here is strong and with anything like fair hope of success would do fine work, but men who have become dispirited cannot be induced to make so good a fight as when their hopes are full." Lee cursed "the army of croakers, fault-finders and gloomy prophets" at home that had "failed to comprehend the stupendous magnitude of the resistance the rebellion is able to present and does present." Unreasonable demands prevailed; he also blamed "semi-secessionism in the northern journals."[24]

"All reports stating the Army of the Potomac is demoralized and unwilling to again face the enemy are false," contended Surgeon William Watson of the 105th Pennsylvania Infantry. "The troops were never in finer spirits and more desirous of engaging the rebels. But I fear we have a long period of inactivity—as a winter campaign in this latitude of mud and rain is impracticable."[25]

Watson's optimistic assertion notwithstanding, the army's morale status was arguable. Most asserted it was adequate; hardly anyone asserted it was good. Many argued for or against "demoralization," using terms like "discouraged," "disheartened," "dispirited," and "heart-sick." Reports, letters, diaries, and memoirs confirmed the army had hit its nadir.

"The soldiers were discouraged," reported *Boston Journal* correspondent Charles Coffin. "They knew they had fought bravely but there had been mismanagement and inefficient generalship. Homesickness set in and became a disease."[26]

---

24 Lee family papers in BV 121, FSNMP.

25 Paul Fatout, ed., *Letters of a Civil War Surgeon* (West Lafayette, IN, 1996), 76-77. BV 112, part 13, FSNMP, letters of an unknown soldier of the 140th Pennsylvania Infantry.

26 Richard Wheeler, *Voices of the Civil War* (New York, NY, 1976), Chapter 14, "Lincoln Turns to Hooker," 242.

"All the surrounding forests had disappeared," a reporter explained, "built into huts, with chimneys of sticks and mud, or fagots [bundled wood] in the stone fireplaces constructed by the soldiers, who also built mud ovens and baked their beans and bread." LOC

So, too, did discontent with leadership—from Burnside all the way up. "Both officers and men do not hesitate to call the President a damned old imbecile fool and openly advocate an overthrow of the government in Washington," wrote Capt. Charles Bowers of the 32nd Massachusetts Infantry. "Governor Andrew, Senators Sumner & Wilson are called damn fools, damned rascals & damned liars, fanatics, abolitionists."

The weather, too, took another turn for the worse, echoing the frosty sentiments of the army. "The winter was severe, the snow deep," Coffin reported. Yet the weather was little different than that endured by the men from Philadelphia or Pittsburgh, and it didn't vary greatly from those in southern New York, Ohio, Indiana, Illinois, Michigan, or Wisconsin. New Englanders had all certainly seen worse.

"All the surrounding forests had disappeared," Coffin continued, "built into huts, with chimneys of sticks and mud, or fagots [bundled wood] in the stone fireplaces constructed by the soldiers, who also built mud ovens and baked their beans and bread."

Franklin J. Sauter of the 55th Ohio Infantry recounted the tough slog it took for his unit to get settled. Arriving after the Mud March, they were shuffled from place to place until, after a week, there were finally assigned a spot to settle in. "[T]he [camp] ground is laid of[f] in Stile. Four men are to [mess] together in one hut, 10 by 7 feet. Our men are still all to work building there huts," Sauter explained. After rain and snow on the 27th and 28th, he continued, "Detailed twelve men to help build us a hut. Have to carry our timber up a Steep hill. Verry hard work." Sauter and his comrades finished the following day.[27]

"These army cabins had a variety of style," recalled the historian of the 24th Michigan Infantry almost three decades later. "Some were dug out of a steep bank; others made of small logs. They were about eight by ten feet in size and five feet high, with shelter tents for roof and gable coverings. The hillsides," he continued, "furnished good fire-places, which were furnished with stone, and had mud and stick chimney. The spaces between the logs were plastered with mud which soon hardened.

Three to four comrades "cooked, ate, slept, and passed . . . time" in each structure, continued the historian for the Wolverine regiment. The soldiers fashioned rough floors and bedsteads from cracker boxes. Pine and cedar boughs became their mattresses, and bayonets stuck in the ground served as candle holders.

"There was much suffering for want of food and clothes, largely the fault of rascally government contractors and inspectors who were usually in collusion to force upon soldiers articles of shoddy make-up and material," explained the regimental history. "The shoes frequently had for soles scraps and shavings of leather, glued or pasted together, which went to pieces in one day's march in mud or rain. Their pantaloons and other clothing were soon in shreds or 'out all around,' because of shoddy material."[28]

Death and Sickness

"Death is upon our track, and almost every day sees its victim taken to the grave," worried a surgeon named Daniel M. Holt on January 2, 1863, from a "Camp in field near Fredericksburg, Va." Dr. Holt, attached to the 121st New York Infantry, continued: "Yesterday two, and to-day two more were consigned to their last resting place, and still the avenger presses harder and harder claiming as his victim the best and fairest of men. There are quite a number waiting at the river bank to be ferried over, and it makes my heart sad to think that I can in no way delay their passage."[29]

---

27 BV 198, part 2, FSNMP, Journal of Captain Franklin J. Sauter, Company B, 55th Ohio Infantry.

28 Orson Blair Curtis, *The History of the Twenty-fourth Michigan of the Iron Brigade (Known as the Detroit and Wayne County Regiment)* (Detroit, MI, 1891), Chapter VI, "Winter Headquarters at Belle Plain," 106-107.

29 Greiner, *A Surgeon's Civil War*, 63.

At least 3,500 soldiers died during the Army of the Potomac's "Valley Forge" winter. Soldiers were typically buried in small cemeteries. Eventually, they would be disinterred and moved to Fredericksburg National Cemetery. LOC

Holt was reflecting on a scene that was becoming all too familiar in the cold, overcrowded Federal camps. Death, now commonplace, took increasing tolls. Later, it would be estimated that at least 3,500 men would die in the "Valley Forge."

"One of the most affecting scenes of camp life was a funeral which occurred one wintry day," recalled Lieut. Jessie Bowman Young of the 84th Pennsylvania Infantry. "[A] burial party, formed of the company to which the dead soldier had belonged, with other comrades from the regiment, lovingly bore or followed his body to the grave that had been dug not far away . . . on a neighboring hill." They marched through snow and slush and stood respectfully by the open grave. They had no chaplain, so they stood silently until one spontaneously sang, "Rock of ages, cleft for me, Let me hide myself in thee." One after another, they joined in sorrowfully.[30]

Similar scenes took place seemingly everywhere in the camps. "We have been called upon to pay the last tribute of respect to various members of our Regiment," wrote a

---

30 Wheeler, *Voices of the Civil War*, Chapter 14, "Lincoln Turns to Hooker," 242-243. Wheeler does not specify a unit. NPS/CWSSS lists Jesse B. Young as second lieutenant, 84th Pennsylvania (M554, Roll 136).

member of the 15th New Jersey on January 9. "One particularly, a member of Co. F, last Monday morning rose in perfect health, and ere the sun had sunk to rest he was sleeping in the embrace of Death." The regiment also received notice from an Alexandria Hospital of the death of another soldier from Fredericksburg wounds—the fourth in their reduced company of hometown friends. He and a pair of colleagues—"L.A.V." and "Little Mack"—regularly wrote to *The Hunterdon Republican*, sadly ticking off the death- and sick-lists.

Death was not always unwelcome. On January 17, Alfred Davenport of the 5th New York Infantry, rejoiced in one unpopular officer's demise. Reflective of bad relations and poor morale, he stated, "I have been reading in the N.Y. papers lately eulogies of our late Captain Cartwright, but to set the record straight, as I see it, all hands were glad to hear of it."

Wounds, sickness, and disease haunted the men, too. Hospital populations ranged from 45,000 in the period after Fredericksburg down to between 4,000-7,000. The hardier types lived with war wounds and injuries. Weaker ones gained discharges "on surgeon's certificate" or for "general disability," and melted into civilian populations.

Soldiers damningly reported increased self-inflicted wounds: "two members of Company I, while on picket post, by some means discharged their pieces, wounding them both seriously—one has since had his right hand amputated and the other, one of the fingers of his right hand." These acts were "done on purpose, expecting by this means to get a discharge . . . . Such cowards should have their heads shaved and be drummed out of the service."

There were also legitimate accidents. Samuel Conrad of the 127th Pennsylvania Infantry, for instance, was injured when walking guard—he fell into a hole from which his comrades had extracted clay "to plaster their shanties." Exposure took its toll, too, as the Virginia winter hardened.

Generalship and Comradeship

Higher up the chain of command, Burnside's personal experience proved to be a microcosm of the Army of the Potomac's. The weather not only bedeviled him, it had made him a laughingstock. His organizational efforts had proven cumbersome and ineffectual. Most problematic of all, the plummeting morale festered as barely concealed political infighting.

Historian Stephen Taaffe has categorized the Army of the Potomac's corps commanders into four overlapping groups: McClellanites; those owing allegiance to the Lincoln Administration; opportunists; and those who rose on merit. Of those groups, the McClellanites constituted about fifty percent. Divided by such factions, the army's leadership became its own worst enemy. Lincoln, shrewd politician that he was, understood that, and he instinctively tried-out new combinations of men from the four

Edwin Forbes sketched a typical infantry soldier on guard: William J. Jackson, Sgt. Maj., 12th New York, on duty at Stoneman's Switch on Jan. 27, 1863. *LOC*

groups in hopes the illusive "correct-mix" might surface. Lincoln most wanted fighters who could produce victory through teamwork. The army needed to be apolitical and beyond abnormal careerism. Thus far, a solution had not emerged.[31]

The situation came to a head in late December, three weeks prior to the "Mud March." Generals John Newton and John Cochrane, using their political connections, paid a secret visit to Secretary of State Seward, a crony of Cochrane's, to express their concerns about Burnside's generalship. Seward took them directly to Lincoln, where they pressed their case for Burnside's removal. The "dispirited condition of the army

31 Taaffe, *Commanding the Army of the Potomac.*

was the want of confidence in the military capacity of Gen. Burnside," they contended."[32] By bypassing the army's chain of command, open revolt had made its way to the White House.

When Lincoln asked Burnside about the accusations, he refused to give up the informants, but Burnside uncovered their identities by simply checking the list of officers who'd been granted leave. Cochrane soon found himself shuffled out of the army, although the shrewd Newton somehow managed to survive. Another of Burnside's most vocal opponents, left wing commander Maj. Gen. William B. Franklin, also found himself without a job. The bitter Franklin pointed fingers at everyone above him. "[T]he administration intended that Burnside should move forward at any cost, and did not care how many lives were lost, or what good were done only so that there was a fight," he groused. "In other words it was determined to pander to the radical thirst for blood which has lately been so rife."[33]

Despite the purges, fractiousness continued within the army. Strife seemed eternal between officers of the combat arms (infantry, cavalry, artillery); the combat and combat support (intelligence, signals, engineers) elements; and the combat and service support (quartermaster, commissary, ordnance, railroad, steam boat) elements. Distinct divides existed between staff and line, echelons of command, and laterally between organizations and units of the same type. Confused Army-Navy relations exacerbated things even further.

Historically, generals and those aspiring to be generals solved such problems. Without "generalship"—directing, consolidating, motivating (reward and punishment), forcing cooperation, coordination, and integration of efforts, and leading by example— the army would continue to be consumed in internal frictions. Effective generals made the best of the internal realities. Poor ones exacerbated problems by creating, condoning or rewarding bad behavior. At troop levels, generals needed support from officers and soldiers and "comradeship"—working together in common cause and purpose.

The glue binding the army together was "pride." Soldiers needed self-pride and unit pride, branch pride, and army pride under the wider umbrella of patriotism. When that pride became divisive or destructive, it destroyed teamwork and cooperation. For example, on January 15th, William Wheeler of the 13th New York Battery expressed pride in himself, his unit, and his branch—and in doing so revealed how little he thought of other units and branches "I enjoy the artillery service very much; it is the only arm in

---

32 Congressional Committee on the Conduct of the War, *Report of the Congressional Committee on the Operations of the Army of the Potomac: Causes of its Inactions and Ill Success. Its Several Campaigns. Why McClellan was Removed. The Battle of Fredericksburg. The Removal of Burnside* (New York, 1863), 24.

33 Mark A. Snell, *From First to Last: The Life of Major General William B. Franklin* (New York, 2002), 163.

which intelligence is needed in every rank, and an officer of artillery has really a fine wide field for study," he wrote. "I have in my own section fine young sergeants and corporals, whom it is a pleasure to bring forward and perfect in the elements of our branch, and who fully answer the description which Victor Hugo gives of the sergeant of artillery, in the fifth volume of his Les Miserables: 'Of fair complexion, with very mild face, and the intelligent air peculiar to that predestined and formidable arm.'"[34]

Any pride was a beginning. Effective generals and senior officers could build on it and develop comradeship at every level. This required time, patience and good examples. General and senior officers on whom men had come to depend needed to avoid ill-timed, negative words—demons that, unfortunately, permeated this army.

The army's mood had been dour and morose during the period from Fredericksburg to the "Mud March." The army had not achieved necessary levels of generalship, comradeship, or mutual trust leading up to its "Valley Forge." All had turned from Burnside—except for the IX Corps—and began to face the prospects of the long, hard winter and a harder spring. Those looking ahead to expired service terms welcomed any day without a march into the enemy guns. For the rest, the future promised only uncertainty.

But faint glimmers of hope soon rose on the horizon.

34 CHJHCF. Cites, "Letters of William Wheeler of the Class of 1855, Y.C., N. P., N.D., 1875. Letter of 1/15/63, 379."

Chapter Three |

Go Forward and Give Us Victories

Joe Hooker hardly seemed like anyone's ideal model of a savior. With piercing blue eyes and a clean-shaven jaw, some soldiers considered Hooker "a very dashing" officer. Yet the hard-fighting reputation that had earned him the nickname "Fighting Joe" was apparently matched by a reputation for hard living and loose morals. The general, complained one officer, was "a man with no firm moral force."[1]

Hooker commanded the Army of the Potomac's Center Grand Division, but he owed his position to seniority and solid political clout, and not to General Burnside's good graces or friendship. The two men were military-political rivals who had little regard for one another. Burnside, who had declined two prior offers to command the army, finally accepted the third offer to lead it, at least in part, because he thought Hooker "manifestly unfit" for the job. Hooker, for his part, predicted that the new arrangement with Burnside at the head of the army would not last long. According to Maj. Gen. George G. Meade, "Hooker gave one or two hits at Burnside, and rather hinted it might not be very long yet before he was in command."[2]

His belief that the wrong man had been promoted was one Hooker took to the grave. "[Burnside's] administration was a blunder and worse than a blunder," Hooker complained about fifteen years after assuming command and less than a year and one-half before his death. "I question if he knew where to begin to make reforms and elevate his command at the end of his three months service [any more] than he did at the beginning." During those three months, Hooker continued, "the Army [of the Potomac] . . . never degenerated so rapidly . . . for not less than a third of Burnside's

---

1   John Haley, 17, ME, *The Rebel Yell & the Yankee Hurrah*, p.57; Walter H. Hebert, *Fighting Joe Hooker*, 167-8.

2   Couch in B&L 3:106; Meade, *Letters*, 1:332.

Relentlessly ambitious, Maj. Gen. Joseph Hooker maneuvered for attention and promotion throughout the early years of the war, yet he backed up his bluster with effective battlefield performances. *LOC*

army had disappeared from the field, and those that remained were conspiring to destroy the patriotism and devotion of those that remained."[3]

"[Burnside] needed but a few weeks more to finish the Army of the Potomac," Hooker lamented. "Its end was close at hand."[4]

The only thing that could save the army—indeed, save the Union itself—was a dictator who could make hard, unilateral decisions, Hooker told a newspaper reporter, certain his comments would circulate. It was "not for this, but in spite of it" that Lincoln called on him. On January 25, after the usual behind-the-scenes political jawboning, War Department General Order No. 20 announced the relief of major generals Burnside, Sumner, and Franklin from their duties and assigned Hooker to command of the army. That same day, general-in-chief Halleck, who had opposed Hooker's selection, icily advised Hooker the president desired an interview at the Executive Mansion "as early as possible." Halleck and Hooker had been contemporaries at West Point and in California. Their California history, in which Halleck had prosecuted Hooker in a court-martial, promised trouble.[5] Hooker had been acquitted, but their poisonous relationship lingered.

At forty-eight years old, Hooker had amassed an impressive military record despite significant obstacles. A Massachusetts native and grandson of a Revolutionary War officer, he had graduated from West Point in 1837. He rose to first lieutenant and achieved a distinguished record in the Mexican War, earning three brevet promotions

---

3   FSNMP, Hooker to Samuel Bates, June 29, 1878 letter, in Hooker Papers, 70-71.

4   Ibid.

5   *OR*, 25, Part II, 3. T. Harry Williams, *Lincoln and His Generals* (New York, NY, 1952), 210, 211. Marszalek, *Commander of All Lincoln's Armies*, 165-175.

through lieutenant colonel. By June 1849, he was an assistant adjutant general in the Pacific Division. California witnessed a severe career downturn for Hooker, though. After a prolonged leave of absence (1851-1853), he resigned in February 1853 to become a Sonoma farmer. Although apparently contented, a combination of personal and business calamities brought him down. In 1858, Hooker unsuccessfully attempted to rejoin the Army.[6]

Not until August of 1861, after the outbreak of civil war, did Hooker finally return. After heavy personal lobbying—and despite Lt. Gen. Winfield Scott's opposition—Hooker was commissioned brigadier general of volunteers (two places higher than another previously failed military careerist, U. S. Grant). Hooker fought well at Williamsburg and in the Peninsula where he commanded a III Corps division under Maj. Gen. Samuel Peter Heintzelman. Reportedly, a telegrapher, omitting a dash in a reporter's headline, accidentally bestowed Hooker's nom de guerre, "Fighting Joe."[7] While he disliked the nickname because he thought it made him sound rash, his men loved it because they felt it captured their fighting spirit. Hooker didn't limit his conflict to the battlefield. He also caused universal discord in relations with superiors and peers. Just that autumn, he had clashed with Burnside at Antietam and Fredericksburg—good reasons for Burnside's enmity.

Although warranted, a more complete biographic summary of Hooker is beyond this work's scope; however, a brief summarization of his character is necessary—for it was character (actually the lack of it) that ultimately sank Hooker's wartime fortunes. Historian Thomas P. Lowry provides a balanced perspective: "Hooker was a maze of internal contradictions. His virtues were numerous. He brought spirit, discipline, and sanitation to demoralized divisions, he had personal courage . . . . But, on the other hand, his acid tongue, his arrogance and high-handedness, manifested in part by drinking, gambling and womanizing, diminished his potential for greatness."[8]

Whatever his flaws—a question requiring continuous review and revision—army gossips believed he drank too much and kept a headquarters of questionable morality and virtue. He had certainly employed the worst kind of politics to manipulate and maneuver himself into this command. His many detractors intentionally found little good to say about Hooker's morals and are thus less than fully credible. Hooker's

---

6   Warner, *Generals in Blue*, 233-235.

7   As the story goes, the headline was supposed to say "Fighting—Joe Hooker," but the telegrapher didn't transmit the dash, so the headline appeared "Fighting Joe Hooker." Hooker lost his punctuation, but gained dash of another sort.

8   Thomas Lowry, M.D., *Sex in the Civil War: The Story the Soldiers Wouldn't Tell* (Mechanicsburg, PA., 1994) 145-149. Lowry reiterates Halleck's and Hooker's ominous prewar California history.

supporters were kinder, but with the same lack of complete credibility. There was a general consensus, however, that he was truly a fighter. Many therefore gave him the benefit of the doubt—but little more, at least to start.

Change in Command

"Burnside has been relieved at his own request, and Hooker put in his place," wrote Republican Congressman William Parker Cutler of Ohio, a Lincoln loyalist, on January 26. "Our Potomac army is so far a failure, and seems demoralized by the political influences that have been brought to bear upon it. All is confusion and doubt. The President is tripped up by his generals, who seem to have no heart in their work. God alone can guide us through this terrible time of doubt, uncertainty, treachery, imbecility, and infidelity."[9]

On that same day, from "Camp near Falmouth, Va.," Burnside issued General Order No. 9, relinquishing army command. He praised his soldiers' "courage, patience, and endurance" and generously exhorted them to support their new commander, whom he described as a "brave and skillful general who has long been identified with your organization."[10]

Simultaneously, Hooker issued General Order No. 1, also from "Camp near Falmouth, Va.," asserting awareness of his arduous duties and identifying with his soldiers, with whom he had "shared . . . the glories and reverses." Hooker added, "In the record of your achievements there is much to be proud of, and, with the blessing of God, we will contribute something to the renown of our arms and the success of our cause." He requested their "cheerful and zealous co-operation" and unqualified loyalty —things he had conspicuously denied others. Sympathy for Hooker would be easier—thrust as he was into leadership of a demoralized, beaten army—were it not for his (sadly typical) burst of bombast: "In equipment, intelligence, and valor the enemy is our inferior; let us never hesitate to give him battle whenever we can find him."[11]

For an army that had consistently failed to destroy enemy forces despite numerical, technological, and material superiority, Hooker's praise was retrospectively excessive. For an army that had suffered a long series of defeats and humiliations, Hooker's exhortations might have been more reserved. Hooker might particularly have been more temperate denigrating his more successful Rebel adversaries.

---

9 Rufus Dawes, *Service with the Sixth Wisconsin*, 118.

10 *OR*, 25, Part II, 5.

11 Ibid.

The new army commander finished his order by conveying "cordial good wishes" to the departing Gen. Burnside. Anyone aware of Hooker's relationship with Burnside and his previous behavior could legitimately question Hooker's sincerity. Those who had fought Lee's soldiers might also question his military judgment.

Captain Charles Francis Adams, Jr., of the 1st Massachusetts Cavalry, expressed a pessimistic view consistent with many at that point: "The Army of the Potomac . . . will fight yet, but they fight for defeat, just as a brave, bad rider will face a fence, but yet rides for a fall . . . . There is a great deal of croaking, no confidence, plenty of sickness, and desertion is the order of the day." Adams, the scion of two American presidents, traced this state to Fredericksburg, the "Mud March" and frequent command changes, adding revealingly, "McClellan alone has the confidence of this army."[12] Adams' words betrayed a larger truth: the Army of the Potomac still wrong-headedly longed for a new Napoleon to ride in on a white horse, magic plan in hand, and take them to victory.

A more balanced view soon came from Lt. Josiah Marshall Favill, 57th New York Infantry: "Since General Hooker assumed command, we have frequently seen him, and he appears to be looking after affairs. He is a fine appearing soldier, with a smooth shaven face, and, as a division commander, has been very successful. He is a high liver, has a reputation for gallantry, and keeps a good many society people about his headquarters. Anything, of course, is an improvement on Burnside and we all hope Hooker may prove a success." Addressing the lingering charge that McClellan was "killed-off" by the newspapers, Favill argued McClellan had "killed himself" by believing his overblown reputation.[13]

One of Hooker's first orders of business was his January 25 audience with the president. Importantly, part of their discussion focused on whether Hooker should command merely the Army of the Potomac or the entire Department of Washington and Upper Potomac. This offer, made freely by Lincoln in the beginning, was destined to haunt Hooker's command status five months' later. Despite the offer of bigger and more prestigious responsibilities, though, Hooker wisely recognized the army's revival would require all of his available time, skills, and energy.[14]

Less prudently, Hooker requested he report directly to the president and not through Halleck, a slight that certainly made Halleck an even greater bureaucratic enemy. Although somewhat justified by their earlier animosities, this request should have forced Lincoln to reconsider Halleck, Hooker, or both. Lacking clear replacement

---

12 Worthington C. Ford, ed., *A Cycle of Adams Letters, 1861-1865* (Boston, MA, 1920), Volume I, 241.

13 BV 196, part 1, FSNMP: Favill, *Diary of a Young Officer.*

14 Walter H. Hebert *Fighting Joe Hooker* (Indianapolis, IN, 1944).

candidates probably curtailed such presidential thoughts. Splitting vital command and control was equally risky. For example, the following day Gen. Heintzelman complained of ineffective ties between his Defenses of Washington and the Army of the Potomac. The Washington Defenses then stretched far beyond the capital—from Maryland (Monocacy to Annapolis to Piscataway Creek) and across the Potomac to Virginia ("Goose Creek, Aldie, the Bull Run Mountains, Cedar Run and the Occoquan"). Heintzelman, perhaps unaware of the Lincoln-Hooker interview, essentially made a case for unified command. Heintzelman's communiqué instead tilted Halleck's attention toward direct control of the Army of the Potomac by the War Department and making the Washington Defenses a separate military department. Heintzelman, a former superior of Hooker's in a seniority-driven Army, likely had his own agenda. Regardless, a clear relationship between the two commands was needed since the Defenses provided most of the combat service support, reinforcements and replacements for the army.[15]

By forcefully ordering Hooker and Halleck to cast-off their poisoned past, Lincoln might have made them cooperate—a critical step toward strategic success. Unfortunately, he missed the opportunity to bring them into line. As beneficial as it would have been to simplify and clarify the command situation, President Lincoln faced more basic concerns. Foremost on his mind were thoughts he'd articulated in a letter to Hooker on January 26—the same day Burnside and Hooker had swapped general orders. Lincoln's note was the most extraordinary political-military command message in American history:

Major-General Hooker:

General: I have placed you at the head of the Army of the Potomac. Of course I have done this upon what appears to me to be sufficient reasons, and I think it best for you to know that there are some things in regard to which I am not quite satisfied with you. I believe you to be a brave and skillful soldier, which, of course, I like. I also believe that you do not mix politics with your profession, in which you are right. You have confidence in yourself, which is a valuable, if not indispensable, quality. You are ambitious, which, within reasonable bounds, does good rather than harm; but I think that during General Burnside's command of the army you have taken counsel of your ambition, and thwarted him as much as you could, in which you did a great wrong to the country and to a most meritorious and honorable brother officer. I have heard, in such a way as to believe it, of your recently saying that both the Army and the Government needed a dictator. Of course, it was not for this, but in spite of it, that I have given you the Command. Only those generals who gain

15 Heintzelman's correspondence is in OR, 25, part II, 3-4. Williams, *Lincoln and His Generals.*

successes can set up dictators. What I now ask of you is military success, and I will risk the dictatorship. The Government will support you to the utmost of its ability, which is neither more nor less than it has done and will do for all commanders. I much fear that the spirit which you have aided to infuse into the army, of criticising their commander and withholding confidence from him, will now turn upon you. I shall assist you as far as I can to put it down. Neither you nor Napoleon, if he were alive again, could get any good out of an army while such a spirit prevails in it. And now beware of rashness. Beware of rashness, but with energy and sleepless vigilance go forward and give us victories.

Yours very truly, A. Lincoln[16]

Hooker rationalized Lincoln's letter as "fatherly," although there's reason to doubt his sincerity because it's likely he made his characterization to Lincolnite reporter Noah Brooks knowing it would make its way to the president's ears. The only possible objective interpretation of such a private, direct communication from a commander-in-chief to a principal subordinate was that Lincoln had serious reservations about Hooker; was under no illusions about his prior behavior; and was watching Hooker with a jaundiced, if hopeful eye. A saving grace was that Hooker took Lincoln's admonition as a challenge. That did the country greater good.[17]

Lincoln was not oblivious to the troubles Hooker faced in his new command. Speaking to a ladies' group around that time, the president said: "I have no word of encouragement for you. The military situation is far from bright, and the country knows it. The fact is, the people have not yet made up their minds that we are at war. They have not buckled down to the determination to fight this war through. They have got it into their heads that they are going to get out of this fix, somehow, by strategy . . . and no headway will be made while this state of mind lasts."[18]

As usual, Lincoln grasped reality and made his point plainly. The people, and by extension their citizen-army, acted as if victory would come to them. An underlying national weakness was exposed: the inability to endure a long, brutal, frustrating war. The days of endless optimism and bloated pseudo-patriotism had passed. After two years, it should have been brutally obvious to the remotely perceptive that this war

---

16 *OR*, 25, part II, 4.

17 Hebert, *Fighting Joe Hooker*. Hebert quotes reporter Noah Brooks, Lincoln's friend and author of *Washington in Lincoln's Time* (New York, NY, 1895), 45-56. Under the sarcastic chapter title (Chapter XI), "Administrative Joe," Hebert devotes only 13 pages to Hooker's "Valley Forge" command.

18 Wheeler, *Voices of the Civil War*, Chapter 14, "Lincoln Turns to Hooker," 249. The quote itself comes from reporter Charles Coffin, who covered the president's talk.

would last until military victory was achieved. Lee and company certainly weren't going to just give up, lie down, or "go away," and those gray-backed soldiers living just beyond the far bank of the Rappahannock would continue to fight well as long as nerve, sinew, and energy lasted. The main hope—and hope was all there was at that point—was that the Federals could improve sufficiently while the Confederates diminished.[19]

"General Hooker was much admired in the army," wrote Maj. Rufus Dawes of the 6th Wisconsin Infantry. "He was grand in his personal appearance and military bearing but his assignment to the command did not restore confidence in the country."[20]

Thus officially began one of America's most critical periods of military command. Lincoln, the commander-in-chief, personally held the high command together while supporting his appointee. Using considerable political powers of persuasion, guile, patience, and acumen, Lincoln reduced as much back-biting as possible and provided necessary political-military direction and resources for Hooker to repair his broken and dispirited army and prepare to defeat Lee—whose army still waited across the narrow Rappahannock.

"It was in view of those difficulties that I trembled at the task before me, in entering upon so important a command," Hooker said, sounding a note that almost seemed like humility.[21]

The Union Army's "Valley Forge" Officially Commences

Eighty-six years later, after intensively studying Lee's army for half that time, Dr. Douglas Southall Freeman reduced all military leadership to three components: "know your stuff; be a man; look after your men."[22] On Freeman's first point, Joseph Hooker assuredly—if somewhat surprisingly to some observers—knew his stuff: how to command, administer and plan. Freeman's second point meant exercising good character and judgment while commanding. "Fighting Joe" demonstrably failed in

---

19 Ibid.

20 Dawes, *Service with the Sixth Wisconsin Volunteers*, 118.

21 FSNMP, Hooker to Samuel Bates, June 29, 1878 letter, in Hooker Papers, 70-71.

22 The sequencing in Freeman's quote has varied. A 2007 *Parameters* (U. S. Army War College) article by Richard Swain relates: "Douglas Southall Freeman... phrased the same thoughts more informally. 'Know your stuff. Be a man. Look after your men.'[*] 'Know your stuff' is about competence. It involves both training and education, the former involving mastery of practical skills and the latter development of intellect so these skills can be applied in proper order in the endless series of new challenges and unique contexts a military officer will confront as he or she progresses through a military career." (* cites: Douglas Southall Freeman, Chapter 15, "Leadership; Lecture of May 11, 1949," Stuart W. Smith, ed., *Douglas Southall Freeman on Leadership*. Newport, R.I., 1990, 205-14.)

judgment, character, and prudence yet, aided by his patriotism and professionalism (and that of subordinates) he proved "man enough" for this job. It was Freeman's third point, looking after your men, where Hooker distinguished himself most.

Immediately upon taking command, Hooker rapidly and wisely addressed gaping shortfalls in his soldiers' material and physical care and comfort. Rations were increased and vastly diversified. Fresh meat and vegetables suddenly appeared everywhere in abundance; soft bread from newly constructed field bakeries replaced hard-tack; mail and packages from home were expedited; and the U. S. Sanitary and Christian Commissions were encouraged to spread their supplies and spiritual and physical nourishment. Hooker even tried, though with less success, to get his troops paid on a more regular and timely basis.

Hooker's worst problem remained the massive desertions. They had to be quickly contained for the army's survival. On Hooker's first day in command, he was informed that some 85,000 soldiers (3,000 officers and 82,000 enlisted men) were unaccounted for in his army. These numbers included those lost though desertion, absence- without-leave and in Washington hospitals. They may have also included some of the sick in Stafford hospitals. In total, the absences comprised anywhere from 58-62 percent of the army at that point.

Initially, Burnside's "grand divisions" lingered: two army corps grouped together with artillery and cavalry to form the Right, Center, and Left wings of the army. Sumner turned over command of the Right Grand Division to Maj. Gen. Darius Nash Couch, accurately pronounced as "gallant and able." Sumner's soldierly loyalty to his superiors had been uniquely solid. His headquarters flag, flown at Fort Sumter and carried with distinction afterward, including at his Stafford headquarters ("Phillips House" and "Lacy House"), was struck for the last time. Its torn pieces were sent to Army comrades.[23] Meade replaced Hooker as commanding general of the Center Grand Division. Franklin was temporarily replaced by Maj. Gen. William F. "Baldy" Smith as commander of the Left Grand Division. Major General Franz Sigel commanded the Grand Reserve Division.

On January 29, Hooker's General Order No. 2 announced his new staff of sixteen: Maj. Gen. Daniel Adams Butterfield (chief of staff); Brig. Gen. Seth Williams (assistant adjutant general—AAG); Lt. Col. Joseph Dickinson (AAG); Brig. Gen. James A. Hardie (judge advocate general); Brig. Gen. Henry J. Hunt (chief of artillery); Brig. Gen. Marsena R. Patrick (provost marshal general); Col. Rufus Ingalls (chief quartermaster or

---

23 Warner, *Generals in Blue*, 489-490. A. Conner's collection includes a May 7, 1863, U. S. Military Telegraph telegram transmitting a piece of the flag and relating its provenance to Capt. George C. Morton, 5th New York Cavalry, commanding the escort for Maj. Gen. Heintzelman in the Washington Defenses.

Joseph Hooker chose Brig. Gen. Daniel Butterfield as his chief of staff. It proved to be one of Hooker's shrewdest command decisions. Butterfield served effectively in that capacity, but his style and political allegiances made him widely unpopular in many circles of the army. LOC

CQM); Lt. Col. F. Myers (deputy CQM); Col. H. F. Clarke (chief commissary); Surgeon Jonathan Letterman (medical director); Capt. Samuel T. Cushing (chief signal officer); Lt. D. W. Flagler (chief ordnance officer); and four aides-de-camp: Maj. William H. Lawrence, Capt. William L. Candler, Capt. Alexander Moore, and Capt. Harry Russell. Many, including Butterfield, Williams, Hunt, Patrick, Ingalls and Letterman were outstanding officers in their respective specialties.[24]

Butterfield's selection as Hooker's chief of staff was most important, as "Little Dan" brought disciplined order and operational and troop awareness to army headquarters. Aged 31 years, Butterfield was the son of John Butterfield of the Overland Mail Company. Prior to the war, he had superintended the eastern division of the American Express Company—a business background that gave him a "genius for organization and the promotion of big enterprises."[25]

Butterfield's rapid military rise from first sergeant to major general by November 29, 1862, meant he had served at all command levels through corps. Wounded as a brigade commander at Gaines's Mill—an action for which he later received the Medal of Honor—he returned by Second Manassas to command his brigade. He rapidly succeeded to division command (October 1862) and corps command (November 1862). Butterfield commanded the V Corps at Fredericksburg and in the "Mud March."

Historian Stephen Taaffe summarizes Butterfield: "Although he was efficient and energetic in his new duties, many officers resented his imperious manner, which was all

24 OR, 25, part II, 6.

25 Hebert, *Fighting Joe Hooker*, Chapter XII, 171-172.

the more galling to some because he had so little prewar military experience."[26] Imperiousness, arrogance, and sarcasm in Butterfield were somewhat understandable as he brought to the army the alien style and culture of "big business." Criticism of a lack of "prewar" experience seems thinner. Butterfield had as much relevant wartime command experience as any of his critics, and his meteoric rise was wholly merited. Butterfield simply wasn't a West Pointer or of "the Old Army's" erstwhile lieutenants and captains now commanding corps and armies. Butterfield's real weakness, rather, was that he shared some of Hooker's worst traits and thus provided no counter-balance to his commander. Still, the two worked effectively together.

Relations were less harmonious between the army itself and the War Department. A flurry of brief notes between Halleck and Hooker readily betrayed their extraordinarily awkward relationship. Halleck launched the first salvo on January 29: "Will you be in Washington soon, or shall I arrange to meet you at Aquia on business?" Hooker responded on January 30: "Have no business requiring my presence in Washington, but will meet you there or at Aquia, as you may desire." Halleck responded later that day: "As some of the matters on which I wish to meet may require a reference to the War Department or to the President, I will meet you here at your earliest convenience." By day's end, Hooker finally relented: "I will be in Washington to night, and report in the morning."[27]

Losing Men By Design and Detachment

Four days into Hooker's administration, Confederates still didn't know about the change in command on the other side of the river. On January 30, Gen. Robert E. Lee requested that two British observers be granted permission to pass through the lines. His request was incorrectly addressed to "Maj. Gen. Ambrose E. Burnside, Commanding United States Forces."[28]

On that same day, as he swapped correspondence with Halleck, Hooker unveiled his most important priority reform for the army by addressing the lingering problems with leaves of absence by officers and men. Specifically, he alluded to an 1862 War Department general order, No. 61 that said leaves of absence could not be granted except to prevent death or permanent disability. Hooker wrote that Burnside had allowed grand division commanders considerable latitude and discretion because the

---

26 Taaffe, *Commanding the Army of the Potomac*. Taaffe's study outlines Hooker's actions (and foibles) and ascribes great importance to Butterfield's role as chief of staff.

27 *OR*, 25, part II, 9.

28 Ibid., 37.

Army's adjutant general permitted Burnside to authorize "leaves for a short period." Referring to a lack of uniformity in following such instructions, Hooker drafted and enclosed a new order, and "by it much desertion would be stopped, and a more contented feeling pervade the army."

Hooker's General Order No. 3 promulgated rules for "officers empowered to grant leaves of absence." These limited all leaves to a maximum of 15 days' duration— effectively 10 days at home for soldiers from Maine, New Hampshire, Vermont, Ohio, Michigan and "States west of the last named" with longer travel times. Hooker reserved the power for himself to approve leave for corps, division, and cavalry brigade commanders. He limited furloughs to one brigade commander in a corps; one field officer (majors and above), and two line officers per regiment; and one officer per battery or detachment at a time. Enlisted furloughs rewarded those with excellent records and limited them to two men per 100 present-for-duty in a regiment, battery, or detachment at a time. Until an officer or soldier returned on time, the next one from that same command could not depart. These furloughs, regardless of problems in initiating or administering them, would rate among the best of Hooker's reforms.

Eight days after the order was issued, each regiment, battery or detachment was required to provide a full accounting of men absent from duty for any cause. Such lists would be reckoned as: officers and enlisted men who were furloughed; detached; absent sick; wounded/in hospital; and deserters. Lists were consolidated by brigades and divisions.[29]

With his army already riddled with desertion, Hooker got news from Halleck on January 31 that his army was being further diminished: IX Corps was being reassigned to Maj. Gen. John Adams Dix at Fortress Monroe. This reduced the Army of the Potomac from eight to seven corps, none of which were at full-strength. Halleck also informed Hooker that the peripheral commands at Harpers Ferry and the Shenandoah Valley were being shifted to Maj. Gen. Robert Cumming Schenck's command, headquartered in Baltimore. Heintzelman continued to command the Washington Defenses. To complicate things further, Halleck told Hooker that these detached forces were unable to withstand major Confederate assaults and so Hooker was required to reinforce them if necessary, although they could not support him in turn. Halleck added that, per Hooker's recommendation, the Pennsylvania Reserves of V Corps would be transferred to the Washington Defenses in exchange for an equal number of Pennsylvania troops. Halleck told him to request transportation to make the exchange, and to transport IX Corps to Fortress Monroe. "In regard to the operations of your own army," Halleck added, "you can best judge when and where it can move to the greatest

29 Ibid., 10-12.

advantage, keeping in view the importance of covering Washington and Harpers Ferry either directly or by so operating as to be able to punish any force of the enemy sent against them." Halleck enclosed a copy of his January 7 letter to Burnside that embodied the general-in-chief's "views in regard to the duty of the Army of the Potomac to act against the enemy in its front whenever circumstances will permit."[30]

Halleck's letters fully justified harsh judgments of him by contemporaries and historians. As Navy Secretary Gideon Welles bluntly put it, Halleck "originates nothing, anticipates nothing... takes no responsibility, plans nothing, suggests nothing, is good for nothing." Lincoln, Stanton, and McClellan were less flattering—yet Halleck inexplicably remained.[31]

Inactivity and Antagonism

"I am afraid I gave you too sombre a view of the state of things," wrote Chaplain John R. Adams of the 5th Maine Infantry. "It is a Christian duty for me to look on the bright side, and to encourage others to do the same, and I have labored to do both." Adams had little sympathy for gripers: "before the [Mud] march there was much despondency, for idleness in camp begets fretfulness and croaking. But on the march, and after the march, these very persons will complain the more, for they have marched through the mud, and have been wet and galled, and have accomplished nothing." Well, that wasn't quite true, he decided: "We have demonstrated to the people of the North that there is such a thing as Virginia mud!"

Complaining of strife over McClellan and partisan politics, Adams supported the Administration and fathomed the army's strengths: "If called to fight, our men would not shrink from doing their duty. The mass are truly loyal. Our commanding officers are in a critical state just now. We want some decisive victories to turn the scale." He faulted debilitating camp inactivity: "The men are demoralized by having nothing to do."[32]

By that point—January 31—the many behind-the-scenes maneuvers initiated by Hooker and Halleck were underway[;] but as yet, the changes had made little impact on the men themselves, who still wallowed in various degrees of malaise. "[P]atriotism has oozed out through the pores opened by the imbecility of leaders, and the fatigues and disappointments of a fruitless winter campaign," wrote Dayton E. Flint of the 15th New

---

30 Ibid., 12-13.

31 Warner, *Generals in Blue*, 196. Halleck's new nickname became "Old Wooden Head."

32 BV 354, part 7, FSNMP, *Memorial and Letters of Rev. John R. Adams, D.D., Chaplain of the Fifth Maine and the One Hundred Twenty-first New York Regiments During the War of the Rebellion, Serving from the Beginning to its Close* (Privately Printed, 1890), 98-99.

Jersey Infantry, encamped near White Oak Church, on January 27.[33] Lieutenant John H. Stevens of the 5th Maine Infantry lamented on January 30: "We seem to be shut out from the rest of the world."[34]

There were undeniable pockets of resilience, though. Where good generals and officers led well, men clung to their esprit and to their comrades. Soldiers commonly adhered to good generals and colonels, and carried their favorite political leaders with them. Colonel Walter Phelps of the 22nd New York Infantry, on January 29, spoke for that group: "I never saw the brigade in better condition than they are today. I think I can say so of the Division. I hear much said about the demoralization of the army. I have never seen anything of the kind in this division, it may exist elsewhere, but I don't believe it. If there is any demoralization, I know it is among officers rather than men and I think it is only another name for camaraderie." Phelps remained convinced that "the government has the wealth, the men, and the ability to crush this rebellion . . . . We are not as united as the South—but we have the ability and the inclination to overcome them. The only difficulty is this government will not allow the army to accomplish anything. It is an evil acting disgrace to this country that persons high in office at Washington should have sacrificed the interests of that country—Stanton & Lincoln &c. I cannot say more on the subject"—although he did, making an inevitable plea for McClellan's return.[35]

Distrust of the Administration was not only found at lower levels of the army. Maj. Gen. George Meade on January 30 revealed: "A good deal of excitement exists in the army from a report prevailing that the provost marshal of Washington, or rather the head of the detective police in his department, is in the habit of systematically opening the letters received and written by officers . . . . I have endeavored to the best of my ability to do my duty, and I have never said a word to any one around me that the most hypocritical fool could find fault with." Major generals' mails were probably not being molested, but enlisted men's boxes were regularly checked for contraband civilian clothing—evidence of impending desertion.[36]

---

33 Dayton Flint Letters, Civil War Miscellaneous Collection, U. S. Army Military History Institute, Carlisle Barracks, Pennsylvania; derived from Manning, *What This Cruel War Was Over*, 87.

34 Gladys Stevens Stuart and Adelbert M. Jakeman Jr. *John H. Stevens, Civil War Diary*, (Acton, ME: Miller Books, 1997).

35 CHJHCF. Cites: "Letters of Walter Phelps to "E," January 29, 1863, BV 215, [part 7], FSNMP."

36 CHJHCF. Cites: "George G. Meade Jr., *The Life and Letters of George G. Meade*, (New York: Scribners, 1913), Volume I, p 353."

"Rounce" from the 4th New York Cavalry noted that they'd received two month's wages. "Notwithstanding We have three month's pay due us yet," he added. "O, it's a 'big thing' to get money, but a bigger thing when you can't buy anything after you get the money."[37]

"Rounce's" cynicism was indicative of the eroding confidence soldiers had in the government they served. Field and company officers felt it, too. Captain Charles Francis Adams Jr. of the 1st Massachusetts Cavalry expressed the common view: "The *New York Herald* may say what it pleases, but the Army of the Potomac is at present demoralized. Even I can see that, small means of observation as I have. You have no idea of the disgust felt here toward the Government." He bemoaned troubles of McClellan, Fitz John Porter, Burnside, Sumner, and Franklin, adding, "all this that Hooker may be placed in command, a man who has not the confidence of the army and who in private character is well known to be – I need not say what." More ominously, he added, "I earnestly hope [the Government] will now break up the army, else some day it will have it marching on Washington."[38]

Adams's potshot at the *New York Herald* wasn't isolated. Relations with the press were strained, and not a few of the newspapers' detractors wore stars. Yet the papers and the army were entwined in a symbiotic—some might even say parasitic—relationship. A *Herald* reporter named Richardson told of "hundreds of pens"—correspondents with the army.[39] Some were "unauthorized hangers on" (Halleck's term). Others lived in the camps and tried to capture soldier perspectives. Some wrote from a political or personal slant. Most merely attached themselves to some general and lived well on army supplies and support. While regular officers most distrusted reporters, the scribes enjoyed popularity among volunteers, many of whom, contemplating postwar political careers, sought hometown publicity. Richardson presciently recommended a corps of war correspondents with official standing, capable of living and traveling with the army, and able to purchase provisions and forage at officers' rates. As it was, though, the detente between the army and the journalists was delicate at best. S. M. Carpenter reported to the *Herald* on January 21 that a Mr. Demming of the Associated Press was arrested that morning at army headquarters on the orders of Secretary Stanton and hauled off to Washington. Charges were vague, but

37 Ibid.

38 CHJHCF. Cites: "Washington Chauncey Ford, ed., *A Cycle of Adams Letters* (Boston and New York: Houghton Mifflin, 1920), Volume I, p 250." BV 354, part 8, FSNMP.

39 CHJHCF. Cites: "The Press in the Army, an entire section of cards; those used here are from Albert D. Richardson, *The Secret Service: The Field, the Dungeon, and the Escape* (Hartford, CT, 1865), 304.

he was deemed a "dangerous man" whose "future reports . . . will be detrimental to the cause of the country."[40]

January 31 brought a fuller accounting of the army's strengths—and those of the other forces in the general capital area. In aggregate numbers (present and absent), it revealed that Hooker was ultimately able to draw on a maximum of 326,750 men. Of these, 194,061 officers and men were present for duty in various headquarters and attached cavalry, artillery and special troops units; three grand divisions; and a grand reserve division. The Washington Defenses had 44,538 present for duty. This meant that 149,523 men were at Hooker's disposal in the Rappahannock sector alone.

However, the same official records list a total of 177,490 officers and men "present for duty, equipped" in infantry (145,818), cavalry (14,072) and artillery (17,600). Subtracting the Washington Defenses infantry, cavalry, and artillery (30,346) in that same status report, Hooker would have 147,144 combat arms troops alone on the Rappahannock front—more than generally related. Efforts to tabulate actual numbers of men in the Army of the Potomac proved extraordinarily difficult. Pettifogging accounting methods of the diminutive "Old Army" never yielded acceptable tallies.[41]

"The Army to Set Men Free" Fights the Emancipation Proclamation

The end-of-January musters naturally did not include statistics on racial prejudice or ethnic animosities or political biases, but they, too, were "present for duty." Enormous amounts of venom had been released thirty days earlier with the Emancipation Proclamation. The soldiers making up the army came from an American society that was racially prejudiced against blacks, free or enslaved, and ethnically bigoted against immigrants—especially Irish and Germans who had arrived post-1840s, but "others" as well. The underclass of white farmers, laborers, or mechanics comprising most of the army did not welcome the thought of four or more million black or a million immigrant competitors absorbing their postwar land and jobs. Until January 1863, that outcome had been unlikely, and the working poor had at least shared a common racial "superiority" bond with the upper- and middle-classes. Especially among War Democrats, Lincoln's proclamation threatened livelihoods and political sensitivities. That feeling intensified with the sudden appearances of thousands of strange looking and sounding "contrabands," now dependent upon them for work and sustenance.

---

40 CHJHCF. Cites: "Letters of S.M. Carpenter to Mr. Hudson, of the *Herald*, James Gordon Bennett [publisher of the *Herald*] Papers, Library of Congress."

41 *OR*, 25, part II, 15-36.

Throughout January, reflections flew from varied perspectives. Edward W. Whitaker of the Harris Light Cavalry, 2nd New York, related on January 8: "The slaves are all going to Washington leaving brutal masters and overseers and lazy mistresses to raise their own crops and dress themselves." He reported fifty-three had passed his outpost in a single night, ending with "Emancipation!! How the darkies rejoice."[42] On January 14, Lt. George Breck wrote to the *Rochester Union and Advertiser*: "The emancipation edict has had its share of discussion in our camp, as we presume it has in other camps, for soldiers will discuss political matters, even if they have been told it is out of character for them to do so." Breck felt proclamation discussions transcended politics and that "military necessity" had combined with "justice" to compel its "enunciation." He questioned whether soldiers saw how this aided the Union cause, since it really didn't liberate slaves within their control (although it did). Breck sagely added, "We hope the best results may flow from the Freedom policy. Anything to help crush this atrocious rebellion and give us back the good old Union. If presidential proclamations will accomplish this, let them come thick and fast!"[43]

News and images emerged and reached the nation. Breck had previously described the early January exodus of former slaves from King George County. On January 31, a million *Harper's Weekly* readers saw a full-page rendition of the same scene captured by artist A. R. Waud and photographer David B. Woodbury in Stafford County, entitled "Contrabands coming into camp in consequence of the Proclamation." Such scenes bred curiosity and pity among the soldiers, and America took note.[44]

Many soldiers, acting out of human decency, aided freed slaves whether they cared about them or not. Most of the freedmen hired by the army were treated little better than they had been as slaves; but, pointedly, they were paid—most, for the first time in their lives, and they could now keep all they earned. However small, it was a first breath of freedom.

All treatment of "contrabands" was not benign. A few were demonstrably mistreated, effectively returned to slavery. One (hopefully rare) example was Horace Emerson of the 2nd Wisconsin Infantry. "I did not pay my nigger anything," he wrote on January 31. "I made him do all my work for nothing and he done the washing for the

---

42 BV 329, part 1, FSNMP, Letters of Edward W. Whitaker, 2nd New York, "Harris Light Cavalry."

43 CHJHCF. Cites: "Letters of Lt. George Breck to *Rochester Union and Advertiser*, compiled and transcribed by John Hennessy and Richard Becker."

44 Noel G. Harrison, "In the Wake of December's Disaster: Photography after the First Battle of Fredericksburg," in *Fredericksburg History and Biography* (Fredericksburg, VA: Central Virginia Battlefields Trust), Volume No. 8, 2009, 112-121.

co. and they paid me so I am ahead on the Black cuss."[45] Emerson may have been the lowest of the species, but among poor and uneducated "Slavocrats," these were common feelings. Francis Edwin Pierce of the 108th New York Infantry, had written five days earlier: "I don't object to fighting every day in the year, and at the end of 3 years would willingly lay aside my life, provided the war is conducted for the restoration of the Union and the constitution as it was, but it is plain to be seen that this has become a mere political war and is waged principally for the benefit of a sectional political party, and that the administration pays no attention whatever to the constitution—then I am done." That semi-lofty sentiment was followed by "I will not jeopardize my life or become an invalid for life from exposure and fatigue, hunger and cold, simply to restore 3,000,000 of the brutes to freedom."[46]

Clearly, such views didn't come from reading the proclamation. Lincoln was explicit that war aims remained restoring the Union by suppressing the rebellion. What he added was a new "war measure" to free slaves, including compensating slaveowners who returned to the Union. Lincoln's provision for black troops was another "war measure."

Paradoxically, those who railed against the proclamation and black soldiers soon called for the draft to reinforce depleted Federal units. That draft would add only about 45,000 white soldiers to the ranks. By contrast, Lincoln's measure would add nearly 180,000 black soldiers. The 500,000 slaves in the District of Columbia and the loyal Border States were handled separately as non-rebellious Union places still under constitutional protections. Captain Isaac Plumb of the 61st New York Infantry had preemptively answered Pierce and the others on January 1: "Our Northern traitors tell us we are fighting for the Negro. Those traitors would sooner see the country disrupted and lost than have the institution of slavery die." On January 12th, he wrote: "For one I would be willing to have my life saved by a black man, yes a Nigger if you will, and I would fight by his side in such a cause as this."[47] More and more soldiers saw it that same way.[48]

---

45 CHJHCF. Cites: "Letters of Horace Emerson to his brother, Clements Library, University of Michigan."

46 CHJHCF. Cites: "Blake McKelvey, ed., "Civil War Letters of Francis Edwin Pierce of the 108th New York Volunteer Infantry," in Rochester Historical Society's *Rochester in the Civil War* (1944), 150-173.

47 CHJHCF. Cites: "Diary of Capt. Isaac Plumb, 61st NY, Civil War Miscellaneous Collection, USAMHI; quoted from Furgurson, *Chancellorsville, 1863: The Souls of the Brave*, 14."

48 Looking back from August 1863, Stephen Pingree of the 4th Vermont Infantry spoke for many. He said although he "once doubted the *policy* of this war, I never doubted the *right* to maintain the Union." Then he added, "I once doubted the policy of the Negro soldier bill and,

Many soldiers, including many War Democrats, finally rationalized non-abolitionist views for the sake of the cause. A January 14 speech by Col. Ross of the 20th Connecticut Infantry outlined key arguments: African slavery was the cause of the rebellion and the war; the oath sworn before God on entering service required obedience; and anything which hurt the Rebels worked for ultimate victory. Anti-abolitionists accommodated their views and logic, as well: by defeating the South's dominant slaveholder class—the planter aristocracy, which was the leading political, social and economic force—and depriving them of their wealth (slaves, lands, businesses and houses), the rest of the South would inevitably crumble and fall. On that pragmatic basis, the army's soldiers continued to set men free—not from altruism or humanitarian motives, although some felt that way, but to end "the cursed rebellion."[49]

In January 1863, despite the recurring rhetoric, this army was far from "crushing" anything, except perhaps its own morale and effectiveness.[50]

Onward Christian Soldiers

Another force rallied around the army—not angels certainly, but an army of God nevertheless. Many were like O. P. Case of Hartford, Connecticut, who arrived in Washington on January 24. The next day, pass in hand, he traveled via the steamer *Wilson Small* to Aquia Landing. Visiting the camp of the 16th Connecticut, he found relative Lowell M. Case hospitalized with typhoid. Case next visited the 21st Connecticut Infantry. After traveling through the army's camps, he took a steamer from

---

in fact, of the emancipation policy of the Gov't. . . . Today, I believe in not only the justice but the policy of a war to restore the Union. I believe not only in Universal Emancipation . . . . I have faith in the effectiveness of Negro troops . . . . I hate slavery and believe by destroying it we weaken the Rebellion." (August 2, 1863, Stephen M. Pingree letter to Augustus Hunton in "Lyndon State College Collection," Pingree (Pingry)-Hunton-Sickney Family Papers (1832-1962), MSA 135, Folder 6, Vermont Historical Society, as quoted in Robert G. Poirier, *They Could Not Have Done Better: Thomas O. Seaver and the 3rd Vermont Infantry in the War for the Union* (Newport, VT, 2005), 76.

49 CHJHCF. Cites: "The 20th Regiment, C.V.," *The Waterbury American*, January 16, 1863, Col Ross speech."

50 The army's condition at January's end is summarized by John Hennessy. He traces sources of discontent ("an astonishing breadth of complaints"); concerns about generalship (poor battlefield performance) and leadership (inability to motivate and inspire); concerns over administration and congressional meddling (especially McClellanites); political disputes; and racial disputes. Saving graces, however, were detectable: continued allusion to final victory; Hooker's aggressiveness (juxtaposed with his self-promotion and denigration of others); and rehabilitation of the army's "psyche and organization" through furloughs, additional medical reforms, and better food Hennessy, "We Shall Make Richmond Howl."

Point Hospital.[51] "Here they have moved almost all of the sick from the Connecticut regiments and the regiments of the Army of the Potomac," he wrote on January 28. "The tents are on elevated ground, and it looks like an immense camp meeting; but, unhappily, it is composed of sick soldiers and there is more crying than singing. This is called the General Hospital of the Army of the Potomac . . . . The sick average about 600 in each corps, making in all about 4,000 sick soldiers. This does not comprise one half of the sick—only the worst cases." Case estimated the hospital's costs at roughly $255,000. He mentioned "wood buildings, consisting of cooking houses, dispensaries, &c," equipped with stoves and beds.[52]

Also on the 28th, another Hartford man, Rev. L. B. Rockwood of the American Tract Society, wrote from "Falmouth, Va.": "Co-operating in my work with the Christian Commission, we occupy a tent at the Falmouth Station, fifteen miles from Acquia Creek, and but one mile from the city of Fredericksburg. The great army of the Potomac lies to the right, left and rear of us, extending in each direction for many miles." Unlike the soldiers, he saw possibilities in old Stafford: "Before being desolated by the ravages of war, this country must have been one of great beauty. Even at this season, the scenery from the surrounding hills is very fine." Pressing needs abounded, he observed, and on the previous Sunday, he'd refused a request to preach to a regiment in order to help prepare and distribute food to 600 sick men on their way to Aquia Creek hospital. Two days earlier he had filled his haversack with tracts and the *American Messenger* and passed them out to picketing troops, noting, "One of the men sent the Messenger I had given him and a daily over to Fredericksburg in a truce boat." Rockwood lauded the army's desire for "good reading." "No one can be here for a single hour, and not see the value, and pressing demand for just such work as we are attempting to perform for the thousands of the sick and needy in this great army," he wrote.[53]

Succor came all the way from the top, too. The U. S. Christian Commission (USCC) sent a new leader to the army. John A. Cole, a "General Field Agent for the Christian Commission," provided field reports with a unique view of army-USCC interaction. "Back to my work again," he wrote from Washington on January 31. "I find everything [in the USCC] much changed for the better, the operations more extended and better system every where . . . . I expect I shall be requested to act as general superintendent of

---

51 Today's Marlborough Point.

52 BV 314, part 50, FSNMP, O. P. Case's January 28, 1863, letter in the *Hartford Daily Courant* of January 31. Lowell M. Case of the 16th Connecticut was described as "(last year organist of the 4th Church)."

53 BV 314, part 51, FSNMP. Despite having also been written on January 28, L. B. Rockwood's letter was to the same paper as Case's and it appeared in the February 4, 1863, edition.

the work at Falmouth and Aquia Creek and think I shall consent to take it as all here say I must. I shall not be in Washington much I presume, but shall have just those opportunities for work that I want."[54]

Within the army's ranks were good men, patriotic and faithful to their sworn duty and their God. Facing adversities—lost battles and unfulfilled leadership—they persevered and kept the faith. One was Thomas White Stephens of the 20th Indiana Infantry. His diary, unlike so many others, was clear and prayerful, uncomplaining and insightful. He was a young man tested by physical privation, illness, and battle.[55] On January 15, he reported what became a regular routine: "Up before day, went into the woods, and bowed in secret prayer. Felt my Savior near. An hour thus spent!" This preceded afternoon company drill (skirmishing) and brigade drill. After a hard night of wind and rain, he related on January 16, "This morning, up early and went to the woods, bowed in secret prayer, felt it good to spend the moments thus. – Thank God, that here, I find him so near, and his love so great to me."[56]

Two days later, what must have seemed like divine retribution took place: the 1st Brigade—which included the 20th Indiana—witnessed a deserter from the 63rd Pennsylvania being punished. The man, branded with a "D" on his thigh, "was drummed out of U. S. service, to the tune of the 'Rogue's March'." Stephens' regiment had missed the Mud March and, as a consequence, he spent time engaged in various duties around camp. The change in army command, when it came, passed almost without his comment. "Recd news of Genl. Burnside's resignation. Genl. Hooker takes his place.—Gens. Sumner and Franklin are relieved," he noted.[57]

Among the more high-minded men of the army, like Stephens, these were weeks to be endured. Notably, he did not complain, gripe, or bellyache, but persevered with illness and did not shirk his duties—not that he always saw it that way. "O how far short

---

54 BV 91, part 13, FSNMP. USCC General Field Agent John A. Cole's "Army Letters."

55 Stephens' regiment saw action in North Carolina at Newport News (ground action in the famous fight between the CSS *Virginia* and USS *Monitor*) and on the Virginia Peninsula. Taken prisoner and kept for five weeks at Libby Prison and Belle Isle in Richmond before exchange, he missed several of his regiment's bloodiest fights. The 20th (and presumably Stephens) fought at Groveton (August 29), Second Manassas/Bull Run (August 30), and at Chantilly (September 1). Spared the horrors of Antietam, the regiment arrived at Falmouth by November 19, and went on to fight at Fredericksburg that December.

56 BV 106, part 3, FSNMP. "The Civil War Diary of Thomas White Stephens, Sergeant, Company K, 20th Regiment of Indiana Volunteers," edited by Paul E. Wilson and Harriet Stephens Wilson (Lawrence, KS, 1985). William G. Cutler, *History of the State of Kansas* (Chicago, IL, 1883) at www.kancoll.org/books/cutler/shawnee/shawnee-co-p41.html (accessed July 12, 2009).

57 Ibid.

I come of doing my duty," Stephens wrote on Sunday the 25th after attending a "good, earnest sermon in the 63rd Pa." "Lord help me."[58]

"A Regular God Forsaken Country"

Another reality soon settled over the army at January's finale: wartime Stafford, Virginia. A 4th New York cavalryman named "Rounce" wrote from "Camp in Two Foot of Snow, near [Alcock,] Va." on the army's dangerous outpost line west of Hartwood: "We are now in the woods of Virginia, and likely to stay here till the war is over, contending with numerous outlaws who infest this section, committing all sorts of depredations: murder, rapine, arson, robbery; and meeting plunder with philanthropy. Such as may be properly termed fleet-footed robbers and human butchers to whom we give prisons and parole. It is unsafe to go two miles from camp, as the infernal Rebels lie in ambush."[59]

Afoot in an alien and inhospitable land, far-removed from familiar places, family and friends, W. A. Guest of the 124th Pennsylvania Infantry, painted a colorful, if linguistically challenged picture on January 30:

> I will give you a histery about the people down here. The niger are all taken out of this state and the wite people all alike. The men what is dressed in reb uniforme an the girls looks as if they had been used fore a house-cloth or making to wipe out an oven. I was out on picket…an I went to a house to buy a pie an I see the dirties girl there that I ever saw. One of them had on a soldiers blouse fore a shimmy an a pair of pant fore drawers an had a frock over them an a pair of government shoes an the dirt was about an inch thick on her face an neck. There was about a dosen of youngster running about crying with cold an hunger. I pittied the little children but the old ones I did not fore they could stand the cold better than the children. Well all the way on the march i did not see but three houses on the road. It was nothing but woods an bushes an pines all the way along the road an it was a regular god forsaken country fore it is nothing but mud an bushes as far as I have [seen] in the state an it is the same as far as I can see.[60]

A more literate soldier of the 140th Pennsylvania concurred: "If they leave we will too and I think we may fall back to Washington and let them have this God forsaken country." Positively commenting on imminent issue of Springfield rifles, he added, "I

58 Ibid.

59 William B. Styple, ed., *Writing and Fighting in the Civil War: Soldier Correspondence to the New York Sunday Mercury* (Kearny, NJ, 2000), 164.

60 BV 112, part 2, FSNMP, letters of W. A. Guest.

have made up my mind that it will all be over by the fourth of July. If it isn't over by then, I would not give much for this army for it is badly discouraged and out of heart."[61]

The weather and terrain continued to plague the soldiers. On January 29, the same Pennsylvanian wrote: "We have four or five inches of snow here with the mud nearly twice that deep under it. I never saw such mud in my life. However the sun is shining and the snow will leave us soon. But the mud will stay with us." Soldiers still yearned for "Little Mac"; this one pronounced McClellan "the only man who can get a good fight out of this army." But he left that door open: "If they don't give us McClellan or someone the army has confidence in this army may turn into an armed mob and throw down their arms and go home."[62]

Month's End: The Army Blames Nearly Everybody and Everything

In a turbulent month, the Army of the Potomac had recovered from a tremendous battle loss; suffered a humiliating and frustrating encounter with adverse weather and terrain; and found itself with a new commander. These experiences had left the army broken and in despair, with many units and men on the edge, if not in the abyss of demoralization.

"I am tired of this way of carrying on war and if this Army [is] here much longer there will not be over half their number left on account of desertions," wrote John Morton of the 17th Michigan Infantry on January 13. "Nearly all of the soldiers are disgusted with Lincoln's mode of warfare and if I ever get a chance there will be one less in the Northern Army." But thirteen days later, on January 26, Morton was not talking about deserting. Rather, he was thinking ahead to postwar life in Iowa or Kansas after receiving a homestead farm for his presumably honorable military service. He also reported his health was "getting better," and he was soon going to be able to resume regular duties. The pump of reform had been primed and began to drip, if ever so slightly.[63]

They were all young men, even the officers and generals, and they were, by nature, impatient; as such, they scarcely noticed positive incremental steps by leaders to correct situations or relieve their suffering. As commanding general, Hooker hit the ground running, but his orders and reorganizations and reforms were not yet widely evident during his first six days of command. In all their blaming, the men could not yet see—those who saw it at all—beyond "hope" for a better future.

61 BV 112, part 13, FSNMP, letters from an unknown soldier in the 140th Pennsylvania.

62 Ibid.

63 BV 106, part 5, FSNMP.

They blamed the government, both the Lincoln Administration and the Republican-dominated Congress. They blamed the Emancipation Proclamation. They blamed the War Department. They blamed their state governments (when they differed politically). They naturally blamed top generals. McClellanites and anti-McClellanites debated a restoration. Burnside passed by so quickly that only old friends and loyal troops defended his reputation. They blamed a lack of victories. They blamed intra-army factors, especially commissaries (poor food), quartermasters (shoddy clothing and equipment and forage), and paymasters (too little pay, too seldom disbursed). They blamed the weather and the ground—with some justification, as it seemed to them that God and nature conspired against them. They also blamed the newspapers as disloyal and a source of demoralization. They even blamed the poor downtrodden escaped slaves, who had contributed nothing to their misery. Strangely, they did not much blame Lee or his army. They also did not blame themselves (beyond intra-corps struggles).

"I expect before six weeks to know that the Army of the Potomac is entirely broken up, as it has been a humbug since its formation," reflected Priv. John Weiser of the 130th Pennsylvania. "There is too many troops in one body for any one man to handle."[64]

Even though Hooker did not know of Weiser's concerns, he was about to prove him wrong.

64 BV 112, FSNMP. Weiser's account is in part 8.

Chapter Four |

Suffering

A_S winter deepened from January to February, the weather bit deep into the army. "The weather is terrible, and fluctuates from wet to dry once or twice a day," shivered William Taylor of the 100th Pennsylvania. "In my last I believe I stated that it was very cold, and that it was likely some of us would freeze. So it was. Three men of the 29th Mass encamped beside us froze to death that night. It has now been raining and sleeting for 36 hours."[1]

With the February deep freeze, soldiers' attitudes only hardened. "The severity of the weather is nothing compared with the frigidity of our hearts toward the administration and war department keeping men all winter in shelter tents and deeding them hard tacks & salt beef," wrote James Woodworth of the 44th New York early in the new month. "It is an outrage on humanity and one that will live in the hearts of those composing the army of the Potomac until disease and the bullet have consummated its extinction."[2]

An 8th New York Cavalry trooper, "Genesee," who'd arrived in Stafford on January 13 from the Washington Defenses, quickly took the measure of the army. "As far as my observation extends," he wrote on February 8, "the soldiers are heartily sick of soldiering and of the war; the exceptions are very few both of the old and new regiments. The romance of a soldier's life disappeared long since, and the knavery, fuss and feathers, petty tyranny and annoyance of modern warfare, is a poor substitute for the generous and chivalric spirit we are accustomed to associate with the military leaders and followers of olden times and as far down as our own revolutionary contest." He complained about pay and outlined other grievances, including a sweeping

---

1 Taylor letter 6 February 1863. FSNMP collection.

2 CHJHCF cites: "Letters of James Woodworth to his wife Phebe, Clements Library (Schoff Collection), University of Michigan."

Winter brought its own miseries—as if sharing space with 100,000 other men wasn't challenging enough. Proper shelter was an ongoing concern. LOC

condemnation of "this wretched war which was conceived in iniquity and has been carried on by incompetency."[3]

Just a day earlier on February 7, Edwin O. Wentworth of the 37th Massachusetts reflected a similar attitude. "I am satisfied that the South cannot be whipped back into the Union," he decided. "If the abolitionists were out of power, peace, and a reconstruction of the Union would be comparatively easy. I wish the present administration were out of power. I am glad I did not elect it." He conjectured, wrongly but enthusiastically that war would make 90 percent of the soldiers into Democrats.[4]

Soldiers were beginning to take more note of the change that had taken place at army headquarters, though. "There is much talk & comment on the recent changes in commanders," reported Lt. Henry Grubbs of the 155th Pennsylvania Infantry, passing along some campfire talk centered on the army's new commanding general. "'Fighting Joe' Hooker has command of the army but most of the men seem affraid of him & think

3 BV 317, part 6, 8th New York Cavalry letters to the *Rochester Daily Union and Advertiser*, February 13.

4 CHJHCF cites: "Edwin O. Wentworth Papers, L.C. [presumably Library of Congress]."

he is too rash & anxious to fight but I think he is a sound man, not afraid of the enemy and a good General, & the 'Rebs' will have to do their best if he gets after them."[5] Their concerns about Hooker's rashness correlated with President Lincoln's secret letter to Hooker on January 26. What might the soldiers have thought had they known they shared the same views as their president, whom many of them distrusted?

"General Burnside has been relieved and Gen'l Hooker has taken command," wrote Elisha Hunt Rhodes of the 2nd Rhode Island in his February 1 diary entry. "A few more changes and I suppose the people north will think the war ended."[6] For Rhodes, the change in command merited only a third-place mention in his list of events for the day. Like most soldiers, Rhodes was occupied by more day-to-day concerns.

"An order was received today stating that two officers at a time from each Regiment would be allowed leave of absence," Rhodes wrote. "At this rate my turn will come in about one month. I have already sent up my applications and hope to see my home before long." He then went on to describe a log house built for him by the men of his Company D. "On the first floor we have a fireplace and table. Upstairs on a shelf we have a bed and a ladder to reach it. The floor of the second story only covers a part of the room and in fact is the bed. The walls are of hewn timber with spaces filled with mud. The roof is pieces of shelter tent. We moved in this evening and feel very happy in our new home."

Not everyone was so happy. An infantryman with the 140th Pennsylvania recounted that "there has been five or six in this regiment shot their fingers off."[7] Such actions rendered subsequent infantry service impossible, but risked courts-martial. Nor was the dissatisfaction limited internally. On February 1, the same Pennsylvanian wrote of tension between his regiment and one of the locals. "Our Colonel is acting Brigadier now for a short time and has his headquarters at an old sesh's house a half mile from camp," he reported. "He took me and nine men out for a guard. It is a splendid house and property and we planted old glory in the yard and the lady of the house was going to tear it down. I objected to that and she gave it up." After they set up their tents, she threatened to let her cows loose on them. She was dissuaded by the threat that the bovines would be summarily bayoneted.[8]

Contact with all Rebel females was fruitless, or so believed Jacob F. Smith of the 127th Pennsylvania Infantry. In a February 5 letter, he bemoaned that "the last young lady I have seen was when we were in Fredericksburg and she said Everything is lovely

5   BV 232, FSNMP. Henry Grubbs Papers.

6   Rhodes, ed., *All For the Union*, 91.

7   BV 112, part 13, letters from an unknown 140th Pennsylvania soldier in FSNMP.

8   BV 112, part 13, unknown soldier of 140th Pennsylvania Infantry letters, FSNMP.

when the Yankeeys ant about. So you can see how welcome we were." The February chill, it seems, came not only from the weather.[9]

Army and Navy, Desertion and Smuggling

Although the soldiers were not happy about being in Stafford, Virginia, General Hooker ramped up efforts to maintain them there. He recognized desertion as perhaps the army's greatest malaise, and his earliest reforms looked to address the problem. "The greatest vigilance is now exercised to prevent its continuance," explained a soldier with the 70th New York, "and cavalry and infantry patrols are continually scouring the country on the look-out for such characters. A great number have already been taken."[10]

On February 1, Hooker took matters one step further, eliciting help from the Navy to help in his retention efforts. Under Hooker's direction, Chief of Staff Butterfield wrote to Lt. Cdr. Samuel Magaw, First Division of the Potomac Flotilla[:] "General Hooker desires that you should use every exertion to stop the passage of small boats conveying deserters from the army across the Potomac." Butterfield explained that large numbers crossed the Potomac in small boats above and below Aquia Creek. "Any person detected in this effort by your efforts . . . may be turned over to the provost marshal at Aquia Creek," he offered. "It is believed that spies and contraband are conveyed across the Rappahannock below the lines of our army. If you can destroy the small boats and means of traffic across the Rappahannock . . . you will render an important service."[11]

Pertinent information on deserters crossing the Potomac River came from Col. Charles Candy, commanding a XII Corps brigade post at Dumfries in Prince William County, north of Stafford. Candy reported deserters on rafts crossing to Maryland from between Quantico Creek in Prince William County and Chopawamsic Creek in Stafford County. On January 25, Candy wrote to Gen. Heintzelman, "Excuse the suggestion [to detach a blockading boat to search for deserters], but I feel a personal pride in putting a stop to desertions." Candy's sound suggestion was not pursued.[12]

---

9 BV 112, part 6, FSNMP, letters of Jacob F. Smith.

10 CMC 70 NY "Our Army Correspondence" in *Pittsburgh Evening Chronicle*, 2/26/63; FSNMP Ms. 05313.

11 OR, 25, part II, 36-37. Magaw was incorrectly addressed by Butterfield as the flotilla commander (Commodore A. A. Harwood commanded at that point).

12 *Official Records of the Union and Confederate Navies in the War of the Rebellion* (Washington, DC, 1897), Series I, Volume 5, Operations on the Potomac and Rappahannock Rivers (Dec. 7, 1861 -July 31, 1865), 218-239. Hereafter cited as ORN; NPS/CWSSS, relates Colonel Charles Candy was in 66th Ohio Infantry, M552 Roll 16.

Butterfield's request netted similar results. Magaw responded to him on February 3, promising to assist on the wrong river, the Rappahannock, where "contrabandists" were pulling their small boats into the thickets during daytime and venturing out at night.[13] Magaw made no mention, though, of Butterfield's reference to the Potomac. Smuggling—not desertion—was the Navy's main misplaced concern. Naval records reveal the Potomac Flotilla's unfortunate late-January preoccupation with smuggling.[14] However, most of the reported smuggling on the Potomac took place well down-river from Stafford, diverting naval attention from the area where Hooker felt it would be of most use.

Exemplary of Army-Navy miscommunication was an even on February 21 when the sutler schooner *Mail* was stopped at Georgetown carrying 428 dozen cans of strong drink masquerading as milk—"a villainous egg-nog," accused one teetotaling observer. The cargo was bound from Belle Plain in Stafford. Amazingly, three soldiers aboard, identified as belonging to the 1st, 6th, and 19th Maine Volunteers, attracted little scrutiny as potential deserters. The event sparked a flurry of naval activity until at least the end of February. Magaw, with the USS *Freeborn* and *Dragon*, checked out the Butterfield-requested positions, but once again on the Rappahannock River and not on the Potomac River. [15]

Another series of events demonstrated how easily Army-Navy resources could be distracted. Answering General Lee's January 30 letter requesting safe passage for two foreign officers through the Army of the Potomac, General Halleck on February 3 directed Hooker that, "Foreign officers will not be permitted to pass our lines without a pass from the War Department, and such passes are given only on the application of the minister or diplomatic agent who represents their Government." The British officer—the "Lord Huntington" of Lee's letter—was now called "Lord Hartigan" in naval reports. Colonel Leslie retained his correct identity. They had grown impatient waiting for authorization and made a preemptive move. Captured aboard the *King Philip* on February 8 by the U.S.S. *Dan Smith* while "landing from the Virginia shore," claimed one observer, the British officers were forwarded by the Navy to Washington, where "the merits of the case will be decided by the military authorities." The list of those captured with the British officers suggests their vessel's use by the Confederate Signal

---

13 Ibid.

14 Colonel Herman Haupt of the U. S. Military Railroads had also reported extensive smuggling, but had not given much attention to deserters. Herman Haupt, *Reminiscences of General Herman Haupt* (Wright & Joys, 1901).

15 *ORN*, 226-227.

Corps and Secret Service, operating freely between Aquia and Potomac Creeks and southern Maryland.[16]

While the Navy's cordon continued leaking deserters, Hooker was still confident enough by February 6 to declare, "desertions from this army are now at an end, or nearly so." He must have felt lingering pangs, though, because on February 18, he expressed alarm to Brig. Gen. Alpheus S. Williams (in temporary command of the XII Corps). Hooker received word that "large numbers of deserters escape through our lines upon the road between Potomac Creek, Chopawamsic Creek, Dumfries, and Occoquan." He ordered Williams to picket the area "so carefully" as to prevent any passage of lines, paying close attention to sutlers or anyone passing themselves as "telegraph repairers." "[I]nstruct your pickets to shoot all deserters or persons attempting to pass our lines who do not, on being challenged, answer the summons of the sentinel, and submit to examination by proper officers," he added. It is not known whether he issued deadly force orders to other commands.[17]

Lingering Illnesses and Medical Concerns

If desertion remained one of the army's great malaises, disease remained the other. As the army hunkered into the cold February, the medical drama—featuring death from disease, sickness, and the malingering effects from wounds—continued.

"No one knows how we suffer out here," lamented "Ferris," a soldier with the 83rd New York Infantry, writing on February 8 from "Camp Near Fletcher's Chapel" (King George County). "If one is sick, he must remain out here; if he gets well, it is a miracle." Unhappy with obstructions to furloughs—he likened getting one to climbing to the moon—Ferris worried about mounting sick lists and overflowing hospitals. "[N]o less than forty men have died at the General Hospital at Acquia Creek in one single day," he claimed.[18]

A comrade's death lurked in every crude shelter. On February 15, James S. Graham of the 140th Pennsylvania Infantry wrote about the death of his friend and messmate, Issac Donelson, who had died two days prior after coming down with a fever three

---

16 OR, 25, part II, 37-38. All of those with records connect to activities described in Tidwell et. al., *Come Retribution*, which explains linkage to the Confederate Secret Service.

17 OR, 25, part I, 50-52, 86; BV 354, part 7, FSNMP, *Memorial and Letters of Rev. John R. Adams, D.D.,* 100-101. The second letter was on March 9, 1863.

18 Styple, ed., *Writing and Fighting the Civil War*, 166-167. FSNMP historian Eric Mink related: "Fletcher's Chapel is located just across the Stafford County line, at the intersection of Caledon Road ([Va.] Route 218) and Fletchers Chapel Road. It, like White Oak Church, was a prominent landmark in the Union camps, especially for the [I] Corps."

weeks earlier. Donelson languished in a hospital for two weeks, attended the whole time by friends and a cousin. "About an hour befor he died I was standing beside his bed and I asked him if he would not like to see some of his folks," Graham wrote. "Yes he said he would but he said he would never see them in this wourld but I want you to tell them to prepare to meet me in heaven where I expect to be befor morning and tell them goodby for me. These were the words he spoke." Graham hoped his friend had passed to a better world "where there is no more war." They shipped his body home. "I miss him like a brother." Graham added. "There has been more died since he died with the fevor."[19]

Like other aspects of the army, reforms began slowly—but they were, indeed, coming. At January's end, the War Department's surgeon general had admonished the army's medical director, Dr. Jonathan Letterman, to properly mark those soldiers who died with a "strong card" that had their name, company, and regiment affixed to their breasts. Resources were strained, though. In response, on February 10, Letterman ordered changes that would, he hoped, help keep better track of hospitalized men: he ordered the Windmill Point Hospital (Marlborough Point) to ship its "seriously sick men" to Washington, shut down corps-level hospitals, and establish division-level hospitals and medical depots.[20]

Like the army's medical system, the United States Christian Commission was becoming more systematic, too. General Field Agent John Cole combined religious zeal with practical belief that they could aid soldiers' spiritual and physical conditions. "The wickedness exhibited in an army in a single day is such that I feel more and more the necessity of the Christian Commission," he testified on February 10. He had just visited Windmill Point Hospital where more than 4,000 sick soldiers suffered terribly and many died. "They all love our Ch. Com. and all surgeons, nurses and all are ready to do any thing for us."[21]

"We have from three to five delegates there all the time," Cole continued optimistically. "[M]any lives I believe have been saved within the past three weeks and many souls have passed from darkness into light. We believe that a great revival has commenced here, God grant it!" He also proudly reported establishing a laundry operation that supported 3,000 patients per week at Windmill Point. The men, he

---

19 BV 121, FSNMP, Lee Family Papers, Letter of James S. Graham, 140th Pennsylvania Infantry, February 15, 1863 to Aunt Mary Ann Lee, Hickory, Pennsylvania.

20 Surgeon Justin Dwinelle Papers, FSNMP, Letter of January 29th, endorsed by Dwinelle on February 8 from the Windmill Point II Corps Hospital.

21 BV 91, part 13, FSNMP. USCC General Field Agent John A. Cole "Army Letters," 1861-1866.

added, were grateful for "Testaments and papers" contributed from home and perceptively recognized the efforts of women laboring there.[22]

Like most civilians with the army, though, Cole seemed oblivious to the extent to which his delegates drew on army resources. He seemed oblivious, too—perhaps willfully—to the problems his delegates caused for the medical staff, exaggerating the esteem showed them. Contemporaneous accounts by Surgeon J. Franklin Dyer, for instance, described some of the friction. Dyer recalled asking the civilians to help move sick soldiers into tents from the rain, and the civilians merely went inside and prayed for the rain to stop.[23]

Restoring Honor and Pride

Soldiers at war become increasingly influenced by personal pride and pride in their units—in this case, regiment, brigade, division, and corps. That pride begins at the unit level. Thus far, Hooker had attempted mainly organizational efficiencies, but on February 2, he instituted a change intended to aid the cultivation of pride on the unit level: He contacted the War Department Adjutant General's Office about implementing a general order for inscription of battle-honors on regimental and battery colors.[24]

"Most, if not all, the regiments and batteries now in the service with this army are entitled to distinction," Hooker buoyantly explained. He recognized his soldiers' military honor was now embodied in their colors. The banners, carried by units everywhere and under all conditions, embodied their units' combat records. Once soldiers identified with their colors, they would fight harder and longer to protect them. "No better incentive could be given to the army for future effort than this honorable recognition of their past services," Hooker concluded.[25] One of Hooker's most important steps was appealing to soldiers' pride and causing them to fight for their unit, leaders, each other, and the memory of fallen comrades.

Restoring confidence in leaders and cause was vital, from the top down. On February 2, Cyrus H. Forwood of the 2nd Delaware Infantry bemoaned drinking and carousing: "Officers had too much of the ardent on Saturday which added to their incompetency." Drinking was a common problem among officers and, to a lesser

---

22 Ibid.

23 Chesson, ed., *J. Franklin Dyer, Journal of a Civil War Surgeon.* Dyer's accounts were traced to Dr. Justin Dwinelle at Windmill Point.

24 The original order, General Order No. 19, was issued on February 22, 1862.

25 *OR*, 25, part II, 37-38.

extent—owing to controls—among enlisted men. Forwood was especially bitter about it, though, because too much liquor among the officers had caused a mix-up in the relocation of their camp grounds, and now the men had to move all of the huts. Forwood's condemnation was justified given his two years' experience and early enlistment. "For do you know that four months more will fill up my three years," he wrote on Valentine's Day. "And then farewell to the muddy, boggy, blood stained sacred soil of Virginia. Sacred yes. The soil of Virginia is sacred, sacred to the memory of the many heroes who have fallen in the defense of our country." Suddenly sympathetic, he added: "Virginia has paid in treasure, and in blood, more precious than all treasure, a heavy price for blindly following the teachings of a few unprincipled men who sought only their own advancement and the slavery of their fellow men."[26]

Similar subtle changes were creeping in elsewhere amongst the men. Depressed on January 29, John Weiser of the 130th Pennsylvania showed improved morale in a February 8 letter from "Camp near Falmouth, Stafford County, Va.," after a better meal of soft bread, cold chicken, and hot sausage. Two days later he noted that he'd sent a cap and coat home for cleaning, to be returned via a comrade. "If I never get home," he added, "do keep them as a relic of my belonging to the Army of the Potomac, something I am and shall be ever proud of."[27]

Dispositions and Activities

On February 2, Halleck informed Maj. Gen. Dix at Fortress Monroe that IX Corps was to be assigned to him. As the IX Corps prepared to leave the Army of the Potomac, Hooker saw an opportunity. Anxious to be rid of Maj. Gen. William F. Smith—who was temporarily commanding VI Corps—Hooker suggested on February 3 that Smith be appointed to command the departing IX Corps. During the exchange, he also recommended Maj. Gen. John Sedgwick, who was "with the Ninth Corps without assignment," to command VI Corps. Halleck pointedly replied on February 4 that "Major-General Burnside is the permanent commander of the Ninth Corps"—a skillful bureaucratic reminder that Burnside, then on leave, remained in-play.

The Hooker-Halleck exchange also included a seemingly helpful warning from Halleck, who stated that greater care was necessary if Hooker and the War Department wished to limit leaves. Far too many requests came to the War Department, he said,

26 Russell P. Smith, ed., "Cyrus Forwood and the Crazy Delawares at Fredericksburg," *Fredericksburg History and Biography*, Volume IV, 2005, 20-21.

27 BV 112, part 8, letters of John Weiser.

On February 12, 1863, the IX Corps loaded aboard troop transports at Aquia Landing and sailed for Newport News. The long month-and one-half journey put the soldiers back under the wings of their former commander, Ambrose Burnside, who had been reassigned to command of the Department of Ohio. Note the coffins in the foreground. LOC

which could neither determine nor limit the parameters of General Hooker's General Order No. 3.

The shift of the IX Corps away from the Army of the Potomac gave Hooker yet another reason to reexamine the disposition of his entire force. Of particular interest was the Grand Reserve Division, commanded by Maj. Gen. Franz Sigel. Conforming to Hooker's January 28 orders, Sigel reported his dispositions on February 2. His forces were not deployed as operational reserves, but rather they served as the main firewall against enemy incursion toward the Courthouse and Aquia Creek.

The cavalry of the Grand Reserve Division—a de facto brigade of about 1,000 men commanded by Col. Louis P. di Cesnola—guarded the army's far right flank "at Allcock, near Hartwood Church." The cavalry brigade drew supplies from Falmouth Depot and foraged in western and northwestern Stafford. Cavalry outposts and videttes, deployed to the southwest and west, tied in with the XI Corps picket line of Brig. Gen. Carl Schurz' Third Division. Schurz' division, including Schimmelfennig's First Brigade and Krzyznowski's Second Brigade, was deployed "between Hartwood Church and Maria" (probably meaning Berea). They too were supplied from Falmouth "over the same roads as the cavalry." The Third Division's left joined the right of the

Union Pickets along the Rappahannock River,
with the spires of Fredericksburg visible on the far shore. LOC

Brig. Gen. Adolph Wilhelm von Steinwehr's Second Division, centered in Falmouth in the "immediate vicinity of the supply depot." Two brigades of the XI Corps' First Division were at Brooke Station guarding the railroad and Potomac Creek Bridge and Belle Plain, respectively. They drew their supplies from depots there.

One division and one brigade of the XII Corps were at Stafford Court House, facing west and drawing supplies from Hope Landing, five miles distant, and food from Brooke Station on a four-mile, partly-corduroyed road. A brigade of the XII Corps' Second Division was near Aquia Landing and drew supplies from there. The other brigade of that division was at Dumfries in Prince William County and it drew its supplies from Otterback's Wharf, four miles from Dumfries. Sigel pointed out that the road to the wharf was at times impassable, but "constant exertions" kept it open.

The brigade at Dumfries was deployed defensively around the village. Sigel noted about 300 cavalrymen assisted the deployed infantry and artillery there and were establishing videttes out to a distance of 2-3 miles. The 17th Pennsylvania Cavalry, detached from di Cesnola's command, was deployed from Aquia Church to Stafford Court House. Six companies guarded western approaches—from Stafford Store to Potomac Creek—and three detached companies were at Occoquan in Prince William County. All infantry brigades had thrown out pickets, and those at Aquia Landing and

Belle Plain protected the logistic facilities. XII Corps pickets also defended the area parallel and one mile west of the north-south Telegraph Road.[28]

Outpost duty—picketing and military responses—was the responsibility of Sigel's Grand Reserve Division's chief of staff, with control exercised by officers-of-the-day at the corps, division, and brigade levels.[29] These officers checked picket posts daily. Officers-of-the-day of divisions and brigades checked pickets at night. On the defensive perimeter, one or two infantry sentinels guarded every road, trail or cross-country approach. They were backed up by relieving pickets (15-36 men) positioned 100-200 yards behind the sentinel line. A main picket position backed-up these troops in a defensive position. Where substantial enemy advance was possible, defenses included "a general reserve of one or two infantry regiments, with one or two sections of artillery and some cavalry." Special pickets, per Sigel, were positioned at key points, principal roads, fords and bridges and/or for the purpose of connecting and supporting relieving pickets.

Corps commanders and the "commander of the Grand Division patrols and scouts" controlled tactical reserves through positioning and commitment instructions. Out beyond the infantry were cavalry outposts, usually controlled by company commanders; outer-most were videttes, cavalry pickets of one or more cavalrymen acting as mounted sentinels. The cavalry thus provided early warning to infantry pickets and main positions. Cavalry also conducted "regular patrols" with 5-25 men. Sigel listed these: from Hartwood and Allcock to the Rappahannock fords (Richards and U. S. Fords in Stafford and Kelly's Ford in Culpeper County); from Aquia Church to Stafford Springs, Rock Hill Church, and "Spottsville" (Spotted Tavern); and the Telegraph Road towards Dumfries. Cavalry in Dumfries and Occoquan sent patrols into the depths of Prince William County.

Sigel also revealed that at various times some 15-30 "scouts"—a military euphemism for spies—were assigned to the Grand Reserve Division headquarters and deployed north and west looking for Confederate formations. Lastly Sigel described regimental camp security—essentially posting guards under regimental officers-of- the-day. Such guards defended camps and prevented unauthorized departure and entry. Grand division, corps, division and brigade provost marshals positioned their own guards, patrolled, and arrested stragglers. Miscreants were "punished at once by a field officer [major or higher] of their regiment, under authority of General Orders No. 91,

---

28 OR, 25, part II, 39-40. Allcock, as stated, was closer to Spotted Tavern than Hartwood Church. Telegraph Road followed roughly the track of today's U. S. Route 1, which, ironically, is today named Jefferson Davis Highway.

29 At the corps level, officers-of-the-day were on a five-day rotation; at the division and brigade levels, they were on a daily rotation.

from the War Department." Camp police, regular inspections and drills completed troop routines.

Sigel's report offers insight about Union defenses in Stafford. Typically regarded as a static "encampment," with men shivering helplessly in huts, the Union dispositions were actually alive with thousands of individual and group actions, most of them centered around security. Hooker's defensive scheme for the Army of the Potomac was not static in concept or execution.

Presumably leaving the XI Corps' First Division in place, Sigel on February 4 ordered the Second and Third Divisions to march to Potomac Creek on February 5 and encamp there for the night. In the same order, he directed the corps' cavalry to follow—somewhat curious as the December 31 order-of-battle showed no cavalry assigned to the corps, and the Grand Reserve Division Cavalry was already deployed. Likely "the cavalry" referred to was another part of di Cesnola's command.

Hooker was repositioning and concentrating the XI Corps along the Stafford Court House to Falmouth line, protecting the heart of his defensive perimeter, Aquia Landing. The Dumfries and Occoquan detachments were left in place. The XI and XII Corps would thus be more effectively positioned on-line and constitute general operational reserves or a tactical second defensive echelon if Lee advanced or sent large cavalry raids from either the west or the south. They were thus better positioned to defend Aquia Landing, Hooker's "back door" for evacuation and resupply.[30]

The Rappahannock Station Expedition:
A Micro-Study in Hooker's Early Command

Although then in command for only nine days, Hooker took an aggressive role in operations. On February 4, he ordered Meade's Center Grand Division to conduct a division-sized "reconnaissance" raid to Rappahannock Station (now Remington in Fauquier County).

Hooker's decision was based on a February 2 reconnaissance by the XI Corps' cavalry, which had scouted from Allcock along the Marsh and Warrenton Roads. Arriving at Morrisville, the force split and followed two different roads to Mount Holly Church and, from there, to "Kellysville Ford." Guided by a "good scout" named Hogan, the Federals engaged some Confederate cavalry, saw another 50 and captured a prisoner. They also spotted a Confederate pontoon bridge across the river. By the time they reported back that evening, they'd found a Confederate cavalry brigade at U. S. Ford and another at Rappahannock Station—later identified as from the Rebel brigades

30 *OR*, 25, part II, 39-40.

of Wade Hampton and Fitzhugh Lee, respectively. Brigadier General Julius Stahel reported the findings, corroborated by a Confederate prisoner, on February 3.[31]

To Hooker, the words "pontoon bridge" must have leapt from the report. It indicated a Confederate crossing in force, with infantry, artillery, supplies, and cavalry. He must have had reservations, however, as he prudently ordered the man who had seen the pontoon bridge to go with Meade's forces. It must have been enormously embarrassing, then, given the new army commander's vigorous actions, that Stahel—who had shown sound initiative by sending another reconnaissance—soon discovered the "pontoon bridge" report was in error. The Federals had mistaken a working party in a boat or boats at the Orange and Alexandria Railroad Bridge on the Rappahannock. "I am sorry to see exaggerations sometimes even by those officers whom I consider among the best," Stahel apologized. His commander, Sigel, immediately informed Hooker, who then had Butterfield inform Meade of the error. Hooker did not, however, call off the reconnaissance. "[T]he major-general commanding directs that the reconnaissance be made as ordered," Butterfield ordered—perhaps to banish further doubts or to "exercise the system."[32] Thus, Meade was instructed to destroy a railroad bridge and segment of tracks that presented no direct threats and could be readily repaired.

Meade informed Sigel that the expedition would pass in close proximity to the Grand Reserve Division's sector. Meade sent two cavalry regiments and an artillery battery west on the Warrenton Road and advanced an infantry division to support them. He placed an infantry brigade at Grove Church (Fauquier County), where the roads to [Ely's] and Kelly's Fords turn off; another brigade at the Deep Run crossing; and a third at Hartwood Church. Additionally, Meade gave the infantry division commander "a regiment of cavalry, with which he will picket all the fords and approaches to them, from the United States to Kelly's Ford."[33]

Meade then ordered Col. John Baillie McIntosh of the 3rd Pennsylvania Cavalry to take the two regiments of cavalry and an artillery battery to Rappahannock Station and "destroy the railroad bridge, and completely destroy the railroad for a mile or more from the river" in both directions. McIntosh was informed he would be backed up by an infantry division, temporarily commanded by Brig. Gen. Joseph B. Carr, and a cavalry regiment deployed from Hartwood Church to near Deep Run. That cavalry commander was to watch the fords, especially for enemy crossings, and render warning and aid

---

31 OR, 25, part II, 45. "Good scout" Hogan may have been Pvt. Thomas H. Hogan, 9th New York Cavalry. (NPS/CWSSS; M551, Roll 65).

32 OR, 25, part II, 45-47; see 46 for Brig. Gen. Julius Stahel's report, the basis of Meade's reconnaissance.

33 Ibid.

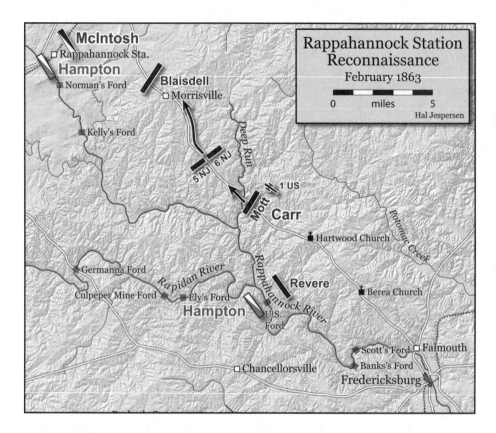

McIntosh, if he withdrew. Meade ordered McIntosh to take two days' rations for the men and one day's for the animals. In a postscript, he told McIntosh to expect an officer and an enlisted man who had served on Stahel's February 2-3 reconnaissance force, both of whom would accompany him.

Meade wrote to Carr ordering him to carry out his mission and to take three days' rations, 60 rounds of ammunition per man, and ambulances rather than wagons. Carr was further instructed to post strong infantry pickets near the cavalry pickets and maintain communications; keep cavalry pickets well back from the river; and prevent civilian communications with the enemy by posting guards at houses. Once Carr informed Meade of the dispositions, the commander would have McIntosh direct a regiment to report to Carr at Hartwood Church.

Meade's plans were solid, and his instructions were clear and competent. He may have been overly prescriptive in his instructions to McIntosh and Carr— perhaps reflective of army relations or his anxiety about over-extending these forces. Additionally, Meade demonstrated flexibility by adjusting his plan based on his cavalry subordinate's input prior to the operation: when McIntosh reported that

Rappahannock Station Reconnaissance (February 1863). New to command, Joseph Hooker ordered a reconnaissance in force in the direction of Rappahannock Station to test the Confederate position and his own internal organization. Most of the details of the raid remain a mystery because of lost reports, but Federals counted the excursion a success despite horrible weather. Supporting McIntosh's cavalry, Blaisdell's brigade moved up to Rappahannock Station just in time to watch the opposing cavalry forces clash. Mott's brigade never made it to the battlefield, and Carr's third brigade—Revere's—was apparently diverted to guard U.S. Ford against possible counter-raids against the column's flank. (Historian Kristopher D. White assisted with the preparation of this map.)

he had only 600 men in two regiments, Meade directed Carr to add another cavalry regiment, suggesting the 1st Massachusetts Cavalry.

That may have precipitated the next change: McIntosh promised Meade that if General Carr would give him three companies of the cavalry regiment attached to him, he would secure all fords above Ely's. McIntosh also informed Meade of a strong cavalry reserve at Hartwood. Meade endorsed McIntosh's recommendation that an infantry brigade planned to be at Hartwood Church should be deployed near U. S. Ford. All of this suggested an effective cavalry commander, and one whom Meade trusted.[34]

"[I]t took almost every man to furnish the detail," said a member of Third Pennsylvania Cavalry, which made up part of McIntosh's expedition. Many of the accompanying infantrymen felt foreboding. "The ground was frozen stiff, and the men were not a little concerned to know what this sudden call in mid-winter might portend," said a member of the 1st Massachusetts Infantry.[35]

They set out in a violent snowstorm. "Snow falling very fast," the Pennsylvanian recalled. Sometime after 3:00 p.m., though, it turned into a cold rain, "which froze as it fell, and made things particularly nasty," a member of the 1st Mass Cavalry added. All in all, it was bad weather for movement: "The roads are very deep and almost impassable."[36]

---

34 OR, 25, part II, 47-49. Warner's Generals in Blue, 300-301.

35 History of the Third Pennsylvania Cavalry, Sixtieth Regiment Pennsylvania Volunteers, in the American Civil War, 1861-1865, Vol. 3, Pt. 4 (Philadelphia: Franklin Printing Company, 1905), 162; Warren Handel Cudworth, History of the First Regiment; Massachusetts Infantry, from the 25th of May, 1861, to the 25th of May, 1864; Including brief references to the operations of the Army of the Potomac (Boston: Walker, Fuller & Co., 1866), 346.

36 Benjamin William Crowninshield and Daniel Henry Lawrence Gleason A History of the First Regiment of Massachusetts Cavalry Volunteers (Boston: Houghton, Mifflin and Co., 1891), 111; History of the Third Pennsylvania Cavalry, 162.

The V Corps, camped near Stoneman's Switch in Falmouth, was ordered to do a reconnaissance-in-force in weather that turned into a bitter blizzard. LOC

The next day, "in view of the present storm," Butterfield notified Meade that Hooker gave him discretion to recall his force. Meade's men continued on under clearing skies. "Hopes are now entertained of having fine weather," the Pennsylvanian reported.[37] Their destination was Morrisville, a crossroads beyond Hartwood Church. "In all the reconnoissances made this winter, Morrisville was a well-known point for camping or assembling," a Massachusetts man reported. "The name foreshadows quite a place; the fact was that the town consisted of one house and a barn. Here a road branched toward Kelly's Ford, a favorite crossing place on the Rappahannock River."

A portion of Sigel's picket line rested in the area, and although Meade had warned Sigel that the expedition would be moving through, word didn't trickle down to the men in the column that the Reserve Corps pickets would be nearby. When Sigel reported to Butterfield that his picket line had been attacked by enemy cavalry, Butterfield feared that it had actually been McIntosh's cavalry force, not Confederates.

Full details of the expedition remain a mystery. The reports of McIntosh and Carr were "not found" for inclusion in the Official Records. Carr's three brigades—Blaisdell, Mott, and Revere—seemed to advance without being in full contact with each other. Revere's brigade apparently shifted from Hartwood Church to watch over the crossing

37 Ibid, 163.

at U. S. Ford, per McIntosh's suggestion to Meade. Mott's brigade, ordered "to march on secret service"—a term generally reserved in both armies for out-of-the-ordinary reconnaissance missions, raids, etc.—arrived at Hartwood Church at around 3:00 p.m. on February 4, then marched another three hours toward Grove Church, bivouacking at Deep Run. Justin Dimick's Battery H, of the 1st United States Artillery, joined Mott as the brigade resumed its march at 8:00 a.m., reaching Grove Church at 10:30 a.m.[38]

By then, Blaisdell's brigade had made it all the way to Morrisville. They had bivouacked overnight in the woods, then moved close to the ford "to prevent any attempt by the enemy to cut off [the Federal cavalry's] retreat," one of them wrote. They arrived just in time to watch the fight erupt between McIntosh's troopers and their Rebel counterparts under Hampton. Confederates tried to cross the bridge "when a volley from the Union carbines emptied several of their saddles, and arrested their progress, and another compelled them to beat a precipitate retreat." Falling back, they reformed and brought up infantry, but Federal fire forced them back again. "The Union cavalry rode upon the bridge, at which the rebels began to destroy the other end," the Bay Stater wrote. "Seeing they could not get over, our cavalry likewise aided in the work of its demolition, and it was speedily on fire from end to end." "[T]he cavalry . . . succeeded in destroying the bridges, after something of a fight, in which several men were killed and wounded on both sides," a member of the First Massachusetts Cavalry summarized.[39]

Mott, meanwhile, sent two infantry regiments as backup—the 5th and 6th New Jersey, under the 5th's Col. W. J. Sewell—to occupy the crossroads near Morrisville. But with the action at the bridge wrapped up, Mott received orders to withdraw to camp at 6:00 p.m. He sent his artillery first and marched the infantry at 8:00 p.m. to within one mile of Hartwood Church.

From "the other side of the hill," a Confederate report from Brig. Gen. Wade Hampton to Maj. Gen. J. E. B. Stuart on February 7 fleshes out the chronicle of events with a somewhat different version. Hampton related the Federals had "endeavored to destroy the bridge, but were foiled in their attempt. . . . Just at dark a party got under the bridge on the opposite side of the river, behind the abutments, and cut a few of the posts, attempting to fire the timbers at the same time. In the meantime a vigorous attack was made on my pickets, who got into the rifle-pits, and held their ground resolutely."

---

38 *OR*, 25, part I, 7-9. Justin E. Dimick served in the U. S. Artillery at Fredericksburg and Chancellorsville. The Division Artillery, 2nd Division, III AC [Capt. J. E. Smith] (New Jersey Light Artillery, 2nd Battery; New York Light Artillery, 4th Battery; 1st U.S. Artillery, Battery H; and 4th U.S. Artillery, Battery K) did not include a Dimick's battery.

39 Cudworth, *History of the First Regiment*, 346; Crowninshield and Gleason, *A History of the First Regiment of Massachusetts Cavalry Volunteers*, 111.

The Federals were driven off at the cost of one Rebel wounded. "I regret that the condition of my horses did not allow me to follow them," Hampton added— revealing much about the overall condition of his force. "All is quiet along the lines to-night."[40]

On the clear, cool morning of February 7, the Federals all headed back to camp. Mott resumed the march, reaching his destination by 3:00 p.m. He commended his units' performance and good morale during the suddenly changing weather: a severe all-day snowstorm interspersed with rain and hail, extreme cold, and even periods of sunshine and thaw—all of which produced terrible marching conditions. The cavalrymen, too, had performed well under poor conditions. "From their appearance, they seem to be tired and worn out, riding almost day and night for the past three days through storms of snow and rain," a member of the 3rd Pennsylvania Cavalry said. "Notwithstanding all this, the column pushed forward . . . accomplished the duty for which they were sent and returned to camp without the loss of a man." Lacking McIntosh's and Carr's reports, Hampton's report alone assesses the expedition's overall cost: the Rebels "captured 25 prisoners in the last few days and killed 6 of the enemy."

For his part, Meade counted the venture a success in his February 10 report, and he praised the "energy and promptitude of these officers and their commands."[41] But if Hampton was correct, then six Union soldiers lost their lives and twenty-five men spent time rotting, or worse, in Southern prison camps because a bad bit of intelligence—one disproved by additional reconnaissance—had triggered Hooker's chilling words: "the major-general commanding directs that the reconnaissance be made as ordered." For all the emphasis Hooker placed on taking care of his men, troop care goes beyond merely seeing after their rations and dry socks; it includes not risking their lives and safety on feckless missions. Generalship sadly requires high risk, but actions must be worth those risks. By sending an infantry division, four cavalry regiments, and an artillery battery to embellish a mistake, Hooker fell far short of that American standard.

Where Elephants Roam

While the Rappahannock Bridge expedition was underway, IX Corps regrouped at Fortress Monroe. An exchange of Pennsylvania troops with the Washington Defenses took place. Hooker noted the Pennsylvania Reserves had enlisted for three years and, in fair exchange, he wished comparable replacements. He "would be pleased" if the 34th Massachusetts under Col. George D. Wells was ordered to the army, it "having served in

---

40 *OR*, 25, part I, 52-53, 54.

41 *History of the Third Pennsylvania Cavalry*, 163.

my old division for a long time." As planned, Maj. Gen. William F. Smith also shipped off to Fortress Monroe, and General Sedgwick assumed command of VI Corps.

"As desertions from this army are now at an end, or nearly so, I respectfully recommend that no infantry from my command be sent to Maryland," Hooker added. "The dragoons now there, in my opinion, is a sufficient force to arrest all deserters attempting to make their escape from service in that direction." He asked for direct command over any further infantry regiments needed in Maryland.[42]

Halleck, never one to pass up the chance to rile his erstwhile subordinate, certainly must have had this in mind when he wrote to Hooker on February 17. "Application has been made to exchange the Tenth Maine and Twenty-eighth New York for two regiments now in Maryland," he said innocently. If Hooker approved the move as "beneficial for the service," Halleck would have the orders prepared "as soon as the roads are passable." Hooker responded to this mundane request sharply: "After my experience in exchanging the Pennsylvania Reserves, by which I gave 270 more officers and men than I received, no further exchange will be made with my consent."[43]

Halleck then pried Heintzelman away from his duties supervising the Washington Defenses in order to respond to Hooker's short-change assertion. Heintzelman pointedly stated that he had been ordered to replace the Pennsylvania Reserves with "Pennsylvania troops" and that Company F of the 27th Pennsylvania Infantry had been "excepted from the order" by Halleck. Escalating things, he pointed out that on departure day, Company K of the 150th Pennsylvania had been retained by order of President Lincoln as a personal guard. Dragging in governors, Heintzelman explained that he had no authority to send troops from other states. His coup de grace was mentioning that Brig. Gen. Abner Doubleday, Hooker's subordinate, was aware of these transactions, and the "numbers at my disposal were well-understood by Doubleday when he made application." The missing numbers, he added, were expected to be made up by returning convalescents and stragglers—a group Hooker had personally pronounced moot.

Two days later Hooker's staff inevitably drew Doubleday into the fray. Assistant Adjutant General Williams passed along Heintzelman's letter together with Hooker's order. "The general commanding directs you report what agreement was entered into by you with General Heintzelman with regard to the Pennsylvania Reserves," Williams wrote. "Your especial attention is directed to that part of General Heintzelman's letter which alleges that the exchange was to be for Pennsylvania regiments and no others, irrespective of numbers." Doubleday was asked if he understood that Hooker was to

42 OR, 25, part I, 50-52.

43 Ibid., part II, 83, 87-88.

receive fewer officers and men than he sent and his reasons for not having given his personal attention to the matter.

Doubleday had already hinted that the defunct Maj. Gen. Franklin, at the time commanding the Left Grand Division, had authorized his Washington trip. On February 20, Doubleday responded that he'd always understood that equal numbers of Pennsylvanians were to be exchanged and was surprised to find otherwise. In passing, he invoked Pennsylvania's governor who had become interested in the exchange— forcing state pride to furnish equal numbers. Doubleday threw a little kerosene on the fire by stating that he believed Heintzelman hadn't favored the exchange. He would have pressed the matter, but Maj. Gen. John Fulton Reynolds had taken exception to his being in Washington and compelled his return.

All told, a petty argument over minor affairs between the two most senior officers had drawn in and affected the relations of at least a half-dozen of their busy subordinates and more staff officers, invoked the names of a president and a governor in vain, and produced absolutely nothing of value. The likes of Hooker and Halleck relished the jousting, but comparatively innocent middlemen got bumped by the bureaucratic elephants romping in the weeds. Those elephants would continue to clash, showing off the worst of themselves to the detriment of the army, in the months to come.[44]

Reorganizing the Failed "Grand" Experiment

Through all the minor conflicts—military and political—army reorganization rolled on. With the IX Corps' departure on February 5, the death knell was sounded for grand divisions. Hooker's General Order No. 6 awkwardly eulogized:

> The division of the army into grand divisions, impeding rather than facilitating the dispatch of its current business, and the character of the service it is liable to be called upon to perform being adverse to the movement and operations of heavy columns, it is discontinued, and the corps organization is adopted in its stead.

Grand divisions had accomplished but one thing: four rather than eight commanders reported directly to the commanding general. Any efficiencies gained by the arrangement had been outweighed by the additional staff bureaucracy. By reorganizing the army into seven corps, Hooker opted for more direct communication, but a greater span of control. The order announced that I Corps would be commanded

---

44 Ibid., part II, 83, 87-88.

by Maj. Gen. John F. Reynolds; II Corps by Maj. Gen. Darius N. Couch; III Corps "temporarily" by Brig. Gen. Daniel E. Sickles; V Corps by Maj. Gen. George G. Meade; VI Corps by Maj. Gen. John Sedgwick; XI Corps by Maj. Gen. Franz Sigel; and XII Corps by Maj. Gen. Henry W. Slocum.

"To-day an order is issued abolishing grand divisions and returning to the system of corps," wrote Meade in a letter home. "This is what I expected and accords with my ideas of what is best for the efficiency of the army. Baldy Smith has been relieved of his command and Sedgwick takes his corps—cause unknown, but supposed to be his affiliation with Franklin, and the fear that he would not co-operate with Hooker."[45]

As four Grand Division headquarters were eliminated, staff officer changes followed. A Federal general's personal staff (aides-de-camp), often relatives, generally went with him. The remaining staff officers became "unemployed." Compounding the injustice, these officers had usually been selected by merit for their positions. For example, the staff of the erstwhile Right Grand Division dissolved. On February 6, Maj. Gen. Couch, keeping his own staff, reported the availability of lieutenant colonels J. H. Taylor, chief of staff; C. G. Sawtelle, chief quartermaster; William W. Teall, chief commissary; and Paul J. Revere, assistant inspector general; along with lieutenants Alonzo H. Cushing, topographic engineer; and Ranald S. Mackenzie, engineer officer. All but Mackenzie were on-leave.

Couch mentioned another complication: Sumner had expressed a desire "to apply for entire staff, should he be assigned by the President to another command."[46] Because Sumner was very senior, this further dampened the staff's assignment options. They were no doubt prepared for these events—the army's generals came and went frequently—but allegiance and loyalty often led to exile and abandonment. Staff responsibilities were barely standardized, so staff officers who worked well for one general didn't necessarily know how to work effectively for another, and staff officer training had not yet been developed. Those who had cultivated or left relationships in subordinate commands might hook-up with new assignments, but that too caused ripple effects displacing or cutting-off others.

Sumner's former staffers were men of definite ability. Sawtelle and Paul J. Revere would be breveted generals; and, by war's end, Lt. Ranald Slidell Mackenzie would rise to brigadier general and command a cavalry division; in fact, by 1865, General U. S. Grant would hail him as the most promising young officer in the army at 25. Mackenzie, meanwhile, remained in engineer duties and Cushing returned to the 4th U.S. Artillery.

45 Ibid. See also Meade, *Letters*, 353.

46 Sumner was reassigned to a position in Missouri but died of a heart attack on leave at his daughter's house in Syracuse, New York, before assuming his new responsibilities. He was 66.

In another reorganization measure, Hooker returned artillery to corps control and eliminated the direct command authority of Brig. Gen. Henry J. Hunt, who was retained as "Chief of Artillery" with organizational and ordnance management responsibilities. This reorganization of the artillery would later have enormous negative consequences. Hunt had demonstrated at Fredericksburg the effectiveness of concentrating the reserve artillery under a unified command. Hooker, consistent with many senior infantry commanders, still believed artillery was best used when parceled out to the corps and divisions. Whether as a salve or based on merits, Hooker encouraged the War Department to provide brevet promotions for each corps' chief artillery officers.

Creation of the Cavalry Corps

On February 5, Hooker turned his re-organizational eye toward the army's cavalry. "The cavalry of the army will be consolidated into one corps," he ordered. As one exception, Hooker extended Col. di Cesnola's independent cavalry sector on the army's southwestern flank in Hartwood and west "until further orders."[47]

Mud-slogging infantry—who joked they'd "never seen a dead cavalryman"—likely chuckled when they recalled the total Federal cavalry casualties at Fredericksburg of two killed and six wounded. Infantry sarcasm aside, effective 19th-century generals knew heavy cavalry casualties did not herald victory any more than light casualties indicated a lack of action. Cavalry was the most complicated of that period's combat arms.

In Europe, cavalry often made up entire standing armies on the premise that infantry formations could more quickly be mobilized, trained, and deployed than horsemen; therefore, cavalry had to be kept at the ready. If correct, America had not learned that lesson. The prewar Army of 1861 contained a meager six-regiment Regular Army cavalry force, recently reorganized from two dragoon, one mounted rifle, and three light cavalry regiments. This was far too small a force to facilitate wartime expansion. Few militia cavalry units were more than parade-ready, and the Regulars' 100-man cavalry troops were too large and unwieldy for novice commanders (troops would soon shrink to 82 men). Common wisdom mandated two years were required to bring cavalry units to full military usefulness. Arming, equipping, and training a volunteer cavalry regiment was inordinately slow—and the Union Army's cavalry would ultimately expand to 252 regiments, one battalion, and 161 independent companies.

As important as manpower issues were, cavalrymen (and others) needed horses to ride. Although the North had a horse population of about 4.7 million to pick from, acquiring enough mounts and training them for cavalry duties became a labor and

47 Ibid.

industry unto itself. Needless to say, the 1861 Army lacked horse training and care facilities and veterinary services to cope with astronomical force expansion. Further, the manufacturing base was unprepared to generate huge amounts of specialized equipment needed to put and keep cavalry in the field.[48]

Leaders were also desperately needed—making Fredericksburg's casualty list a deeper sting. One of the two cavalrymen killed was Brig. Gen. George D. Bayard, who, along with Brig. Gen. John Buford, had contributed virtually all of the Union cavalry's limited wartime progress. And Buford, the best surviving cavalry leader, now led the smallest element in the new cavalry corps.[49] Moses Harris, a Regular Army cavalry officer and Medal of Honor recipient later recalled that, prior to the February 5 reorganization, cavalry was "at the disposal of generals without experience, who still further divided it, so that each brigade, almost, was provided with its troop or squadron whose duty it was to add to the importance of the general by following him about, to provide orderlies for dashing young staff officers and strikers for headquarters."[50]

The army's cavalry needs were glaringly apparent. Continually bested by Stuart's Rebel cavalry—notably organized as an independent force that could be rapidly concentrated, strike deeply, and deploy in mounted or dismounted maneuver—the Federals needed rapid development. Sadly, the Union cavalry's main function early in the war—inadvertent as it was—was limited to providing Confederate cavalry with upgraded weapons and equipment. Tactically, Federal horsemen were routinely used for mundane "palace guard" headquarters-related security missions. They screened and guarded flanks of marching and camping infantry rather than forming advance guards or reconnoitering well ahead and to the flanks. They were administratively buried and tactically stifled in an infantry-focused army. Their reporting was muddled because it went directly to many infantry commanders who seldom exchanged it with adjacent or higher headquarters. Because of organizational diffusion amid infantry brigades, divisions, and corps, their logistics and technical equipping were uneven. Unable to train or operate as units and large units, they could not develop internal leadership.

48 Brig. Gen. Theodore Rodenbough, U. S. A. (Retired), "Cavalry of the Civil War: Its Evolution and Influence," 16-38; Capt. Charles D. Rhodes, U. S. A., "The Federal Cavalry: Its Organization and Equipment," 38-70 in Miller, ed., *The Photographic History of the Civil War*, vol. 4, *The Cavalry*. Regimental statistics are drawn from Phisterer, *Statistical Record of the Armies of the United States*.

49 "The Army of the Potomac's cavalry," argues Wittenberg, "was never used efficiently or effectively during the first two years of the war." Wittenberg, *Union Cavalry Comes of Age*, Chapter 1, "Formation of the Cavalry Corps: Army of the Potomac, February 1863," 1-39. He dates the turnaround from the Hartwood Church engagement in Stafford.

50 Capt. Charles D. Rhodes, U. S. A., "The Federal Cavalry: Its Organization and Equipment," 38-70, in Miller, ed., *The Photographic History of the Civil War*, vol. 4, *The Cavalry*.

Promising young cavalry officers were lost in infantry commands. There, they had little chance to learn by experience or even shared experience from other cavalry leaders. Like their infantry brethren, the cavalry branch had suffered from the previous 20 years spent in widely separated Western posts and Eastern garrison duty. Rising cavalry leaders, like their infantry counterparts, had never seen, let alone led, the larger formations that were staples of a major war. Wartime progress was glacial. However, by February 1863, Federal troopers could fight on foot or mounted; expose their valuable horses only in massed charges, and employ carbine, revolver, and saber to good effect.

In his autobiography, General William Woods Averell articulated the wartime role of American cavalry:

> Reliable information of the enemy's position or movements, which is absolutely necessary for the commander of an army to successfully conduct a campaign, must be largely furnished by the cavalry. . . . The duty of the cavalry when an engagement is imminent is especially imperative—to keep in touch with the enemy and observe and carefully note, with time of day or night, every slightest indication and report it promptly to the commander of the army. On the march, cavalry forms in advance, flank and rear guards and supplies escorts, couriers and guides. Cavalry should extend well away from the main body on the march like antennae to mask its movements and discover any movement of the enemy. . . . Cavalry should never hug the army on the march, especially in a wooded country, because the horses being restricted to the roads, the slightest obstacle in advance is liable to cause a blockade against the march of the infantry. In camp it furnishes outposts, vedettes and scouts. In battle it attacks the enemy's flanks and rear, and above all other duties secures the fruits of victory by vigorous and unrelenting pursuit. In defeat it screens the withdrawal of the army and by its fortitude and activity baffles the enemy. . . . In addition to these active military duties of the cavalry it receives flags of truce, interrogates spies, deserters and prisoners, makes and improves topographical maps, destroys and builds bridges, obstructs and opens communications, and obtains or destroys forage and supplies.[51]

Averell, to his credit, was not merely a walking cavalry manual. In December 1862, he had proposed a large-scale Federal cavalry raid against Richmond. Received well, the raid was obviated by Stuart's Dumfries and Fairfax Station raid.[52]

Few outside the cavalry understood its sheer physical exertions. Operating beyond the range of direct material supply or comforts, their duty cycle was endless: outpost;

---

51 Wittenberg, *Union Cavalry Comes of Age*, 4-5, derived from Edward Eckert and Nicholas Amato, ed., *Ten Years in the Saddle: The Memoir of William Woods Averell, 1851-1862* (San Rafael, CA., 1978), 328-329.

52 Ibid.

picket; flank and rear security; reconnaissance and other "expeditions" securing flanks and gaining information; and courier and escort. Unless routinely rotated and rested, men and horses wore down quickly. Their misery increased with provost patrols to pick-up stragglers and deserters; impromptu missions to carry messages or supplies; and endless care and feeding of their strong-but-fragile four-legged conveyances. Men could be stretched and pushed beyond their limits in crises; but, the horses, knowing neither cause nor comrade, could not be reasoned with or inspired into greater performance. They gave everything they had, and then broke down or died. When not rested, fed and looked after, the equines simply ceased functioning.

During the "Valley Forge," cavalry operations were some of the most important. "The infantry lose more men by the casualties of battle, but the cavalry nearly make up for it in excessive duty and exposure," said Thomas Lucas of the 1st Pennsylvania Cavalry. Corp. John B. Weston of the 1st Massachusetts Cavalry grumbled, "I got in night before last from a 3 days scout and a more uncomfortable 3 days and nights I never passed. I was in the saddle 20 hours out of 24." Weston's captain, Charles Francis Adams, said, "I . . . dare not go and look at my horses. I know just how they look, as they huddle together at the picket-ropes and turn their shivering croups to this pelting northeaster. There they stand without shelter, fetlock deep in slush and mud, without a blanket among them, and there they must stand—poor beasts—and all I can do for them is to give them all the food I can, and that little enough. Of oats there is a sufficiency and the horses have twelve quarts a day; but hay is scant, and it is only by luck that we have a few bales just now when we need them most."[53]

In February, the army's cavalry, primarily the divisions of Pleasonton and Averell, guarded the extended western flank from Falmouth to Hartwood Church with outposts and videttes along the river and in greater strength at Banks Ford, U. S. Ford, and Richard's Ford. To the east, cavalry operations extended well into King George County. Brigades established rotations by squadron and watched for enemy movements; stood in reserve; and rested and cared for their animals in camps.[54]

The new cavalry corps brought new military requirements. Most were positive— e.g., flexing untried wings in independent reconnaissance operations and developing more aggressive and knowledgeable leaders. Restructuring also required new administrative actions. Clerks, adjutants and quartermasters drooled over new procedures and advancement possibilities as all command and staff positions were now all filled by cavalrymen. Bureaucratically, old orders and directives had to be acquired,

53 All quotes from Wittenberg, *Union Cavalry Comes of Age*, Chapter 2, "A Restless Winter: The Battle of Hartwood Church," 40-70.

54 Ibid.

copied, disseminated and retained in voluminous files. An example was a hand-written extract of the earlier, field-printed General Order No. 10, on the subjects of leave and desertions:

> A full register of all officers and men absent on Leave, furlough or on account of Sickness will be kept at the Head Quarters of each Regiment with the date of departure and return. These registers will be carefully examined by officers inspecting the Regiments and abstract will be sent to the Corps Head Quarters every Saturday. Corps Commanders will carefully examine the same, and report to these Head Quarters all cases of unauthorized absence. A Register of Deserters will also be kept at Regimental Head Quarters and an abstract of the same transmitted weekly to Corps Commanders.[55]

The man Hooker selected to head the cavalry corps was 40-year-old Maj. Gen. George Stoneman, then commanding the First Division of the III Corps. A New Yorker from Chautauqua County, Stoneman was in the West Point Class of 1846, where he was "Stonewall" Jackson's roommate. Classmate Darius Couch later noted their "unobtrusive, meditative dispositions, not putting themselves forward, rather thinkers than talkers." Stoneman was recalled as "esteemed by his personal associates as a generous-hearted, whole-souled companion."

Stoneman had not served in Mexico, but rather in Western cavalry assignments. Couch recalled Stoneman's "reputation of being a highly accomplished officer of the Cavalry service." Another former commander complimented him as being "universally respected by all [the unit's] Officers, and indeed I may say with truth, was the most popular officer in it."

At the onset of the war, Stoneman commanded a garrison at Ft. Brown in Texas; refusing an order to surrender to Confederate forces, he instead led his men northward to safety. Stoneman eventually earned promotion to brigadier general and appointment as the army's "Chief of Cavalry" under McClellan, who noted Stoneman had overcome "vexatious obstacles arising from the great deficiency of Cavalry arms and equipments, and the entire inefficiency of many of the first regimental officers appointed."[56]

McClellan and Stoneman's habitual misuse of cavalry reflected poorly on Stoneman, though, who found himself consistently outmatched by his Confederate

---

55 Original order dated December 21, 1863; at the 2nd Cavalry Division of the newly formed Cavalry Corps, Army of the Potomac, it was verified by H. C. Weir; at the 1st Brigade, 2nd Cavalry Division, it was verified by Capt. William H. Rogers, AAAG. Henry C. Weir, a Medal of Honor recipient, listed as "Henry G." in NPS/CWSSS. Author's collection.

56 Darius Couch, *Twenty-Sixth Annual Reunion of the Association of Graduates of the United States Military Academy at West Point, New York, June 10, 1895* (Saginaw, Michigan: Seenan and Peters, Printers and Binders, 1895), 25-28.

counterparts. By the summer of 1862, Stoneman found himself commanding infantry, instead. By December of that year, by default of his seniority, he found himself in temporary command of III Corps in Hooker's Grand Division, which saw little action during the battle of Fredericksburg.

Stoneman's command selection was presumably based on previous personal and professional connections with Hooker, appropriate rank and seniority, and his extensive cavalry experience. Given the task and time available, however, Hooker would have been better served by a younger and more aggressive figure with more practical understanding of Civil War cavalry operations, such as John Buford, but the internal politics of the army—at that time, in particular—made such a choice impossible.[57]

Assuming command of the new cavalry corps on February 7, Stoneman had a daunting task and little time. By February 10, he assessed his corps' strength at 517 officers and 10,593 enlisted men present for duty. The aggregate present was 13,452 and the aggregate present and absent was 17,166. A supplemental report of "present for duty equipped" listed all cavalry in the army with 425 officers and 9,633 enlisted men, of whom 389 officers and 8,553 enlisted men served in the cavalry corps proper. Additionally, the artillery of the cavalry corps, serving 12 guns, had eight officers and 442 enlisted men.[58]

By February 12, the cavalry corps' reorganization status was reported in its General Order No. 4. Artillery was to be moved to the mouth of Aquia Creek, as close to the railroad as possible, to be constituted into an artillery brigade for the corps. No commander was designated—"senior officer present" was the only designation listed—and quartermaster and commissary appointments were ordered formed. The artillery brigade was charged with acquiring and maintaining supplies of food and fodder. The corps was notified that pack saddles had been requisitioned so that the supplies of the entire command could be fully mobile and not be completely dependent on slower, heavier wagons.[59]

The corps' initial structure was to be three cavalry divisions of two brigades each "as nearly equal in effective strength as possible;" and a reserve cavalry brigade and artillery brigade. The First Division (Pleasonton) was headquartered at "Aquia Creek Church" and was composed of the 6th, 8th and 9th New York Cavalry Regiments; 8th Illinois Cavalry Regiment; 8th and 17th Pennsylvania Cavalry Regiments; 3rd Indiana Cavalry Regiment; and one squadron of the 1st Maryland Cavalry Regiment.

---

57 Later in the war, Lincoln, Stanton, and Grant (when he became general-in-chief) became more creative in working around seniority issues.

58 *OR*, 25, part II, 59, 65, 71-72, 75, 77-78.

59 Ibid., 82-83.

The Second Division (Averell), headquartered at Brooke Station, consisted of the 1st Massachusetts Cavalry; 1st Rhode Island Cavalry; 4th New York Cavalry; 6th Ohio Cavalry; and 3rd, 4th, and 16th Pennsylvania Cavalry.

The Third Division (Gregg), headquartered "near Belle Plain," consisted of the 1st Pennsylvania Cavalry; 1st New Jersey Cavalry; 1st Maine Cavalry; 1st Maryland Cavalry (minus one squadron); 2nd and 10th New York Cavalry; and "independent company."

Oriented toward the Rappahannock, the three divisional areas of responsibility were: First Division to the army's right; Second Division to the center; and Third Division to the left. Brigadier General John Buford commanded the Reserve Brigade, collocated with corps headquarters and comprised of the 1st, 2nd, 4th, 5th and 6th United States Cavalry Regiments. The 6th Pennsylvania Cavalry ("Rush's Lancers") were directly subordinated to cavalry corps headquarters "for the present."[60]

Stoneman expressed his desire for officers and men "to fit and perfect themselves for the most vigorous and rapid movements." Finally, he ordered them to turn in to the quartermaster department defective horses and those sick animals that couldn't be made available within a reasonable time.

Apparently the cavalry's initial geographic orientations did not last long. On February 14, Pleasanton wrote to Gregg that he was sending a regiment relieving Gregg's pickets on the left and asking for specific orders that would be in effect. Pleasonton added a postscript: "Phillips' house burned down to-day." Burnside and Sumner were now truly "gone" in the smoke and ashes of their former headquarters.[61]

A typical divisional organization was recorded on February 16 in General Order No. 13 for Gregg's Third Cavalry Division:

First Brigade (Kilpatrick)
2nd New York Cavalry
10th New York Cavalry
1st Maine Cavalry

Second Brigade (von Kielmansegge)
1st Maryland Cavalry
1st New Jersey Cavalry
1st Pennsylvania Cavalry

60 Ibid.

61 Ibid.

The "independent company" (Orton's District of Columbia Cavalry) was attached to division headquarters for orderly and general duties. Gregg ordered brigade commanders to organize their brigades "with a view to their permanency."[62]

Reorganization of the cavalry facilitated smaller and more numerous raids. The new cavalry corps was also capable of greater flexibility reacting to intelligence coming directly from army headquarters. A report by Hooker to the War Department on February 19 noted Confederates had been conscripting in the Northern Neck, establishing a supply depot at Heathsville, and receiving mail from Baltimore. In response, a Federal cavalry reconnaissance dispatched southeasterly into Westmoreland County captured horses and mules (turned over to I Corps); captured provisions (turned over to commissary); and contraband (people and property turned over to the army's chief quartermaster). U. S. Government mail bags were also recaptured. There had been a naval component to the raid, too: Hooker asked the Potomac Flotilla to send a vessel up the Rappahannock to capture or destroy the vessels moving supplies "from the Neck to the enemy." These operations took place February 10-16.[63]

Major William H. Medill of the 8th Illinois Cavalry and Capt. Craig W. Wadsworth of Reynolds' staff added further details. Medill's report, more understated than Hooker's, noted that they'd arrived at Westmoreland Court House too late to catch the reported conscription, but they captured two cavalrymen, two conscripts who were paroled on the spot, and some illicit supplies—"tobacco, sugar, coffee, saltpeter" and "nearly fifty barrels of villainous whiskey." Apparently after tasting, Medill had the whiskey and saltpeter destroyed. They camped at Westmoreland Court House that night, then rode to Warsaw in Richmond County, where they captured two 40th Virginia Infantrymen and horses, while capturing the "post office in full-blast" (the 40th Virginia's colonel, John Mercer Brockenbrough, reportedly barely escaped). The Federal horsemen then reconnoitered "Fleetwood Academy" aided by a list of locals eligible for conscription. After camping that night, they returned to Stafford on the thirteenth.

Medill also reported a "very large trade in contraband goods of every description" between Maryland and Virginia and Rebel depots at Union in Richmond County and

---

62 Ibid. The order was signed by Capt. H. C. Weir, AAG, who had apparently been moved from 2nd to the 3rd Division amidst all that "permanency."

63 *OR*, 25, part II, 86. Also see 12, 15, and 16. The Northern Neck physically consists of the lower four counties in the peninsula between the Potomac and Rappahannock Rivers (historically it also includes Stafford and King George Counties). Union Village got its name because it was at the junction of Westmoreland and Richmond Counties. It was later renamed Village. Hague (established in 1824 in eastern Westmoreland and named for a Dr. Hague). Raus McDill Hanson, *Virginia Place Names: Derivations and Historical Uses* (Verona, VA: McClure Press, 1969), 173, 210.

Hague in Westmoreland County. He added there were "probably 500 Confederates at home in the counties below this one on furloughs and deserters." The Rebels were sending 20-30 partisan rangers at a time across the Rappahannock rounding-up stragglers and deserters. Medill noted that pro-Union families provided information when "properly approached." He cited "two families named Swisher, another named Conde, and Rev. G. H. Norton."

Horses and men were scarce, having been subjected to four previous drafts, but roads and forage were adequate for a large cavalry force, so Hooker sent out a second reconnaissance. Captain Wadsworth, Reynolds' aide-de-camp, was ordered to go with Capt. Moore and two squadrons of the 8th New York Cavalry on February 13. Arriving at Westmoreland Court House at noon that day, they pushed on to Warsaw hoping to intercept mail or smuggling. Wadsworth learned of a "regular line" between Richmond and Hague, and they captured a Marylander with dress goods. They took four prisoners—one from the 9th Virginia Cavalry, two from the 40th Virginia Infantry, and one from the Signal Corps. Wadsworth noted "the latter was on duty, watching the Potomac River; the other three were on furlough." Wadsworth, confused by the abundance of Lees in the cavalry, reported that "General F. Lee's brigade is stationed in Essex County, opposite Richmond and Westmoreland Counties." He mistook Fitzhugh Lee for William Henry Fitzhugh "Rooney" Lee, who commanded his brigade there. At Machodoc Creek on February 14, the squadrons learned that a Dr. Samuel E. Spaulding of Leonardtown, Maryland, described as "the wealthiest and largest trader on the Neck," had just departed. They returned on February 16 with 17 captured horses and a mule.[64]

It is not known precisely what intelligence was gleaned from all of this cavalry reconnaissance, but the extant record of the Confederate Signal Corps and Secret Service and "Secret Lines" corroborates some of the names, places, units, and patterns involved. "Secret Line" operatives, when not conveying spies, correspondence, critical supplies, key personnel, and information into Maryland, were busy upriver rowing Federal deserters across the Potomac. Cross-Potomac covert activities also took advantage of Westmoreland County's Machodoc Creek, Rozier Creek, Mattox Creek, Bridges Creek, and Pope's Creek, as well as Potomac and Aquia Creeks in Stafford. The Federals, especially the Navy, believed these were "smuggling" and other criminal activities, rather than an intricate web on special communications lines connected to covert groups and individuals in Virginia with Maryland, Washington, Delaware, Baltimore, Philadelphia, New York, and Canada. The Northern Neck, from the Chesapeake to Stafford County, was a focal point for this activity primarily because of

64 Ibid.

its ties to Robert E. Lee and his intelligence system. All used this network to move up and down the Eastern seaboard with impunity. The 9th Virginia Cavalry and 40th Virginia, throughout the war, were connected to Confederate "secret service."[65]

Compared to covert Confederate operations, the Federal cavalry's role in intelligence gathering proved to be its most challenging post-reorganization shortfall. Historian Edwin C. Fishel suggests that reconnaissance successes were largely attributable to John Buford's earlier influence. Key personalities drove successful reconnaissance in both armies; however, Union commanders evidenced greater systemic deficiency. Fishel adds that, while army commanders considered the cavalry their most important intelligence source, they routinely found other tasks for it. A counter-argument was that cavalry was needed for security of the main body. Lost in discussion was the best combat information derived from skilled contact with the enemy. Active reconnaissance—pushing enemy contact close to full engagement to find a weakness or opportunity—produced the best intelligence.

In fairness to Joe Hooker, however, he inherited an inadequate and inefficient intelligence-gathering system. His predecessors had all failed to develop systematic intelligence approaches. Hooker's reforms still relied too much on technical means (such as reconnaissance balloons and signals intercept) rather than combat reconnaissance and human intelligence; the Confederates generally still performed better. Their "home-court advantage"—familiarity with the terrain and access to cooperative populations— was significant. General Lee, who was at heart a battlefield planner, cavalryman, and topographic engineer, guided operations with a deeper appreciation for good reconnaissance, weighing combat risk, terrain, and the effects of weather.[66]

A rising star in the Federal cavalry, Capt. Wesley Merritt of the 2nd U. S. Cavalry, later reflected:

From the day of its reorganization under Hooker, the cavalry of the Army of the Potomac commenced a new life. Before that time it had become so accustomed to meet and be overpowered by superior numbers that at times it took the numbers for granted, and left some fields to inferior foes. In its new form and numbers it avoided no enemy of any arm of the service; for, while it could contend always successfully with the enemy's cavalry, it was always sufficiently strong and confident of its powers to make a stubborn fight and a dignified retreat in the face of even an army.

65 Tidwell, Hall and Gaddy, *Come Retribution*, and Tidwell, *April '65*.

66 Edwin C. Fishel, *The Secret War for the Union: The Untold Story of Military Intelligence in the Civil War* (Boston, MA, 1996), Appendix 2.

"This new found confidence and enthusiasm," adds cavalry historian Eric Wittenberg, "spread throughout the newly created Cavalry Corps. Its time had come."[67]

Intelligence Reorganized

Cavalry operations hinted at systemic deficiencies in Hooker's intelligence-gathering operations. But he had already begun to address the larger problem in other ways. Among his other reorganizations and reforms, Hooker initiated a fundamental restructuring of the army's intelligence service.

The need could not have been greater. In McClellan's time, Allan Pinkerton and his colleagues sent spies hither and yon, producing over-inflated enemy strength estimates. With McClellan's relief, they left, taking virtually all of the acquired knowledge and information on the enemy with them—presumably to write self-congratulatory tomes justifying their suspect work. A lone, fortuitous exception, John C. Babcock, remained with the army's intelligence service. As a result, Burnside was left with virtually no intelligence support as his army ventured into Confederate Virginia. He futilely complained that operations had driven their best sources of information, the "contrabands," south beyond reach, and he hastily patched together an inadequate intelligence staff for his Rappahannock campaign.

The improved Federal cavalry force mandated a better intelligence system—one worthy of the name—to acquire, evaluate, and interpret information from cavalry, agents (spies and scouts), infantry reporting, captured newspapers, prisoners, intercepted signal and telegraph messages, and reconnaissance balloons. This operational and tactical intelligence required integration with strategic intelligence from the War Department—basically derived from Federal spies and Lafayette C. Baker's detectives. A running feud between Baker and provost marshal Brig. Gen. Marsena Patrick hampered cooperation, but relations moderated. Occasional information from the Navy and State Departments also assisted. These tentative efforts had to be orchestrated.[68]

Patrick became the lynch-pin of Hooker's and Butterfield's new intelligence system. A model of rectitude with a passion for nocturnal order—he was an insomniac —the 51-year-old Patrick found his desire for quiet continually challenged by chaotic

---

67 Wesley Merritt, "Personal Recollections—Beverly's Ford to Mitchell's Station, 1863," in Theophilus F. Rodenbough, ed., *From Everglade to Canon with the Second Dragoons* (New York: D. Van Nostrand, 1875), 285, quoted in Wittenberg, *Union Cavalry Comes of Age*, 31-32. Merritt, in Warner's *Generals in Blue*, was in a good position to judge because he had served as an aide-de-camp to generals Phillip St. George Cooke [Jeb Stuart's father-in-law] and George Stoneman.

68 Fishel, *Secret War For The Union*, 275-297, 298-310, 311-339.

The Bureau of Military Information: Col. George H. Sharpe, John C. Babcock, unidentified, and Lt. Col. John McEntee (left to right). Although the photo was taken in August of 1863, by the spring of that year, Sharpe, Babcock, and McEntee had already made significant strides in intelligence gathering. LOC

camp life. In the best traditions of the service, he who complained the loudest found himself "in-charge" of fixing the problem. Trapped in the unpopular post of provost marshal general, Patrick corralled deserters, stragglers, and malingerers and limited intrusions by spies, sutlers, and newsmen. His work against desertion required direct cooperation with Washington provost marshals and Eastern Seaboard police. He also exercised some control over river transportation and commerce. Limiting potential deserters' access to civilian clothing even led Patrick to take control of mail security.

On February 4, John C. Babcock, the lone holdover from the Pinkerton regime, provided Hooker with a report on "secret service department" duties. Guided by Babcock's report, Hooker and Butterfield placed the issue firmly in Patrick's hands: "organize and perfect a system for collecting information as speedily as possible." A line officer at heart, Patrick did not find the work satisfying. "I am trying to make up a system of Secret Service," he wrote, "but find it hard to organize where there is so little good material." Future trouble was suggested when he added: "I do not fancy the class of men & think they do not fancy me." This brought forth an age-old American military quandary pitting conventional military leaders against characters yearning to act freely or unhindered within structured military boundaries. Patrick sought a capable handler for the eclectic assortment of intelligence hard workers, prima donnas, and malcontents,

Brig. Gen. Marsena Patrick was strict but fair in his role as provost marshal of the Army of the Potomac. During the army's occupation of Fredericksburg in December 1862, he tried (largely in vain) to stop soldiers from looting the city. Expanded powers bestowed by Hooker allowed Patrick to bring much-needed discipline to the army during the early months of 1863. *LOC*

not to overlook a few frauds attracted to unsupervised work. The citizen-army always seemed to yield an indispensable smart man or two (oddly, they were usually lawyers).

In this case, it was Col. George Henry Sharpe of the 120th New York Infantry, whom Patrick appointed on February 11, 1863. Sharpe combined a legal background with service as a regimental commander. With a rigorous mind and a basic military knowledge gained as a regimental commander, he was a distinct asset. Interestingly, Sharpe spent time during his alleged "decision-making period" consulting with Col. Daniel T. Van Buren at Fortress Monroe and in Baltimore discerning ways to infiltrate spies as "deserters" or "smugglers" into Rebel territory.[69]

Patrick's strength was in operational security—denying information and access to enemy intrusions—which was now fortuitously a priority, as it worked hand-in-glove

69 Ibid. See also: www.cia.gov/library/publications/additional-publications/civil-war/p16. htm (accessed September 11, 2010).

with information-gathering and intelligence analysis. Developing an intelligence system was vital; however, it was equally important to employ counter-intelligence in order to stop interminable leakage of army data. Security was improved by exercising greater control of newspapermen, sutlers, and civilian aid volunteers and by limiting contacts with Stafford's populace. On February 13, Hooker informed Patrick he wanted "all trading establishments, peddlers, &c., within the lines of the army, except regularly authorized and appointed sutlers" broken up and sent out of the lines that day. After 24 hours, all "goods, wares, and horses" would be confiscated and benevolently split between the army's three general hospitals at Aquia Landing, Belle Plain, and Windmill Point. Revealingly, Hooker's headquarters were apparently unaware those hospitals had been closed down by Surgeon Letterman. That same day, Hooker warned the Adams Express Company in Washington to place invoices on incoming packages and stop mailing civilian clothes, which assisted in desertion, and intoxicating liquors to soldiers. However, the letter specified there would be no change in officers' packages policy—presumably meaning intoxicating liquors would continue to flow to them. Hooker asked War Department assistance in clamping-down on forged passes and limiting authorizations to one known officer each in the War Department and Military Governor's Office. Further centralizing, on February 17 Hooker assigned Patrick control of the entire Washington-Stafford mail service.[70]

Historian Edwin Fishel characterized Hooker, Butterfield, and Patrick as a "triumvirate" overseeing army intelligence activities. The term triumvirate suggests a certain unrealized synergy, though. Patrick shared reservations about Hooker's (and Butterfield's) moral standing.

Patrick and Sharpe did not know each other. Sharpe's new boss, Patrick, did not enjoy good relations with Butterfield even though Sharpe did. However, Patrick had developed an undeniable eye for counter-intelligence.

On February 5, Patrick met with a group of New Yorkers, including Col. John Morgan, former owner of the Eagle Gold Mine in southern Hartwood near the U. S. Ford. Morgan provided valuable local references for loyal men. On the other side of Stafford County, largely through his own devices, Patrick had zeroed in on the cross-river spying operation of Mrs. Jane Gray of "Traveller's Rest." He regularly tried to catch her in the act, only to be spotted and welcomed for tea by the charming matron. Patrick's spy-catching had a major flaw, in any case: Despite his dour demeanor, he was kind-hearted and trusting, and this did not serve him well in ruthlessly rooting out espionage.

---

70 *OR*, 25, part II, 73-74, 84.

Sharpe was not "Patrick's man," per se. One account, based on his diary, suggests Patrick felt Sharpe was "Tricky and full of all sorts of Policy," presumably pertaining to Sharpe's "lawyerly" ways. Col. Sharpe was powerfully tied to Butterfield and, in his new position, directly reported to Butterfield and Hooker. Sharpe's ties to Butterfield may have been prewar political New York in origin, and his military roots lay in Hooker's old division. He did not have many combat merits, as Sharpe's regiment had only recently come from the Washington Defenses, played a brief combat role at Fredericksburg, and slogged through the "Mud March." A Republican and alumnus of Rutgers and Yale, Sharpe also had potentially dangerous ties to key Washington men, including Congressman John Steele—his law partner—and Secretaries Seward and Stanton. Those associations, especially with the latter two members of the president's cabinet and inner circle, inevitably engendered misgivings among senior military men. Such palace intrigues confounded good intelligence work and created distrust. [71]

Once engaged, however, Sharpe moved aggressively. He combed the army for potential spies, recruiting three from the 3rd Indiana Cavalry: sergeants Milton Cline and Daniel Cole and Pvt. Daniel Plew. From Ohio units he recruited infantry Sgt. Mordecai P. Hunnicutt, a former detective, and artilleryman Henry W. Dodd. A New Yorker, D. G. Otto, formerly a schoolteacher in the South, was provided by Maj. Gen. Sedgwick. The army also fielded a number of civilian spies. Some, like Jackson Harding and Joseph M. Humphreys, were holdovers. Stafford County's home-grown Union spy, J. Howard Skinker of "Oakley," returned from D. C. exile. Others included Spotsylvanians Ebenezer McGee and Isaac Silver. Maj. Gen. Heintzelman contributed his most effective spy from the Washington Defenses, Ernest Yager. Sharpe added Capt. John McEntee, an Ulster County neighbor, as a report writer and interrogator. A brilliant choice, McEntee had also served in Patrick's old brigade in the first Federal occupation of Stafford in April-September 1862. Knowing the ground and the Stafford people aided Patrick's and McEntee's effectiveness. This made a good start, but Sharpe lacked adequate time to validate his agents' reliability.[72]

Briefly known as the army's "Secret Service Department," Sharpe's organizational title thus conflicted with Baker's in Washington. It was soon changed to the lower-keyed "Bureau of Military Information." Sharpe maintained a civilian payroll, paid from the War Department's Secret Service Fund, which detailed his staff and spies. John C. Babcock received $7.50 per day; Skinker got $5.00; and Humphreys $4.00, all above the standard $2.00 wage for agents. The payroll also listed several "colored" employees paid $1.00 per day. Since a mess was known to have been established, they

---

71 Fishel, *Secret War For The Union.*

72 Ibid.

may have been cooks or teamsters. Fishel notes, however, that two—Dabney Walker and Louis Battail—had protested the low wages, suggesting "they may have been used as agents," but they did not file a claim.[73]

This recalls an 1882 work, Anecdotes, Poetry and Incidents of the War: North and South 1860-1865, which discussed a freed slave, "Dabney," and "The Clothes-Line Telegraph." In this light, the subtly bigoted account is worth quoting:

> In the early part of 1863, when the Union army was encamped at Falmouth, and picketing the banks of the Rappahannock, the utmost tact and ingenuity were displayed, by the scouts and videttes, in gaining knowledge of contemplated movements on either side; and here, as at various other times, the shrewdness of the African camp attendants was very remarkable.
>
> One circumstance in particular shows how quick the race are in learning the art of communicating in signals. There came into the Union lines a negro from a farm on the other side of the river, known by the name of Dabney, who was found to possess a remarkably clear knowledge of the topography of the whole region; and he was employed as a cook and body servant at headquarters. When he first saw our system of army telegraphs, the idea interested him intensely, and he begged the operators to explain the signs to him. They did so, and found he could understand and remember the meaning of the various movements as well as any of his brethren of paler hue.[74]

According to the account, Dabney's wife and daughter were positioned as laundresses with a Confederate headquarters. They had worked out a series of signals to be displayed on clothes lines where she hung her laundry. Thereafter Dabney became highly informed about events and plans on the far shore, despite never being absent from camp. He explained his code system to inquiring officers and continued to provide accurate information during the "Valley Forge."[75]

Without apparently knowing of the 1882 account, Fishel seems to have confirmed Dabney's role, at least in its particulars. "A spy had been placed in Fredericksburg, from where she (there is evidence that she was a Negro woman) was to communicate across to Falmouth by means of a simple 'clothesline code,'" Fishel writes. "Babcock described it to Butterfield: 'A clothesline with one piece denotes that the forces in the vicinity of

73 Ibid.

74 Ruth Coder Fitzgerald, *A Different Story: A Black History of Fredericksburg, Stafford, and Spotsylvania, Virginia* (Fredericksburg, VA, 1979), 87. Motives and sources of this 1882 article were unknown; however, articles of that period tended to disparage or make light of black people's activities. The 1882 article was reprised in B. A. Botkin, *A Civil War Treasury of Tales, Legends and Folklore* (Promontory Point, NY, 1960).

75 Ibid.

Fredericksburg are on the move. An empty line denotes that they have all gone away. Two pieces shows that they are in force as they have been since the fight, three pieces that they are being reinforced. One piece has been displayed all day yesterday and today, till 4:00 p.m. when observer came away.' Butterfield wired Hooker in Washington that 'Sharpe's signals' indicated an enemy move."[76]

Sharpe's "all-source" analytical activities are likened by Fishel to those of George Washington in the Revolutionary War—an ironic comparison as Lee was employing Washington's system to a finer point. "Sharpe not only reported the findings of the three collection functions under his own control [espionage, interrogation, and scouting/military spies]," Fishel summarizes, "but also merged them with the products of six other types of collection—cavalry reconnaissance, balloons, Signal Corps observation stations, flag-signal interception, examination of Southern newspapers, and reports telegraphed by neighboring commands." Regardless of shortcomings, a basic military intelligence system was being cobbled together.

Perhaps a bit over-generously, Fishel ascribes the "history-making invention of all-source intelligence" to Hooker's innovations. The reforms certainly moved in the direction of producing decision-facilitating intelligence from a mass of fog; however, effective use of all intelligence sources remained elusive for a century. Reform, it must be recalled, requires a beginning, and for the Union Army it began with Sharpe's "Valley Forge" efforts. Sharpe's reforms—like those of Hunt with artillery and ordnance, Letterman with medical service, Butterfield and Williams with administration, Ingalls with logistics, and Haupt with transportation—paid increasing dividends to the army and Union cause.[77]

Despite the significant strides forward, reporting problems persisted. On February 21, II Corps Commander Maj. Gen. Darius Couch exposed one such vulnerability. "I telegraphed you last evening that the pickets had reported that sixteen pieces of artillery and eleven pontoons were seen passing through Fredericksburg down the river," he wrote to Hooker. "The information did not get to me until twenty-four hours or more after the movement was observed—as stupid a thing as ever occurred in military history. It is but a specimen of how military duties are done by a great many officers in my corps." Couch complained of a lack of attentiveness by his officers. "Upon personal investigation, I find that the movement of pontoons and artillery was seen by so many that nobody reported the fact," he confessed. "The general officer of the day was

---

76 Ibid. Fishel, *The Secret War For The Union*, 314; Chapter 13, 653, fn 11 cites: "Babcock to Butterfield, March 11, 1863, BMI"; *OR* 25, part II, 135-136. A Babcock memorial article (Mount Vernon, NY, *Argus*, November 20, 1908) notes "a Negro woman spy communicated with Babcock by means of a 'clothesline code,' but the account gives no time or place."

77 Fishel, *Secret War For The Union*, Chapter 13, covering February 1-March 8, 1863.

Colonel Frank, one of our most sterling officers." Couch confided in his commander and trusted him to process this candid assessment with seriousness in hopes that, together, they could solve the problem.

The reply from AAG Williams demonstrated that Hooker utterly missed Couch's point. "Major-General Hooker directs me to say that it is a most extraordinary report," he chided. "The general cannot think you expect him to bring your officers to a sense of their duty. He trusts that you will have no delay in bringing the officer who neglected his duty to trial and punishment. It is of the utmost importance to him to know if the enemy have any pontoons, and, if so, how many and where they are. He desires that you should communicate with him without delay all reliable information you can obtain upon this point."

This necessitated Couch's painful response addressing both intelligence and command issues. Of the former, he wrote, "I am unable to report anything in addition to that of yesterday, but having directed a more diligent inquiry, will inform you as soon as it comes in. The men I questioned yesterday were not positive that pontoons were seen, but thought they were. As for the artillery, one man counted thirty-two six-horse carriages that he supposed were artillery, but could not see the guns." Couch then got to the heart of matters. "I did not intend for the major-general commanding to understand that I wished to throw off the responsibility of disciplining my command, but rather for him to be informed as to the difficulties in the way of duty," he explained, "as, for instance, this most unwarrantable neglect of duty occurred under the best picket officer I have, and as good a one as I ever knew, and, too, at a time when we were endeavoring to perfect our picket system, and thought we were successful."[78]

Williams' response from Hooker certainly ensured that no further confidences would be coming from Couch—a grievous problem considering Couch was, by his seniority, Hooker's second in command. By treating a corps commander as a neophyte needing a tutorial—and as one unaware that pontoon bridging movements were significant indicators—Hooker ensured he would only receive either the barest facts or overly confirmed data. Embarrassed, Couch and his subordinates would check such reports better. But, in such an atmosphere, reports would be held too long, thereby increasing the risk of surprise. When in doubt, Couch and his men would likely avoid communicating at all—which was the surest path to intelligence failure. Commanders and staffs needed to implicitly trust one another so they could work together. This episode betrayed Hooker's major personality flaw, and greatly reduced his command effectiveness.

78 OR, 25, part II, 93-95.

Changes Below the Surface

Beneath the surface of Hooker's large-scale reorganizations, change continued to ripple through the army. Top echelon re-shuffling obscured almost endless shifts within the brigades and regiments.[79] Key officers came and went.

Lieutenant Elisha Hunt Rhodes, between February 7 and 18, shed light on command changes—and picket duty—in the 2nd Rhode Island. From February 7-10, they picketed along the Rappahannock's banks. "I went in command of Co. 'D' and with three companies occupied a plantation house near the river," Rhodes recounted. "We kept fires burning in the fireplaces and it was not so bad afterall. The men occupied the Negro quarters. As firing at pickets is forbidden by each side the men were allowed to go down by the river banks. We did not allow our men to talk to the Rebels, but they kept up a stream of questions. They were anxious to know where the 9th Corps had gone. It seemed queer to see them only a few yards away in their gray clothes." Rhodes remarked on the quality of their band music. The Rebels, he said, were anxious to get New York newspapers and coffee, but the Federals refused. Returning to camp they found a new commander, Col. Horatio Rogers Jr., formerly of the 11th Rhode Island. "He seemed to be much surprised when he learned of our late troubles [with Governor Sprague] and that we were opposed to having him come to us as Colonel," Rhodes admitted. After speaking with some officers, Rogers cleverly sent Lt. Col. Goff home to the governor with a request to appoint him colonel and send Rogers back to the 11th. Instead of forcing the change, Rogers disarmed the opposition, won the respect of the regiment, and continued to command the 2nd.

Incessant regimental changes tossed up both forth good and bad men. Good men in citizen-armies have ambition, but not careerist ambitions to further advancement at any price. Citizen-soldiers tended to focus more on the possibilities of command or what they could do if given command. Such men demonstrated respect for citizen-soldiers under their control and wanted to handle them well and with minimal losses. One of these was Maj. Henry Livermore Abbott of the 20th Massachusetts, who wrote on February 8: "I am in command of the regiment . . . . Oh, by jove, you don't know how much I would give to be permanent commander of this regt. & I can hardly imagine greater bliss than to be commander of a regt. in which all the companies were as good as my own."[80]

---

79 See, for example, highlighted order-of-battle command changes in Appendix 2.

80 CHJHCF. Robert Garth Scott, ed., *Fallen Leaves: The Civil War Letters of Major Henry Livermore Abbott*, (Kent, OH., 1991), 168.

A better example of an important trend in regimental and brigade command took place in the 3rd Vermont Infantry. The regiment's colonel, Breed Hyde, was allowed to resign to avoid a court-martial. Hyde had been repetitively "absent sick" for most of the unit's actions and this built-up to charges. He was supplanted by Col. Thomas O. Seaver, a Norwich University-trained citizen-officer who had risen on merit. Old Army fuss and feathers and "by the book" administration were replaced with common sense leadership. Seaver's command assumption order was direct: "The Executive of the State of Vermont has confided to me the command of the Third Regiment. I shall endeavor to be worthy of your confidence, and to return his unimpaired." For the next 17 months, Seaver focused on real discipline. As historian Robert G. Poirier expressed it: [during Seaver's tenure] "one is more likely to find punishments for 'not reporting a sleeping sentry'—a corporal was broken to the ranks as a result – rather than lengthy tomes concerning the 'proper wearing of cross belts.'" Around that time, Col. Lewis A. Grant of the 5th Vermont moved up to command the First Vermont Brigade. When predicated on merit, such promotions were almost always successful as the men knew the officer's character and achievements and more readily accepted their leadership.[81]

Where Eagles (and Turkeys) Soar

Of the most colorful characters to rise to prominence during the Civil War, none rose so high—quite literally—than the remarkable Thaddeus Sobieski Constantine Lowe. "Professor" Lowe, an early aeronautical pioneer, had achieved success early in the war by conducting aerial reconnaissance using hot air balloons.

In April 1861, Lowe had tested his balloon Enterprise on a flight carrying him some 650 miles in nine hours from Cincinnati, into Virginia, down across North Carolina, and into South Carolina's backcountry. Landing in secessionist territory, Lowe was arrested, but he convinced his captors he was not a spy and they released him. Lowe's misadventure helped him realize an opportunity for useful national service and, bypassing others' efforts, he moved to Washington, D.C., to establish a Union aeronautic or balloon corps. Adept at persuasion, organizing, marketing, and cultivating halls of power, Lowe found believers among the political class. Combining ballooning with telegraphy in a demonstration at the President's Mansion on June 17, 1861, Lowe sent the first airborne telegraph message to the president: "we command an extent of country nearly fifty miles in diameter." This brought presidential endorsement and, of course, more demonstrations. Some of Lowe's former competitors joined his effort, but the stodgy Army bureaucracy, struggling to grasp advanced technologies like breech-

---

81 Poirier, *They Could Not Have Done Better*, 78-79. Grant offeres an excellent example, leading his men in meritorious service in such battles as Second Fredericksburg and the Wilderness.

"Professor" Thaddeus S. C. Lowe's aeronautic corps employed a new technology with mixed success. Rather than support Lowe in his efforts to work out the kinks, Hooker marginalized him. *LOC*

loaders, was not keen to take on aerospace warfare. Lincoln nevertheless persevered and essentially forced General Scott and company to form the Aeronautics Corps.[82]

Lowe himself somewhat missed the main point of a war. He moved his organization ahead with the idea of flying balloons over enemy lines and forces—the ones that actually shoot bullets—and returning with information. Thus he had to worry about getting shot at by both sides, going and coming back, as exemplified by his earliest flight, from Arlington House, which resulted in a shoot-down by Federal troops. Soon thereafter, the Army's Bureau of Topographical Engineering, Lowe's initial supervisors, discovered that hot air in Washington, although never in short supply, was expensive. Nevertheless, Lowe's aeronauts developed their craft in operations on the Potomac and in the Virginia Peninsula in the spring and summer of 1862 respectively.

Lowe's group remained idle until September 1862, when McClellan again became the principal field commander. Despite his belief in balloons, they were deployed too late for Antietam. With McClellan's final relief and Burnside's succession to command, the balloon corps languished. The aeronauts were ordered to the Rappahannock and

82 Charles M. Evans, *War of the Aeronauts: A History of Military Ballooning in the Civil War* (Mechanicsburg, PA, 2002), Chapter 14, "Thaddeus Lowe's Last Battle," 263-287.

took up a position near the Phillips House in Stafford, and remained there through Fredericksburg. Burnside feared tipping his hand and ordered the balloonists not to show themselves, denying any possible pre-battle intelligence usefulness.

During the battle itself, the balloons were used badly and to little effect. Significantly, however—given later developments—Dan Butterfield, then commanding V Corps, ascended with a balloon for some command reconnaissance. "That was of great value in making dispositions and movements of troops," he later declared. After Fredericksburg, on December 22, a balloon reconnaissance confirmed that Confederates remained across the river in-force. During the "Mud March," the same wind and rain that sank the army's fortunes kept the aeronauts grounded.

Although Hooker's promotion brought intelligence and reconnaissance reforms, the balloon corps' fate did not measurably improve. Butterfield, as the new chief of staff, provided some hope for effective use; however, they were administratively subordinated to the Quartermaster Department, and submerged operationally under the army's chief engineer, Lt. Cyrus B. Comstock. Comstock had made some ascents during the battle, and he believed the balloons had some value in gathering topographic information. However, no one yet perceived the value that might result from integrating their reconnaissance results with other intelligence sources. To further complicate matters, sometime in February 1863, Lowe was summoned to appear before a Congressional committee investigating the balloon corps.[83]

On February 3, Lt. S. Millett Thompson of the 13th New Hampshire recalled a tale of collateral, if humorous, damage suffered because of the balloons. "David Hogan of 'E' has an experience that he can never forget," he wrote. "His round of duty takes him near regiment's sinks and cesspools [i.e., field latrines]. A large shell, intended for one of Professor Lowe's balloons, falls into one of them and bursts there, and scatters about two cartloads of the vile contents for rods around, nearly burying Hogan out of sight. Hogan is unhurt, beyond a scare, but his clothing and appetite are utterly ruined."[84]

Back to Reality: The View From the Bottom

What began as a winter of discontent, by mid-month, had become a season of change. Reorganization rippled up and down the ranks, and reforms began, albeit slowly, to pay off dividends. Hooker reminded the War Department on February 15

---

83 Ibid.

84 F. Stansbury Haydon, *Military Ballooning during the Early Civil War* (Baltimore, MD, 2000), 344; S. Millett Thompson, *History of the Thirteenth Regiment, New Hampshire Volunteer Infantry, in the War of the Rebellion, 1861-1865* (Boston, MA,1888), 106.

that 85,123 men (2,935 officers and 82,188 enlisted) had been "absent from this command when first placed in my charge." Just days earlier on February 10, a head count of the army tallied only 64,684 officers and men absent from duty—a remarkable recoup of a corps's worth of men during the short period of time Hooker had been in command.[85] Those numbers, fresh on General Halleck's desk when Hooker wrote on the fifteenth, provided the army commander with at least some degree of smug satisfaction.

Not everyone was quick to see the benefits or embrace the changes, of course. "The only thing worth mentioning is that the army is made up of Corps now. Grand Divisions are done away with, per orders read to us last evening," groused Ferris, the infantryman from the 83rd New York, who criticized Hooker for "trying to immortalize himself." "Orders, to the amount of bushels are being sent in, and us poor soldiers have to wade up to our knees in mud (evenings) to listen to these documents read." He then attacked the red-tape and poor quality regimental and brigade commanders who created work for the men without considering previous attrition. Ferris' regiment was down to 271 men. He bemoaned a lack of replacements and home support.[86]

But all was not quite hopeless, and among hundreds of thousands of young and energetic Americans, only so much downheartedness and low morale was possible. Problems indeed persisted, but the future looked decidedly brighter. A sense of improvement hung in the air like frosty breath. Indeed, to the common soldier, the great swirl of activity in Stafford must have seemed as if the "the modern age" was coming alive.

"I can see for miles up and down the Potomac," wrote James P. Stewart of Knap's Pennsylvania Battery E on February 10, 1863. "Vessels coming and going, under full sail and others with a full head of steam driving ahead, giving an occasional puff of their whistle. All bustle and confusion about the [Aquia] landing as the 9th Army Corps is going out on transports for Fortress Monroe or New Bern [North Carolina]. See a steamboat back out with a band playing and colors flying, it's grand I tell you. And then again the Rail Road passes just in stones throw from our camp, the Locomotive screeching and puffing. Trains loaded with soldiers, both going and coming. All this work going on."[87]

---

85 *OR*, 25, part II, 77-78, and part I, 65.

86 Styple, ed., *Writing and Fighting the Civil War*, 166-167.

87 James P. Stewart, February 10, 1863, letter, quoted from James P. Brady, comp., *Hurrah for the Artillery! Knap's Independent Battery E, Pennsylvania Light Artillery* (Gettysburg, PA, 1992), 197. Jane Conner, *Lincoln in Stafford*, 36.

Not that it was all work. Snowball fights led the winter games, just as baseball would break out in better weather. One soldier of the 19th Massachusetts Infantry recalled one such February 1863 snowball battle that included a new multi-racial wrinkle:

Another jolly time I recall. One day a light snow had fallen, and the men began to snow-ball. Soon companies were engaged and then the right and left wings of the regiment were pitted against each other. I was with the left wing and we were holding our own when the drum corps re-enforced the right. Up to this time headquarters had been spectators, but they became excited, and joined the right wing. With such re-enforcements, the battle would soon be lost to us, but I remembered that some twenty of our negro servants were in rear of the hospital tent, and went to them and offered bounty if they would enlist. They hesitated, but I assured them that I would stand the blame if they joined our forces. Having loaded every one with an armful of snow balls, I charged over the hill and attacked headquarters by the flank. If anyone doubts the bravery of colored troops he should have seen my army that day. They rushed upon the foe, regardless of who it was. Their ammunition exhausted, they started on the charge with heads down, and butted all before them. Headquarters vanished. The right wing gave way, and the left held the field. It was the first battle won by colored troops in the war, and proved they could fight if well officered.[88]

Change, it seems, came in many forms. More was on the way.

---

88 CHJHCF. John G. B. Adams, *Reminiscences of the Nineteenth Massachusetts Regiment* (Boston: 1899), Chapter 7.

Chapter Five

Great Advances

Never did February of 1863 feel more like the Revolutionary era's Valley Forge than on February 22 which, ironically, was also George Washington's birthday.

"It commenced snowing about dark last night & when we got up this morning we found a pyramid of snow about three feet high in one corner of the tent. And an extra blanket of the same material covering our persons," shivered one Union soldier, Edwin B. Weist, 20th Indiana Infantry, at Camp Pitcher. "The snow is deepest I remember to have seen it for several years."[1] If that didn't evoke imaginings of the snow-swept winter at Valley Forge, cannon fire soon did. "Washington's birth day was celebrated by a salute of thirty four guns from different batteries in the neighborhood," Weist reported. The 34-gun salute honored the pre-secession Union. Consistent with Lincoln's wishes, the national flag and such salutes never subtracted the 11 Confederate States.

America's greatest founding father had also been Stafford's most famous resident. His boyhood home, later known as "Ferry Farm," was situated on the banks of the Rappahannock in Stafford. Indeed, the river that separated the two armies was the one that a ferry had regularly crossed and where Washington, as a boy, allegedly threw a coin from the farm to Fredericksburg.[2] Federal troops occupied the grounds where the famous cherry tree, if chopped, would have been chopped. Vestiges of what they incorrectly believed were the Washington farm buildings were still visible.

---

1 Jane Conner, *Lincoln in Stafford*, 36. The Diary of Edwin B. Weist (transcribed by Gordon Bradshaw of Mayer, Arizona).

2 In actuality, Washington threw a stone, not a coin as the popular tale was later remembered. The point is probably moot as most historians believe the story apocryphal. It was possible, as retired Washington Senators' pitcher and manager Walter Johnson replicated the legendary feat using coins on February 22, 1936, with two of the three hitting the Fredericksburg side.

George Washington. The general's boyhood home, Ferry Farm, sat on the Union side of the Rappahannock River. The few buildings there served as a physical reminder to the men in both armies about the nation's founding principles. Both viewed Washington as a hero. LOC

Both armies sincerely believed Washington was their spiritual father— at once the creator of the Federal Union and leader of the First American Revolution. Postage stamps, patriotic envelopes, and stationary on both sides bore his image. One of the three most popular types of privately purchased identification disks worn by Union soldiers bore his profile and birth date. Meanwhile, the Great Seal of the Confederacy depicted Washington's lone, mounted image and the date of the Confederacy's formal creation: February 22, 1862, the anniversary of Washington's birth. Even as Union soldiers heard the boom of the salute, the ammunition-deprived Confederate artillery responded on that same day with a small salute of their own.[3] Band music was also heard from the Rebel side.

"The birth day of our great Father, Geo. Washington!" wrote a diarist from the 122nd Pennsylvania Infantry, encamped at Stoneman's Station. His prose, while romanticized, was nonetheless sincere:

Our large guns have not forgotten the memorable day that brought forth the innocent babe which in its early youth manifested those rare qualities which mark the man. The Right Arm of the gallant army which secured us our liberty is still cherished in 'the hearts of his countrymen.' The troubles which he predicted, & against which he so warmly & earnestly bade us to strive have, in spite of his warnings, ripened to more than he dared apprehend. The house in which was born [sic] this noble 'Chief' stands but two miles from where we encamp, & is occupied by rebels [meaning the owners]. Time has wrought a wonderful change; the grounds which were trod by the very embodiment of innocence & truth &

3   Fishel, *Secret War for the Union*, 303, cites Marsena Patrick's diary of February 22, 1863, and relates the fact of the Southern artillery's response.

afterwards enjoyed by the standard of gallantry and virtue are now nourishing traitors, plotting to destroy that Government which was established for the security of their rights and liberties.[4]

Ironically, the diarist was quoting "Light Horse Harry" Lee's tribute, "First in War, first in peace and first in the hearts of his countrymen." As it was, the "rebels" and "traitors" on the opposite bank of the river were commanded by Light Horse Harry's son, Robert, born just a few miles from Washington's birthplace on Virginia's Northern Neck.

R. E. Lee grew up trying to emulate everything about our first president. He even married into the Washington family. His mother-in-law, Molly Fitzhugh Custis, was born and raised at Stafford's "Chatham" (known during this war as "Lacy House"), overlooking Ferry Farm, the Rappahannock River and Fredericksburg. This and other ties linked Lee to Stafford. As executor for father-in-law George Washington Parke Custis's estate, Lee had been the de facto curator of the primary national collection of Washington memorabilia. No doubt for inspiration, Lee carried one of Washington's swords in his military baggage.[5]

As idealistic as the Pennsylvanian had been in his diary, he wasn't blind to the day's weather. "The snow is 10 or 12 inches deep and the weather is very cold," he wrote. "The boys are content in their little tents, so the streets are clear from all animals in shape of soldiers."[6] Others made mention of the poor conditions, too. "[A] heavy snow storm visited the country around Fredericksburg and added somewhat to the discomforts of the army," reported Sidney Morris Davis of the 6th U.S. Cavalry. "As this was the anniversary of Washington's birthday, we had expected a sort of holiday, but the chilly blasts and driving snow obliged each of us as were fortunate enough to be off duty to keep under our frail shelters."[7]

In fact, the weather did much to steal the Federals' celebratory thunder. Lieutenant John H. Stevens of the 5th Maine, accustomed to northern New England winters, mentioned that the regiment had been called out to hear Washington's farewell address

---

4   BV 152, Pennsylvania, part 2, FSNMP, Joseph Franklin Mancha Papers. The birthplace "house" was actually in Westmoreland County at Pope's Creek. Even the standing building in Stafford was not the original Washington farm house. Ferry Farm was on ground originally in Stafford, then King George, and again in Stafford County at the time of the Revolution.

5   Richard B. McCaslin, *Lee in the Shadow of Washington* (Baton Rouge, LA, 2001) provides a more complete exposition of Lee-Washington connections.

6   BV 152, Pennsylvania, part 2, FSNMP, Joseph Franklin Mancha Papers.

7   Cooney, ed., *Common Soldier, Uncommon War*, 291-300.

and a prayer from the chaplain. Other diarists, however, seemed only to notice the cold.[8] "On the 22nd we started at seven in the morning in four inches of snow and I never saw it snow and blow so hard in my life," wrote a soldier from the 140th Pennsylvania Infantry. "It snowed about 18 inches and we were from seven until two o'clock going six miles. Sometimes we went through drifted snow shoulder deep." He added ruefully, "I thought the weather could not be any worse, but I was wrong."[9]

"There's about a foot of snow on the ground and it's falling yet," exclaimed Lt. Sam Partridge of the 13th New York Infantry. "How I've pitied the pickets today, how I pity them tonight—no tents, no fire, no comfort—lonely and vigilant. There's a picket of 2,000 some four miles out. [Lt.] Col. [Francis A.] Schoeffel is in command of the whole—214 are from this regiment. It took a mounted messenger four hours to come in this morning."[10] The 24 year-old graduate of the City College of New York found the blizzard particularly shocking because, just days earlier, he'd sensed a taste of spring. "Since the last snow storm we have been enjoying warm pleasant days and very cold, very damp nights, and I spent every moment I could out of doors enjoying the sunshine," he'd written about the days leading up to Washington's birthday:

> In the afternoon I was riding cross country from Stafford Court House and thinking how soon the tulip trees and azaleas and cotton woods, and magnolias, would be in blossom and how dense the foliage would be, and looking at the briar thickets and Virginia creepers, and the laurel bushes growing on the edges of the cypress swamps, and thinking how many in striving for the laurel crown, had found a grave beneath the gloomy cypress. It was so warm and so pleasant that I rode slowly for the sake of enjoyment. In the woods furthest from camp, I saw robins and quail and started from the cedar brush two or three rabbits, not hares such as run in New York but genuine rabbits.[11]

This description belied oft-heard statements that the surrounding landscape had been denuded of trees.

"It snowed here on the 22nd, but it did not stop with four or five inches, it was a foot or more," bemoaned Pvt. Samuel Trimble of the 4th Pennsylvania Cavalry; he wrote from (aptly named) "Camp Mud and Misery" on February 27. "[I]t is pretty much gone by now. The roads are near belly deep with mud and when horses get so near done

---

8 BV 354, part 8, FSNMP. Gladys Stevens Stuart and Adelbert M. Jakeman, Jr., *John H. Stevens, Civil War Diary* (Acton, ME., 1997).

9 BV 112, part 13, letters from an unknown soldier in 140th Pennsylvania Infantry, FSNMP.

10 BV 146, FSNMP, No. 36, Samuel Selden Partridge Papers.

11 Ibid.

out that they can't get along they just shoot them and let them lay there." The opportunity for Americans in both armies to share their common history soon faded. Instead, Washington's birthday exposed civil war sorrow among a patriotic people.[12]

As a counterpoint, in Richmond, Jefferson Davis's January 5, 1863, speech to "the People of the Free States by the President of the Southern Confederacy" had set that same February 22 as the effective date for a counter-emancipation. The most tyrannical document ever issued in America, it at once enslaved all free-blacks in the South and promised capture and enslavement of any blacks in free-states subjected to future Confederate operations—relegating such military actions to nothing more than "slave-hunts." For anyone taking note, there was no longer a question about whether this war centered on slavery.[13]

Extra! Extra!—"From Hooker's Army"

On February 17, a "newsboy" had attempted to sell New York Tribune copies in the 25th New York Infantry's camp and was summarily booted-out. A soldier-correspondent from the 13th New York Infantry, signed as "Scorer," confirmed the incident to the *Rochester Union and Advertiser*, but added, "No paper has ever been excluded to our knowledge."[14]

In fact, the army and the press had convoluted relationships. Important factors in those dynamics included a newspaper's political leanings, posturing by particular officers, and personal relationships between soldiers and editors and reporters.[15]

Such shifting tides sometimes meant papers were, indeed, banned from camps, regardless of Scorer's personal observations. "The N.Y. Times is now allowed to come to the Army but the Herald is not," reported Charles Brewster of the 10th Massachusetts Infantry on February 23, "and I am glad of it for it is a treasonable paper anyway and ought to be suppressed entirely." Six days' earlier, Maj. Holman S. Melcher of the 20th Maine Infantry wrote, "You have no idea how much injury that ——— (can't

12 BV 210, FSNMP. Trimble was mustered in and out of service as a private (NPS/CWSSS - M554 Roll 123).

13 Broadside, Jefferson Davis Papers, University Library, Washington and Lee University, Lexington, VA., quoted in Ervin L. Jordan, Jr., *Black Confederates and Afro-Yankees in Civil War Virginia* (University Press of Virginia, Charlottesville, VA, 1995), Appendix C, 319-320.

14 CHJHCF: Cites: "Letter of 'Scorer,' Feb. 17, 1863 to the *Rochester Union and Advertiser*, edition of February 26, 1863.

15 James Perry's *A Bohemian Brigade: The Civil War Correspondents—Always Rough, Sometimes Ready* (Wiley, 2000) and Brayton Harris's *Blue & Gray in Black and White* (Brassey's, 1999) both offer excellent overviews of the press during the Civil War.

Soldiers built a dizzying array of makeshift shelters to protect themselves from the winter. The fact that any trees were left standing seems almost astounding. NPS

do justice by any adjective in our language) *Herald* is doing to the army. I have got so mad at it, that I won't buy or read one." In contrast, he lauded the *Baltimore Clipper* and *Philadelphia Inquirer* as "sound-hearted and patriotic." Before long, Hooker himself would take an unwelcomed interest in the press. "I wish that you could choke the newspapers," he had written to Secretary of War Stanton in early December, presaging his later actions as army commander. "They are a nuisance in their effect on certain minds."[16]

The soldiers themselves, believed to provide unvarnished and less self-serving views than official reports and biased reporting, were deemed reliable sources by editors of like mind in a trusting age. Consequently, their letters were popular in hometown newspapers and proved to be influential in shaping public opinion.

That shaping sometimes took the form of scolding. Surgeon Wiggin of the 17th Maine, writing on February 19 in the Lewiston (Maine) *Daily Evening Journal*, was repulsed by home front negativity and called the perpetrators "denouncers of the war. If these men were in the army, they would soon depend from a convenient tree. The army

16 CHJHCF: 1. Cites: "David W. Blight, ed., *When This Cruel War is Over: The Civil War Letters of Charles Harvey Brewster* (Amherst, MA: University of Massachusetts Press, 1992), 2, citing "William B. Styple, ed., *With a Flash of His Sword: The Writings of Major Holman S. Melcher, 20th Maine Infantry* (Kearny, NJ: Belle Grove Publishing, 1994), 20; Joseph Hooker to Edwin Stanton, December 4, 1862, Edwin Stanton Papers, LC.

brooks no sympathy with traitors." The army was neither demoralized nor disloyal, he argued, and men returning from furloughs were refreshed to be away from hometown despair. "[T]he army believes in emancipation," he asserted, "and sees easily through that rotten logic that calls the war a fight for the black man, when in reality it is the black man fighting for us!" Disloyal officers were being dismissed, and "Hooker now has Generals who will co-operate with him and he will lead the army to victory." Finally, he hoped the South would continue its obstinacy and thus strengthen Union resolve to defeat the efforts of the "Peace Party in the North" to negotiate a "pro-slavery peace."[17]

These conclusions may have been premature, but the better army elements were already in-line with them. Another section of the paper's first page, entitled "From Hooker's Army," related:

> Intelligent observers returned from visits to the Army of the Potomac, not of curiosity but of patriotic solicitude, are confident of the future under the vigorous command of Gen. Hooker. They report noteworthy symptoms of the moral reorganization, manifestly in progress with the material reorganization of the force. Conversion has somehow been experienced by most of those officers who were vocal with disaffection over McClellan's removal. A consciousness that a strong governing mind is over all pervades every department of the army. There is not a regiment that does not feel the influence of the idea that the commander is invested with the power, and overflowing with the will, to dismiss the feint-hearted and the incompetent and promote fighting men into their place. The confidence of the troops grows daily, that whenever Hooker fights he will smash at one blow the rebellion in Virginia; and this confidence is well founded. He will give the rebels such a fight as has never been on this continent.[18]

While encouraging and perceptive, Hooker had not yet commanded for a full month. Only additional time and evidence would validate such a turnaround.

More often, especially in the quiet winter months, the soldier-correspondent focused on self-comfort and offered letters much more prosaic in nature. "Nothing of interest has transpired since my last [letter], and we are still domiciled in the little habitations which we have erected with our own hands upon lands donated to us for that purpose by the benevolent Uncle Sam," wrote a II Corps soldier, signed as "G," on February 17th from "Head-Quarters Provost Guard, Gen. French's Division, near Falmouth, Va." He continued with additional interesting detail:

17 BV 355, part 7, FSNMP, *Daily Evening Journal*, Lewiston, Maine, Thursday Evening, February 19, 1863, No. 264, 1.

18 BV 355, part 7, FSNMP, *Daily Evening Journal*, Lewiston, Maine, Thursday Evening, February 19, 1863, No. 264, 1.

These habitations, though rude in their appearance, present an air of comfort to the soldier, and, considering the limited facilities for constructing them, reflect much credit upon the ingenuity and skill of the builders. The only materials used being mud, logs, and the ordinary Shelter tents for roofing. They usually dig from two to three feet under ground, with a capacious fire-place, which affords ample heat in the severest winter. The furniture consists chiefly of shelving, made of cracker boxes, placed upon which may be seen numerous tin cans, bottles, etc., relics of the sorry dishes of preserves, pickles, jellies, etc., which they once contained. Some of the huts are supplied with bedsteads, constructed of poles, and being softly covered invite the soldier to Nature's calm restorer, "balmy sleep." The number of occupants to each hut is from two to four persons, these mutually perform the agreeable offices of cooks, wood-choppers, laundress, chambermaid, bottle-washer, and kindred employments.[19]

"G" humorously suggested a domestic revolution was underway in which these young men would be in great postwar demand as husbands. He then complained of being charged for new clothing they were issued after the Seven Days' battles in July 1862. Ordered to destroy their old clothing, they complied and were summarily billed from their scant and infrequent pay. An injustice, but he concluded, "It is done, and there is no use in groaning about it." Such "complaints" expressed with humor suggested a different spirit was emerging.[20]

Food for Man and Beast in Hooker's Army

On February 6, Hooker issued General Order No. 8 limiting fodder and fresh beef levies on local citizens. Acquisitions beyond the newly prescribed limits were deemed plundering and pillage. The order mandated that soldiers leave civilians with at least a six-month- supply of food, calculated at a rate of 1.5 bushels per person, including employees.

General Order No. 9 followed on February 7. "Flour or soft bread will be issued at the depots to commissaries for at least two issues per week to the troops," it instructed. "Fresh potatoes or onions, if practicable, for two issues per week. Desiccated mixed vegetables or potatoes for one issue per week." The soft bread from numerous soldier bakeries popping up in and around the camps was especially morale-building. The hated, weevil-infested "mummies of hard crackers" were the subjects of most men's complaints. The order came with a clear signal—at least as clear as army-speak went: If a

19 Ibid.

20 Styple, ed., *Writing and Fighting the Civil War*, 167-168.

Rather than "push" supplies out to units, the commissary department set up stations that "pulled" units in to centralized supply locations. *LOC*

commissary failed to provide the rations, Hooker had spelled out, commanders were ordered to report the name of the commissary officer, who then had to explain himself in writing. He needed to prove that the rations "were not on hand at the depot for issue to him" or "otherwise to satisfactorily account for his failure." Hooker and Butterfield had witnessed first-hand Burnside's vague, un-enforced edicts. Knowing that logistical bureaucrats responded best to the spur from senior officers, Hooker gouged them.[21]

Although this army had supplies, it had difficulty moving and distributing them efficiently. It had not learned to "push" critical supplies to forward positions and relied exclusively on "pull"—that is, it didn't actively distribute supplies beyond depots. Supplies could therefore sit at a depot indefinitely if troops didn't go there to retrieve them. Responding to "numerous complaints . . . by commanders of batteries and cavalry regiments," chief quartermaster Rufus Ingalls demonstrated the difference between "pushing" and "pulling" in a February 20 dispatch. The commanders complained "that their animals have suffered at different times for want of a sufficient supply of forage, and that every exertion had been made by them to obtain it."[22]

Ingalls would have none of it. "It is well known that an ample supply of grain and a part of hay ration have been at the principal depots, which could easily have been drawn and taken to camp by packing. At this time there is plenty of hay and grain," he said. "Battery and cavalry commanders should in the future see that their commands are supplied (whenever the roads will not allow hauling in wagons) by packing with a

21 Ibid.

22 See Warner, who described Ingalls as "perhaps the only person in a position of great responsibility who gave satisfaction to every commander of the Army of the Potomac." Warner, *Generals in Blue*, 245-246.

Goods came to Aquia Landing by boat down the Potomac River and were offloaded onto railroad cars that carried the supplies south along the U.S. Military Railroad from Aquia Landing to the army. LOC

portion of the animals for the benefit of the whole, and should always send an officer to attend to this matter in person. They should also see that the protection is afforded the animals by building shelters of some kind, and no excuse should be taken for neglect of this duty."

Ingalls, he felt, held up his end of the bargain—i.e., getting supplies from Washington-area logistical bases to the army's Stafford depots by water, rail, and road. That in itself was a logistical achievement.[23] In food alone, the army each day required about half a million pounds of field rations for the men and one million pounds of feed and forage for the animals. If Ingalls got the supplies to and received them in Stafford depots, it was up to individual units to pick them up. Resupply of the troops, therefore, remained dependent on units picking up and moving supplies cross-country.

23 *OR*, 25, part II, 55, 57.

Stafford's road networks (to stretch the term) were at best inadequate, however, and essentially hopeless during any sort of foul weather. All logistics movements were proportionately difficult. Therefore, units often went without essential supplies while ample stores sat in depots just five or ten miles distant. Despite its wealth of supplies and its formidable transportation logistics, the Army of the Potomac frequently failed in distribution.

The fact remained that the Quartermaster Department was a separate bureaucracy, accountable primarily to itself. Commissary and quartermaster resupply ultimately devolved to a given commander's energy and efforts. Unless senior officers rode the system hard, this condition persisted. The acid test was food in the hands of the troops. Although improving, letters clearly show such efforts were uneven.

Other subsistence means existed during the "Valley Forge," though—namely foraging for food for man and fodder for beast. Sidney Morris Davis of the 6th United States Cavalry discussed these issues at some length in his 1871 memoir. Davis arrived in Stafford in November 1862 and pulled his share of picket duty, initially below Hartwood near U. S. Ford. There, he freely made contact with the locals, and recorded a number of humorous encounters with the Monroe family. Mrs. Monroe told him that, as he meant them no harm and had respected their persons and property, she would be as helpful as possible. Her husband, although a "strong Union man," was serving as a Confederate soldier. During occasional grubbing, Davis interacted with the family and delighted in their ignorance: Mrs. Monroe once asked him if Abraham Lincoln was a white man, and inquired whether Rebel general Thomas "Stonewall" Jackson was actually a man or some kind of god or angel. "They belonged to that class of uneducated southerners known before the war as 'poor white trash,'" Davis assessed. In concert with prevailing Democrats' attitudes, he believed the Staffordians were innocent victims of a war in which they had no stake. He marveled at their prejudices, especially against "abolitionists."

Under "Winter Quarters—Unhappy Days," Davis described his experiences after mid-January: "Hooker was popular among the soldiers on account of his military reputation. Whether or not overrated as to his abilities in the field, one thing soon became evident—on this occasion he seemed to understand what was needed to meet the emergency that was upon us." Trooper Davis highlighted Hooker's reforms, especially his "system of furloughs" and the improved food quality, particularly fresh soft bread.

"I was surprised at the great change for the better that seemed to have taken place —the cheerfulness that had superseded the old despondency," Davis explained. "The men seemed to have been rejuvenated by some mysterious process. They forgot all their disasters, and grew buoyant with hope. The determination to carry on the war to a successful conclusion," he added with some obvious surprise, "which had almost disappeared during the last days of the Burnside control, came to the surface again stronger than ever."[24]

The Defense of Aquia Creek Landing:
A Case Study in Contingency Planning (Part I)

One of the more remarkable episodes of the "Valley Forge" involved contingency plans by Hooker and Butterfield. They recognized Aquia Landing's vulnerability to Confederate offensives or large-scale cavalry raids from the west or southwest. Key to re-supplying and moving troops and evacuating prisoners and the wounded, and with direct ties to steamboats and the U. S. Military Railroad, the landing was a critical point.

An extended north-south movement corridor ran through the center of the Federal perimeter—and offered an open invitation to cavalry raids. Because of a series of cross-compartmented east-west creeks, though, a south-to-north Confederate attack from the Rappahannock was unlikely. The dominant terrain of Stafford Heights complicated matters. Confederate cavalry success wasn't a given, as there were risks of entrapment between Aquia and Accokeek Creeks.

A large attack by Lee from the upper Rappahannock through Hartwood toward Stafford Courthouse and Aquia Landing or a cavalry raid during withdrawal worried Hooker and Butterfield most. The sector was defensible but additional fortifications and troop re-deployments would be needed.

In early February, after detecting the open flank to the southwest in the Hartwood sector, Hooker and Butterfield repositioned XI and XII Corps to protect the army's logistics base and back door at Aquia Landing. Lt. Cyrus Comstock, the army's chief engineer staff officer, was sent to improve defenses.

On February 2, they received Comstock's incisive analysis—a solid example of the contingency planning by engineer staff officers of that day. The defense of Aquia Creek Landing might be necessary in two cases, Comstock said: "First, in case of embarkation with our rear guard strongly pressed by the enemy." More optimistically, he added "Second, in case of an advance from it as a base, to resist raids."[25]

The first option required defensive actions, especially if a rear guard of less than 5,000-8,000 Federals were employed or if the enemy could gain the "hill overlooking Aquia Creek" and deploy artillery. "The difficulty can be overcome by occupying a defensive line running from the point where Accokeek Creek becomes impassable

---

24 Charles F. Cooney, ed., *Sidney Morris Davis: Common Soldier, Uncommon War: Life as a Cavalryman in the Civil War* (Bethesda, MD, 1994), 291-300, 307-319, 323.

25 *OR*, 51, part I, 979.

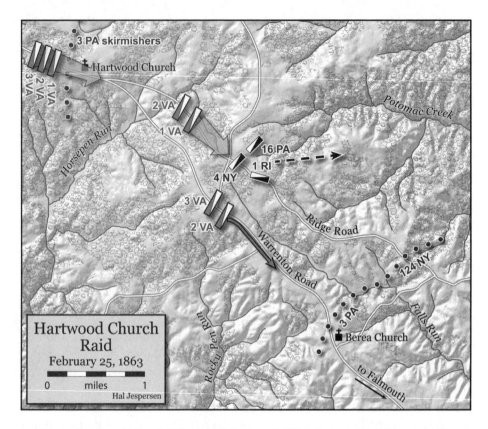

Hartwood Church Raid
February 25, 1863

0 miles 1

Hal Jespersen

nearly north to Aquia Creek," Comstock believed. "This line would still leave a hill near the Watson house outside of it, from which Aquia Creek Landing could be seen by the enemy's artillery." On that hill, he recommended "a small redoubt for 100 men and no guns. The line in question should consist of a slashing, with short portions of breast-works of logs and earth at points where they should see the slashing well, and three small redoubts. The largest of these redoubts would be on the road from Aquia Landing to Stafford Court House, about a mile from the landing, and should cover six guns. The other two should be between this and the railroad and should each cover about six guns."[26]

Redoubts, earthen fortifications with a flat side that faced the direction of defense, could contain infantry and artillery. Ideally they formed part of a defensive network connected with infantry entrenchments and internal roads. The total line Comstock envisioned would be about a mile and a half in length and could be held by 3,000 men against a strong attack. In support, gunboats could control Brent's Point, on the north

26 Ibid.

Hartwood Church Raid (February 25, 1863). Despite bedraggled horses, Confederates chose to press their home field advantage by pushing against Federal defenses near Hartwood Church, one of the westernmost outposts of the Army of the Potomac. Under Brig. Gen. Fitzhugh Lee, some 400 handpicked men from several Confederate cavalry regiments pushed through poor weather and caught Federals at the church by surprise. Driving them back to stronger defenses around Berea Church, the Southern troopers finally called off the raid when they came up against reinforcements from the Federal III Corps. Despite the significant changes recently implemented in the Federal cavalry corps, the rout at Hartwood Church demonstrated that much work remained to be done.

side of Aquia Creek. He estimated the redoubts would require ten days for construction and the rest of the work would be done in four. Comstock figured on a work force of 1,500 men, provided they were not changed during the work.[27]

The engineer also wanted to secure vulnerable points on the railroad line from raids, anticipating a cavalry raiding force of about 2,000 men and six guns. Two of the redoubts he referred to, one each on the Stafford Court House Road and near the railroad, should remain to the last and the gunboats must also remain. "At Potomac Creek bridge and Accokeek Creek bridge, however, redoubts should be built, each capable of holding 250 men and two guns," he concluded. "Construction for each of these redoubts would require 400 men for ten days."

On February 7, consistent with Comstock's recommendations, Butterfield ordered General Slocum of the XII Corps to "detail a brigade of at least 1,200 effective men, with the full complement of officers, for temporary duty at Aquia Creek, in the construction of works to cover the depot of supplies." They were to camp between Aquia Creek and Stafford Court House and prepare to begin work by February 9. Butterfield directed the commanding officer to report to Comstock, as "chief engineer officer of the general staff," for instructions. Slocum likewise received a copy of those instructions on February 8; highlighting their priority, Slocum was to "acknowledge receipt of this dispatch."[28]

Lieutenant Comstock assigned the work to Lt. C. E. Cross, commanding the Regular Engineer Battalion, ordering the engineers to construct "a redoubt near Watson's, another near where the Bruce house stood, and a third on the bluff at the south end of the line pointed out a few days ago." He wanted cover for three guns at the Bruce house to control the Falmouth railroad "and yet be covered from guns across the

27 *OR*, 25, part II, 56.

28 Ibid.

ravine." Comstock authorized Cross to call on lieutenants Mackenzie and Suter for assistance.[29]

Typically, construction of fortifications and corduroyed roads fell heavily on infantry units. Engineer units primarily focused on design and supervision of fortifications and pontoon bridging. Infantrymen naturally resented this type of work, although those accustomed to hard labor sometimes welcomed a break from camp routine. On the other hand, difficult labor in harsh weather took unsurprising tolls on men's health.[30]

At least the army possessed enough pioneer tools for the work. On February 18, Hooker specifically ordered all corps commanders to keep a reserve of 750 shovels, 250 picks and 500 axes— a total of 1,500 implements—in addition to the "complete equipment of pioneers of brigades." Hooker further stressed "strict accountability."[31] The work necessary to bring the contingency plans to life was soon completed.

The Hartwood Church Raid

Even as Hooker prepped Aquia Landing against a possible Confederate attack or cavalry raid, Rebel cavalrymen prepared a raid probing the Federal perimeter's western extremity. In that sector, Confederate cavalry patrols roamed freely from the Rappahannock north to Warrenton and Brentsville and small Rebel units regularly probed the Federal army's outer defenses. In contrast, the Union cavalry, which had earlier scouted out to the west at Allcock Mills in Stafford and toward Rappahannock Station and Kelly's Ford, had settled into a purely protective mode largely avoiding advances into hostile territory beyond their defenses.

Rebel operations were increasingly limited by shortages of able horses and food and fodder. But, compared to their Federal counterparts, Stuart's men still dominated in large part because of their home-field advantage. Historian Homer D. Musselman relates an "extensive spy network existed in Stafford" that reported Federal troop movements. He quotes Capt. Frank W. Hess of the 3rd Pennsylvania Cavalry, who said, "Every inhabitant in this county was in full sympathy with the enemy, and no matter how frequently the posts of our videttes were changed and the reserves moved, it was

---

29 *OR*, 51, part I, 985.

30 *OR*, 25, part II, 87. Herman Haupt, *Reminiscences of General Herman Haupt* (North Stratford, NH, 2000), 147, 154, 158-170. The vestiges of at least eleven redoubts exist today, three in the Stafford Civil War Park, which opened in April 2013.

31 Haupt, *Reminiscences,* especially see Chapter IX, "Opening Operations under General Hooker," 184-187.

but a short time until the precise location was known . . . on the other side of the river." Musselman adds that women and children took a special patriotic pride in spying.[32]

Most Confederate cavalry actions were conducted below regimental-level, most commonly with less than a company engaged, and no significant penetrations of Union defenses took place. That changed on February 25, however, when one of the most significant combatant actions of the "Valley Forge" erupted around Hartwood Church. It was only a brigade-sized Confederate cavalry raid, yet historians regard Hartwood Church as a major benchmark in the cavalry war for both sides.

Hartwood Church was the outermost cavalry post in the southwestern corner of the extensive Federal perimeter. It sheltered men, horses, grain, and rations. Further west, cavalry videttes guarded approach routes. To the east, around Berea Church, Federal infantry maintained picket lines. Situated along the Warrenton and Marsh Roads, Hartwood Church-Berea Church was a main movement corridor toward Falmouth or toward Stafford Courthouse and Aquia Landing. The cavalry could detect and delay the potential enemy advances Hooker and Butterfield had anticipated toward the courthouse and landing.[33]

However, the Federal cavalry presence did little to keep the area secure. Confederate scouting parties conducted guerrilla operations, destroying Union communications lines, threatening cavalry outposts, and attacking targets of opportunity. "There are scattered over the country between the right flank of the army and the railroad many young rebels, who assemble, mount, and form scouting parties at the shortest notice," warned Brig. Gen. Averell. "Upon the approach of any superior force they are suddenly transformed into idle, loitering citizens, without arms, and professing great ignorance of the country."[34]

Meanwhile, deep within the perimeter, distractions were piling up for an army commander who had already centralized too much tactical control. Hooker was in Washington at the Willard Hotel on February 23 and returned to Stafford the following day to find a mountainous amount of paperwork. Hooker spent February 24 attending to that mountain—even as a Rebel cavalry brigade began moving toward Hartwood Church.

Also distracting Hooker, his artillery chief, Brig. Gen. Hunt, anticipating a campaign toward Richmond, had proposed a plan organizing a siege train on a pattern used in the Peninsula. It involved grouping artillery of heavy- and siege-gun calibers,

---

32 OR, 25, part II, 87. Haupt, *Reminiscences,* especially see Chapter IX, "Opening Operations under General Hooker," 184-187.

33 Musselman, *Stafford County in the Civil War,* 50.

34 Ibid.

heavy howitzers, and heavy mortars with sufficient transport and logistics, such as pre-stocked ammunition and other supplies, for independent offensive action aimed against Confederate fortifications and strong points. Alternatively, Hunt informed Hooker that the army's artillery needed 3,487 recruits to complete existing batteries.

Further, incoming information from a scout on February 24 informed Hooker that Longstreet's troops were now at Suffolk and on the Carolina coast; Stuart was near Warrenton; and Jackson was in Staunton contemplating a raid with Stuart into Maryland.

On the twenty-fourth and twenty-fifth, Hooker appraised Washington, employing his new intelligence bureau's estimates, of the overall picture: "Information from deserters, contrabands and citizens for the past two or three days, when compared and collated, seems to corroborate the following statement: That the enemy have decreased their forces in our front; that two or more divisions of Longstreet's corps have gone to Tennessee and South Carolina; that the enemy are under the impression that we are evacuating from Aquia, leaving a sufficient force to keep Lee's army in front of us." Foggy conditions, he added, had inhibited balloon operations and roads were impassable for reconnaissance. A few hours later Hooker sent a correction—confirmed by balloon reconnaissance—that Jackson was still across the Rappahannock in Spotsylvania and Caroline counties.[35]

While Hooker dealt with these and other issues, the inconvenient Confederates under Brig. Gen. Fitzhugh Lee left their base near Culpeper, crossed the river, and approached Hartwood. Lee actually commanded picked men in detachments from the 1st, 2nd and 3rd Virginia Cavalry Regiments, a combined force of about 400 troopers (probably limited by available horseflesh).[36]

Fitz Lee's cavalry brigade's condition was exemplified by Col. Thomas Taylor Munford's 2nd Virginia Cavalry. The 2nd had been at Fredericksburg in December 1862; made the Christmas raid on Dumfries, Occoquan, and Fairfax Station; and was on picket duty in January 1863. Earlier in February, the regiment braved snow and cold and moved to Waller's Tavern in Spotsylvania County before picketing the Rappahannock. On February 11, they had fought a particularly harsh combination of snow, hail, and rain. Probably because of these hardships, Munford himself led the 2nd's contingent.

More specifically, Fitz Lee took his command from Stevensburg, in Culpeper County, on February 24. Crossing the Rappahannock at Kelly's, they moved along the Warrenton Road from Morrisville through a daunting 15 inches of snow. On February

35 Musselman, *Stafford County in the Civil War*, 50.

36 *OR*, 25, part II, 95, 97-100.

25 at around 9:30 a.m., Fitz Lee divided his force and ordered their approach toward Hartwood along two parallel roads that surrounded the church.[37]

Federal cavalry were changing guards at noon when the Confederates struck the church outpost. The Federals were not on heightened alert due to the severe weather, and their videttes mistook Lee's column—clad mainly in stolen light blue overcoats—for fellow troopers. Allowing them to approach too closely, the Federals were surprised and quickly over-run, although one account depicts raiders creeping up on the far videttes through the snow and capturing them. Responding Federals were trapped in file formations, unable to maneuver in deep mud and snow, and were soon driven back toward Berea. "[C]onsidering the [poor] conditions of the roads," a Northern observer sardonically noted, "[we] made very good time to the rear."

Fitz Lee's troopers rounded up prisoners and horses, moved forward, and scattered the reinforcing 16th Pennsylvania and 4th New York Cavalry Regiments. The 3rd Virginia Cavalry detachment foiled at least one counterattacking Federal force by charging on Lee's order. "Routed them," Fitz later boasted, albeit tersely, "and pursued them within five miles of Falmouth, to their infantry lines. Killed and wounded many of them. Captured 150 prisoners, including 5 commissioned officers, with all of their horses, arms, and equipments." His successive charges, he crowed, "were splendidly executed."[38]

Further Federal resistance delayed the Confederates until 7:00 p.m. when Fitz Lee's cavalry finally reached infantry defenses near Berea Church. The III Corps infantrymen "opened fire on the assailants, and drove them back with loss," reported their commander, Brig. Gen. Dan Sickles. "The attack was not renewed," he added and "a detachment of our cavalry, estimated from 60 to 100, was cut off by the enemy and made prisoners." Col. Benjamin P. Bailey of the 86th New York, whose troops were among the Federals engaged, explained in his report that Northern cavalry had passed through the infantry lines and engaged Fitz Lee's men with pistols at 20 yards.[39]

The Rebels then disengaged and withdrew in good order to Morrisville. The successful raid cost the Confederates 14 casualties, while they captured 125-150 Yankee cavalrymen, their much-needed horses, weapons, and equipment, and whatever supplies lay about.[40] Jeb Stuart's endorsement to Gen. Robert E. Lee pointed to Fitz Lee's ability and gallantry in rapidly deploying after receiving a telegraphed order on the evening of the twenty-third, and overcoming "extraordinary obstacles and difficulties in

---

37 Wittenberg, *Union Cavalry Comes of Age*, Chapter 2.

38 Robert J. Driver Jr. and H. E. Howard, *2nd Virginia Cavalry* (Lynchburg, VA, 1995).

39 *OR*, 25, part I, 21-26.

40 Ibid.

the way of success—a swollen river, snow, mud, rain, and impracticable roads, together with distance."[41]

This first major test of the new Federal cavalry corps had arrived at the Army of the Potomac's doorstep. While trying to flog his cavalry corps into action, Hooker requested Maj. Gen. Heintzelman at 6:30 p.m. to send additional cavalry from the Washington Defenses out to the west at Catlett's and Rappahannock Stations. Heintzelman complied, "sending" 2,000 cavalry in that direction—although they did not depart until the following morning.

All the remaining actions by the cavalry corps were after the fact, too late, and feckless. At 7:30 p.m. on the evening of the twenty-fifth, Hooker alerted Couch's II Corps to "send a good brigade of infantry up to Berea Church" where a force of enemy cavalry had approached the picket lines. Stoneman and Averell were responding, he said, cautioning Couch not to "get in collision" with them. Averell, then at Potomac Creek heading for Hartwood, was separately ordered to follow the Rebels and cooperate with Stoneman in attacking them. Other Federal cavalry were alerted, too, lest the feared breakthrough toward Stafford Court House take place, revealing Hooker's greatest concern.[42]

The XII Corps was alerted and its temporary commander, Alpheus Williams, was instructed to guard against Fitz Lee's advance. An advance by Hampton was also reported. Cavalry and infantry units as far north as Dumfries reacted. Hooker boldly asserted, given the reported condition of Confederate horses, "We ought to capture every one of them."[43]

Butterfield provided Averell some combat information and added typical army headquarters bombast: "General Hooker says that a major-general's commission is staring somebody in the face in this affair, and that the enemy should never be allowed to get away from us." The same message went to Pleasonton, whom Stoneman had ordered forward to work with Averell. Pleasonton's men began moving at 2:30 a.m. on February 26; however, he didn't plan to move his headquarters beyond Aquia Church where he would be at 8:00 a.m. This rightly irritated Butterfield, who sarcastically blasted Stoneman. "The accompanying dispatch just received from Pleasonton," he snarled. "His brilliant dash and rapid movements will undoubtedly immortalize him! It

---

41 Ibid. Musselman, *Stafford County in the Civil War*. An alternative view, drawing on staff officer H. B. McClellan is in Edward G. Longacre, *Fitz Lee: A Military Biography of Major General Fitzhugh Lee, C.S.A.* (Cambridge, MA, 2005), 96-97.

42 *OR*, 25, part I, 21-26.

43 *OR*, 25, part II, 100-108.

is fair to presume that he failed to receive your orders to push on, otherwise I cannot account for his movements at all."[44]

Pleasonton, reportedly "in position" at Aquia Church by 8 a.m., again incurred Butterfield's anger. "I don't know what you are doing there," Butterfield barked in a 10:15 a.m. dispatch. "Orders were sent you at 11 p.m. last night, by telegraph and orderlies, to push for the enemy without delay, and to communicate with General Stoneman at Hartwood. The enemy have recrossed the river, at Kelly's Ford probably, and Averell is pursuing them. Get your orders from Stoneman."

Stoneman, traveling overnight to Hartwood with his aides, caught up with the Reserve Brigade and sent a message forward urging them to move faster to link up with Averell. By 4:30 a.m., that was effected, and Stoneman ordered the brigade and division forward under Averell while he remained at Hartwood Church with "a portion of the Reserve Brigade." Stoneman then began—impotently, as it turned out—to cast about in all directions. He sent a "quadroon" to Richards' Ford, but information soon arrived that some Confederates had already swum their horses across there. He sent a squadron of troopers via Warrenton Road toward Spotted Tavern searching for enemy passage north toward Dumfries, but they found no trail in the snow. He also sent three officers to Pleasonton telling him to return to camp. He even planned for Averell to go out to destroy the (irrelevant) Rappahannock Station bridge with axes borrowed from II Corps.

It's hard to reckon whether Stoneman or Hooker was more frustrated. Stoneman heard from his commander at 6:30 a.m. on the morning of February 26: "[I]n the event of your inability to cut off the enemy's cavalry, you will follow them to their camp, and destroy them." Befuddled at the prospect of an impromptu raid into enemy territory, Stoneman nonetheless mustered his available forces, intending to lead all but 500 on a raid. While underway, he received at 4:45 p.m. new orders from Hooker, sent at about noon, to "return to camp." The hapless Stoneman complied, bringing an end to the flurry of counterproductive activity.[45]

From the Confederate perspective, the Hartwood Cavalry Raid was an undoubted tactical success, but it played an important role in the maturation of the cavalry for both sides. Modern historians, such as Edward G. Longacre in *Fitz Lee: A Military Biography*, rank it as the beginning of Fitz Lee's final rise to prominence as a major cavalry commander. Meanwhile, historian Eric Wittenberg says the raid spurred the Federal cavalry to higher levels of raiding and performance. In the short-term, though, the raid showed Hooker and Butterfield how little their 20-day-old cavalry creation had

44 Ibid.

45 Ibid.

progressed and how far it had to go. They should have concluded that Stoneman, Pleasonton, and Averell were not part of the solution. Countering a raid that hit fast and withdrew quickly required immediate reaction and anticipation by pre-positioned reserves. None of that happened.

At another level, this was merely a sparring episode between two armies in winter defensive postures during a strategic pause. Its true effects were over-blown on both sides. From his limited perspective, Emmet M. Irwin of the 82nd New York Infantry described it most appropriately: "Everything is quiet I believe in the army with a few exceptions. Our cavalry picketts were drove in last Wednesday, some of them came in our camp as hard they jump. The rebel cavalry followed them as far as the infantry picketts then wheeled about and off again. The 124th were out at the time."[46]

Within the camps, in the depths of the great perimeter, there was even less concern—none, in fact. On February 25, when the raid at Hartwood started, a soldier in the 2nd Wisconsin Infantry was far more interested a closer skirmish. "The boys have lively times by snow-balling," he admitted. "The [company] streets are lined with men each with a snow-ball, ready to throw at the first shoulder-strap [i.e., officer] that presents itself."[47]

The Scouting Party from Centreville

Heintzelman, as requested, had dispatched a cavalry force from the Washington Defenses in reaction to the Hartwood raid. Remarkably, they didn't depart until the following day and neither participating cavalry commander was informed to that effect. Had they moved swiftly, they might have had a chance of success because Confederate scouts and agents expected Union cavalry reconnaissance from the army's perimeter to the east, not from Centreville. However, ordered to Catlett's and Rappahannock Station as Hooker and Heintzelman had discussed, their movement (like Stoneman's from Stafford) was far too slow to catch Fitz Lee's force.

In overall command, Col. Percy Wyndham of the 1st New Jersey Cavalry formed a temporary brigade. Colonel George Gray of the 6th Michigan Cavalry was ordered to take six companies of his regiment to Fort Scott where he would be joined by Col. Norvell's 5th Michigan Cavalry. They arrived at Fairfax Court House by 3:00 p.m. on February 26, and Wyndham's aide told them to move to Centreville. They bivouacked and, on the morning of the 27th, joined a detachment of the 18th Pennsylvania Cavalry and took the road to Warrenton crossing Bull Run. They linked up with detachments of

46 Ibid.

47 Letter to his sister from Private Emmet M. Irwin. Author's Collection.

the 1st (West) Virginia and 5th New York Cavalry Regiments. Those three regiments, along with the 1st, 5th, and 6th Michigan Cavalry, were formed into a second brigade for movement. Effectively a cavalry division, they moved through Warrenton at about 3:30 p.m. on February 27 and pushed about five miles down the Orange and Alexandria Railroad and camped for the night. On Saturday, the twenty-eighth, they moved 25 miles without a halt toward Falmouth, arriving at 2:00 p.m. Gray reported the cavalry had frequently moved off the direct road, which heavy snow and rain had turned into mud, searching for enemy signs. The composite command then approached the Federal perimeter from the southwest and headed east to Falmouth.

At Falmouth, after arranging resupply, Wyndham turned over temporary command to Gray and inexplicably resigned; his resignation was accepted; but, just as inexplicably, it was revoked by Heintzelman.

The column moved out again on Monday, March 2, for Stafford Court House. After crossing the Occoquan River, Wolf Run Shoals, and Fairfax, it returned to Washington. "Not having any knowledge as to the object of the expedition, I am, of course, unable to say whether or not it was accomplished," Gray exasperatingly concluded, "We did not see the enemy."

Wyndham's report was even more befuddled—confusing as to whether he and Gray were actually on the same operation. The scouting party was delayed waiting for the Michigan cavalry near Bull Run, he recounted. Then his advance element briefly engaged and scattered a squad of enemy cavalry before encamping on Licking Creek, where he spotted enemy "squads and videttes" across the stream. On the morning of the twenty-eighth, they marched toward "Elk Run and Spottedville," where he learned that "the main force of the enemy had already crossed the Rappahannock, taking with them 100 prisoners." Wyndham also learned from seven Rebel prisoners that Fitz Lee had led a raid with 600-800 troopers against the rear of Hooker's army. Wyndham at least figured out what had happened after the fact; Gray apparently never did.[48]

Drill, Inspect, and Review

Another Hooker-Butterfield reform aimed to expand and energize the army's inspectors-general. On February 28, the army was fully mustered and most, if not all, units were inspected. Lieutenant Sam Partridge provided a spirited description from the 13th New York's camp. "The last day of every second month is muster day, when all the troops are mustered for payment," he explained. "Regiments are paraded, wheeled into column of companies, ranks opened, officers and sergeants to the front of their

48 http://www.secondwi.com/fromthefront/7th%20wis/1863/7th%20feb%2063.htm (accessed September 14, 2003). Author is listed only as "S.J.M."

companies, colors to the front, music to the rear, Field and Staff to the front, and the mustering officer calls the rolls of each company." Each man answered or was accounted for, and men, arms, accouterments, and equipment were inspected. Partridge described "lots of other flummery" accompanying administrative work.[49]

"Major Throup of the Michigan 1st mustered us and he was as particular as if he cared something about it," Partridge said in a tongue-in-cheek description of the inspection:

> He handled every man's gun, tried with the rammer every case where he suspected there was an atom of dust in the barrel, and was disappointed if he couldn't find a speck of rust on the bayonet. He looked into every cartridge box to see if the prescribed 60 rounds were there, and into every cap pouch to find a corresponding number of percuss[ion caps]. If the underside of the lock guard below the trigger was dirty, he regarded the possessor of the piece in the light of a culprit who ought to be put into the wooden hoss cavalry for an hour. [A punishment combining pain and humiliation where a soldier was forced to ride a large saw horse decorated as a horse, sometimes with an exaggeratedly large wooden saber.] If a man had a button off his jacket he gave him a terrible jaw. If the edge of the shirt showed above the jacket he couldn't find words to express his disapprobation of slovenliness . . . . The Field and Staff had to accompany him in his inspection, and as he was so thorough it took several hours.[50]

Partridge, to his great joy, was excused to attend to his duties, including dispatching "3,200 whiskey rations to the pickets, some five miles away." This required two and a half barrels, sent on a wagon with eight mules. Twelve hours and five breakdowns later, they reached the thirsty pickets. "When they got back," Partridge added, "the wagon looked like one great lump of mud, and you couldn't tell whether it was drawn by mules, hoses [horses], or camels."[51]

To observers at the range of 150 years, the antic parades, musters, and inspections of the army in the field, beset with unforgiving weather and terrain, may seem quaint and pointless. There was a fine balance, but field soldiers needed to be held accountable for their equipment and discipline, and frequent inspections were necessary. Parades were practice battles. Lacking such exertions, a citizen-army could degenerate into a mob. Partridge's reasonably good spirited description further suggests a renewal of spirit,

---

49 *OR*, 25, part I, 38-40.

50 BV 37, Samuel Selden Partridge Papers, FSNMP.

51 Ibid.

necessary for citizen-soldiers to accept routines associated with the discipline imposed on them.

Even among the relatively isolated XI Corps—arriving later and with its large German contingent—there was a subtle shift in esprit. A Philadelphia paper, The Press, captured it during a review of the corps by Hooker. "The day was as genial as though it were in the month of May. The sun appeared to shine more brightly than usual, and as it reached its meridian height the troops were drawn up in line," the paper's correspondent wrote. "The array was characterized by more than ordinary splendor. As General Hooker rode up, mounted on his beautiful white charger, he was saluted with the applause of the whole line, the band playing 'Hail to the Chief.' By his side was General Sigel, on his handsome black steed. The display was extremely imposing." The site chosen for the occasion, the Stevens's farm, was "most admirably selected," the paper said. "It was a large open level, skirted on all sides by stately forests of green pines, which added much to the éclat of the occasion." The review of the corps took place by division. "Much commendation was bestowed upon them for their efficiency in drill and their soldierly appearance," wrote the reporter. Perhaps it would have been better for the XI Corps if time could have been frozen right there and then.[52]

The experiences of Lt. Franklin J. Sauter of the 55th Ohio Infantry, recorded during the last half of February, reflect a similar renewal. The regiment was encamped near Brooke Station. On February 10, "a verry fine day," Sauter was refused a pass to go to Aquia Landing as too many officers were already gone. He did receive his pass the following day, though, rainy and cold as it was. He and two others walked six miles to Aquia Landing where they purchased a ham, had dinner, watched the hustle and bustle of the depot, and boarded a return train. The train split and stranded them, though, so they walked back to camp in the dark, noting they "got muded all over."[53]

On February 12, Sauter sent $14 home with a furloughed soldier and received two letters—one each from Ohio and Kentucky. He, his captain, and a captain and lieutenant from another company, decided to mess together. They "hired a negro to cook," agreeing to pay him 18 dollars a month. They built a cook shed next to their hut and Capt. Bement paid the first month's expenses. "[O]ur darky is a verry good cook. Get up a good meal," Sauter wrote.

On February 13, he purchased a new journal book. On that "verry fine day" they received orders to erect company signs of evergreens on each company street. The following day, February 14, he wrote, "Today is Vallentine day, and havnt received any

---

52 Ibid.

53 BV 198, part 2, FSNMP, Journal of Captain Franklin J. Sauter, Company B, 55th Ohio Infantry.

yet, nor don't exspect any, but I have sent one." On the fifteenth, Sauter, as regimental officer of the day, received orders to maintain quiet. He placed a sign on a tree: "don't ride through these streets" to keep horsemen from riding through company areas.

Things picked up February 16. They had an officers' call at 11:00 a.m. to prepare for a review. An hour later they marched one mile from camp and "formed a line of Battle. General Hooker is reviewing Officer." Sauter commanded the brigade's first company as they passed in review in column of companies. He noted the presence of generals Sigel, Stahel, and McLean and their staffs. Later that day, two more officers joined their mess, now numbering six.

On the seventeenth, he happily traded his watch for a revolver. On the eighteenth, his high spirits continued when he received two letters and two Valentines. His euphoria didn't last long, though. "the water is running through our tent, and our Chimney Smokes," he recorded. "A verry bad and on comfortable day. The Capt. has the blues and I haint much better." They rebuilt their chimney; added a seventh officer to the mess; and Sauter wrote home sending along a copy of the *Army Register*—all on the nineteenth. February 20 brought two copies of the *Perrysburg Journal* in the mail. He sent on a copy of the *Fostoria News*, his hometown paper, to Wisconsin and enjoyed the company of a lady visiting his captain. He received news of a promised furlough and a Lt. Patrick visited him in hopes of swapping for it. Sauter refused.

"Snowed all day Last night," Sauter wrote on February 22. "Snow twelve inches deep. Dull times. We were Strardeld by heavy Canonading. Thought the rebles were making an attack, but were mistaken." He got the point: "this was Washingtons birthday and our Batterys fired a national salute."

February 23, a "fine day," brought another inspection, this one by a Maj. Riley. Sauter cut "a big pile of wood for exersice" afterward. Although he'd intended a riding tour of Stafford Court House, Sauter found himself on brigade guard. He commanded half of the guards—85 men—defending a three mile-stretch along the Falmouth-Aquia rail line. He did not sleep during that very cold night.

On February 25, he shot a turkey with his revolver and socialized. He and Capt. Bement received blank pay and muster sheets on the twenty-sixth and spent the evening filling them out. During that long, rainy day, an ambulance crossing the creek was washed away. They rescued the horses. Sauter sent in his furlough application and planned to start home to Ohio the following Sunday. On Friday 27, muster rolls completed, they held officers' school. He borrowed some money from one man and agreed to take some home for another. The twenty-eighth was muster and pay day. They marched about a half mile, held another inspection and a review, and mustered for pay. His captain went to Washington, leaving him in company command. He conducted another officers' school and visited a friend.

The seemingly humdrum snapshot of Sauter's February, like other accounts, suggests something far more profound was going on beneath a banal surface: Hooker's reforms had broken the despondency of a broken army. It was now once again possible to get back to business, even if business wasn't all that exciting.

The transition wasn't always smooth, and it seeped unevenly through the army. The 24th Michigan, a new regiment in the Western "Iron" Brigade," offers an example. "A Virginia winter is a makeup of a variety of frost, rain, snow, slush and mud, sandwiched with sunshine and heavy gales," wrote regimental historian Orson Blair Curtis. "One day clear and mild, the next a fierce cold northeaster sets in, with a dashing snow storm for a few hours which turns to drizzling rain, producing a knee depth of red clay mud, almost impassable for man or beast."[54]

The regiment was encamped at Belle Plain's "Camp Isabella," named in honor of Col. Henry A. Morrow's wife, "who brightened camp life by her genial presence during the winter." The early days of February saw "frequent details . . . for artillery, pioneer and ambulance service," and gathering fuel for heating and cooking became a preoccupation. Manpower shortages, created by "deaths, discharges and sickness," required replenishment. Morale was improved by camp music and better food, off-setting at least a little the dull winter, drills, and picket duty. Despite difficulties gaining passes, ladies "graced the camp" and "occasional friends" visited the sick. [55]

February 21, however, was specifically remembered as "a day of painful interest, in the execution of court-martial sentences upon seven members of the Brigade." Curtis described the brigade-level punishments. "Its five regiments were drawn up inclosing a hollow square, within which the offenders were brought under guard. After a few remarks from brigade commander Solomon Meredith, their sentences were read. "For misbehavior before the enemy, etc.," five of the men were to forfeit all bounty and pay, have their heads shaved, and be drummed-out of camp. The other two were drummed-out only. One of the latter came from the 24th Michigan. The regiments were drawn up in two lines and the seven cowards, with uncovered heads, were marched between. A line of guards with reversed muskets preceded them, and closely behind followed a guard with pointed bayonets a few inches from them. At the quickstep, the band played the "Rogues March," and the disgraced men "were sped out of camp, amid the scorn and contempt of their late comrades."

Regardless of the invigorated efforts of the inspectors-general, and the back-to-business attitude of the army in general, pockets of poor behavior and poor morale lingered—fueled in part, suggested Curtis, by the poor attitudes and anti-war sentiments outside the army. "A distinctive anti-war party had arisen in the North to

54 Ibid.

55 Curtis, *The History of the Twenty-fourth Michigan,* Chapter VI, "Winter Headquarters at Belle Plain."

oppose every war measure of the government," Curtis wrote. "Clement L. Vallandigham, a member of Congress from Ohio, was the leader of this faction. They flooded the army with letters encouraging desertions, and discourage enlistments." While the South tolerated no division of sentiment, Curtis believed, the North fought both the rebellion and an "enemy at home."[56]

Yet the "enemy" lurked within, too. One persistent doubter, Albert E. Higley of the 22nd New York Infantry, had judged the sum of his own experiences and had come up empty of any redeeming qualities. A War Democrat who had been briefly attracted to Lincoln's banner, he had honorably volunteered early and "saw the elephant" in brutal combat. Sensing less home front support and glory than he had anticipated, Higley started second-guessing, and he unloaded his concerns in a vitriolic letter penned on February 25:

> Saturday's paper says "it is supposed that as soon as the conscription act is passed that a call will be made for six[ty?] or eighty thousand more troops and that it is expected[.] [T]he Soldiers whose times will soon expire will offer themselves as substitutes for unwilling conscripts." I'd smile—yes I would laugh quite heartily to see myself taking the place of an "unwilling conscript." I never knew one yet that I would do it for. I am very much like the nigger (pardon me I should have said colored gentleman that is the term now). You know he said "I love the white girl, and the black. And I love all the rest. I love that gal for loving me; but I love myself the best.["] I would like to see the man who had money enough to hire me to stay in the army. Talk of bounty—There is not money enough in the United States Treasury to hire me to remain in the Army six months after my term of service expires. Who could name the amount that would pay me for the hardships I have endured for the past twelve months? Who could name the amount that would pay me to stand in a field for two hours, with the dead and dying on all sides—exposed all the while to a murderous fire. I repeat the question what amount would be necessary to pay me for Bull Run, Rappahannock Station, Fredericksburg and then the marches—the heat & cold the hunger and thirst – the danger and suffering naturally incident to an active campaign. No one. And would I take the place of one of those prating abolitionists or peace democrats because they had unfortunately been forced to do something except stay at home and abuse our Generals. No—a thousand times NO. I would as soon cut off my right hand. Perhaps you will think this rather strong—but it is not half as much as I feel but cant write as well as I can think or talk. When Lincoln ran for the Presidency I did what I could to elect him by carrying a lamp &c and when he called for volunteers I shouldered a musket as readily as I did the lamp and I feel that I have done my duty in that respect. But if Lincoln were to run

for President again I would as soon vote for Dan Orcutt and as for carrying a musket after my term of service expires: I shant do it thats all.[57]

Assuming he didn't desert, Higley was a fairly typical Union soldier, prepared to do his duty and complete his term of service. However, no amount of army reform was going to purge his disillusionment.

Month's End

While antiwar efforts of Vallandigham and other home-front "enemies" might have indicated a growing disillusionment in the North, that sentiment gave the rest of "Yankeedom" a reason to examine their own feelings about the war—and by late February 1863, something was becoming clear. Northerners began to grasp that greater intensity and commitment by its army, its navy, and its people would be needed to defeat the South. The Federals had suffered initial over-confidence and thought that Rebel sentiments did not—in fact, could not—run so deeply as to endlessly persist. Northerners had truly underestimated the war potential and visceral hatred of their Southern foes. Now, respect for their implacable Rebel enemies was increasing. So, too, was the understanding among Northerners that only battlefield victories and the destruction of the underlying Confederate socio-economic infrastructure could bring the bloody conflict to a close.

Delusions of easy victory had finally dissolved in Stafford's mud. But something else happened in that mud, too: The army's fighting spirit had begun to revive. Discipline and training were accepted in a businesslike manner by the soldiers and junior officers. The army was returning to its work and its war.

"The mud is drying up somewhat and I suppose that Joe Hooker will start us as soon as possible," wrote Amory Allen of the 14th Connecticut Infantry from "Camp Near Falmouth, Va." on February 16. Allen had just "had the good luck or bad luck as you may call it to be promoted to 1st Corporal of Co. I." Allen continued: "I was very glad to receive a letter from you and was very glad to learn that you were all well. But I have neglected to write for some time for two reasons. Firstly, I have had no stamps, secondly have had not much time after drilling twice a day, etc. We are living very well now to what we have been. We have all the soft bread we can eat and potatoes and onions and fresh beef and beans. We have got about 6 quarts of beans on hand now and 6 loaves of bread. It is warm and pleasant here today." And, he noted, "We have been paid off." Arguably, life in the army could not get much better, although Allen did express one down note: "I do not think that I

57 Ibid.

THE EMBLEM OF THE FREE.

Both sides laid claim to Washington's legacy while celebrating his birthday across the river from each other. One Northern song, "The Emblem of the Free"—alternatively called "The Traitor's Dream"—is typical of the kind of patriotic fanfare that made the rounds. The "emblem" was the American flag and the traitor Jefferson Davis. According to the Library of Congress, "The illustration, based on the song, shows Davis asleep in a chair at right, about to be crowned by a winged demon, Lucifer, who stands behind him. At Davis's feet is a kneeling woman who presents him with an American flag. In the background the specter of George Washington looks on. Washington points toward Liberty and two female attendants (center), who appear in an aura of light. Liberty has a halo of stars, and holds another American flag. On the far left two Revolutionary War soldiers huddle next to a campfire, "your vet'ran sires, Encamp'd at Valley Forge, Exposed to winter's storms." *LOC*

can get a furlough. Very few get them and then only for 10 days from the time that they leave until they get back and that is too short a time to be at home. I think it would hardly pay for so short a length of time. I should like to see you all and think of you all daily."[58]

Despondent and defeated soldiers do not write strong letters home, they do not make fun of military "flummery," and they do not think in the long term. Disheartened men do not march well or draw favorable comments for their drill and appearance.

---

58 CHJHCF. Cites: "Joan F. Aldous, editor, *The Civil War Letters of Albert E. Higley* (Glens Falls, NY, 1986), 226."

These soldiers were starting to sense that the train was back on the track. There would be derailments and diversions, true, but they were now headed in the right direction. "[T]he army may as a mass have dim ideas of principles or rights, but they do know that they have been working and fighting in this cause, and they do not propose to give up and own themselves thrashed, just because their friends at the North are unwilling to make some slight sacrifices also," wrote William Wheeler of the 13th New York Battery. "I believe in the North's being made to feel the war, which she has not yet done as a nation, and to really offer up something to win this great, almost infinite good."

Wheeler articulated the two most important things that had come into focus for the Army of the Potomac: it was feeling a better about its own condition, and it was becoming decidedly less tolerant of home front dissonance. Too many had died in camp and battle and too many were suffering privations and sickness to permit anything less than full support from the Northern population.

"With regard to the state of the country, I think it is not by any means so unfavorable as many of our friends at home seem to suppose," Wheeler continued; "we have made great advances in our opinions upon many subjects, such as drafting, arming of the negroes, etc., and I hope to see the campaign carried on in the spring with a vigorous policy and to a successful issue. The army will obey every properly issued and communicated order from head-quarters; so long as the President and the Secretary of War are all right, Congress may blow, legislatures may resolve, and knots of rebel sympathizers may make a show of resistance, but it will amount to nothing."

Wheeler's letter, written on Washington's birthday, evidenced a mature and rational mind and a good sense of the America he had left behind. His was a new understanding of what was required: "[I]f violent resistance be made to the enforcement of the draft, we can easily spare a couple of veteran regiments who would enjoy nothing more than to drag out concealed rebels and stay-at-homes, and make them bear their share of the burden." He even declared he wouldn't mind deploying to New York, where he recalled "a fine position for artillery on Broadway below Canal Street, commanding the street as high as Eleventh, and the balls would ricochet splendidly on the hard pavement."[59]

As it was, the army ended February right where it had begun—physically, at least—confronting infernal mud, fickle weather, and an uncertain enemy situation. But in other ways, the Army of the Potomac had come a long way, thanks to highly significant reforms, important restructuring, and a demonstrable shift in attitudes.

March would provide important answers as to how far the army might still progress, and whether its progress would be sufficient.

---

59 BV 119, part 1, FSNMP, The Civil War Letters of Amory Allen, 14th Connecticut Infantry (II AC).

Chapter Six |

Improving Spirits, Deep Beliefs

On the third of March, 1863, Capt. Franklin J. Sauter finally got to go home on furlough. His revealing story was typical of the thousands who were finally able to squeeze in such visits. A member of the 55th Ohio Infantry, Sauter had spent the two previous days absorbed in regimental inspections. Naturally anxious about departing, he worried some unexpected duty or emergency might arise, but at 2:30 p.m. on March 3, he received the all-clear and set out on what would be a long journey. It did not begin well.

He and a "Capt. Wickham" departed together, walking the eight miles to Aquia Landing, but missed the departing steamboat by just ten minutes.[1] Trying again the next day, Sauter took a railroad car from Brooke Station back to Aquia Landing, where he caught a 2:00 p.m. boat to Washington. By four, after an unusually fast boat ride, he was on a train bound for Baltimore. By nine, he was boarding a crowded train for Harrisburg, Pennsylvania. In the bustle, he lost his haversack, packed with opera glasses and precious letters home from his soldiers. He noted, too, that a "poor discharged soldier's" pocket had been picked of $150.

Sauter detrained in Harrisburg at 2:00 a.m. on the 4th. An hour later, he boarded a train for Pittsburgh, arriving at noon on the 5th. There, he was treated to a free lunch by the Soldiers' Aid Society. "Of course I went," he recorded. "Found many Soldiers sitting around the room with a sqare bord on their laps, and 6 or 8 Ladys handing vutals around, and enjoyed myself well." He left Pittsburgh at 1:00 p.m. for Cleveland, Ohio, where he arrived about 8:00 p.m. and "staid at the Angeir house all night." On March 6, he left at 9:00 a.m. and arrived at Toledo at noon. After a two-hour layover, Sauter departed for Perrysburg, where he arrived at 3:00 p.m. "[F]ound my folks all well and

---

1 The story of Franklin Sauter on this page and the next all comes from his journal. BV 198, part 2, FSNMP, Journal of Captain Franklin J. Sauter, 55th Ohio Infantry.

they were glad to see me;" he wrote, "their was a General Shaking of hands and kissing, etc. etc."

Sauter spent seven-and-a-half days at home. The only problem he reported came on March 12. His journal entry reported a party at his house with too many ladies—an unsatisfactory ratio of two to one—but he enjoyed himself.

On March 14, Sauter began his return trip, leaving Perrysburg at 3:00 a. m. His travel took him by way of Toledo, Fremont, and Fostoria, where at last he arrived at noon to another rousing welcome round of handshaking that hurt his right hand. His Fostoria visit included dinner, tea, and a sleep-over. The following day he hired a team and departed. Stopping at Beltsville to warm up, he encountered several former comrades who entertained him and put him up. On the sixteenth, Sauter packed a trunk loaded with 14 pairs of boots and packages bound for men in the 55th Ohio. A former sergeant took him to Fremont in a one-horse wagon. There he purchased two American-made watches and three others totaling $111. He left at five and arrived in Cleveland at 8:00 p.m. To save money, he and another soldier slept in a single room at the American Hotel.

On March 17, at 7:00 a.m. Sauter made his way from Cleveland to Pittsburgh, Harrisburg, and Washington, where he arrived late that night. At 9:00 a.m. the next morning he checked his trunk for the midnight steamboat ride to Aquia Landing. After getting a pass from the provost marshal, he discovered the boat would not leave until the next morning, so he checked into the Planter's Hotel and attended a theater performance of Hamlet at "Grovers Theater." At 9:00 a.m. on March 19, Sauter reached Aquia Landing about noon. He spent as much time traveling during his exhausting 15-day furlough as he had relaxing at home.

On his way back to camp, Sauter discovered Captain Bement had resigned as company commander, and Sauter had been named in his stead. The men welcomed Sauter back with a hearty cheer.

The next few days kept Sauter busy. He sold all of the watches he had purchased except an American one, which he kept. He retrieved some luggage he had lost on his return trip and, a few days later, received news that the haversack he'd lost in Baltimore had been found, too. On March 20, while riding the regimental quartermaster's horse to Falmouth Station, Sauter observed the balloon Washington aloft, declaring it "quite a Curiosity" and "the first one I had ever seen." He also learned that his regimental commander, Col. John C. Lee, was commanding the brigade.

Life was looking very good for the Ohio captain. Unfortunately, Franklin Sauter had little more than one month to live.[2]

---

2   Ibid.

Command and Control

As appreciated as they were, and as much as they did to improve morale, furloughs remained a hot topic in the Union Army's uppermost echelons. On March 3, Hooker fired the latest salvo in an ongoing exchange with Halleck over who had authority to approve them. Halleck contended only Hooker's headquarters—and not his corps commanders—could authorize leaves and furloughs. Hooker replied by reiterating that, upon assuming command, he had issued General Orders on February 7, 1863, with detailed instructions regarding leaves and furloughs. He had delegated authority to carry out his directives to his corps commanders. "If officers holding these high positions cannot be intrusted with this duty, it seems to me they should be replaced by others who can," he noted. He pointedly reminded Halleck that "[t]he delay incident to applications for leave will be appreciated when you are informed that my camp is nearly 100 miles in circumference and, if acted on immediately on their receipt at these headquarters, would . . . delay the departure of the applicant eight and forty hours."

On March 5, Halleck bureaucratically retorted by citing War Department General Orders Nos. 61 and 100 of 1862, which denied leave-granting authority to army and corps commanders except on surgeon's certificate. This authority was only to be granted by the secretary of war, Halleck reiterated, and had only been relaxed in Hooker's case and that of Maj. Gen. William Rosecrans in the West. "To give it to your generals of army corps and refuse it to other commanders of armies and departments would not be just," contended Halleck, presumably backed by Stanton. "Last reports show that 9,692 officers are now absent from their commands. It is the determination of the War Department to diminish this number by retaining to itself the power to grant leaves and by refusing them except in the most urgent cases." Halleck was arguing that, regardless of how stupid the regulation was, it would be enforced uniformly and fairly.[3]

Hooker's leave policies, though—built on the sound leadership premise of punishing poor performance and rewarding better–than–average performance—were instrumental as part of his overall effort to improve the army's discipline and sagging morale. "Orders were read on parade relative to the different regts who were par excellence and vice versa on inspection, the giving and withholding of leaves of absences, etc.," observed Lt. John H. Stevens of the 5th Maine Infantry on March 5, confirming that Hooker's inspectors-general were in fact succeeding. "'Virtue is its own

3   *OR*, 25, part II, 118-119, 123.

reward,'" he explained. Indeed, but Hooker's improved furlough system didn't hurt, either.[4]

Hooker identified regiments and batteries whose inspection results had merited continued leaves and furloughs (or not). Those regiments with high inspection marks were: 1st, 2nd, and 20th Massachusetts Infantry Regiments; 10th and 19th Maine Infantry Regiments; 5th and 10th New York Infantry Regiments; 5th New Jersey Infantry Regiment; 111th Pennsylvania Infantry Regiment; 3rd Wisconsin Infantry Regiments; and 1st Minnesota Infantry Regiment. Fourteen artillery batteries were similarly praised. At the discretion of corps commanders, the units could authorize increased durations and numbers of soldiers on leave per General Orders No. 3.

Substandard were: 12th, 21st, 23rd, 26th, 34th, 35th, 42nd, 59th, 60th, 78th, 88th, 104th, 105th, 107th, and 145th New York Infantry Regiments; 29th, 68th, 69th, 124th, 125th, 132nd, 136th and 155th Pennsylvania Infantry Regiments; 27th Indiana Infantry Regiment; and 32nd Massachusetts Infantry Regiment. In these regiments no further leaves would be granted and officers on leave would be recalled until corps commanders could certify improvements. The same applied to 11 artillery batteries.[5]

Assuming these inspections were fair, this was an exceptional leadership move. Unit recognition has been cited as a major step forward in winning support. Even in the patrician and strongly War Democrat 20th Massachusetts Infantry, one officer related, "We have received the greatest honor yet" for "general excellence."[6] In a similar good move, leaves issued under this order would be specifically marked "in pursuance of Paragraph VI, General Orders No. 18, Army of the Potomac"—thus recognizing the bearer's and unit's special achievement.

Hooker ordered the cavalry corps to conduct similar inspections and to issue similar results. He regulated infantry outpost duty: corps would make details for three-day periods. Formal guard mounts would take place; officers and men would be issued three days' rations; a surgeon would be detailed; and no officer or soldier could return to camp during the period except as special couriers and for emergencies (both with passes). No sick men would be returned without surgeon's certificate. As leave returns were conditioned for others' departure, Hooker ordered all leave extension requests denied. Late returnees would be court-martialed. Hooker also established a more thorough system of identifying returned deserters.[7]

---

4 BV 354, part 8, FSNMP. G. S. Stuart and A. M. Jakeman Jr., eds., *John H. Stevens, Civil War Diary.*

5 *OR*, 25, part II, 119-122.

6 Miller, *Harvard's Civil War*, 226.

7 *OR*, 25, part II, 119-122.

Despite Hooker's earlier pronouncements to the contrary, though, desertion continued, even as morale improved. Desertion even took place in his old corps. On March 5, Hooker ordered Brig. Gen. Dan Sickles to catch and return the "late deserters from the Third Corps." He told Sickles to wire Heintzelman in Washington and Schenck in Baltimore to cover all bridges, boats, and avenues. He advised checking all travelers, especially those coming through southern Maryland, and that "deserters will be generally found in citizens' or negroes' clothes, with forged passes." Hooker also wanted provost guards to check rail cars headed north. This crackdown reflected his continuing concern and willingness to escalate enforcement.[8]

Men in the camps noticed such efforts. "Deserters are being brought back by hundreds," noted II Corps surgeon Frank Dyer, "and any officer or man staying away beyond his time is instantly brought up [on charges] on his return, and if he cannot give a reasonable excuse, is recommended for dismissal if an officer or other punishment if an enlisted man. This tends to bring them back on time."[9]

During his jousts with Halleck, Hooker also issued omnibus General Orders No. 18 on March 3, setting right a number of other army internal discipline matters. He required corps, division, and brigade commanders to clean out nests of enlisted men being used as servants, orderlies, and extra-duty men. He mandated use of the "contrabands" within the army "as laborers, teamsters and servants, whenever practicable," and those not so employed should be turned over to the provost marshal general for disposition. This released more soldiers for line duties. Although falling short of more active military roles, it also gave substantial numbers of former slaves' opportunities for service. Hooker's reference to "citizens, non-residents" without permits was less clear; however, his order to remove them from camps was unambiguous. He next required strict accounting of funds within regiments and batteries for hospital uses and prescribed punishment for abusers.[10]

As part of his ongoing efficiency efforts, Hooker clarified procedures for dispatching intelligence on enemy movements while also reducing transmission time. Such reports were to be marked "important" and sent by telegraph where available. When doubt existed concerning the telegraph's condition, couriers were also sent. Wherever suspicion warranted, incoming officers' packages had to be opened (but in that officer's presence). Sutlers' business was confined to their appointed regiments. Violators' goods would be confiscated—half went to the informer and half to the informer's regimental hospital fund. Sutlers fraudulently invoking officers' names or

8   *OR*, 25, part II, 123.

9   Chesson, ed., *J. Franklin Dyer, Journal of a Civil War Surgeon*, 63-64.

10   *OR*, 25, part II, 119-122.

orders to purchase or sell contraband articles would be similarly punished. Lastly, Hooker ordered that public business within an officer's purview be conducted promptly and without delay. These orders, when applied with integrity, wrought better discipline and order.[11]

Hooker's corps commanders responded positively to Hooker's top-down push for a tighter operation. It helped that a number of the more prominent "McClellanites" were gone. Dan Sickles was Hooker's only close ally amongst the army's corps commanders. The army's other corps commanders—Reynolds, Couch, Meade, Sedgwick, Howard, and Slocum— represented an evolution in meritocracy. They were competent generals who'd properly advanced into their high positions and, whatever their opinions of Hooker, they all could organize, train, prepare, and develop their corps into better fighting formations than they had received.

Post-reorganization command reforms were bearing fruit. They renewed spirit in a demoralized army by exercising practical, common-sense leadership and promoting the troops' material welfare. Simply implementing Hooker's reforms enhanced the army's fighting spirit, if only in one corps or division at a time. But these subordinates evidenced more demonstrable character and ability. That, in turn, meant they could pick and develop subordinates more effectively. They produced top-to-bottom results by setting proper behavioral examples that could be emulated. Excepting inevitable errors in personnel selection, such men also appointed or retained division and brigade commanders on merit.[12]

Further Signs of Thaw in The "Valley Forge" Winter

At the division level, the situation looked good to Surgeon Frank Dyer of the II Corps' 2nd Division. "I think the army is in much better condition than when Hooker first took command," was his qualified assessed. On March 8, Dr. Dyer observed that the corps hospital at Aquia Creek had been broken up "and we now have division hospitals. Ours is placed just below the hill on which our headquarters are, and we are beginning to put the patients in." The surgeon also expressed satisfaction with some of Hooker's other changes, too. "If the army does not have fresh bread at least four days in the week and vegetables at least five, he will have some good reason from the commissaries," Dyer wrote. "There is a far better state of things since Hooker took

---

11 OR, 25, part II, 119-122.

12 Taaffe, *Commanding the Army of the Potomac*.

command," he repeated. "We want a good victory to encourage the country. Things have looked blue about long enough. It is time for the tide to turn."[13]

Chaplain John R. Adams of the 5th Maine and 121st New York reflected a similar optimism on March 9. "I am happy to tell you that our army is in a good condition, in good health, and in good spirits—better than for months," he wrote. "There is confidence in General Hooker, and the men will go where he will lead them. I trust it will be to victory, and the crushing out of the Rebellion. We are pleased to see an improved state of feeling at the North . . . . This is very hopeful. I hope that something will be done now to good effect."[14]

"Let us hope and pray that when we do move it will be to victory," wished Surgeon Daniel M. Holt of the 121st New York Infantry on March 16, summarizing army morale and readiness in perhaps premature terms. "Hooker says he will drive the rebels out of their entrenchments or he will send his army to a hotter place than they were ever in here below. We are in fighting trim and ready for the fray: Not a man speaks doubtingly or despondingly in view of the 'impending crisis.'" Holt believed the men felt "a decisive battle" was coming and were ready. He knew the cost would continue to be high: "many—very many noble sons of the Republic will be stricken down, and the soil [will] drink deeply the blood of the truest, finest and most devoted of America's freemen." His main thoughts were equally patriotic: "There appears to be but one sentiment here, and that is to fight. Thank God no copperheads disgrace the field or service however plenty they be at home. Only spike their mouths and chain their tongues at the North, and we will attend to their more honorable brethren in the South. It is hard to fight two battles at the same time—one in the front and the other in the rear." Holt, like the rest of the army, looked increasingly hard at the antiwar faction: "I hate them worse than the enemies in front, and would sooner see a field strewn with their blackened, putrid carcasses, than those we are fighting down here."[15]

Gardner Stockman of the 5th Connecticut Infantry wrote a letter on February 26, published in *The Waterbury American* on March 13 that reflected the shifting mood in the context of the "Valley Forge." "[T]he booming of artillery from the batteries of our own division, echoed by hundreds of guns from miles around, informed the few genuine residents that are left in this section of Virginia, that the memory of Washington still lived among the ranks of their invaders," he wrote:

13 Chesson, ed., *J. Franklin Dyer, Journal of a Civil War Surgeon*, 63-64.

14 BV 354, part 7, FSNMP, *Memorial and Letters of Rev. John R. Adams, D.D., Chaplain*, 101. This was the March 9, 1863, letter.

15 CHJHCF. Cites: "James M. Greiner, Janet L. Coryell, and James R. Smither, ed., *A Surgeon's Civil War: The Letters of Daniel M. Holt, M.D.* (Kent, OH: Kent State University Press, 1994), 81.

And to one standing in the midst of the encampments, looking around upon the little huts cottered up of pieces of pine sticks and the mud of foresaid, and covered with the bits of cotton sheeting, ironically styled "shelter tents," the wood cut illustrations of the "Winter at Valley Forge," which adorned Parley's history in school-boy days, was forcibly brought to mind, and the admiration then felt for the hero and his companion heroes of that never-to-be-forgotten campaign, is felt to have been still more deserved than when it was the height of boyish ambition to have an opportunity to emulate their glorious example. And indeed the parallel between the situation of this army and that of the band of Revolutionary worthies is not by any means far fetched.

Stockman exaggerated, but was sincere in his comparison of the Revolutionary period with his own:

It is true that the soldier of the present day is perhaps better clad than were his predecessors of '76, but wherein else we have the advantage of them it is difficult to discover—for they had the certain knowledge that the hearts of their countrymen, who were not with them in the field, were sympathizing in every beat with their efforts, to console and encourage them. While, on the contrary, almost every male from the North brings us some new evidence that the war is becoming a burden too heavy for our stay-at-home friends to bear, and that the soldiers who were sent out a year, or a year and a half ago, with congratulatory speeches and complimentary cheers, and earnest adjurations to "carry the old flag through every Southern State," and the assurance that they should be supported and their hands held up till victory crowned their efforts, cost what it might, will return (those who return at all) to receive a chilling reception at the hands of faint-hearted and discouraged tax-payers, who having wearied in well doing, wish they had never put their hands to the plow—added to the scornful sneers of those who, sympathizing with rebellion in the beginning, would rejoice in the successful triumph of treason, and exult in the discomfiture of those who have risked health and life in the honest effort to maintain the right.[16]

"R," a 20th Connecticut Infantry soldier, writing on March 8, addressed negative comments published by a "returned soldier." "R" did a point-by-point refutation, pronouncing false a statement that Company A would vote Democrat, adding: "No Republican member of Co. A is here to fight for party power . . . When the war is over the American soldier will go home to peaceful pursuits of an American citizen, stronger

16 BV 313, part 123, FSNMP, *The Waterbury American* of March 13, 1863. The letter is signed "G. Stockman" (Gardner Stockman, NPS/CWSSS, M535 Roll 15). The letter is captioned "From the 5th Regiment, C.V.", postmarked "Stafford Court House, Va., Feb. 26, 1863."

in his love of his country, for having battled in its defense, and will cast his vote for those principles of truth and right founded on the broad basis of universal freedom and eternal justice, come under what name they may." He dismissed the belief the war must end in compromise: "I am sure that the soldiers of the Army of the Potomac will never submit to any compromise, except on terms of full and perfect submission to the laws of the United States, and till this is acceded to by the rebels in arms, will prosecute the war to the bitter end." Then he challenged the assertion that the men opposed the Emancipation Proclamation: "they do believe slavery to be the cause of the war, and that the way to settle it is to strike deep at the root from which it sprung." Lastly, "R" denied allegations the men had suffered at their officers' hands:

> I acknowledge that we have had hardships, privations and suffering, but it was not from any neglect on the part of our superiors, but a result consequent upon a winter campaign. I believe our soldiers never endured greater privations since that dreadful winter at Valley Forge, than they have experienced this winter. And yet long and weary marches, insufficient shelter, and scanty food, have not called forth a murmur of discontent, or a complaint from those who have been used to every comfort and luxury of happy homes.

He concluded, "I believe I have uttered the honest sentiments of all those who have come to battle for the dearest rights that ever nerved freemen to high and heroic deeds."[17]

Major Rufus Dawes Speaks Out For The Army

On March 10, Maj. Rufus R. Dawes of the 6th Wisconsin, who had first prophesied the Union Army's "Valley Forge" on Christmas day three months earlier, left on a 15-day furlough to Marietta, Ohio. On March 16, responding to a citizens committee's request to speak on "the war and the state of the country," he gave the most significant and relevant testimony by any participant. "Is the Army of the Potomac demoralized?" was how the Iron Brigade officer began his talk, delivered with undeniable integrity and a thorough knowledge of the army's condition. Dawes gave the home front crowd both barrels, and every word is memorable and worth reprinting here in full:

---

17 BV 313, part 126, FSNMP, letter from "R." of the 20th Connecticut Volunteers, which appeared in the Friday, March 27, 1863, edition of the same Waterbury newspaper as fn 6 above. "R" served in Company A of the 20th. Thus two men from different Connecticut regiments perceived the "Valley Forge" connection at the same time.

I have belonged to the Army of the Potomac during almost the whole of its existence, and I have no hesitation in saying that in point of discipline and general efficiency, the standard is higher this winter than ever before. I think the men are in better spirits. There are several reasons for this opinion. They are now old soldiers, inured to the toils, hardships and dangers of the service, and skillful in making the best and most of comforts with which they are provided. The paymasters have been around this winter and arrearages have been paid up. Nothing is more disheartening and demoralizing to the soldier than to feel his family is suffering at home for want of his small and richly earned wages. The men are better provided this winter with good and healthful rations, that at any time before in the history of our army. Fresh bread, onions, potatoes, and fresh beef are regularly furnished in addition to the old stipend of hard tack and side meat. An encouraging system of furloughs, as a reward of soldierly conduct, has been instituted. You can hardly realize with what satisfaction the soldiers hailed general order number three on the subject of furloughs. In short, the soldiers feel that their personal comfort and happiness, so far as attainable in the army, is being looked after and they feel encouraged. Breaches of discipline and soldierly conduct have been more surely punished this winter than usual. Orders have been enforced against political discussions, and disrespectful and treasonous language towards the government or superior officers. Copperhead newspapers no longer monopolize the circulation among the soldiers, and, by the prompt dismissal of disaffected and disloyal officers, the army is being purged of the damnable heresy, that a man can be a friend to the government, and yet throw every clog in the way of the administration and the prosecution of the war. No, the Army of the Potomac is not demoralized nor has it ever been.[18]

"How does the army like General Hooker?," continued Major Dawes. "They like him," he went on,

Because he is "fighting Joe Hooker." They like him because of the onions and potatoes he has furnished them, and they like him because he is the commander of the Army of the Potomac, and they expect him to lead them to victory. Victory is what we want no matter whether Hooker, Burnside or McClellan leads us. The bones of our comrades and dear friends are bleaching all over the battlefields of the east. We have marched and we have countermarched, toiled and suffered, without realizing the hopes and expectations of the country. Now we want, and we expect, under "fighting Joe," such a triumph as will place us right upon the records of history, and the glory and blessings of which will repay us for the disasters and sufferings of the past. The fighting of an army depends more upon the courage and good faith of subordinate commanders than seems to be understood throughout the

18 Dawes is not being disingenuous. Men in the better units often refuted "demoralization" in their regiment, brigade, division or corps. Few defended the army as a whole. Dawes's recent personal views, reflected in this speech, were extended to the larger army.

country. From such, or many other causes, General Hooker may fail, but, we feel his heart is in the work, that he is a fighting man and we have great hope.

Dawes wasn't finished. "How does the army like the Emancipation Proclamation?" he asked, adding:

If there remains any one in the army, who does not like the Proclamation, he is careful to keep quiet about it. We are hailed everywhere by the negroes as their deliverers. They all know that "Massa Linkum" has set them free, and I never saw one not disposed to take advantage of the fact. The negroes will run away if they get the chance, whenever they are assured of their freedom, and that the Proclamation places it beyond the power of any military commander, however disposed, to prevent. Slavery is the chief source of wealth in the South, and the basis of their aristocracy, and my observation is that a blow at slavery hurts more than battalion volleys. It strikes at the vitals. It is foolish to talk about embittering the rebels any more than they are already embittered. We like the Proclamation because it lets the world know what the real issue is. We like the Proclamation because it gives a test of loyalty. As governor Andrew Johnson, of Tennessee, says: "If you want to find a traitor North, shake the Emancipation Proclamation or the writ of habeas corpus at him and he will dodge." We like the Emancipation Proclamation because it is right, and because it is the edict of our Commander in Chief, the President of the United States.

How does the army like the conscription law? They like the conscription law or any other law that promises to fill the shattered ranks of their battalions. As soldiers anxious for military glory, we want our army strengthened, so we may achieve military success. As patriots, we desire such a force put in the field this summer as may conquer a peace. The old regiments, reduced by battle and disease to mere skeletons, are looking anxiously for recruits. Each has its own record, its own battles inscribed upon its banners, and each wishes to retain its own identity, which it can only do by being filled up. We hail the act with joy, because it indicates a determination on the part of the Government to meet the crisis. We feel encouraged and feel hopeful. Our soldiers need encouragement as well as reinforcement. They want to feel they are sustained and sympathized with by their friends at home. Nothing, in my opinion, has been more demoralizing to the Army of the Potomac, than letters from home to soldiers, advising them "to get out of it, if they can,—that they have done their share,—and that the war is to be hopelessly protracted." If you wish success, write encouraging letters to your soldiers. Tell them that they are engaged in a good and glorious cause, cheer them on as enthusiastically as you did when they entered the service as volunteers. Tell them that victory will be sure to crown their faithful efforts. Do not fill the ears of your soldiers with tales of troubles and privations at home, caused by their absence. Worse troubles would come to you should the rebel arms prevail. Many a poor fellow is brought before the severe tribunal of a court martial, whose greatest crime is listening to and obeying the suggestions of father and mother at home. We like the conscription law because it brings matters to a focus. If it can be enforced, we shall bring an army into the field that must sweep all before it. If it can not be enforced, the future is very hopeless.

"What does the army think of the Copperheads? They think that any citizen of the North, who by word, deed, or influence, throws a clog in the way of an earnest and vigorous prosecution of the war, so long as there is a rebel in arms, gives aid and comfort to the enemies of his country and deserves their fate," argued Dawes, who continued:

> The army is unanimous in this opinion. The chief hope of traitors South, now is in the co-operation of traitors, North. The war is now being prosecuted on correct principles, and for a great purpose, the re-establishment of the republican government throughout the land on the basis of free institutions, and the eternal overthrow of a monied aristocracy based on slavery. The consummation of so great an enterprise will be a step forward in the history of the world. The world is moving forward, and carrying us with it. We can not resist the progress of events. However prejudices of the Copperheads may be galled at the policy of the government or the conduct of the war, all of them of sound judgment are realizing that they have but one salvation, to stand by the government in its peril. Our enemy is too strong, too earnest, too much determined to rule or ruin, to admit of any compromise or half way ground. The traitors at home, who clog the government in its righteous struggle, will go down in history with infamy. If the voice from the army helps to open their eyes to this fact, I beg to add my voice again. We want to fight this war until we conquer a peace on terms that will be honorable, and a peace that can be lasting. The traitor who aids and comforts the enemy by standing in the way of this, has our heartiest contempt as a coward, who dares not maintain his true principles by an honorable appeal to arms. Do not expect overwhelming victories of us. The rebel army in our front is too skillful in maneuvering, too expert in retiring, too strong in bayonets, to be "gobbled up or bagged." Your Army of the Potomac will go out this spring, purged of disloyalty, the men stronger in health, and better in spirits than ever before. Remember that the same men are there who charged again and again the deadly rifle pits at Fredericksburgh, who swept over the crest at South Mountain, and who struggled on the bloody fields of Antietam. The army is more anxious for victory than you can be, and rest assured that when it is again called to battle it will do its duty.[19]

The War of Words Against "Traitors at Home"—Part I

While Dawes was on furlough, President Lincoln issued a general amnesty for deserters and absentees. Some histories give its date as March 10, 1863. Hooker, on March 20, however, referred to the President's proclamation pursuant to "the

---

19 Dawes, *Service With The Sixth Wisconsin Volunteers*, 124-128.

twenty-sixth section of the act of March 3, 1863, pardoning all soldiers now absent without leave from the army who report at certain posts before April 1." The March 3 date is supported by reports of returning deserters. As the Emancipation Proclamation encouraged slaveholders back into the political Union, Lincoln's amnesty proclamation offered military redemption to deserters. Both were "war measures." Hooker suggested to the Army Adjutant General that the amnesty should also include those undergoing arrest, trial, and punishment; however, all such reprieves should include forfeiture of pay and allowances for missing time.[20]

Regardless of nuances, Lincoln's edict provided the opportunity for a mass return to arms and a second chance at salvaging military honor and reputation. The "rights and wrongs" and effects on morale could be argued endlessly; however, this army badly needed trained men. The deserters, given reflection and reprieve, might wish to "undo" abandonment of cause and comrades.

"I suppose the North has lost faith in this army," wrote Sgt. C. Hickox of the 27th Connecticut on March 11. "Well, there's some reson for it to be sure, but thank God we haven't lost faith in ourselves. The men who carry the muskets in this army are not half so badly demoralized as those who stay at home and grumble at us, and of whom we expected better things." He cursed the newspapers and home-folks who were "beginning to grudge their dollars where we have not hesitated to give our lives." He added, "Next to killing rebels, I'd like to go home and shoot copperheads." The antiwar faction found little or no sympathy in the army.[21]

Dawes' and Hickox' views were fairly universal. Communities, friends, and hometown newspapers received at least a million letters written during the "Valley Forge." Letters from "Camp near Falmouth," "Falmouth," "Camp Opposite Fredericksburg," "Stafford Court House," "Potomac Creek," "Hope Landing," "Aquia Creek," "Hartwood Church," "White Oak Church," "Belle Plain," "Brooke Station," "Camp Pitcher," "Kane's Landing," and a host of other Stafford County places chastised or enlisted support from "friends at home." The army, bearing huge losses and privation, no longer countenanced the "fire in the rear" subverting and sabotaging their war effort. Dawes (and his comrades who made similar speeches and resolutions) and Hickox (and his comrades who wrote such letters) proved soldiers at war could influence homefront support.

Drawing the army into national politics may have been considered wrong by some; however, that was a gross misunderstanding of the nature of America's military. The

---

20 *OR*, 25, part II, 149.

21 BV 182, part 3, letters of Sgt. C. Hickox to his cousin, Miss Charlotte Hickox of Solon, Ohio.

citizen-army was just that. Professional armies in peacetime avoid taking sides politically, but a citizen-army—as envisioned and established by the founding fathers—was composed almost entirely of volunteers. Such an army could not and should not, by definition, sacrifice its right to speak directly to the people. This citizen-army played for the highest stakes, risking everything, and sacrificed disproportionately to achieve its mission. Morale had been kicked into the gutter—or, more appropriately, a Stafford mud-hole—and they had every right, and indeed the moral obligation, to communicate their views to those who had sent them to war and on whom they depended for support.

Individual opinions, letters and speeches were one thing, but this period witnessed another phenomenon: mass unit resolutions against the Copperheads. During late February, companies of the 20th Indiana Infantry had issued resolutions against the "traitors at home."[22] That trend expanded in March.

An Empire State regiment issued "An Appeal to the People of New York" in the *Rochester Democrat and American*. Twenty-six members—from colonel to second lieutenants to enlisted men—who styled themselves as "representing every county from Lake Erie to the ocean," signed the resolution from "Headquarters, 44th N. Y. S. V., Camp near Falmouth, Va., March 9th, 1863." Their words struck home: "We can no longer keep silence. A sacred devotion to our country—an ardent love for our homes—and above all, an abiding faith in God, bid us speak." For nearly two years, they had suffered, periled, and endured "all things, for the sake of our common country." They left homes, businesses, and lives left behind, and sacrificed on the march, in camp, in battle, and in hospitals. "You told us to go," they wrote, "that God would be with us, and that your most fervent prayers would follow us. Encouraged by your words of patriotism, of hope, of faith, we came to the war. After suffering thus much in behalf of you, and your children, and the nation's honor, dear alike to us all, will you withhold from us, now, your sympathy and support?—Will you join with those, worse than traitors, at the North who cry 'peace' when they know there is no peace, nor can be none, till this unholy rebellion is crushed?"[23]

Private George B. Wolcott, a member of the 44th, wrote a letter home on March 10 that reflected the unit's sentiment. "Having with regret witnessed the dissensions and strife among political [enemies?] up North," he wrote, "we the members of the 44 Regt. yesterday originated and signed a petition to the people of N.Y. State denouncing their want of faith in the [existing?] conflict, and sent them from the field words of encouragement and cheer (which they ought to have done to us) and bade them have

22 BV 182, part 3, letters of Sgt. C. Hickox to his cousin, Miss Charlotte Hickox of Solon, Ohio.

23 CHJHCF. Cites: "Rochester *Democrat and American* of March 18, 1863, in which this letter appeared.

more faith in God, and sustain us in our efforts to crush the Rebellion and cease to cry for peace on any terms, for this was only to be attained by fighting for it."[24]

That same day, the 11th New Jersey launched a protest against pending "Peace Resolutions" in the state's legislature. The men attacked the politicians for desiring a "dishonorable peace with armed rebels seeking to destroy our great and beneficent Government, the best ever designed for the happiness of the many." They "fully recogniz[ed] the impropriety of a soldier's discussion of the legislative functions of the State," they admitted, yet deemed it their due "that the voice of those who offer their all in their country's cause, be heard when weak and wicked men seek its dishonor."

Only the Union guaranteed liberty and independence, the regiment maintained, and the war "commands" homefront support. The "Peace Resolutions" were "wicked, weak, and cowardly" and aided the rebels; they regarded as traitors alike rebels in arms and "secret enemies of our Government" at home; and they condemned reports that claimed the army was demoralized and clamoring for peace. "We put forth every effort, endure every fatigue, and shrink from no danger, until, under the gracious guidance of a kind Providence, every armed rebel shall be conquered, and traitors at home shall quake with fear," they resolved, "as the proud emblem of our national independence shall assert its power from North to South, and crush beneath its powerful folds all who dared to assail its honor, doubly hallowed by the memory of the patriot dead."[25]

The 24th Michigan unanimously adopted a resolution on March 11 drafted by a committee of three captains, two lieutenants, and Col. Morrow.[26] "We have heard with astonishment that a feeling is fostered in the North and West, adverse to a vigorous prosecution of the war," they wrote, worried that "unless checked by the patriotism of loyal citizens . . . the government shall be compelled to make peace on dishonorable and disastrous terms." The Michiganders resolved that no termination of war short of unconditional surrender and return to Union was acceptable. They called on the government to use "its vast resources in a vigorous prosecution of the war." They discarded "all former differences of party or sect and unite with the loyal citizens everywhere in restoring our blood bought union." They noted "with regret and indignation," efforts to "discourage the volunteer soldier," and they recognized "no difference between such traitors and those in armed rebellion." They endorsed the draft and offered to execute the law (and resisters, if necessary). "[T]he Army of the Potomac

24 BV 110, part 12, FSNMP; letter of March 10, 1863, from George B. Wolcott of the 44th New York Infantry Regiment.

25 Henry Steele Commager , ed., *Documents of American History* (New York, NY, 1945), 427-428.

26 Regimental historian Orson B. Curtis noted they were "all Democrats except Captain Edwards."

is neither 'disorganized' nor 'demoralized,'" they concluded, "but at this moment is as efficient in discipline as any army in the world."[27]

The 24th Michigan belonged to the Iron Brigade, which similarly passed a resolution on March 11. "That, toilsome as soldier life may be, and much as we long for the society of our families and the endearments at home, we feel it our duty to carry on this war to the bitter end," the brigade's resolution read, "and whatever the consequences to ourselves, do not desire peace until the last rebel in arms has vanished from our soil." They warned "our friends at home to beware of the traitors in their midst, and never forget that the first duty of a good citizen and true patriot is a maintenance of his rightful government." Pointing out that, "[t]he blood of thousands of our friends, already sacrificed upon the altar of our country, cries aloud to you to follow their glorious example and fill the thinned ranks of an army which will never submit to an inglorious peace," they called for "vigorous prosecution of the war until the last rebel in arms is subdued, and the stars and stripes float over every inch of territory of the United States." They endorsed conscription and supported governmental acts "having for their object the effectual crushing out of this rebellion." The brigade adopted the resolution with such a resounding "aye" that it startled the horses of the general and his staff.[28]

As Gardner Stockman of the 5th Connecticut Infantry had written in late February to *The Waterbury American*, so too did his entire regiment on March 10. Their letter bemoaned politics at home in which they had been unable to voice opinions or vote. They felt their compact with the people was compromised and unfulfilled. They charged treason "upon our native soil," adding, "we have so far fulfilled our promise to you" and "those who remain clustered around the torn and riddled banner of Connecticut which you entrusted to our care, and which has never been disgraced, still hold the contract good." The 5th remembered "those who have gone down in the headlong charge, and closed up in the ranks of death—those who sleep in soldiers' graves," and asked, "shall it be said that Connecticut requited her brave sons with cowardice?" The letter urged residents not to vote for the antiwar nominee for governor.[29]

Two weeks later, on March 24, the 14th Connecticut Infantry sent a resolution to the American clarifying the political allusions in the 5th Connecticut's letter. Thomas H. Seymour, nominated for governor by the Democratic Party on an antiwar platform, had aroused the 5th's ire. Remarkably, where the 5th opposed Seymour outright, the 14th's

---

27 Curtis, *The History of the Twenty-fourth Michigan*, Ch. VI, "Winter Headquarters at Belle Plain."

28 Ibid.

29 CHJHCF. "*The Waterbury American* of March 20, 1863."

letter corrected the impression that it was supporting Seymour. Captain I. R. Bronson, commanding the regiment, stated this resolution had been "unanimously adopted by officers and men present for duty, with the exception of less than a score of enlisted men." However ambiguous, the resolution's core went for the heart: "[W]e utterly abhor and despise, as the meanest of all treason, the effort that is being made in many parts of the North to take advantage of the reverses and consequent temporary discouragement of our people, to bring about a dishonorable peace, which would give up in substance the whole question we have been fighting for." The regiment refused to "acknowledge ourselves to have been in the wrong from the beginning, and make the blood of our brave and beloved brothers, slain in this conflict, virtually blood spilled by our own murderous hands." They held "these home traitors to be worse than the armed traitors we meet in the field, a disgrace to our people, a 'fire in the rear' of our patriot army." They called on "our friends at home, all true and loyal men, all real Democrats, without distinction of party, to rise in their might and put down these enemies with the ballot, while we try the bullet upon the comparatively more open and honorable enemies to the southward."[30]

Some regiments naturally had conflicted views on war opposition. Schisms could still separate the War Democrat majority from their Republican allies, and there were even a few discernible Peace Democrat influences within the army. In the 26th New Jersey Infantry, for instance, such a rift opened between officers and enlisted men. "[W]e are in favor of peace," resolved the officers, "but there is but one basis of peace with the rebels, and that is unconditional submission to the government which their and our fathers established, and that we mean to fight for such a peace and no other." Compromise was deemed impossible because it meant "dissolution of the Union, and would be a miserable and disgraceful death by suicide of the grandest government the world has yet beheld." Opponents were branded "traitors and rebels in disguise," and attacked as, "Those who do all they can to oppose the war, to embarrass the government, to prevent vigorous measures, to weaken credit or magnify our defeats and glorify all the successes of our enemies, to discourage enlistments, to denounce the enrollment, to disparage and slander the officers charged with the administration of public affairs, to fill the public mind with distrust, apprehension, and a desire for a disgraceful peace; to outrage and libel the army now in the field; and leave it to perish unsupported in the struggle, or finish the contest as best it may; and in short, all who by such infamous means have justly entitled themselves to the disgraceful distinction of the sinister name Copperhead."

30 Ibid., April 3, 1863."

This resolution was accompanied by another from Sgt. Mjr. Cummings, who claimed that the officers' resolution had not been put squarely before the regiment—so "the majority of the enlisted men" passed one of their own.

On March 24, an open letter went to a Lancaster, Pennsylvania, newspaper from the "Non-commissioned officers of Company K" of the 122nd Pennsylvania Infantry —"Col. Hambright's Regiment"—that "represents the views of the men of that company, and, so far as we have been able to ascertain, the sentiments of the entire regiment, with perhaps one or two exceptions." The letter read: "As we notice in almost every northern paper which reaches us, and in many of our letters, something concerning the Copperheads, we begin to think as you and all loyal men say, that while the soldiers are watching in the front, there is an enemy in the rear." Their considered view was that, "if some of these traitors at the north were out in the field, as they should be, instead of distracting and dividing public sentiment, and opposing the Commander-in-chief, this war would soon be over." Subversion provided hope to "the rebels in our front." They condemned those leaders in Lancaster who held what the NCOs perceived as antiwar meetings. "Talk about the 'despotism' of the President!" they scoffed. "Why, if our good old [Andrew] Jackson was at the head of affairs, in these times, these cowardly traitors, who insult that flag which our forefathers fought, bled and died for, by offering sympathy to its enemies, would be hung as high as Haman, for his last regret on his death bed was that he had not served the South Carolina traitor Calhoun in that way." The 122nd suggested that they would deal similarly with the Copperheads and "their treasonable plots" upon their return home. "The 122nd is composed of good material," they concluded, "but their hearts are too much devoted to their country to 'stay at home and vote,' as many others were persuaded to do by men who, we now learn, are rank Copperheads." Describing themselves as "hard-working men," they now labored "in a glorious cause and we will be ever ready to work to save our country from further desolation and utter ruin."[31]

Typical of the opinions junior officers held were those written on March 8 to the *Hartford Evening Press*, by Capt. Samuel S. Woodruff of the 20th Connecticut Infantry, whose letter appeared in the paper on March 18. Woodruff lashed out at copperheadism at home and praised the patriotism of his fellow Union soldiers. "There is but little excitement with us, except when we hear from the cowardly sneaking treachery of our enemies in the rear, who are doing more to prolong this war than the enemies in front," he wrote. "What is it that makes them so bold and confident now? Is it because 20,000 loyal citizens have left the state of Connecticut in arms and marched to the rebellious states of our country, to support our national flag and to sustain the best government

---

31 CHJHCF. "*Lancaster Daily Express* of March 28, 1863."

that ever existed on God's footstool?" Woodruff bemoaned citizen-soldiers being denied participation in the political fray. "This job is not going to last much longer, and then we will attend to the rebels at home," he warned. His duty commanding corduroy road construction from Aquia Landing to his brigade's camp allowed him conversations with the entire brigade's soldiers; thus he felt well-informed that they were not "demoralized, discouraged and disgusted" at that point. "They talk as sensible men always do," he concluded. "They talk about war and about home. They would be glad to have the war come to an end and return home, but they have no idea of ending it in disgrace to themselves or their country; they are as loyal and as ready to fight the battles of their country as they have ever been. Of course there are some growlers and fault-finders, who are good for nothing at home or in the army . . . . God bless them; truer men never entered the field."[32]

Some newspapers—almost all with specific political affiliations—and any members of the public who had their own political agendas doubted such truth. Rather, they contended that some of the resolutions and open letters were not credible, genuine expressions of the troops' true feelings. And no American "grass roots" effort can be excluded from a possibility of political tampering or instigation. For example, the *Hartford Daily Times* on March 24th wrote: "We do not have room for all the letters from our soldiers in the field that come pouring in upon us. A pile of forty or fifty of these letters on our desk attests to the true feeling of the soldiers. The attempt to palm off on our Connecticut people a set of humbug resolutions, got up at the behest of ax-grinding politicians, excites indignation among the mass of the soldiers."[33]

Objectively, a disconcerting amount of common language and common arguments ran through the resolutions, which might suggest a common source of "guidance." Resolutions could have been influenced by higher commanders pressing subordinates to speak out against the antiwar movement. But, that seems less likely than what might be termed a dominance of "group views" within units. And, even if there was command-influence, wouldn't that also suggest a greater organizational effectiveness and unity than is generally credited to the army at that point? Intuitively, there must have been some Peace Democrat-influenced views among the officers and soldiers; but, there was no known evidence of any unit in its entirety stating a case or declaring support for the Copperheads. What was later termed "group think" was highly possible

---

32 BV 315, part 68, FSNMP. Capt. Samuel S. Woodruff wrote from "Camp of the 20th Conn. Vols., Stafford Court House, Va."

33 CHJHCF. Copy of original; as cited in text. It is arguable; but, given the war's outcome, soldier letters advocating Peace Democrat or Copperhead agendas may simply not have survived in equal numbers.

in 1863, as well, but it was unlikely that so many private letters would have shared common views if they were not sincerely felt.

Indeed, surviving anti-Copperhead resolutions and letters are so pervasive as to cause wonder whether there was any out-and-out opposition to the war in the military. At some level there must have been. The individual example of Maj. Henry L. Abbott of the 20th Massachusetts Infantry suggests as much. Abbott was identified as having pronounced "copperhead" tendencies; however, his attitude had nuances. According to biographer Anthony J. Milano, Abbott believed in an "educated aristocracy fit to rule" and that the "Harvard Regiment" major was "fighting the war to restore the Constitution's guarantee of private property North and South." Ironically, Abbott was in line with Confederate reasoning on the other side of the Rappahannock. That is not to denigrate Abbott or his service, as his views were consistent with Democratic Party elites such as George McClellan, and he was certainly patriotic. (Abbott would be killed fighting in 1864 during the Overland Campaign.)[34]

The War of Words Against "Traitors at Home"—Part II

Public resolutions and open letters were one thing, but writing to loved ones and speaking in presumed confidence were more reliable barometers of the army's true feelings. They also wrote to local newspapers directly or their relatives posted letters in the papers. "Valley Forge" complaints against the antiwar movement became increasingly common. Copperheadism had become one thing—perhaps the only thing—on which this citizen-army united and collectively opposed.

"As for the class called 'copperheads,' let them beware . . ." threatened a 126th New York infantryman writing on March 4 to his Rochester newspaper, "for they shall reap in bitterness, ruin and sorrow the harvest they are now sowing. The nation has sacrificed too much, suffered too much, is too near the end, to desist from its efforts now. Let them know if there is no martial law in the North, when the brave boys of this army come home they will make it." He then added: "There is not a man at the North of common intelligence and honesty, who thinks that peace can be found except through the bloody way of victory." Of the Copperheads, he concluded, "They are too mean to

---

34 BV 145, part 3, FSNMP, which includes an August 26, 1990, letter to the chief historian Robert K. Krick from Anthony J. Milano stating his intention to publish a book on Abbott and his views. That project does not appear to have come to fruition; however an article in Volume III of the *Civil War Regiments* journal was published. Anthony J. Milano, *Copperhead defiance from a Yankee officer: private letters of Major Henry Livermore Abbott, Harvard College, class of 1860, Twentieth Regiment, Massachusetts Volunteer Infantry, 1861-1864* (Harvard University Thesis, 1987). Milano referred to Abbott as an "arrogant young patrician."

live, too wicked to die, and they can find no sympathizers among the men of the 126th New York Regiment."[35]

On March 6, Capt. Henry F. Young of the 7th Wisconsin Infantry wrote to his father-in-law, who shared it with the local Union Club in Patch Grove. They asked to have it published. Young, a War Democrat who had supported Stephen A. Douglas in 1860's election, wrote he was, "very glad indeed to hear that the people of Wisconsin, that is the loyal portion, are getting waked up once more for if ever this nation needed the support of every loyal man that time is now." Given his prior politics, he remarkably added: "Congress has placed almost unlimited power in the hands of the President; that's just what was wanted. Now let the loyal people of the North sustain him; let them come out in their might and frown down all opposition; if the opposition can't be frowned down put it down in some other way, for it must go down; if men must be traitors notify them to leave the country and send them South, give them over to the tender mercies of their lord and master Jeff Davis."

Young admitted that people might "think these extreme measures," but he vowed by them: "[B]y the eternal I go in for any and every means to put down the rebellion. I now go in for arming every Negro within our lines and all that will after be coming in [and] form them into companies, regiments and brigades, giving them the same rights and privileges as white soldiers." He called for vigilance committees in "every town and county in the loyal states . . . authorized by the Governors . . . [to] be held responsible for the good conduct of all citizens" with the "power to suppress all newspapers that in any way or manner oppose all efforts being made to suppress the rebellion." Young then remarked, the "action of the Copperheads in the West and North-west has raised a howl of indignation in the army that will yet blast every man of the infernal clique to everlasting disgrace and their names to infernal infamy."[36]

Still conflicted about the emancipation objectives and new mission, War Democrat Anthony Graves of the 44th New York Infantry wrote to the Albany Evening Journal on March 19. His words, even more direct than his officers and NCOs, represent important movement in troop attitudes. "What can these people of the North be thinking about?" he asked. "They must know by this time that there can be no peace until the Rebellion is put down; and as for the nigger, they should not think about him. If they would only look at it in the true light, they would see that the niggers are the greatest

---

35 The writer's name has unfortunately been rendered unreadable in the copy used. CHJHCF. Copy of original; cites the *Rochester Democrat and American* of March 11, 1863, portions of which are also obscured.

36 www.secondwi.com/Copperheadpages/copperheads.htm (accessed on April 20, 2009).

opponents we have to contend with. Take them away from the South and we accomplish a great part in putting down this Rebellion."[37]

His next sentiment was most revealing. "For my part, I have made up my mind that, this Rebellion must be put down and the Union again united," he wrote, "and to accomplish this, we have to fight, and all we ask of the North, if they will not help to do it, is to keep their mouths shut, and not cry so much about the movements of the Army, asking why they don't do this, and why they don't do that."[38]

"Little Mack" of the 15th New Jersey Infantry wrote with word-play facility—if not all the facts—in the March 13th edition of the *Hunterdon Republican*. "I cannot but notice an article in your last paper, referring to political intriguers that have sent circulars to corrupt the army, among them the 15th," he began. "They may debate in Congress whether the army is composed principally of Democrats or Republicans,"

but the true political complexion of the army is, they Know Nothing but the Union; and the Copperhead wing of the Democracy will work in vain to demoralize this army, with all their attempts at armistices, compromises and "nigger" excitements. They cry, it is a pity, a shame, to war against the South, who are our brethren—yet it is a fact well known that the Rebel army is partially composed of negroes. Do the sympathizers with the South call them their brethren? Oh no! Then why not the North put negro to fight against negro? Or if these Northern traitors think that it would be impolite to send this race against the noble chivalry, let them come themselves and help restore the Union through this, the only means of securing a lasting peace. It is easier to fight on the Rappahannock than it would be—as it would be most certainly—to fight on the banks of the Delaware.

We or they must rule this Union; and now we must decide which—whether this is a Government for white men, as Democrats say it is, or whether (as Mason of Mason and Slidell fame, declared "we should call the roll of our slaves at the base of Bunker Hill") make it a Government for black men. We must combat the doctrine that the Constitution carries property in slaves everywhere, or our Democrats (not Union, but Copperheads) will have riding in the same car the negro slave as waiter to his Southern master. And yet they would cry it was the fault of the Abolitionists, who are laboring instead of having them spread over

---

37 CHJHCF. Cites: "*Albany Evening Journal* of March 30, 1863."

38 Ibid. Graves's letter also addressed conscription: "In speaking of the Conscript law, you say that 'it is regarded by some as an unjust act and that you are not without fear that its enforcement by the Government will meet with opposition.' Of course, some would have to find fault with it; and as for putting it in force, if the authorities will only send some of us up there, we will put it in force d—d quick for them."

the country, to have them sent out of it, where they will never trouble Mr. Copperhead again. But I am not a politician, so I will close and return to the news.[39]

The view that the Confederacy had enlisted black *en masse* was spread by newspapers such as *Harper's Weekly*. Distant observations of Rebels—once described as "the dirtiest band of men known on earth"—probably created those false impressions.

David Acheson of the 140th Pennsylvania, writing on March 25, was more succinct. "The Army of the Potomac is, I believe, the most democratic army we have," he declared, "and yet were it called upon to give an opinion concerning the copperheads of the north, it would give forth such a cry of hatred and disgust as would make the traitors tremble." Another man in the 140th had written two days earlier: "All it wants now is for the North to put its shoulder to the wheel as one man and the rebs' days are numbered. In three months treason will be wiped from the face of God's earth and the old flag over every state in triumph. But some of the letters . . . coming here from friends from home (the copperhead class) has done more harm than all the sickness in the army. The copperheads write . . . discouraging stuff to their friends here."[40]

By mid-March 1863, renewed fighting spirit and morale—so lacking after the "Mud March" in mid-January—were now certainly apparent. Demoralization had met with hope in January; forward progress had been made by mid-February; and Hooker's and Butterfield's efforts had gained greater effect by early March. Although their fundamental patriotism and political pragmatism had not yet fully manifested, the message was becoming abundantly clear: the war had to be brought to a conclusion on the corpse of the Confederacy, and the people of the North and West had but one option: support the war effort by every exertion. Amazingly, the army was now telling the people back home to support them—or else.

"Fine Times for a Few Days"

On March 1, the 96th Pennsylvania ended its month-long fatigue duty and guard tour on Windmill Point. Corporal Evan M. Gery recorded the regiment leaving the point, crossing Potomac Creek on boats, and reestablishing camp at White Oak Church. There, it was evident Hooker's troop care covenants had become routine. The men drew soft bread four of every six days and alternated days drawing potatoes and onions. Packages were regularly being received from his home back in Pottsville, Pennsylvania,

---

39 The (cited in text) letter from "Little Mack" was written on March 2, 1863, and is found in BV 109, part 8, FSNMP.

40 The quote from David Acheson is from CHJHCF, which cites: "Sara Gould Walters, *Inscription at Gettysburg (140th Pennsylvania)* (Gettysburg: 1991), 72."

although oddly taking about a month to reach Stafford. Their month of absence made the changes in camp seem all the more dramatic.[41]

Even as Hooker's reforms trickled down, much of the army's routine remained the same. "Since the first of the month we have led a very quiet life," penned Lt. Elisha Hunt Rhodes of the 2nd Rhode Island Infantry on March 12. "Drills take place when the weather will permit, but mud and rain is generally the rule. I shall start for R.I. before many days now I hope. It is a good time to leave, as we have nothing to do." His captain was on court-martial duty and Rhodes again commanded Company D. He remained long enough to celebrate his birthday—a significant milestone in survival, as he noted in his diary: "I am a man today, for it is my birthday and I am twenty-one years old. I have a birthday present—a leave of absence for ten days, and I appreciate it very much."[42]

Abel G. Peck of the 24th Michigan provided a rare mention of marksmanship training from "Camp Isabella": "We have been having fine times for a few days. We have been out shooting at a target. The Colonel was out with our company yesterday. He is a gay fellow, as the boys say. He makes more sport than all of the rest of us put together. We think he is a very fine man."[43]

A more intricate and humorous discussion of marksmanship training appeared from Emerson F. Merrill of the 72nd New York Infantry:

> We had a shooting match yesterday. A Colonel offered a prize to the three men within a hundred that should mark the best. Three shots at the distance of forty knots or two hundred yards. He gave the man [who] made the best shots 25, to the second best 15, and the third best 10. There were 200 men that shot, three shots apiece, in all 600 shots, several of which hit the target. Out of all the men that shot there were only 4 that hit the target three times. The prize of 25 was won by a man in Company B, he averaged 15 ½ inches from the center, the second prize of 15 was won by a man in Company [C], the third prize was won by Emerson F. Merrill, Company I. I averaged 17 inches from the center. Remember the whole regiment had been practicing everyday for a week. The two best were selected to be marksmen for the Regiment.

---

41 Gery's complete diary, well-annotated, was published beginning on January 22, 1942 in a series in the *Hamburg* (Pa.) *Item*.

42 Rhodes, ed., *All For the Union*, 92-93.

43 BV 212, part 4, FSNMP, letters of Abel G. Peck, 24th Michigan Infantry.

Clearly there were few Davy Crocketts in the 72nd, but at least they were trying to improve. Merrill added happily, "We get potatoes twice a week, onions twice a week and fresh bread 3 or 4 times a week. I need to stop writing and get some of it."[44]

Army life agreed with Pvt. George Wolcott of the 44th New York. "I am still in enjoyment of excellent health and would you believe it, weight 167 lbs.—19 lbs. more than ever before in my life," he wrote in a letter home. "Gen. Hooker has caused soft bread, potatoes, onions and other vegetable to be served as often as 4 times per week and this together with our pork, bacon, fresh meat, rice, shurger, tea, coffee &c. affords a super abundance of good wholesome food, so it is not strange that one grows and thrives in the army. I often wish that the poor could have what the army throws away, they would fare well on such an abundance of everything. . . . Of course our fare is not so good on a march, but I have no reason to complain so far."[45] Morale was improving.

"[T]he army is gaining in patriotism, health and good sprits daily," wrote Capt. Young of the 7th Wisconsin. "Gen. Hooker is weeding it out, almost every day there are a number of officers dismissed the service; some for absence with out leave, some for incompetency and many more for disloyalty; this is all right; hurrah for Old Joe as the boys call him."[46]

The Strategic Pause and Defense Continues

Even as things looked brighter for individual soldiers, the army's strategic situation as a whole remained as it had since February. So did the weather. "Mud-mud-mud all the time," wrote Pvt. William Guest of the 124th Pennsylvania Infantry, inarticulately but accurately. "The wagons cannot get along nore anything els the way the roads is."[47]

That didn't stop the cavalry, however, which continued security operations attempting to anticipate the next Confederate move. On March 2, Cavalry Corps headquarters ordered Pleasonton's 1st Division to post videttes from the headwaters of Accokeek Creek north to two or three miles above Dumfries. "Genesee" reported to a Rochester newspaper that his 8th New York Cavalry had broken camp at Belle Plain on February 20, traveled north across Aquia Creek to Dumfries, and weathered the severe snow storm of the twenty-second. He recalled that day as one "that will be remembered by us as one of the most trying to the endurance of man and beast since our

---

44 BV 231, part 4, FSNMP, letters of Emerson F. Merrill, 72nd New York Infantry.

45 V 110, part 12, FSNMP; letter of March 10, 1863, from George B. Wolcott of the 44th New York Infantry Regiment.

46 www.secondwi.com/Copperheadpages/copperheads.htm (accessed on April 20, 2009).

47 BV 112, part 02, FSNMP, letters of William A. Guest, Company F, 124th Pennsylvania.

organization." Establishing their reserve camp, they rotated three companies on picket duty. "Our lines extended out westerly some six or seven miles in the middle of a hostile country," he continued, "and as we were compelled to maintain our horses by foraging, the inhabitants of course were only too glad of an opportunity to assist in driving us out." Genesee reported a small foraging party of Company M was attacked on March 2 by "a superior force of mounted men" which took two prisoners. The following day, he added, the 8th New York "sat in our saddles on guard the whole night, expecting an attack at any moment." Nothing happened; they were relieved and returned to camp. They had apparently learned from the cavalry's poor Hartwood response.[48]

Alerts and reactions took place during the following 48 hours, but dismounted Confederates surprised a company-sized group of Federals and made off with 20 horses. "The capture was undoubtedly effected by a portion of Stuart's or White's men," Genesee speculated, "who had been piloted to their destination by some of the skulking bushwhackers, who live in the immediate vicinity, and are always acting as spies, or engaged in shooting single pickets from ambush, a murderous sort of warfare that would disgrace a savage."

Now deployed where they might actually encounter enemy cavalry, Federal horsemen reacted more swiftly to incursions. On the second, Averell's 2nd Cavalry Division was ordered to link-up with infantry picket lines on the Rappahannock and post videttes upstream to Rocky Pen Creek, in front of Berea Church, to Guy's Old Tavern, and finally to the headwaters of Accokeek Creek tying-in with the 1st Cavalry Division. Both division commanders were given identical instructions to establish the line personally or with a highly trusted subordinate, man it, and conduct active patrolling with the best available horses on all approaches. "The general directs me to say that the strength of the force to guard this line must depend upon circumstances, of which you must be the judge, as you will be held responsible that the duty is properly and thoroughly performed," the messages concluded. Although deployments were better, such correspondence revealed lagging levels of trust needed to conduct successful, continuous cavalry operations.[49]

This was important because perimeter activity remained an ongoing cause for concern. At 8:00 p.m. on March 9, Col. Charles Candy reported a small cavalry incursion on the north side of the perimeter at Dumfries, preceded by a red signal observed at the Brentsville Road and Quantico Creek intersection. Candy noticed a lack of cavalry on his flank. Two days earlier he'd notified the cavalry corps that the "entire country

---

48 OR, 25, part II, 116-117. BV 317, part 6, FSNMP, *Rochester Daily Union and Advertiser*, March 13—letters from 8th New York Cavalry are from March 7.

49 OR, 25, part II, 116-117.

between the Quantico [Creek] and Occoquan [River]" was "open to the enemy." A second note recalled that cavalry was supposed to patrol the Telegraph Road from Dumfries to Occoquan every six hours. On the eleventh, Hooker's headquarters warned V Corps of a Confederate cavalry raid aiming to destroy Potomac Creek Railroad Bridge and to prepare. This information came from Stafford's Federal spy, J. Howard Skinker, apparently operating beyond his Hartwood home. Butterfield ordered Stoneman on March 12 to send out a regimental-sized cavalry reconnaissance to the Rappahannock fords as far as Kelly's looking for enemy cavalry activity.[50]

Hooker continued his focus on defensive tactical and operational concerns, but also renewed concrete measures in preparation for future offensives. He returned to the previous month's proposal by artillery chief Henry Hunt and Brig. Gen. Robert O. Tyler to organize a siege train with artillery of heavy- and siege-gun calibers, heavy howitzers, and heavy mortars—along with associated transport and logistics—for the anticipated Richmond campaign. In modern times, these would be referred to as "breakthrough artillery." Hooker realized that southward movement toward Richmond would involve crossing multiple east-west rivers and streams, which were all easily fortified at crossing points. There would also be strongpoints created en route to and around Richmond. By massing this high-powered artillery and providing the artillery groups with their own logistics, Hooker expected them to be more effective in the long run.

On March 7, Tyler provided Butterfield with information dating back to October 1862. From Fort Ward in Alexandria, he now proposed a scaled-back base force of three heavy batteries of four 4.5 inch siege guns each—drawing ten from Fort Ward and replacing those with 30-pounder Parrotts. The remaining two siege guns would come from the Ordnance Department. The assembled train would have four companies commanded by a field-grade officer. Six horses would haul each heavy gun. Two wagons per gun would be needed for 2,400 pounds of ammunition. For powder, one wagon per four guns and one wagon per company would be needed. In all, Tyler wanted a forge wagon B; a battery wagon D; 30 wagons; 32 six-mule teams totaling 192 mules; 80 draught horses; six saddle horses; and a large number of harness sets. Hunt, in October 1862, had wisely added a forge wagon A for shoeing the animals; and suggested increasing the number of animals per siege gun to eight with two drivers for the mixed harnesses. This was a well-designed, mobile force with substantial firepower and its own ammunition resupply and repair/maintenance equipment. Such a grouping could substantially strengthen a major attack.[51]

---

50 Ibid., 35-136.

51 *OR*, 25, part II, 129-131. Tyler had originally envisaged a mixed force of 40 4.5 inch rifles; 10 8-inch, M 1861 howitzers; 10 8-inch, M 1861 mortars; and 10 Coehorn mortars.

One of Hooker's talents (or faults) was his ability to attend to matters large and small. Even as he was thinking big and bold, he managed to find time to continue his peevish correspondence with Halleck over the earlier exchange of Pennsylvania troops. Referring to the February 28 muster report, Hooker claimed he'd been shortchanged 1,233 officers and men. (He had earlier argued the number was 210.) This now included "extra-duty men of the Pennsylvania Reserves" Hooker had initially kept behind before forwarding to Heintzelman. Rubbing salt in the wound, Hooker added that 1,500 officers and men would not make the exchange equal. This may have been his way of claiming Halleck was under a moral obligation. In any case, with offensive operations in the works, Hooker was not prepared to lose any resources that might be available.

This attention to detail and sense of moral purpose were both reflected in another seemingly small incident on March 7. Hooker politely wrote to Robert E. Lee that the bodies of Confederates Surgeon William B. Davies, Lt. Edward W. Horner, and Pvt. George A. Price, all of the 2nd Virginia Cavalry, were in coffins at Falmouth Depot ready for exchange for the body of Union soldier J. C. Newcomer, killed at Fredericksburg on December 13th. The dead were frequently left to the enemy's apathetic care and the elements. Yet here was an example of the civility and decency that both Hooker and Lee embodied. The disposition of four combatants' remains did not matter much in the grand scheme of things; however, four Victorian American families would be eternally grateful for the return of a loved one and a bit of closure—acts denied to many thousands in burial trenches or two-foot field graves. On February 27, Hooker had restricted truce flags to reduce random acts of interaction. Operating within those guidelines, it was still possible to do military business with the enemy.[52]

"They Do Not Complain"

As the flow of soldiers going home on furlough continued northward and westward, a civilian visitor from Lewiston, Maine came south to Stafford. His visit offered a good ground's-eye-view of Joe Hooker's army in those mid-weeks of March. "Com," as he signed his subsequent letter to the *Lewiston Daily Evening Journal*, went by boat to Aquia Landing and searched for the 1st Maine Cavalry. He found their camp about three miles from Belle Plain. He next visited the 20th Maine Infantry at Stoneman's Station. "I met the Colonel, Lieut. Colonel and his lady, Dr. and Mrs. Monroe, and the latter accompanied me to the headquarters, where the 17th Maine [Infantry] is stationed," he reported. "Their location is not a very good one, although they do not complain."

---

52 *OR*, 25, part II, 129.

Camp of the 150th Pennsylvania at Belle Plain. The 150th arrived in March of 1863, and one company was detailed to guard President Lincoln. The men are lined up in the center "street," transport wagons are in the foreground, and choking smoke is rising from the camp shelters. NA

"Com" spent the night in camp talking with the soldiers. The next day, he visited the regiment's hospital and its 20 patients. The day after, he went to the division hospital near the "Phillips House, lately burned" and saw Lowe's balloons. He passed out packages from home to the men. Finally, aided by "Mrs. McK." with her ambulance and orderly, he went to the headquarters of Maj. Gen. Oliver Otis Howard—a Maine native—and visited the general and his aide-de-camp brother. In Howard's tent, Com saw "the daily [Bible] verse sheet, printed so largely that I could read it distinctly from the door. I wish the same could be seen from all the Generals' tents!"

"Remember the brave boys," he reminded readers. "They are . . . far from demoralized; and they, like their General are ready, any time for a move. They have no fellowship for copperheads, and would shoot them if they came here!"[53]   Indeed, howling at the now near-universally hated Copperheads would continue—even as the Army of the Potomac began renewed consideration of the enemy closer at hand.

53 BV 351, part 11, March 24, 1863, letter from "Com" to the Lewiston, Maine *Daily Evening Journal* and published in the Wednesday evening edition of April 1, 1863 (No. 299).

Chapter Seven

Longing for the Spring Campaign

On the morning of March 24, 1863, the II Corps division of Maj. Gen. Winfield Scott Hancock assembled near the banks of the Rappahannock River. Evergreens of pine and laurel and holly stood out among the brown trunks of winter-slumbering maples and oaks. The attention of the men, however, was focused inwardly toward the center of their hollow-square formation. There, three men convicted of cowardice were about to be drummed out. The perpetrators' heads had been shaved on one side, and they bore large boards emblazoned "Coward." Followed by sentries with fixed bayonets, the cowards were marched in front of the lines. "The Rogue's March" thundered in their ears from a hundred drums and fifes. Sgt. C. Hickox of the 27th Connecticut Infantry, part of Col. John R. Brooke's fourth brigade, watched in fascination. "The performance was as ceremonious as a grand review," he later wrote.[1]

The division had formed "in sight of Fredericksburg, and on the ground where Washington had chopped the cherry tree and ridden the colt, and lived and played when he was a little boy," Hickox reported. Probably unknown to him, his lone division outnumbered Washington's entire Valley Forge army.

"Dimly beyond," Hickox later wrote, "we caught the outline of the rebel works as the sunshine lifted gracefully the mist above the graves of our ten thousand Dead."

Watching the public spectacle inflicted on the cowards had its desired effect on Hickox, who admitted he might have played a little possum at the division hospital. "I left the hospital, threw my medicine in the fire, and got well," he admitted in obvious good humor. "The habit of eating is an old one, but having become obsolete among

---

1   CHJHCF. Cites: "*Lancaster Daily Express* of April 3, 1863;" Copy of original. BV 182, part 3, letters of Sgt. C. Hickox to his cousin, Miss Charlotte Hickox of Solon, Ohio.

soldiers, has been revived by Joseph Hooker. For the first time since leaving Washington I have all the good food I want."

He concluded on a darker note, however—one that had become familiar throughout the army: "I wish every copperhead of the North might be made to pass the same ordeal at the point of a bayonet."[2]

While resentment continued to boil toward the threat back home, Federal soldiers more and more cast their gaze across the river toward Fredericksburg and Lee's army in the hills beyond.

*   *   *

Soldiers and officers alike had observed "the Rebels" throughout the "Valley Forge." Being so close for so long, with standing orders not to provoke or engage, both sides had been respectful, and some men had even engaged in occasional humorous banter and antics.

"The rebel officers are tall and nervy, being well dressed, having a fine suit of gray; their badges of rank being upon the coat collars instead of their shoulders, like ours," wrote a member of the 108th New York, "R. E.," to the *Rochester Democrat* and American. "Their soldiers, however, are a motly looking and motly clad lot of 'fellows.' We discovered a goodly sprinkling of Uncle Sam's boys' clothing among them. We couldn't help thinking that they must be either contemptibly mean or awfully hard up, else they would have sufficient pride to choose and demand a military dress—one that should be uniform and national." "R. E." described their officers as talkative and gallant with the ladies.[3]

A recurring theme continued in soldier letters and unit resolutions: the Army of the Potomac harbored a deep respect for its Confederate foes, especially the common soldier of Lee's army. Regardless of their appearance, "Lee's Miserables" had earned the Federals' awe by their battlefield courage.

Cavalry Problems Linger

Not all Confederates sat atop the far heights, however. At 5:00 p.m. on March 14, Daniel Butterfield sent cavalry commander George Stoneman a dispatch from spy Ernest Yager: "Enemy under the impression that this place (Dumfries) has been

---

2   Ibid.

3   CHJHCF. Cites: "*Rochester Democrat and American* of March 20, 1863," in which this letter appeared, dated March 14, appeared.

evacuated and is ravaging the country." Yager noted 250 of Hampton's cavalry were headed toward the Occoquan and moving freely between Brentsville and Dumfries. He had seen no Federal cavalry to oppose them.

Although willing to deal with the situation, a March 15 affair showed that Stoneman's cavalry corps wasn't necessarily ready. A small patrol of the 8th Illinois Cavalry—one corporal and six cavalry troopers—was captured between Dumfries and Occoquan. The patrol had gone to Occoquan at 4:00 p.m. and was returning about 8:00 p.m. About 3 ½ miles above Dumfries, they were ambushed by a dismounted party of 20-25 men "lying in a marsh on both sides of a deep ravine through which they had to pass."

When filing his report about the incident, the regiment's Capt. John M. Southworth guessed that the Federals had tried to run off on foot to avoid capture; three of their sabers had been found nearby.

Stoneman endorsed Southworth's report on the seventeenth and included a tirade. "These annoyances will continue until some stringent measures are taken to clear that section of the country of every male inhabitant, either by shooting, hanging, banishment, or incarceration," he growled. "I had a party organized some time ago to do this, but the commanding general did not at that time think it advisable to send it out."

Lieutenant Colonel David Clendenin was faulted for sending less than a platoon on patrol. In arresting him on March 16, his commander, Alfred Pleasonton recommended that "the rebel partisans and bushwhackers be cleared out from the vicinity of Occoquan and Brentsville [both in Prince William County] by a command from this division. One brigade with a few guns would suffice."

Stoneman wasn't so sure. "A great portion of the country is of such a nature that it is impossible for cavalry to operate in it, and to perform the duty properly will require the cooperation of an infantry force," he predicted in his March 17 tirade. "The country is infested by a set of bushwhacking thieves and smugglers who should be eradicated, root and branch."[4]

Hooker's reply, issued on March 26, was telling. "If there are any of the male portion of the community operating as bushwhackers or guerrillas against our troops, and the facts can be proven, let them be arrested and brought in," he ordered. "The commanding general cannot understand why our cavalry cannot operate where the enemy's cavalry prove so active."[5]

Cavalry duty in the area was not all excitement. "Once more our detachment is engaged in the necessary, but severe, duty of picketing," lamented "Genesee," an 8th

4   OR, 25, part I, 45-47.

5   Ibid.

New York Cavalry trooper, in his March 25 letter to the Rochester Daily Union and Advertiser. To the southwest of Dumfries, the line had been drawn in closer "owing to the great numbers of men required to picket such contended lines as were first formed," he explained. "During our stay in Stafford our horses and selves became much recruited, so the we became prepared to do more effective service considering our little experience than could have been expected from raw troops on their first enterprise."

Enemy activity against the 8th Illinois and 8th Pennsylvania Cavalry Regiments had sparked a sharp response from the 8th New York, which mounted a strong reconnaissance and boldly went out into the forests, sabers clanking. "We crossed Cedar River, where we expected to find the enemy, but he had prudently left in good season, and we were compelled to return to camp, which we reached about 6:00 p.m., having been eighteen hours in the saddle and traveled over fifty miles, through mud and mire in the fruitless pursuit of our wary foe."[6]

Fruitless, perhaps, but the Federal cavalry was becoming more aggressive, and troopers like "Genesee" were sounding far more confident than at the month's beginning. They now operated at night, rode deeper into enemy country, and maintained good order. Their Confederate counterparts still outmatched them, however, due to the eternal motivational difference between soldiers operating in foreign spaces and those protecting their own. Counter-insurgency or rear-area security operations remained illusive. When Union cavalry could or would not venture outside perimeters, then the Confederates—regular or irregular—still owned the night.

Hooker expected more. "I know the South, and I know the North," he contended as part of a furious, windy discussion with Stoneman. "In point of skill, of intelligence, and of pluck, the rebels will not compare with our men, if they are equally well led. Our soldiers are a better quality of men." This North-centric nonsense was followed with a more accurate assessment: "[The Federals] are better fed, better clothed, better armed, and infinitely better mounted; for the rebels are fully half mounted on mules, and their animals get but two rations of forage per week, while ours get seven." With a better cause, he held, "we ought to be invincible, and by God, sir, we shall be!"[7]

No more surprises, Hooker ordered—and he granted Stoneman full arrest, cashiering, and execution powers. Perhaps worst of all, he threatened to take command of the cavalry himself.

All of Hooker's personal flaws were thus revealed. The Cavalry Corps's problems were in leadership, and not in the personnel, horses, equipment, etc. Hooker, however,

---

6   BV 317, part 6, FSNMP. Letters in the *Rochester Daily Union and Advertiser*, published on April 1, 1863 from correspondence of March 25.

7   Hooker's diatribe is from Hebert, *Fighting Joe Hooker*, 186; this was quoted from Frank Moore, *Anecdotes, Poetry and Incidents of the War: North and South 1860-1865* (New York, NY), 305.

was not the solution and neither were his other command selections, excepting Buford and Gregg. At this point, Stoneman and company had commanded for a little over one month. The question facing the commanding general was whether he should have worked with these commanders or replaced them and, if the latter, with whom? The clock was working against a quick fix.

As the month progressed, Hooker received continual reminders of lingering problems. On March 20, Col. Charles Candy of the 66th Ohio, stationed at Dumfries, reported that his scout, Clifford, had witnessed enemy rampaging, "pressing men into their service, and driving good Union families from their homes." Candy asked why no cavalry were deployed there, even promising them food and fodder.

A few days later, on March 29, Hooker received the unwelcome news that Confederate cavalry had again raided far above the Rappahannock. At noon that day, five miles above Dumfries, 100 Confederate cavalrymen attacked Candy's cavalry pickets. Candy reported that eight of the patrol were missing and presumed captured. Details remained sparse: the skirmish occurred on the Telegraph Road, and a deserter from the 5th Virginia Cavalry revealed the Confederates had come from the Rapidan. Major E. M. Pope of the 8th New York Cavalry, commanding the pickets, described the "disaster" as of 6:30 p.m. that evening. He had ordered Capt. C. D. Follett to send out scouts, but Follett found only six men returned after his lieutenant and 11 additional troopers were taken.[8]

Averell's Revenge: The Kelly's Ford Raid

Although the Federal cavalry's overall performance remained uneven and the commanding general's frustrations remained high, there were important signs of improvement.

Fitz Lee's late-February Hartwood Church raid had virtually invited retaliation when Lee taunted his old friend, William Averell. Perhaps motivated by their lackluster Hartwood performance, Fitz Lee's note, Joe Hooker's goading, or all three, some life surfaced in the cavalry corps. On March 16, "pursuant to instructions" from Butterfield, Averell led his 2nd Division—a force of more than 3,000 cavalrymen and six artillery pieces—out from the army's defensive perimeter. They headed for Culpeper Court House, where he hoped to surprise Fitz Lee's cavalry. Averell's orders were "to attack and rout or destroy him."[9]

8   OR, 25, part I, 74-75.

9   Ibid., 47-64.

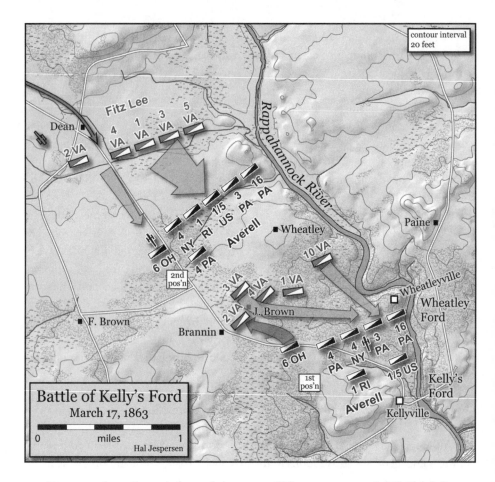

Battle of Kelly's Ford
March 17, 1863

0   miles   1

Hal Jespersen

En route, Averell was informed that some 250 to as many as 1,000 Confederates and one artillery piece were operating north of Brentsville. In response, he requested a cavalry regiment be sent toward Catlett's Station and picket posts be established covering flank approaches from Warrenton, Greenwich, and Brentsville. Inexplicably, this reasonable request was refused, so Averell detached 900 men to secure his flank and turned southwest.

A second concern had to be addressed: Averell's artillery battery had marched farther than the rest of his command—some 32 miles from Aquia Creek to Morrisville—and arrived in poor condition at 11:00 p.m. on the 16th. It required rest and repairs.

Averell had sent forward detachments about 2-4 hours ahead of his main body to check for Rebel scouts and secure approaches to the Rappahannock fords. From Mount Holly Church, Federal scouts observed enemy campfires between Ely's and Kelly's Fords and heard drums beating retreat and tattoo at Rappahannock Station. Confederate cavalry were also reported.

Battle of Kelly's Ford (March 17, 1863). At 4:00 a.m. on March 17, Brig. Gen. William Averell crossed the Rappahannock with 1,800 men, expecting the aggressive Fitzhugh Lee to seek him out for battle. Lee obliged, and after a back-and-forth series of charges and countercharges, the Rebels withdrew three-quarters of a mile. Averell rode after them, and the two sides settled into an extended battle that lasted until 5:30 p.m. Averell withdrew and filed an enthusiastic report. "[O]ur cavalry has been brought to feel their superiority in battle," he asserted. "They have learned the value of discipline and the use of their arms."

In related action, at Morrisville, Lt. Col. G. S. Curtis of the 1st Massachusetts Cavalry was placed in command of all pickets above the Rappahannock. He directed Lt. Col. Doster of the 4th Pennsylvania Cavalry to take 290 men and drive the Rebel pickets toward Rappahannock Station; return to Bealeton; and then post pickets. They encountered only "a small party of guerrillas at Bealeton Station."[10]

At 4:00 a.m. on March 17, Averell's force crossed the Rappahannock with 1,810 men under Col. Alfred N. Duffie, Col. John B. McIntosh and Capt. Marcus A. Reno (1st, 2nd and Reserve Brigades, respectively). Accompanied by the 6th Independent New York Battery, commanded by Lt. George Browne Jr., Averell opted to cross at Kelly's Ford, which he knew best. It took them four hours to reach the ford.[11] There, they found abatis—cut trees overlapped and pointed in the enemy's direction—blocking both banks and "80 sharpshooters" covering the obstacles.

McIntosh dispatched his "ax-men" under Lt. Gillmore of the 3rd Pennsylvania Cavalry to cut away the obstacles, a pointless, time-consuming effort. Afterward, two dismounted squadrons, protected by an empty mill-race near the ford tried three times in vain to dislodge the Rebels. Averell sent other troops to cross a quarter-mile below Kelly's, but the river was too deep to cross and banks too steep to climb.

In desperation, Lt. Simeon A. Brown and 20 troopers of the 1st Rhode Island Cavalry made another attempt at the ford. This time they negotiated the abatis and captured 25 Confederates. On the Federal side, ten men and 15 horses were casualties thus far.

Averell didn't use his artillery lest he alert the enemy "while astride the stream." Once across, he assumed a defensive posture on the far shore—an odd decision on the surface considering his objective was Culpeper Court House. Personally knowing Fitz Lee's character and position, though, Averell expected to be rapidly challenged. His defensive disposition gave him time to water his horses and rest.

10 Ibid.

11 McIntosh's report incorrectly says 6:00 a.m.

When Lee's reaction did not materialize, Averell moved ahead, with Duffie's men leading. A quarter mile forward, they finally spotted the expected Confederate advance. Averell maneuvered the 4th New York to the right and 4th Pennsylvania to the left; ordered both to engage by carbine; and made a section of artillery ready to engage. Averell positioned three of Reno's squadrons in reserve behind McIntosh on the far right. A fourth squadron filled a gap between the 4th Pennsylvania and 4th New York.

Those two regiments initially faltered, but Averell and his staff restored order as two or three enemy columns approached at a trot to his right. There, McIntosh and Gregg attacked. Duffie defended against a Rebel assault with the 1st Rhode Island, 4th Pennsylvania, and 6th Ohio—with the 4th New York in reserve—on Averell's left. Averell took Reno's three reserve squadrons at a gallop to support Duffie. Two squadrons of the 5th U. S. Cavalry and the 3rd Pennsylvania were committed and drove back the Confederates. Due to mud and distance, however, the charge could not bag the withdrawing 300-500 Confederates.

For 30 minutes, Averell regrouped, recovered stragglers, and reset his defenses. Anchored on the road to his left by Lt. Sweatman and his 5th Cavalry Regulars, Averell advanced three-quarters of a mile "from the field we had won." Behind the fire of two guns, the Confederates counterattacked both flanks. The Union advance continued on the right, but the Confederates penetrated on the left. Controlled by lieutenants Browne and Rumsey (Averell's aide), the left held and the advance continued, though slowed by Confederate fires set in the field, which Averell's men beat out with overcoats.

From entrenchments, the Confederates continued fighting with three guns—two 10-pounder Parrots and one 6-pounder. The Rebels successfully coordinated artillery fires with their cavalry advance. The Federals held them off and advanced on the right before encountering infantry positions. Their own artillery, suffering severe technical and supply problems, was out of action and unable to support them. Averell, informed that Southern infantry was on his flank, assumed they planned to encircle him. At 5:30 p.m. he "deemed it proper to withdraw" across the Rappahannock.

On the far bank, Averell tallied Union casualties at 78 killed, wounded, and missing, and guessed that the enemy may have suffered as many as 200 casualties. That number later came in at 133 men and 170 horses of Lee's Brigade—roughly equivalent to Union losses at Hartwood.[12]

Averell's over-enthusiasm was evident:

> The principal result achieved by this expedition has been that our cavalry has been brought to feel their superiority in battle; they have learned the value of discipline and the use of their

12 Ibid.

arms. At the first view, I must confess that two regiments wavered, but they did not lose their senses, and a few energetic remarks brought them to a sense of their duty. After that the feeling became stronger throughout the day that it was our fight, and that the maneuvers were performed with a precision which the enemy did not fail to observe.[13]

Averell pronounced a "universal desire of the officers and men of my division to meet the enemy again as soon as possible."

Unreported, Averell left a retaliatory note for Fitz Lee in response to the note Lee left during his Hartwood Raid. In that first missive, Lee told his Yankee friend he rode a better horse, to visit sometime, and bring coffee; Averell's response announced his arrival and a deposit of coffee.

The raid improved the cavalry corps's morale. Butterfield was impressed, too, but Hooker less so. Typically, he had disapproved Averell's request for an additional regiment for flank security and then criticized him for leaving a third of his men behind. Hooker also felt that Averell could and should have done more.

Averell, given the state of the cavalry, felt he took an important step toward respectability. The raid certainly excited the secretary of war. "I congratulate you upon the success of General Averell's expedition," Stanton wrote to Hooker. "It is good for the first lick. You have drawn the first blood, and I hope now soon to see 'the boys up and at them.'"[14]

To that point, Averell's raid on Kelly's Ford was the war's largest cavalry-on-cavalry fight. But universal joy in Yankeedom exposed the Federals' deep-seated inferiority. After all, this was in the war's twenty-third month. Averell's force outnumbered Fitz Lee's brigade; and they only penetrated at best three miles into the Confederate outer defenses. On the other hand, as Stanton stated, this was an important "first lick" and first steps are seldom decisive. Most importantly, the raid demonstrated the Federals could raid, surprise Stuart's cavalry, and engage their opponents in cavalry battle.

Of equal interest, this raid shocked the Confederates, necessitating rare spin-control on their side. Simply put, the Yankees weren't considered capable of such action. Like many raids, Kelly's Ford's impact was more psychologically than militarily successful. Word was served on Stuart's men: Federal troopers could no longer be assumed to be huddled close to defensive perimeters and campfires.

An unintended consequence of the raid was the death of Confederate Maj. John Pelham. The boy-hero of Stuart's Horse Artillery at Fredericksburg and elsewhere, Pelham had spontaneously joined in the cavalry fight and fell mortally wounded.

13 Ibid.

14 Ibid. Part II, p. 148 for Stanton's full response (March 19).

The death of Maj. John Pelham during a fight with Federal cavalry was of little tactical importance, but the death of the Southern war hero highlighted an important lesson the Federals were trying to make: the days of uncontested Confederate cavalry dominance were over. *LOC*

Boy-heroes, especially well-publicized ones, aided home front morale; but, their deaths had a contrary, often ten-fold impact. "The Gallant Pelham's" death delivered a body-blow to Stuart, his cavalry, and the South. The loss, wrote Stuart, "has thrown a shadow of gloom over us not soon to pass away."[15]

Other Shuffles

The cavalry corps was not the only unit in the army facing trouble. March 18 brought a death-knell for Thaddeus Lowe's Aeronautics Corps. Chief Quartermaster Rufus Ingalls received a letter from inventor "B. England, of 1724 Rittenhouse Street in Philadelphia" that under-bid and over-promised Lowe's operations. Ingalls bucked the letter to Hooker's headquarters, which showed it to an irate Lowe. He penned a lengthy rebuttal—which, of course, became public and led to testimony by disgruntled former Lowe employee Jacob C. Freno, attacking Lowe personally. Such ruminations consumed the balloon corps' time. For Hooker, already unimpressed by the aeronauts, this was more reason for skepticism.[16]

Another figure lacking the commander's confidence, Brig. Gen. Daniel P. Woodbury, commander of the army's engineer brigade, met with grief, too. Woodbury's career had not survived the late pontoon debacle at Fredericksburg. He received no formal blame, but was reassigned to command the District of Key West and Tortugas in

15 Ibid. Stuart quote in *OR*, 25, part II, 858. The story of Pelham's death is recounted in detail in Burke Davis, *J.E.B. Stuart: The Last Cavalier* (New York, NY, 1957), 271-277. Additional reaction can be found in Jeffry D. Wert's *Cavalryman of the Lost Cause: A Biography of J. E. B. Stuart* (New York, NY, 2008), 208-210.

16 Evans, *War of the Aeronauts*.

the Department of the Gulf (Dry Tortugas being unofficially dubbed "America's Devil's Island"). Within 18 months, he would be dead from yellow fever. Brigadier General H. W. Benham filled Woodbury's position with the Army of the Potomac.

More shuffling occurred. On March 20, Maj. Gen. Julius Stahel was reassigned from the XI Corps to the Washington Defenses. Stahel would come back to the Army of the Potomac a few months later as part of the cavalry corps, but Pleasanton would have him removed. Stahel would serve out the rest of the war in various cavalry capacities, eventually earning the Medal of Honor for actions at Piedmont.

Hooker would not name Stahel's replacement until March 31. Special Order No. 87 assigned Maj. Gen. Oliver Otis Howard to temporary command of the XI Corps. The same order placed Brig. Gen. John Gibbon under General Couch's command in the II Corps to take Howard's place.[17] "General Howard is assigned to the command of the Eleventh Corps, formerly Sigel's, and goes tomorrow, taking his two aides, Lieutenants Howard and Stinson," II Corps Surgeon Frank Dyer noted prophetically. "We all regret his leaving very much and fear that the Eleventh Corps may not enhance his reputation. General Gibbon comes here."[18]

The previous day, after two months commanding the army, Hooker added eight more officers to his staff in General Order No. 32: Brig. Gen. G. K. Warren, chief engineer staff officer; Col. E. Schriver, inspector-general; Lt. Col. N. H. Davis, assistant inspector- general; E. R. Platt, Capt., 2nd U. S. Artillery, judge-advocate-general; Maj. S. F. Barstow, assistant adjutant-general; Col. George H. Sharpe, 120th New York, deputy provost-marshal-general; Capt. Ulric Dahlgren, aide-de-camp; and Capt. Charles E. Cadwalader, 6th Pennsylvania Cavalry, acting aide-de-camp.

Two months into his tenure, Hooker continued to render additional efficiencies in logistics, too. On March 19, headquarters announced, in General Order No. 77, that some pack-saddles arrived and were to be issued to the army corps roughly equally except for VI Corps, which got more than any corps. Inexplicably, II Corps received none. Perhaps they had been previously issued. Pack-saddles would be used—two each —by regiments to carry officers' shelter-tents and rations. The rest would be used to carry 2-3 ammunition boxes per horse, depending on relative horse strength. This was a revolutionary innovation, and the general order specified daily loading and unloading drills. Animals detailed to this "ammunition-pack" would be drawn from the ammunition train (and wagons without horses were to be turned-in). This promised a major improvement in mobile resupply of infantry ammunition, allowing the pack animals to move smoothly with the units into action. However, substitution of

17 *OR*, 25, part II, 150, 167.

18 Chesson, ed., *J. Franklin Dyer, Journal of a Civil War Surgeon*, 63-64.

Maj. Gen. Oliver Otis Howard, called "Old Prayer Book" by some of his subordinates because of his strict religious faith, seemed an unlikely choice to lead the XI Corps. Hooker made the choice, in part, because he intensely disliked the other potential candidate, Maj. Gen. Carl Schurz. "I would consider the services of an entire corps as entirely lost to this army were it [the XI Corps] to fall into the hands of Maj. Gen. Schurz," Hooker contended. *LOC*

unpredictable mules—obstinate, but available and sure-footed—initially threatened this reform. The contrary creatures could foil the best logistician's intentions. But, perhaps analogous to the army itself, mules could be re-trained.[19]

Another important reform of the army's ordnance service took place on March 25 under G. O. No. 30. Whether Hooker aimed at readiness for a move or firming-up ammunition- and arms-handling procedures, the forward thinking order required basic loads of ammunition be kept on hand: "Infantry: 140 rounds with that in the cartridge boxes [40 rounds]; Cavalry: 100 rounds for carbine and 40 rounds for pistol with that in the cartridge boxes; and Artillery: 250 rounds with that in the ammunition chest." The 20 rounds previously carried by infantrymen in their knapsacks would be expended in due course, perhaps through marksmanship training, but not replenished. Thereafter, those rounds would be issued on the eve of battle and carried in pockets. After covering the minutiae, the order fixed the main responsibilities on division ordnance officers, who were relieved from other duties to report to division headquarters.

Another valuable innovation resulted: reserve ammunition wagons would be marked with corps and division symbols, and infantry, cavalry, or artillery ammunition wagons would be "color-coded"—representing the branches with horizontal blue, yellow, or red stripes respectively. The army's main ammunition depot would be marked by a crimson flag marked "Ordnance Depot, U.S.A." On the march, when brigades were dispersed, division ordnance officers could detach stores to brigades. Care would be given in battle to deploying ammunition trains to facilitate resupply. Divisions would

19 OR, 25, part II, 148-149.

draw on the army ordnance depot for resupply munitions. Unserviceable and condemned ammunition would be turned in through regimental quartermasters. Division ordnance officers would have a staff with an acting ordnance non-commissioned officer and a clerk. Extra-duty men on ordnance duty would report to him and be kept on his extra-duty rolls. Now, clearly marked mobile resupply ammunition wagons could be moved closer to the units and pack trains.[20]

Another reform came from up the tracks in Washington. Railroader Herman Haupt sent Hooker a copy of instructions he had cut to his chief engineer, A. Anderson. "You will take measures to have everything in readiness to meet the wishes and second the movements of the commander of the Army of the Potomac," he wrote, "sparing no labor or necessary expense to secure the most effective action when called upon, and to provide the materials and men necessary for the purpose." Significantly, Haupt ordered Anderson to assemble the necessary force to support movement, apply to the army commander for details of soldiers, and gain support from the army's chief quartermaster for transportation of all kinds and forage for his animals. "When active forward operations are resumed," Haupt added, "the all-important object will be to secure the reconstruction of [rail] roads and bridges and the reopening of communications in the shortest possible time." Haupt advised Anderson to have all the required men assembled and moved forward; but, to use them constructing or repairing existing lines or assisting in building blockhouses for protection of rail bridges. Oxen, also needed for an advance, would be gainfully employed hauling ties and wood.[21]

Haupt's order is instructive as another indicator of a contemplated offensive, which was exactly what Henry Halleck had in mind. "Old Brains" wrote to Hooker on March 27. "Dispatches from Generals Dix, Foster, and Hunter, and from the west, indicate that the rebel troops formerly under Lee are now much scattered for supplies, and for operations elsewhere," he shared. "It would seem, under these circumstances, advisable that a blow be struck by the Army of the Potomac as early as practicable. It is believed that during the next few days several conflicts will take place, both south and west, which may attract the enemy's attention particularly to those points." Halleck's suggestion that the army could launch an offensive on the basis of his message—even if it originated from Lincoln or Stanton—betrays his feeble strategic understanding. While Hooker was making real progress in every aspect of his army, the general-in- chief of all the armies was puttering.[22]

20 Ibid., 156-158.

21 Haupt, *Reminiscences of General Herman Haupt.*

22 *OR,* 25, Part II, 160-161.

Railroads proved to be the great lifeline of the Army of the Potomac. It fell to Brig. Gen. Herman Haupt to keep them running effectively. *LOC*

Badges of Honor

One of the most important reforms Hooker made came on March 21 in a circular of significant military-historic importance:

For the purpose of ready recognition of corps and divisions in this army, and to prevent injustice by reports of straggling and misconduct through mistake as to its organization, the chief quartermaster will furnish without delay the following badges, to be worn by the officers and enlisted men of all the regiments of the various corps mentioned. They will be securely fastened upon the center of the top of the cap. Inspecting officers will at all inspections see that these badges will be worn as designated:

First Corps, a sphere—First Division, red; Second, white; Third, blue.
Second Corps, trefoil—First Division, red; Second, white; Third, blue.
Third Corps, lozenge—First Division, red; Second, white; Third, blue.
Fifth Corps, Maltese cross—First Division, red; Second, white; Third, blue.

CORPS BADGES OF THE ARMY OF THE POTOMAC UNDER HOOKER.

Corps insignia were first implemented as a way to facilitate organization and order, but they quickly became sources of pride for the men. *NPS*

Sixth Corps, cross—First Division, red; Second, white; Third, blue. (Light Division, green.)

Eleventh Corps, crescent—First Division, red; Second, white; Third, blue.

Twelfth Corps, star—First Division, red; Second, white; Third, blue.

The sizes and colors will be according to pattern.

The circular originated corps/division badges and was the Army's first systematic use of them. Unit pride and morale improvement skyrocketed. The new symbols adorned every soldier and wagon. Fancier versions of corps badges, some jeweler-quality, appeared for sale in New York and Philadelphia. Later, the badges identified the wearer and linked him to his division's or corps' fortunes or misfortunes.[23]

The corps/division badges offered another opportunity in the endless efforts to count the numbers of men in the army. In an effort to determine how many badges the quartermaster's department needed, the army on March 21 tallied the following:

First Corps: 15,510

Second Corps: 15,337

Third Corps: 17,438

Fifth Corps: 15,467

Sixth Corps: 22,076

Eleventh Corps: 12,880

Twelfth Corps: 11,933

Cavalry: 11,937

Total: 122,578

Total, without cavalry, 110,641.[24]

Ten days later on March 31, as part of its routine end-of-the-month reporting, the army took yet another opportunity to reckon its own strength. Headquarters strengths came in as follows: General and staff, 66 officers and two enlisted men; Provost guard, 159 officers and 2,345 enlisted men; Regular engineer battalion, two officers and 351 enlisted men; Volunteer engineer brigade, 28 officers and 544 enlisted men; and Signal

---

23 OR, 25, part II, 152. This was the origin of shoulder and combat patches/badges in the U. S. Army.

24 Ibid., 151. There was intent to have a distinctive corps badge for the cavalry. An elaborate one was developed with crossed sabers on a blue field atop and radiating eight-point star.

Corps troops, 22 officers and 77 enlisted men. The Artillery reserve reported 53 officers and 1,362 enlisted men. The corps reported as follows:

Organization, Commander / Officers / Enlisted Men

First Corps, Maj. Gen. J. F. Reynolds / 972 / 15,586
Second Corps, Maj. Gen. D. N. Couch / 1,013 / 15,893
Third Corps, Maj. Gen. D. E. Sickles / 1,004 / 17,591
Fifth Corps, Maj. Gen. G. G. Meade / 845 / 15,786
Sixth Corps, Maj. Gen. John Sedgwick / 1,204 / 22,384
Eleventh Corps, Maj. Gen. Carl Schurz / 643 / 13,224
Twelfth Corps, Maj. Gen. H. W. Slocum / 711 / 12,452
Cavalry Corps, Brig. Gen. G. Stoneman / 594 / 11,811

Totals (Including HQs and Arty) / 7,316 / 129,408

Present for Duty: 136,949[25]

Rules of War?

Not all of the army's reforms worked as well as the corps/division badges. New rules for paroles and exchanges, in contrast, were simply bizarre. On March 17, Hooker —despite trying to kill Robert E. Lee's nephew that day—sent him a polite communiqué. Adhering to orders and perhaps feeling that Lee's 32-year U. S. Army tenure had endeared him to War Department orders, Hooker enclosed a copy of No. 49, dated February 28. Paroles were to be written in duplicate with correct names and ranks; failing to do so invalidated parole. Only commissioned officers could parole themselves or their commands. Paroles on battlefields—either entire troop bodies or mass prisoner dismissals—were forbidden. "An officer who gives a parole for himself or his command on the battle-field is deemed a deserter and will be punished accordingly," Hooker explained. Officers could only pledge paroles individually, and no non-commissioned officer or enlisted man could give his parole except through an officer. No prisoner of war could be compelled to pledge his parole.[26]

Laughable even then, a prisoner whose parole process was later found invalid by his government was supposed to turn himself over to enemy captivity. No one could pledge to never take arms against his adversary or allies. Parole pledging was voluntary, but not

25 Ibid, 167. Corps staff and troops later wore versions showing all division colors.

26 Ibid, 145.

binding. "Paroles not authorized by the common law of war" were forbidden and pledging unauthorized paroles was punishable. The final paragraph required the order to be sent by all army commanders to current opponents. How such nonsense survived into even the nineteenth century would be worth separate study. No doubt many hours of whale oil were burnt plumbing the depths of "the common law of war." What any of this foolishness meant to the general, field or company officer, or common soldier must be left to dubious conjecture.[27]

"Everyone Has Something to Do"

Even as Averell and his cavalry were making a show of themselves to the west at Kelly's Ford, the Irish Brigade observed March 17 in much lighter fashion—proving that life was not perpetually bleak during the "Valley Forge." St. Patrick's Day offered the Irishmen the chance to relieve the tedium with steeplechase horse racing and sack races It whetted their appetites for food and drink, too. Celebratory fare included "thirty-five hams, and a side of an ox roasted; an entire pig stuffed with boiled turkeys; an unlimited number of chickens, ducks and small game." Ample drinking materials included "eight caskets of champagne, ten gallons of rum, and twenty-two of whiskey"—all to satisfy the hunger and slake the thirst of the lusty Hibernians.[28]

"General Meagher and staff celebrated by giving a steeplechase on the parade ground of the division," recalled adjutant Josiah Favill of the 57th New York Infantry. "A course was carefully laid out, ditches dug, hurdles erected, and valuable prizes offered to the contestants. The conditions were simply that none but the commissioned officers of the division could ride, which was sufficiently liberal." A crowd of officers participated, while "Meagher, glorious in fancy undress uniform liberally covered with gold braid," entertained generals and lady friends. Among the attendees in Hooker's retinue was Princess Agnes Salm-Salm, the wife of Prince Felix, the colonel of the 8th New York Infantry; Favill described her as "a beautiful and fearless horse woman."[29]

The race, with only a few serious falls, was deemed a success. Infantry guards maintained decorum, but festivities lasted into the night, and things finally teetered toward chaos when Meagher and his brigade surgeon challenged each other to mortal combat. Matters assumed a threatening aspect. The following morning, however, when

---

27 Ibid.

28 St. Clair Mulholland, *A Story of the 116th Regiment of Pennsylvania Volunteers in the War of the Rebellion.* (Philadelphia, PA, 1903), 77, as quoted in Jane Conner, *Lincoln in Stafford,* 37.

29 Favill, *Diary of a Young Officer* in BV 196, part 1, FSNMP. Princess Agnes Salm-Salm's story is summarized in Jane Hollenbeck Conner, *Sinners, Saints and Soldiers in Civil War Stafford,* (Stafford, VA., 2009).

alcoholic effects had subsided, the surgeon apologized and peace resumed. To the surprise and disappointment of the brigade, Hooker struck a surprising party-pooper tone that day. "All fast riding and fast movements of wagons through the army were to cease immediately," he said in General Order No. 28. Provost marshals and guards were to enforce the order.[30]

Nonetheless, the St. Patrick's Day festivities inspired non-Irish Pennsylvanians, Michiganders, New Yorkers, Indianans, and Mainers to new celebratory heights. On March 28, the men of Brig. Gen. David Bell Birney's III Corps division extended the limits of frivolity at "Bell Air" with horse racing, greased pole climbing, and sack races. Entertainment also included an "Ethiopian Concert"—a minstrel show. The division erected a 120-by-60 foot reviewing stand, and "real women, be-silked, be-furred, and bonneted" attended the frolics. Reportedly present were Maj. Gen. Hooker, Pennsylvania Governor Curtin, unnamed "distinguished statesmen," and "officers from the different corps." One observer noted that "General Sickles [the murderer] of Key had his lady there."[31]

Peak soldier morale was achieved when companies within a regiment or regiments within a brigade vied with one another to prove or demonstrate themselves best. Within elite units, the goal was to be "the best of the best" without greatly diminishing other units. Competition, unless unhealthy or excessive, defaulted to unit pride, an "intangible" crucial to combat readiness. Of course, pitting one's mettle against the enemy provided the truest test, but for most men in the Army of the Potomac during the "Valley Forge," the enemy was seldom encountered on a day-to-day basis. Thus, standing well among fellow units reflected a competitive edge.

Soldier "Marker" exemplified this when he described the rivalry between the 16th and 27th New York regiments in a letter that appeared in the March 26, 1863 edition of the *Rochester Union & Advertiser.* "The 16th New York," he began, "whose fame is widespread as that of the 27th, and belonging to the same brigade, hails from St. Lawrence county, the home of Preston King, and the hot-bed of Republicanism. Suffice it to say," he continued," two years' service has changed the radical sentiments of its warrior representatives. From the first Bull Run to the present day it has figured in nearly every conflict registered on the banner of the Army of the Potomac and has invariably sustained a fighting reputation. Colonel, now Major General Davies, was the first commander, a strict disciplinarian, and a military man in every sense of the word."

---

30 *OR*, 25, part II, 147.

31 Oliver Wilson Davis, *Life of David Bell Birney, Major General United States Volunteers* (Philadelphia, PA, 1867), 119, 126-127; Gilbert Adams Hays, comp., *Under the Red Patch: Story of the Sixty-third Regiment Pennsylvania Volunteers* (Pittsburgh, PA,1908), 176, both quoted in Jane Conner, *Lincoln in Stafford*, 37-38. BV 317, part 4, FSNMP, Decker letters.

Under Slocum and Davies as the brigade commanders, great jealousy existed between the 27th and the 16th, "as both were worshipped, and with good cause, in the eyes of their own regiment. Since then, the feeling has gradually worn away, leaving only a generous spirit of rivalry between the two regiments."[32]

Morale was also lifted throughout the army by myriad food boxes shipped to soldiers "by loving hands"—a sentiment common at the time. Packages produced universally happy results; however, they also experienced a wide range of success on the tricky path from hearth to hut. Inconsistent Northern mail services, shipper carelessness, corruption by officers and clerks, and physical dangers all conspired to keep packages from waiting soldiers. When one arrived intact, celebrations erupted among recipients and friends (always numerous at that point). When the system failed, results were predictable. An incident in the 19th Massachusetts Infantry was recalled in 1899 with gallows humor: "Some of the boxes had been a long time on the road, and when they arrived the contents were in uncertain condition. It was hard to tell the tobacco from the mince pie." One of the packages had been expected by the regimental adjutant. The officers gathered to see him open it. "The cover was removed and the smell was not quite equal to the arbutus, but we hoped it was only the top. Another box was found inside containing what was once a turkey, but was now a large lump of blue mould. Nothing in the box was eatable." The officers held council and concluded the turkey needed decent burial. The remains "lay in state," a wake was held, and a solemn procession conveyed the body to the open grave. "Negro servants" served as drum major and pall-bearers. The quartermaster, with the carbine reversed, was the firing party; and a chaplain pro tempore was appointed. At graveside, words and poetry sent the turkey to eternity before returning to camp to mourn "for the spirits that had departed."[33]

Colonel Joseph Snider of the 7th Virginia (Union) Infantry reflected on spiritual matters of a more sincere type. "I try to remember God's holy day, though speaking in general terms, a soldier knows no Sunday," he wrote on Sunday, March 15. "And now, while I am writing, the sound of martial music is heard in many directions—and men are marching off to do duty, as guards and pickets for our camp—This would seem verry strange out in Morgantown—but such is the soldier's duty—and such is the necessities of war."[34]

---

32 CHJHCF. Data in text.

33 Adams, *Reminiscences of the Nineteenth Massachusetts Regiment*, Chapter 7.

34 BV 327, part 5, FSNMP, Letters of Col. Joseph Snider (1827-1904), 7th Virginia (U. S.) Infantry. This letter was written from Headquarters, 1-3-II AC, "Camp near Falmouth, Va." West Virginia did not become a state until June 20, 1863, therefore used Virginia in unit title.

Snider wrote with a fondness for the routine he saw around him. "You would be interested, in seeing the smoke ascending from thousands of little log huts—and promenading some of our nicest streets. Our Towns are regularly laid out—and hence we have alleys, Main streets, front streets, broad streets and our Towns have no hotels, no mattresses. No feather beds—a board with a blanket constitutes the beds. There is one particular difference in our towns and others in the country—we have no loafers here—everyone has something to do—and has got to do it."[35]

Sergeant Thomas White Stephens of the 20th Indiana Infantry made March diary entries that showed how busy the typical soldier was.[36] On the first through third, he performed guard, caught up on reading, listened to a good sermon at the 10th Pennsylvania's camp, and noted reconnaissance balloon ups and downs. On the third, the regiment was reassigned to J. H. Hobart Ward's 2nd Brigade; on the fourth, they moved their camp 4-5 miles to near Potomac Creek Railroad Bridge. For several days amid more plentiful wood, they built shelters and settled in. On the eleventh, he favorably noted three comrades' returns from hospital and a dress parade—off-set by some miscreant stealing a set of his washed drawers. Dysentery returned on the twelfth and thirteenth, but he persevered through letter writing, drawing clothing (drawers at .50 cents, and leggings at .75 cents), a haircut from his brother, and modest purchases of tea at the sutler's.

On March 14, Stephens noted increased spirit: "An order, from Gen. Birney was read this evening on dress parade, that Regimental Commanders prepare and send to headquarters a report of all soldiers, who have distinguished themselves on the battlefield, such soldiers to receive a silver cross (medal of valor), to be worn over the 'Red patch' on the left breast." Another order directed that no soldier under arrest or who is reported for straggling could wear the "'Red Patch.'—Only those, who have been in battle, are entitled to wear it."[37]

---

35 Ibid.

36 BV 106, part 3, FSNMP. Paul E. Wilson and Harriet Stephens Wilson, ed., "The Civil War Diary of Thomas White Stephens, Sergeant, Company K, 20th Regiment of Indiana Volunteers."

37 The Kearny Cross discussed by Stephens, honored Maj. Gen. Philip Kearny, who had commanded the division and had been killed-in-action on September 1, 1862. The medal was established for the 1-III AC and consisted of a gold Maltese cross suspended from a red silk ribbon with the motto "DULCE ET DECORUM EST PATRIA MORI" ("Sweet and proper, it is to die for one's country"). This was distinct from the earlier Kearny Medal, for officers who had served under Kearny. On March 13, a second version of the Kearny Medal was established as a "Cross of Valor" for enlisted personnel. The new Kearny Cross was awarded to any Union soldier who had displayed meritorious, heroic, of distinguished acts while facing an enemy force.

On March 15, Stephens's health improved: "Thank God for his goodness and mercy to me. O that I love him, more, who is all love, love." He read his Bible and "Pollok's Course of Time." On the 16th, he read "*Harper's Weekly*", &c." and listened to an Indiana Senate speech read by a Captain Reed. Duty ended with company inspection. Noting heavy cannonading up-river on the seventeenth, Stephens was on picket duty on the eighteenth, reached by a march of 8 miles. He had "precious seasons" of "secret prayer," proclaiming them the "sweetest, best moments of my life, thus spent!" On picket some 25-30 Confederate prisoners were taken. Presumably in picket reserve on March 19 and 20, he read and prayed: "In bowing in secret prayer, today, felt the presence of One I love best, my nearest, best friend. O how sweet thus to commune with my Saviour: with Jesus my Redeemer."[38]

On March 20, Stephens "took a very bad cold, have a cough," but managed prayer and enjoyed a daily ration of beef and soft bread. They returned to camp on muddy roads on the twenty-first. Tired and sick, a good night's rest made him feel better on March 22 (Sunday). His spirits were enlivened by a new cap (.65 cents) and a box from home; the box contained much needed pain-killer, six pounds of butter, tea, a few cakes, box of cayenne pepper, preserves, and arithmetic and grammar books. Also received were: a "Methodist discipline," handkerchiefs, suspenders and dried huckleberries. Stephens gushed, "God bless our kind friends at home." After evening inspection, he turned-in with his *Harper's Weekly*. On the twenty-third he sent a "haversack of things home" with a friend.

His cold persisted. Remaining in his tent, Stephens "used pain-killer pretty freely" before evening dress parade. On the forenoon of March 24, he was subjected to "very close inspection" by one of General Ward's aides. His sickness persisted, so he continued applying the pain-killer. Either because or in spite of it, he felt God's peace and love. On the twenty-fourth and twenty-fifth, Stephens had a headache (he made no connection with the "pain-killer"). He read his Bible and "Pollok's," rating both highly. He described a review three miles away on March 26 for generals Sickles and Birney and Pennsylvania's Governor Curtin. They also received sad news of Maj. Gen. Sumner's death in Syracuse. On the twenty-seventh, Stephens recorded a "general row in the 99 Pa. Regt." after evening roll call in which several were injured. He cleaned his weapon on March 28 and read. The twenty-ninth and thirtieth included company inspection, feeling poorly, company drill, and a noon review for Indiana's Governor Morton and generals Ward and Meredith. Whether for its brevity or content, the troops repaid the governor's short speech with three cheers. Stephens cleaned his weapon again and

---

38 BV 106, part 3, FSNMP. Paul E. Wilson and Harriet Stephens Wilson, ed., "The Civil War Diary of Thomas White Stephens, Sergeant, Company K, 20th Regiment of Indiana Volunteers."

awoke on March 31 to snow. Perhaps favorably, the snow melted quickly and he returned to reading his Bible and Methodist discipline, despite continued stomach sickness.[39]

Henry Butler of the 16th Maine Infantry Regiment described another common activity. "We have been drilling the skirmish drill," he said. "The way we have to do is to practice loading on our backs and then turn on our bellies and fire. Tomorrow morning I have got to go out on picket and stay three days."[40]

"L. A. V.," a soldier with the 15th New Jersey, wrote positively to his hometown newspaper about the twice-daily company and battalion drills, deemed "necessary for our efficiency in the field as well as our health." "The army is fine spirits," he added, "and though disease has made sad havoc in our ranks, we still retain in memory the duty we owe our beloved country, and shall make it manifest at the proper time. Copperheads at the North hold your peace, and we will make peace."[41]

This overall sense of purpose, coupled with Hooker's reforms, did so much for morale that even the grousing took a lighter tone. "Our Co. (Co. F) is acting as Provost Guard to the 3rd Div. 1st Army Corps—Cap't. Mitchell is Pro[vost] Marshal, Gen. Doubleday is commanding the 3rd Div," wrote Lt. William Oren Blodget of the 151st Pennsylvania Infantry on March 21 from their camp near Belle Plain. Blodget sardonically proclaimed Doubleday "deficient considerably" as a commander because he neither drank whiskey, left his command, or refused to fight. That the general refrained from keeping a mistress also struck Blodget as exceptional. He deemed drunkenness and profanity desirable in privates as the government could waste resources confiscating their whiskey and passing out religious tracts. He ridiculed uneven justice for officers and enlisted men; the weather; and the antiwar movement—hoping for another 200,000 men in the field to finish the war. "Every day

---

39 Ibid.

40 CHJHCF. Letters of Henry Butler, 16th Maine Infantry, to his wife, Mary; Castine Public Library, Castine, Maine, http://www.kalama.com/~mariner/front_butler.htm. Evidence of rifle ranges is extensively found in a series of maps in the White Oak Civil War Museum and Research Center, in Stafford, Virginia. This citation may relate to the types of "drills" reflected in letters and diaries. If the many references to "we drilled today" or "drill" relate to actual firing of weapons—and that is not absolutely certain here—then the documentation gap may not be as great. A preferable theory is that marksmanship training proliferated in the late-May to mid-June period in Stafford, after Chancellorsville and prior to departure for Gettysburg. A persistent "Valley Forge" mystery stems from a lack of written documentation on firing practice within the Army of the Potomac, yet the physical evidence is overwhelming and incontrovertible that extensive rifle firing ranges existed throughout the army's occupied spaces.

41 BV 109, part 8, FSNMP. Letters to the editors of (Flemington,) New Jersey, newspapers. This appeared in *The Republican* on April 3, 1863.

increases the disparity of strength and will continue to do so whether we are victorious or not," Blodget concluded. "All we have to do is to call out our men."[42]

A soldier in the 140th Pennsylvania was waiting for that call. "The roads are drying fast, but I can't see anything to indicate a move," he admitted. "Old Hooker hasn't told me when it is going to be, for he does everything sly and we can't tell much about it. He doesn't do like Burnside did, let everyone know his moves, and I think it is the best way."

That didn't stop the Keystoner from wondering: "All the papers say the rebs are starving and their pickets say they have been on half rations for a month . . . [and] they are falling back to Richmond," he continued, "but they appear plenty around here yet. But when Old Hooker is ready we will know how many there is of them and I don't think that will be long... There is a much better feeling among the men and they are all willing to try it again. If the rebs lose Fredericksburg they can never stop us without more men, for they can never get as good a position this side of Richmond."[43]

Corporal Amory Allen of the 14th Connecticut Infantry echoed similar thoughts on March 24. "We expect to move over the river soon and some where else," he wrote. "Old Hooker will not keep us idle long after the mud is dried up for he is an old fighter and the rebels are very anxious to know where he is about to strike the blow." In his letter, Allen revealed his recent promotion to first corporal. "[I] expect to be one of the colour guards and if I do that will excuse me from picket duty and many other duties," he pointed out. Expressing pride in such dangerous duty as color guard demonstrated an important increase in morale.[44]

Captain Frank Lindley Lemont of the 5th Maine Infantry wrote on March 26 with his prediction that the army would move within two weeks. "I don't know where we shall make a strike, or when, but you may rest assured that Hooker's boys will leave their mark whenever and wherever he say the word," he vowed. "There is a good deal of fight in the Army of the Potomac and in the next battle they will show of what mettle they are made. Joe Hooker is a fighting man and so must every man be under him. I don't know as we shall succeed in the next battle, but we intend to and we are under a [general] who will press forward as long as he has a man who can walk without crutches."[45]

42 BV 210, part 15, FSNMP, letters of W. O. Blodget, 151st Pennsylvania.

43 BV 112, part 13, FSNMP, letters of an unknown soldier in the 140th Pennsylvania Infantry.

44 BV 119, part 1, FSNMP, The Civil War Letters of Amory Allen, 14th Connecticut Infantry.

45 BV 230, part 3, FSNMP. Letters of Frank Lemont, 5th Maine Infantry.

The Army and Lincoln Pray

Looking ahead often provoked anxiety, especially in light of past engagements. Marye's Heights, standing beyond the town on the far side of the river, offered a clear reminder of those travails to anyone who happened to forget. Those who had "seen the elephant" in battle intuitively understood that they were all, to use a later infantryman's phrase, "fugitives from the law of averages."

As a result, religion continued its surge through the camps. John Cole, a general agent for the United States Christian Commission (U.S.C.C.), noted the vigor with which many soldiers attended to their spiritual lives, and it invigorated him. "I am well with the exception of a cold and am enjoying my work greatly," he reported early in the month. "Indeed no money could tempt me to leave it, we are being prospered wonderfully, I can almost say that there is a revival at this place, we had a meeting tonight about 200 persons present and a deep interest was manifest, we have a prayer meeting every night and they are well attended, one night every person came to his feet as desiring the prayers of Christians."

Bibles and tracts had been distributed in mind-numbing numbers. Cole had another 80,000 Bibles—a grant from the American Bible Society—about to be distributed by 20 delegates (10 from New England) at four or five "stations." "We find every where a great desire to receive Testaments & books," Cole added, "and we every where meet the most marked consideration from officers and men." He singled out Treasury Secretary Chase and Maj. Gen. Howard for their significant assistance. His report ended: "I trust God will bless us in our efforts. I feel that we need the prayers of the Christian church every where that our labors may be crowned with success."[46]

The U.S.C.C. had been looking after the spiritual—and, increasingly, the material—comforts of these men for over a year. Soldier's aid societies in Northern communities and the U. S. Sanitary Commission added additional food, clothing, and other supplies. Citizens collected, made, or sometimes purchased and forwarded "donations" to the soldiers. For example, from Falmouth, Surgeon J. Wilson Wishart of the 140th Pennsylvania Infantry thanked Miss Helen Lee (a relation of Federal Colonel Lee) on March 24: "It gives me great pleasure to acknowledge the receipt of a number of copies of the Soldier's Hymn Book and also some Tracts, the gifts of yourself."[47]

Civilian volunteers pretty much came and went at will—a freedom of action denied every general, officer, and enlisted soldier. Cole was among those who could do so. He'd

46 BV 91, part 13, FSNMP, USCC General Field Agent John A. Cole, "Army Letters" 1861-1866.

47 BV 121, FSNMP, Lee Family Papers.

spent much of March in the camps but returned to Philadelphia later in the month to rally more aid. "Here again on a flying visit," he wrote on March 29. "Start at Midnight for Aquia again. I am very busy arranging the 'move' that the newspapers assert to be coming soon. I have now about 35 delegates to look after and feel somewhat anxious as to the turn matters may take. But after all we are in the Lord's hands and what is best will be done."[48]

The U.S.C.C. had six stations by then, Cole explained, "and a glorious work at each." At Falmouth, they had a large room near the bridge that once connected Falmouth with Fredericksburg. "Here in sight of that beautiful city we hold nightly prayer-meetings with an average attendance of 150 or 200," he declared. "[A]t another small room where we live, we have a 'Sunday School.' We have gathered in the little 'Secesh' children who have been deprived of any religious instruction, and there teach them our Sunday School hymns and lessons from the Gospel. The parents are very grateful." At another station—"Stoneman's it is called, which is almost in the center of the army"—they held nightly prayer meetings in a long tent or succession of tents. "God has blessed our work here signally," Cole beamed, "many have been converted, the tent is always crowded to overflowing and every night men are awakened to a sense of their lost condition." Finally, Cole spoke of "still another station" where delegates assisted every night "the good Mrs. [Ellen] Harris at the 'Lacy House' her large room there is crowded every night, she is directly opposite Fredericksburg and in almost talking distance of the Rebs."[49]

Curiously, Cole seemed to overlook Stafford's wartime desolation, but he did end with one other important observation: "The army is in splendid condition and Hooker will fight."[50]

Such an assessment no doubt would have pleased President Lincoln, who was thinking that very night on matters of war and peace. On his desk sat a U. S. Senate resolution calling for a national prayer of confession. Lincoln could have handled the paperwork perfunctorily, but instead, on March 30, he chose to make it an expression of abiding faith:

---

48 Ibid.

49 Ibid. Ellen Matilda Orbison (Mrs. John) Harris is subject of a biography being written by Al and Jane Conner. Her prominent Civil War roles were described in Benson John Lossing, *A History of the Civil War* (New York: The War Memorial Association, 1912), Vol. 3, 43; L.P. Brockett and Mary C. Vaughan, *Women's Work in the Civil War: A Record of Heroism, Patriotism, and Patience* (Philadelphia: Zeigler, McCurdy, 1867), 149-152; and Frank Moore, *Women of the War* (Hartford, CT: S. S. Scranton, 1867). Mrs. Harris is also described in several contemporary sources. See www.civilwar.com/union-women/mrs-john-harris.html (accessed July 16, 2009) and www.hsp.org/default.aspx?id+129 (accessed on July 16, 2009).

50 Ibid.

And whereas it is the duty of nations as well as of men, to own their dependence upon the overruling power of God, to confess their sins and transgressions, in humble sorrow, yet with assured hope that genuine repentance will lead to mercy and pardon; and to recognize the sublime truth, announced in the Holy Scriptures and proven by all history, that those nations only are blessed whose God is the Lord.

And, insomuch as we know that, by His divine law, nations like individuals are subjected to punishments and chastisements in this world, may we not justly fear that the awful calamity of civil war, which now desolates the land, may be but a punishment, inflicted upon us, for our presumptuous sins, to the needful end of our national reformation as a whole People? We have been the recipients of the choicest bounties of Heaven. We have been preserved, these many years, in peace and prosperity. We have grown in numbers, wealth and power, as no other nation has ever grown. But we have forgotten God. We have forgotten the gracious hand which preserved us in peace, and multiplied and enriched and strengthened us; and we have vainly imagined, in the deceitfulness of our hearts, that all these blessings were produced by some superior wisdom and virtue of our own. Intoxicated with unbroken success, we have become too self-sufficient to feel the necessity of redeeming and preserving grace, too proud to pray to the God that made us!

It behooves us then, to humble ourselves before the offended Power, to confess our national sins, and to pray for clemency and forgiveness . . . .

All this being done, in sincerity and truth, let us then rest humbly in the hope authorized by the Divine teachings, that the united cry of the Nation will be heard on high, and answered with blessings, no less than the pardon of our national sins, and the restoration of our now divided and suffering Country, to its former happy condition of unity and peace.[51]

Offense and Defense on the Rappahannock River

Demonstrating the true activity of the "winter encampment," on March 25, the 2nd Wisconsin Infantry mounted a riverine expedition southeast into Westmoreland County. Under the command of Lt. Col. Lucius Fairchild, the Iron Brigade soldiers boarded the steamer *W. W. Frasier* at Belle Plain Landing at 4:00 p.m.—26 officers and 241 enlisted men, accompanied by 20 attached cavalrymen. Moving to the Potomac River, they traveled through the night and steamed 60 miles into Confederate-held territory.

---

51 Fornieri, ed., *Language of Liberty*, 796-800.

Anchoring at daylight, the disembarked cavalry reconnoitered for three hours toward Lower Machodoc Creek. The *W. W. Frasier* then moved down river to meet them. The entire force remained three days, commandeering supplies and materiel: 15 horses and mules; 300 pounds of bacon; 230 bushels of wheat; 25 bushels of oats; 15 bushels of beans; 3,000 bushels of corn; two harnesses; two anchors; and a chain cable from a destroyed "rebel schooner."

On the morning of March 28, the cavalry squad and 23 infantry volunteers—presumably mounted on the captured animals—departed under Capt. James D. Wood to return overland. This detachment rode or herded 48 confiscated horses and mules back to Belle Plain by the twenty-ninth. The remaining force had returned by steamer at 8:00 p.m. the previous night. They brought with them four civilians from Richmond County; a Confederate soldier—presumably a deserter—named Everett and his wife and child; another lady and child; and 30 "contrabands" now headed for freedom. While not the stuff of glory, such raids demonstrated tactical creativity and potentially kept the Confederates off-balance. They also secured needed supplies and animals—and deprived the enemy of them.[52]

The raids illustrated one of the very concerns weighing on Hooker's mind. Recalling earlier contingency plans for fortifications to defend Aquia Landing from raids and attacks, Hooker issued detailed instructions on March 30 addressed to commanding officers at Aquia Creek Landing, Accokeek Creek Railroad Bridge, and Potomac Creek Railroad Bridge. A positive action by army headquarters, it was nevertheless written in Hooker's characteristic tone and overly prescriptive style, and although lengthy, it is worth reprinting here in full:

Commanding Officer, Aquia Creek Landing: The defenses of this place consist of a line of slashing, running from King's house, on Aquia Creek, south to Accakeek Creek, strengthened by two redoubts and an advanced redoubt near Watson's house, occupying a position from which the enemy might shell the landing. These redoubts are numbered from right to left, No. 1 being near the Watson house, No. 2 on the Stafford Court House road, and No. 3 near the railroad. The enemy might attack, first, to force their way at once to the depots; secondly, to reach the hills over the depots to shell the latter; thirdly, by shelling depots from the north side of Aquia Creek, and simultaneously engage or threaten the redoubts and shell the depots from the north side. The first two attacks would fail if the advanced redoubt and defensive line were held. To do this, Redoubt No. 1 will have a garrison of 100 men and no guns; Redoubt No. 2 a garrison of 200 men and two 3-inch guns; Redoubt No. 3 a garrison of 100 men and four 3-inch guns, these guns in Redoubt No. 3 being outside the work. There should be a post of one company where the slashing

52 *OR*, 25, part I, 73-74.

ends at Aquia Creek, to prevent cavalry moving along the shore, and a reserve of 800 men near Redoubt No. 2, to move when needed. One gunboat, at least, should be kept at Aquia Creek, to prevent the enemy from putting a battery in position on the north side of Aquia Creek, to shell the depots, and should be assisted by the guns taken from the redoubts and placed on the hills immediately over the landing, these hills completely commanding the north shore of Aquia Creek. In case the defensive line were forced, the gunboat would be of service in the immediate defense of the depots.

The commanding officer will keep up an efficient system of outposts and lookouts, so that there may be no possibility of surprise. It is doubtful if a cavalry raid would attempt to break through the line without first carrying one of the redoubts. The reserve should move to the threatened point, and, keeping a sufficient sub-reserve, take an active part in the defense. If Redoubt No. 2 or No. 3 were attacked, the reserve would form to its right and left, under its cover, and, if the enemy were repulsed, should charge to complete its overthrow.

The guns of these works are intended to fire at the enemy's troops, not his guns. If the enemy should at any time shell a redoubt, the garrison should cover themselves by a parapet, or, if it was certain that no enemy was near, a part might get in the ditches, returning to the work the moment the artillery fire ceased. If any assault was made, the garrison should mount on the parapet and bayonet the enemy back into the ditch.

As Redoubt No. 1 is isolated, and must take care of itself, it should have a good officer in command.

The commanding officer will be held responsible that the works are kept in perfect repair.

Commanding Officer, Accakeek Creek Railroad Bridge: The garrison for the upper redoubt will be 100 men; for the lower, 25 men. When not surrounded by other troops, the commanding officer must take every precaution against surprise, keeping the garrison at the works and maintaining sufficient guards and lookouts both by day and night. If the attack were in the day, an attempt would probably be made to carry the works, as would be difficult to burn the bridge without. This attempt might be preceded by shelling. Ordinarily no reply should be made to this, as the guns are intended to fire at troops, and not to run the risk of being disabled by a superior artillery. The garrison should shelter themselves behind the parapets; or, if it is certain the enemy are not near the works, a part might get in the ditches, returning to the work the moment the artillery fire ceases. If the enemy attempts an assault, as soon as he reaches the ditches the garrison should rush on the parapet and bayonet him as he attempts to ascend.

At night the enemy might try to burn the bridge without taking the works. In this case a part of the garrison of the upper redoubt should move down to the bridge, keeping in good order, and attack the enemy, knowing the ground well. Having a secure place to fall back on, they would have every advantage over him. If the lower redoubt were taken, the bridge would be defended with musketry and canister from the upper.

More men can fight in these works than can well sleep in them. In case of an alarm, all railroad guards and others in the vicinity should at once rally upon the works.

The commanding officer will be held responsible that the works are kept in perfect repair.

Commanding Officer, Potomac Creek Railroad Bridge: The garrison for the upper redoubt will be 75 men; for the lower, 75 men, with two 3-inch guns outside; for the stockade, at the south end of bridge, 50 men, and for the block-house at the northern end, 30 men.

When not surrounded by other troops, the commanding officer must take every precaution against surprise, keeping the garrison at the works, and maintaining efficient guards and lookouts both by day and night. If the attack were in the day, an attempt would probably be made to carry the works, as it would be difficult to burn the bridge without. This attempt might be preceded by shelling. Ordinarily no reply should be made to this, as the guns are intended to be fired at troops, and not to run the risk of being disabled by a superior artillery. The garrison should shelter themselves behind the parapets; or, if it is certain the enemy are not near the works, a part might get in the ditches, returning to the work the moment the artillery fire ceases. If the enemy attempts an assault, as soon as he reaches the ditches the garrison should rush on the parapet and bayonet him as he attempts to ascend.

At night the enemy might try to burn the bridge without taking the works. In this case a part of the garrison of the two upper redoubt should move down to the bridge, keeping in good order, and attack the enemy. Knowing the ground well, and having a secure place to fall back on, they would have every advantage over him.

A good officer should have command of the upper redoubt, which should be held to the last, as, if this were taken, it would be difficult to hold the lower. More men can fight in these works than can well sleep in them. In case of an alarm, all railroad and other guards in the vicinity should at once rally upon the works.

The commanding officer will be held responsible that the works are kept in perfect repair.

Memoranda with regard to the artillery, —The engineers ask for ten guns—six for the defenses of the landing at Aquia Creek and two for each of the railroad bridges. Should it be deemed necessary to move the guns from the works at the landing to fire across Aquia Creek, a field battery should be furnished—two sections of guns, under a captain at

Redoubt No. 3 (Comstock's numbers), one section at No. 2, the caissons, stables, &c., at a central position between and in rear of these . . . .

The captain of the battery at the landing should be directed to have men properly drilled and instructed, and be required to see that the ammunition, magazines, &c., are kept complete and in good order.[53]

Lingering Problems, but Overall Improvement

By March 25, Maj. Rufus Dawes had returned from leave to rejoin the 6th Wisconsin of the Iron Brigade at Belle Plain. "I am safe and sound in camp," he declared. "There are great preparations everywhere in the army for hard campaigning and hard fighting." His former commander, Brig. Gen. Lysander Cutler, now led the nearby 2nd Brigade of the I Corps' 1st Division. In the 6th Wisconsin, the governor had commissioned Col. Edward S. Bragg as commander, Rufus Dawes as lieutenant colonel, and John F. Hauser as major. "The regiment is fine trim this spring," Dawes reaffirmed. "My visit home was pleasant indeed and I shall go into the new campaign with courage and hope, renewed by the sympathy and encouragement I received at Marietta."[54]

Yet the army Dawes returned to had itself been undergoing renewal. War Democrat Lt. John C. Griswold[,] 154th New York Infantry, summarized three months of changes in a March 16 letter:

On our arrival at Falmouth 3 days after the defeat at Fredericksburg we found the soldiers in a condition bordering on insubordination. Some regiments went so far as to declare that they would never go into another fight with the rebels, that there was no use trying any more for we could never subdue them by force, that it was nothing but a damn nigger war, and that sooner it was settled on peace terms the better. My faith in our final success is stronger today than it was 3 months since. All that is wanting is a united effort & a firm determination on the part of the whole people to sustain the government; & it resolves into a mere question of time as to our final success.[55]

---

53 *OR*, 25, part I, 74-75. Importantly, almost all of these places still exist and are mostly accessible for tours. There is also a raging debate extending to the VDHR over the proper name of one of the relic fortifications. Previously unknown to regional history, the memorandum provides tactical and command insights.

54 Dawes, *Service With the Sixth Wisconsin Volunteers*, 129.

55 BV 110, part 23, FSNMP. Letters from/about John C. Griswold.

"I suppose the army is in good Condition now," wrote McClellan-supporter James E. Decker of the 1st New York Artillery on March 23. "If we had little Mac to lead us on we would be all ready for work but I suppose we will have to be ready as it is. Hooker is a good man."[56]

"I think there never was a commander of this army that had the confidence of the whole army to the same degree that Hooker has got," wrote James T. Miller of the 111th Pennsylvania on March 30, "and I expect he will give us a chance to see the elephant before long."[57]

The passing calendar and improving weather made it clear enough that the campaign season was approaching, but more importantly, a sense of expectancy hung nearly palpable in the air, and everyone in the army could feel it. "Everything goes on improving, the weather and the roads, the dispositions of the army," wrote a soldier from the 26th Wisconsin in a letter published in the *Milwaukee Sentinel*, "even the administration seems to be endowed with a better spirit, and with a new enthusiasm, I may almost say, a certainty of victory, we long for the approaching Spring campaign. Hooker is full of energy, and gaining the general confidence. Our cavalry performed some daring tricks, and promises to be of use hereafter. Besides, our infantry and artillery, if well led, are superior to that of the enemy, and with a cheerful heart the patriot may contemplate the future, it dawns."[58]

The coming campaign, predicted the Badger, would be "the bloodiest of the whole war," "fighting will be done with the rage of desperation," and "blood will flow in streams, and many a one of our young regiment will also have to sacrifice his life." Such sacrifice would not be in vain and, "in spite of all impediments, in defiance of all the efforts of your true friends (?) of the North [i.e., Copperheads]," the army would be victorious and destroy the "contemptible slaveholding oligarchy."

The infantryman of the 26th continued:

the soldier does not forget that at this moment he is the only pillar of the country, that all who care for liberty, equality, in short, for the Union, cling to him as the last anchor of hope, and his courage, his zeal increases with danger. He knows very well that under present circumstances, his personal welfare (I will not say his security) is closely allied with the welfare and success of the Union. All that is sacred to man, the love of fatherland, liberty, his

56 BV 317, part 4, FSNMP, Decker letters.

57 CHJHCF. Cites: "James T. Miller, 111th Pennsylvania to his parents and brother, Miller Papers, Schoff Collection, Clements Library, University of Michigan."

58 Here and in the subsequent paragraphs: BV 282, part 10, FSNMP, 26th Wisconsin Infantry Regiment letters to the *Milwaukee Sentinel*. The one cited a March 29, 1863, letter in the edition of April 7, 1863; page 1, column 5.

personal honor, incites him to the fulfillment of his duty, and that he yet wavered, stands as firm as a rock.

Copperhead leaders were conceptually culled from the people. Their "peace" doctrine was, continued the editorial, "Obtained by means of our arms, peace is the glorious aim the patriot strives for, the much wished for end of bloody combats the wearied soldier longs for the regeneration of the Union, the beginning of her everlasting happy continuance. That peace however the peace party can and will procure for us is the beginning of everlasting reproach, disgraceful oppression, and as a necessary consequence, an eternal dissension."

"In the Army as everywhere," the Wisconsinite continued, adding that it was the "general view of the soldiers here,"

> the opinion of the ignorant, uneducated is determined by success only. If our Army is victorious, then our cause is a glorious one, and an immense patriotism takes hold of the masses. But if we are met with misfortune, if we are repulsed, we become discouraged, and the whole story is nothing but humbug! Yes, many among us there are, whose patriotism is solely dependent upon the quantity of the rations, the regular appearance of the paymaster, etc. . . . The disposition of the Army rests alone in the spirit that prevails with the thinking, educated portion of the soldiers and the officers. If this portion is imbued with the right spirit, then all the bearing of ill will from abroad cannot demoralize the Army.

Like Dawes' March 16 speech in Marietta, the Wisconsin infantryman's letter captured the quiet revolution underway in the Stafford camps. "Indeed, all I said in my speech about the army is strictly true," Dawes affirmed back in camp. "I am glad to be on the record in that speech. I don't want stock in anything better than that kind of doctrine just now."[59]

March 1863 ended, then, with universal signs of resurgent spirit and fighting capacity. Most of what Hooker and Butterfield had attempted, and no doubt hoped for, was taking place at the hands of better corps and division commanders. Within brigades and regiments, leadership experience was finally paying off. New, spirited units were reinforcing the old regiments. The cruel winter gave way to spring. Rest and relaxation had improved morale as much as the other steps: better food; more timely pay; better unit pride, cohesion and spirit; the officers and men finally united against a common foe (the Copperheads); positive steps taken to make cavalry, intelligence, picket duty, straggler control, medical service, communications and tactical logistics, and ordnance support all more effective. Objectively, any or all of these measures could have been

---

59 Dawes, *Service With the Sixth Wisconsin Volunteers*, 129.

taken earlier. The grim qualitative realities, an inability to overcome teamwork shortfalls, and an indecisive execution of missions continued to drag on army resurgence.

But, as April rose on the horizon, further improvement awaited, as did a natural desire for action. "Spring time has come, and as the birds and insects give vent to their voices, one is led to think of the good old times in Jersey when peace and tranquility reigned supreme," mused soldier "L.A.V.," of the 15th New Jersey stationed at White Oak Church. "The calm evenings give occasion for many remarks of the following import: 'What a pleasant evening for promenading. O that I were home gallanting a handsome Miss, enjoying nature's splendor, &c."

But his letter soon turned to the serious business on everyone's mind. He knew the entire nation waited to see the army resurgent. "The universal confidence in Joe Hooker will, I believe, insure us of victory," he predicted; "if not, we will try again, for this country must be saved intact, and there shall be no peace until the traitors cease to tread the soil so gallantly won by our Revolutionary sires. The day of compromises is past, and our Independence must be sustained at the point of the bayonet, if necessary."[60]

---

60 BV 109, part 8, FSNMP. Letters to the editors of (Flemington) New Jersey, newspapers. This appeared in *The Republican* on April 3, 1863.

Chapter Eight |

The Finest Army on the Planet

As Speculation swirled about the spring campaign, Joe Hooker quietly and deliberately put the pieces to move the army into place. He played things close to the vest, not even telling key subordinates all the elements of his plans (a practice that would cause significant problems once the campaign did actually get underway). In order not to tip his hand too early, he wrote to the War Department on March 23 with a request designed to help him maintain security and surprise.

"In view of the fact that when this army moves the sudden stoppage of all visitors to this camp would be a preliminary notice thereof," he began, "also that the attention of all officers and men is now absolutely required to be free from the interferences of such visitors, I would respectfully suggest that hereafter the permits to visit this army be restricted to absolute positive necessity, and that permission heretofore granted to females is denied." These measures should be "gradually introduced within the next few days, and not upon the ground that anything is likely to occur." It wasn't clear when the army would move, so one could link it with imminent actions.[1]

But even as Hooker's request to stem the flow of visitors made its way to Washington, Washington's most important resident had begun contemplating a visit to Hooker. President Lincoln had decided to pay a visit to the Army of the Potomac.

As it happened, reckoning who was and wasn't with the army was much on the mind of the War Department, albeit in a different way. Despite the muster numbers submitted on March 21 and 31—in the wake of the corps/division badge announcement, and again on March 31 at the end of the month—the War Department ordered a general muster for all army troops. Hooker's April 2 General Order 34 set the date for April 10.[2]

---

1   OR, 25, part II, 153-154.

2   Ibid., 185-188, 190-191.

One of the unintended consequences of the army's relative proximity to Washington, D.C., for the winter was the constant stream of visitors that flowed in and out of the army. General Hooker, always a political animal, suddenly found the tables turned as politicians besieged him with requests, demands, questions, and suggestions on behalf of soldiers from their respective states. *LOC*

The army also took note of a singular loss. On March 31, word arrived of the death of Maj. Gen. Edwin Vose "Bull" Sumner, the stalwart former commander of the II Corps at Antietam and the Right Grand Division at the battle of Fredericksburg. The 66-year-old Sumner, the oldest of the generals when he served with the Army of the Potomac, was visiting his daughter's home in Syracuse, New York, before taking his new post out west in Missouri. He died there of a heart attack. "Yesterday was kept in Solemnity through this army in honor of the memory of Maj. Gen. Sumner," recalled Lt. James H. Leonard of the 5th Wisconsin on April 1. "He was very much respected by this army, of which he has been one of the chief officers from the time of its organization to a very short time previous to his death. Though we shall never again witness his old grey head as he rides along our lines, we have his example left us, and his name will be remembered as long as the American army has a place in history."[3]

3   BV 353, part 23, FSNMP, R. G. Plumb, editor, "Letters of a Fifth Wisconsin Volunteer," in *Wisconsin Magazine of History*, Volume 3, September 1919-June 1920, 71-72.

Meanwhile, despite Hooker's March 23 request, visitors to the army continued to come and go, albeit the rate of visitation began to taper off. M. T. Peabody of the 5th New Hampshire described a visit by Joseph Moulton, Jr., agent of the American Tract Society, distributing religious materials to the soldiers. He also recounted a visit from Governor Nathaniel Springer Berry, who reviewed their division. Berry promised efforts to furlough the entire regiment. The young soldier knew how difficult that would be. More realistically, he anticipated a paymaster's visit.[4]

The most worrisome visitors to the army came on April 1. In a midnight probe, "a large force of [Confederate] cavalry supported by six guns" tested Sickles' III Corps picket lines along Potomac Creek. And Confederates had given Hooker plenty else to worry about, too: he spent much of the first few days of April sorting through conflicting intelligence about the location of Confederate Lt. Gen. James Longstreet. On April 2, Hooker reported to Secretary Stanton that Longstreet was back with Lee's army; on April 4, Maj. Gen. John James Peck in Suffolk informed Hooker that John Hood's and George Pickett's divisions, which had departed Fredericksburg on March 1, were still there and that Longstreet still commanded. On April 7, Peck reported that he had received new information that Longstreet was moving his First Corps troops from the Petersburg area. The specter of Longstreet would hover over Hooker for weeks to come.[5]

Perhaps the most unusual visitor arrived in a most unexpected fashion. "Our whole regiment goes out on picket tomorrow morning. A regiment goes out at a time and a Doctor goes with them," explained Henry Butler of the 16th Maine in an April 5 letter. "A thing happened on picket the other day that was quite funny. A soldier from one of the New York regiments had a baby. I was not on picket at the time, but I heard about it. She tented with one fellow all the time. She was promoted at the battle of Fredericksburg for her bravery. It seems strange that she was not found out. If she had been examined as close as was we in Augusta, they would have told whether she was male or female."[6]

While that was no joke, at least one soldier did make mention of April Fool's Day. Sergeant W. H. Bond noted the holiday with a snicker: "[T]he 2nd Vt. had a good April Fool played on them. There was a First Sergeants call and orders for the men to get up at

---

4   BV 107, part 14, FSNMP. Miles T. Peabody per NPS/CWSSS served in 5th New Hampshire Infantry, from private to corporal. (M549 Roll 9.) Peabody's note also mentioned his strong desire for letters from home: "I begin to think that you all have forgotten me."

5   *OR*, 25, part II, 185-188, 190-192.

6   BV 316, part 8, FSNMP. Butler Letters, 1863, April 5, 1863 letter.

12 o'clock and wash their feet. Some of them did it. I did not let them catch me though."[7]

Others attended to more serious matters. "You speak of your fear of the negroes that are freed coming up north," wrote Lt. James H. Leonard on April 1, revealed how the emancipation issue was affecting the army's Union Democrats. "I think there is but very little danger of that. Southern climate is better suited to them and if they can live there as free people and get paid for their labor they will stay there in preference to going up North. For my part I want to see the whole of them out of the country altogether. The idea is preached by the copperheads up north that we are now fighting to free the slaves, the exact reverse is true. We free the slaves to stop the fighting." Leonard's views likely represented more than half of the army at that point.[8]

Writing on April 3, "L. A. V." was again insightful concerning the 15th New Jersey's situation. "There is no forward movement yet, but the indications are that it will not be long deferred," he predicted. "A grand review came off today . . . a division review. Brig.-Gen. Brooks commands this division, and accordingly directed its manoeuvres." He reported "Gen. Hooker and staff came dashing by, the bands playing 'Hail to the chief' and the officers and men presenting arms. 'Fighting Joe' is a favorite in the army, and of course all were anxious to get a glimpse of his personal appearance." He rated the review "quite imposing, though we, poor victims, had to keep 'heads to the front,' till the exercises complete."

After making a rare reference to marksmanship training, he lamented Stafford's condition.[9] "The country hereabouts begins to present a very barren appearance, the timber being hewn down for miles around and farms (such as they are) laid waste, leaving here and [there?] log huts to vary the vast scene of desolation," he described. "The inhabitants, mostly of the female sex, are ignorant, but make pretensions of loyalty, telling us that their husbands and sons were forced to enlist in the service of the Confederated (so called) States."

"L. A. V." returned to familiar refrains:

---

7   BV 323, part 7, FSNMP, letters of Sergeant W. H. Bond from Camp near White Oak Church, this one dated April 11, 1863.

8   BV 353, part 23, FSNMP, R. G. Plumb, ed., "Letters of a Fifth Wisconsin Volunteer," in *Wisconsin Magazine of History*, Volume 3, September 1919-June 1920, 71-72.

9   L.A.V.: "yesterday [was] distinguished for 'Target Shooting.' Company A made some very good shots—John F. Servia being best, John Butler Jr. second, and Wm L. Higgins third. The inducement for good shots was that, whoever came nearest the mark should be one day off duty."

(Above and below) President Lincoln joined the Army of the Potomac from April 4-10, 1863. During his visit, he met with many officers, circulated freely amongst the men, and reviewed the various army corps. "Gentlemen," he told General Hooker and his senior commanders, "in your next battle put in all your men." *LOC*

The health of the men is improving, and though disease still prowls among us, we hope by the blessing of God to soon attain our former healthy condition and regain strength and power to lend a mighty hand in crushing this wicked, unholy rebellion.—Fight we must to bring peace to our distracted country, and we ask not the interference of slinking cowards at the North.— To cry peace, peace, when there can be no peace, is 'played out,' and it disgusts the patriot soldier to hear resolutions emanating from men high in civil authority, fraught with treason, as shown in surrendering all we ever contended for.[10]

Lincoln's Visit

April 4, 1863, was the day before Easter. That evening, under iron-gray clouds that threatened heavy snowfall, President Lincoln and a party of six boarded a steamer south for the Army of the Potomac. The *Carrie Martin* usually ran dispatches up and down the Potomac, but it had also carried such dignitaries as Ambrose Burnside and Edwin Sumner on their farewell voyages away from the army. Now, it would carry President Lincoln south on the river to Stafford to perform his most important service to the army's resurgence.[11]

Accompanying the president were his wife, Mary; 10 year-old son Tad; Dr. Anson G. Henry; Capt. Medorem Crawford; Attorney General Edward Bates; and reporter Noah Brooks of the *Sacramento Daily Union*. It was Brooks who later credited the First Lady for what would become the trip's masterstroke of genius: Lincoln would stay with the army. Despite her many detractors, Mrs. Lincoln was politically savvy. She knew her husband could mend political fences among the predominantly Union Democrat generals, officers, and soldiers. She also understood his greatest political gifts were wielding "the common touch" and empathizing with soldiers who had suffered so much defeat and despair. She knew the Emancipation Proclamation had caused a serious rift and that Democrats reacted viscerally. The army's Republicans were onboard; however, the deeply idealistic mistrusted Lincoln's late arrival. Lincoln needed wartime coalition unity. Most recently, he had focused on blocking European recognition, implementing conscription, and enacting amnesty for deserters. Now he was free to interact with the soldiers.[12]

Normally, the trip down to Aquia Creek took three hours, but the snowfall fell so hard the boat was forced to put in on the Prince William County shore. Brooks feared

---

10 BV 109, part 8, FSNMP. Published letter in the *Hunterdon Republican* on April 10, 1863. "L.A.V." was in Company A. He was most certainly Lucian or Lucien A. Voorhees, a sergeant in Company A.

11 Jane Conner, *Lincoln in Stafford*, 39-70.

12 Ibid.

their vulnerability to Confederate attack, but he, Lincoln, and Dr. Henry distracted themselves from their worries by telling old tales until well after midnight.

On Easter Day, April 5, they continued onward. At Aquia Landing, they attracted a crowd; after greeting the throng, they headed at 10:00 a.m. by rail toward Falmouth. Seated unceremoniously on rough plank benches in a converted freight car, the group passed snow-covered hills and thousands of crude shelters near Brooke, Potomac Creek, and Stoneman's, before pulling into Falmouth Station an hour later. Dan Butterfield met them with two ambulances—a visitor's favorite as the ambulences had springs—and a 6th Pennsylvania (Rush's Lancers) Cavalry escort. They took the White Oak Road to Hooker's headquarters, passing the recently burned "Phillips House," and "Little Whim" plantation.

Their hour-long journey from Falmouth finally brought them to the army's general headquarters. Unlimbering themselves from their wagons, they took up occupancy in tents near Hooker's. Undoubtedly tired, Lincoln nevertheless received visiting officers while the irrepressible Tad Lincoln explored—and perhaps continued his Washington practice of charging "10 cents admission" for those wishing to speak to the president.[13]

While interactions with officers were important, Lincoln began his really valuable work on the morning of April 6. He started with visits to the wounded and sick in field hospitals. Six soldiers typically occupied a tent. "[T]he large hearted and noble President moved softly between beds, his face shining with sympathy and his voice often low with emotion," marveled Noah Brooks, who called it "a touching scene, and one to be long remembered."

"No wonder that these long lines of weary sufferers, far from home and friends, often shed a tear of sad pleasure as they returned the kind salutation of the President and gazed after him with a new glow upon their faces," Brooks reported.

The Lincolns made numerous such stops during their time with the army. The hospital visits emphasized Lincoln's humanity and humility, and as news about them spread quickly through the army's closed society, Lincoln's standing rose from visit to visit.[14] Mrs. Lincoln benefitted, too, from her hospital visits—"giving little comforts to the sick, without any display or ostentation, like a gentle, kindhearted lady, as she is," observed VI Corps commander John Sedgwick.[15] Lincoln endeared himself to the units and common soldiers throughout his visit. During troop reviews, the soldiers noticed, he

13 Ibid. Hooker's headquarters, per Jane Conner, were above the present-day intersection of Virginia Route 218 (White Oak Road) and Ringgold Road at Jenny Lind and Myers Roads.

14 Ibid.

15 John Sedgwick, letter to his sister, April 12, 1863, *Correspondence to General John Sedgwick*, 89-90.

removed his hat for passing units, and merely tipped the brim to return the salutes of officers.

At noon on the sixth, on "an elevated plain" somewhere in Stafford, Hooker showed off his newest creation, the Army of the Potomac's Cavalry Corps, in a review. The frustrating search for accurate troop strengths limits precise counts, but the corps paraded 13,000-17,000 cavalrymen and mounted artillery. Daniel Peck of the 9th New York Cavalry called it "the largest and most magnificent military display ever gotten up on the American continent." Mrs. Lincoln arrived in a six-horse-carriage; Tad was mounted on a small pony. The pomp and circumstance, impeded by the inevitable mud, was nevertheless impressive. Brooks recalled "a grand sight to look upon this immense body of cavalry, with banners waving, music crashing, and horses prancing, as the vast column came winding like a huge serpent over the hills past the reviewing party."[16]

Cavalrymen noted Lincoln's appearance as "extremely thin and careworn," "looking sick and worn out," etc.—and naturally commented on his awkward equestrian skills. A later description from in Lincoln's visit captured it best: "Mr. Lincoln on horseback is not a model of beauty such as an artist would select. A more awkward specimen of humanity I can not well imagine," wrote John Haley of the 17th Maine. "It shows him off at a horrible disadvantage. There was a fearful disproportion between the length of his legs and the height of the horse. It seemed as if nothing short of tying a knot in them would prevent them from dragging on the ground. Add to this his round shoulders and a hat stuck on the back of his head, and one can visualize how he looked."[17]

Yet, the president's homely appearance and humble character endeared him to the army's soldiers. "We were all covered with mud," said Capt. Fred Winkler of the 26th Wisconsin, who'd accompanied his XI Corps commander, Oliver Otis Howard, to the cavalry review, "but we saw Old Abe and a little son; they rode out to the reviews at the head of a multitude of generals and swarming hosts of staff officers. Father Abraham is notoriously not a handsome man, but there is that in his looks which says that he is not a common man." That evening, the president was serenaded by military bands.[18]

---

16 Ibid. Jane Conner suggests three likely places: Gen. Birney's headquarters at Belle Plain on the 6th, but perhaps meaning his old headquarters at "Bell Air;" or the Sthreshley Farm (present-day Grafton Village. The latter location is derived from Gen. Marsena Patrick's diary memoirs.) Peck quote is from Wittenberg, *Union Cavalry Comes of Age*, 115, which also relates it took 3-4 hours for the entire cavalry corps of 25 regiments to pass in review.

17 John Haley, 17 ME, *The Rebel Yell & the Yankee Hurrah*, 75.

18 BV 286, part 7, FSNMP. Cpt. Frederick C. Winkler, letter, April 8, 1863; Jane Conner, *Lincoln in Stafford*, 48.

On Tuesday, April 7, Lincoln reviewed Meade's V Corps inside their camps. As the president rode by each regiment in formation at the front of its camp, he must have noted their greatly diminished size. Many infantry regiments, which had begun the war at 800 to 1,000 men, were now down to 200 or 300. Even less-bloodied outfits routinely mustered less than 500 men. Battle, sickness, and desertion had taken their toll, and war's cost was plainly evident in thin ranks and nearby grave-markers. Surveying the assembled masses in their new uniforms and shoes amidst the endless sea of tents, however, must have also provided some hope to the president.

Grand reviews and unit parades accompanied by military bands may seem strange, even quaint, by modern standards, but Civil War armies drew directly from Napoleonic models in which pageantry, symbolism and ceremony were interwoven with esprit and the brutal and bloody business of battle. Review parades, as mentioned, were actually practice battles. At best, they provided the men with necessary spirit, pride, and identity to march gallantly into death's jaws. Intricate troop maneuvers with fancy uniforms and flags, accompanied by bands, drums, and fifes, were the stuff of battlefield glory. Napoleon's armies—with elaborate banners, musical accompaniment, and gleaming weapons and accouterments—were the gold standard of nineteenth century warfare and the beau ideal of many Civil War soldiers, especially those of the general and colonel persuasion. In the ranks there was naturally less enthusiasm—although many who served there caught the bug.

Subsequent wars literally blasted this nonsense from battlefields, but in 1863, the panoply of warfare conveyed great significance. Units maneuvered by drill and arrayed for combat. Flags, used for unit orientation, were evocative rallying points. Color guards protected unit banners, the embodiment of the unit's honor, with their blood. Drums and bugles signaled actions to be taken. Men suppressed fears and marched best into abject slaughter to the drumbeat and fife. Until shells and bullets took effect, this all produced needed focus and energy.[19]

"The Artists of the New York papers were on hand, and I suppose the scene and those which followed will be given the cheap immortality of wood engraving after the veracious custom of those irrepressible gentlemen," Noah Brooks mentioned after one of the reviews. "I ought to say, however, that these artists do really sketch from life most of the pictures of the scenes through which the Army of the Potomac passes. Waud of *Harper's Weekly* and Lumley of the *New York Illustrated News* have quarters with the army and accompany it on its marches." Brooks might well have added, absent the ability to print photographs in newspapers, that these artists brought accurate, graphic war

19 CHJHCF. Quotes J. Staudenraus, ed., *Mr. Lincoln's Washington: Selections from the Writings of Noah Brooks, Civil War Correspondent* (New York, NY, 1967), 162, 154. Brooks refers to the presence of artists Alfred R. Waud and Arthur Lumley.

perspectives directly to American drawing-rooms. Edwin Forbes, another prominent artist, also worked in Stafford.[20]

On Wednesday, April 8, Lincoln reviewed over 60,000 men (some estimates reached 80,000) of the II, III, V, and VI Corps on a large, cleared space on the Threshley farm "Grafton." "It was a grand sight to see so many soldiers, all with guns and bayonets gleaming in the air," marveled Edgar Clark of the 3rd Michigan.[21]

The review lasted for five and a half hours. Simply bringing that sized force together took time as the units marched from their widely-dispersed camps. "We had to go about four miles from our camp to the review ground," reported Edgar Clark of the 3rd Michigan. "We was tired when we got back to camp."[22] "D. S. T.," 27th Connecticut Infantry, left an indelible record:

> Brigades, Divisions and Corps could be seen winding their ways through vallies and over hills, all heading for the great table-land opposite Fredericksburg. When it is remembered that the thousands of acres are almost entirely barren of wood, one may imagine the view which can be had from any prominent eminences. For miles—in fact as far as the eye can reach—could be seen the different divisions and corps, their bright bayonets glistening in the sunlight, looking like scales on the backs of huge serpents creeping through the vallies en-route to a convention of anacondas. As if endowed with intricate mechanism, they crawled steadily up the hill and stretched out on the field, formed into columns, brigade after brigade, division after division, and corps after corps, until the great plain seemed one vast mass of living loyalty. Now, one could form a reasonable estimate of the pomp and circumstance of war.[23]

As units arrived, they marched into place behind pre-positioned corps symbols then patiently waited, braving cold winds sweeping the plain. A 21-gun salute signaled the president's arrival. The troops were alerted, but the salute inadvertently scared the mules, who responded with rebellious noises and spurts to the great amusement of all.

The eclectic reviewing party also offered a kind of comic relief: Lincoln; Hooker, generals and staff; Rush's Lancers; Mrs. Lincoln in a carriage; Tad Lincoln and his new pal, 14-year-old boy-bugler Gus Schurmann; and assorted ladies. "D. S. T." recalled the

20 Ibid. Brooks' comment came on April 12.

21 BV 378, part 1, FSNMP. Edgar Clark, letter, April 9, 1863.

22 Ibid.

23 BV 311, part 81, FSNMP for "D.S.T.'s" description of the April 8th multi-corps review. The description was published in the New Haven *Daily Morning Journal* on Wednesday, April 15, 1863. "D.S.T." was probably was David S. Thomas, who mustered into service with the 27th Connecticut Infantry in August of 1862 as a first lieutenant. M535 Roll 16.

civilians there, too. "There were, as usual, the hundreds of spectators galloping about in search of some favorable eminence for sight seeing," he wrote. "In this crowd I noticed one beautiful lady, dashing hither and thither like a beautiful fairy, looking in this desert of soldiery like a small sized oasis on horseback." He also described "the vast army" standing motionless "while down along the ranks swept the President and Commander-in-Chief, and following in their train a gay cortège of military celebrities. Like a meteor, the cavalcade dash past and float to view amid the glistening bayonets."[24]

The corps formed into columns by divisions closed en-masse, and at shoulder arms, marched off to pass in review. "In this manner," D.S.T. said, "we march past the President, officers saluting, colors dipping, drums beating, bugles sounding, and bands playing—the whole constituting a medley of music and excitement, the memory of which will require a lifetime to efface."[25] Led by massed artillery, all the infantry regiments passed in review. The sea of flags, fifes, drums, bands, and blue-clad troops, with brass buttons and accouterments shined and leather polished, overwhelmed every spectator. "Probably one of the finest and grandest reviews ever seen on this continent," one soldier declared.[26]

"It was a beautiful day, and the review was a stirring sight," recalled II Corps commander Darius Couch. "Mr. Lincoln, sitting there with his hat off, head bent, and seemingly meditating, suddenly turned to me and said: 'General Couch, what do you suppose will become of all these men when the war is over?' And it struck me as very pleasant that somebody had an idea that the war would sometime end." [27]

Lincoln had other poingnant moments as he witnessed the cost of liberty, readily apparent in thinned ranks and bullet-torn banners. "The President looked as if he had hard work to do, being careworn and haggard in appearance," one soldier said.[28] John Haley of the 17th Maine claimed to see the president weeping. "Why he wept I know not—whether he was thinking how many had fallen, or how many will soon fall. It might be neither," he said. "But this I do know: under that homely exterior is as tender a heart as ever throbbed, one that is easily moved toward the side of the poor and downtrodden. He is probably aware that a battle cannot long be deferred."[29]

---

24 BV 311, part 81, FSNMP. (M535 Roll 16.)

25 Ibid.

26 Jane Conner, *Lincoln in Stafford*, 39-70.

27 Couch, "The Chancellorsville Campaign," *Battles and Leaders*, vol. 3, 120

28 Jane Conner, *Lincoln in Stafford*, 39-70.

29 John Haley, *The Rebel Yell & the Yankee Hurrah*, 75.

Confederates must have been reminded, as well. "The ground on which the review took place was in easy sight and almost within cannon range of the heights occupied by the enemy beyond the Rappahannock," noted Wesley Brainerd of the 50th New York Engineers. "What must have been their feelings as they witnessed our solid columns wheel and march past the reviewing Officer hour after hour as they did nearly all that day? As the review was drawing to a close they gave us one round of shell from their nearest battery as much as to say, 'Come on, we are ready for you.'"[30]

If that single boom hit home with Lincoln at all, he heard a strong counterpoint shortly thereafter. As his party returned to camp, they encountered a group of freed slaves along the road. "Hurrah for Massa Linkum!" they cheered. With all its imperfections in process, purpose, and personality, the army was at last truly set on a course to set men free.[31]

On April 9, the president and Tad visited the Rappahannock's picket lines without incident, and in the afternoon, Lincoln reviewed I Corps at Belle Plain. The bright, sunny spring day revealed a spectacular vista of Potomac Creek, open fields, and burgeoning trees. Reportedly, 17,000-20,000 men, 10-12 artillery batteries, and at least three brass bands marched. "The President and his body guard rode on their horses. As they rode by us we presented arms," recounted Henry Butler of the 17th Maine. "The old fellow rode with his hat in his hand. He looked as though he had a great deal of trouble on his mind. His wife and Secretary Chase's daughter was with him."[32] As Lincoln passed through lines of carefully staged soldiers, a citizen-soldier in the 14th (Brooklyn) N. Y. S. M. asked "in a familiar, but not insolent manner" to "have the Paymaster sent along"—a humorous exchange that found its way into the New York Times.[33]

The review not only gave Lincoln the opportunity to inspect the troops, it gave them the opportunity to take stock in themselves. "The health and morale of the army is most excellent," a soldier who called himself "Indiana" wrote to the Indianapolis Journal. "The men are in high spirits, and have entirely shaken off every thought and feeling of doubt and discouragement. They feel that God has committed a trust to their keeping. They are determined in God's name to stand fast by their pledged honor, their heroic

30 Wesley Brainerd, 50 NY EN, 194 of manuscript.

31 Jane Conner, Lincoln in Stafford, 59. Noah Brooks is quoted.

32 Ibid.; BV 316, part 8, FSNMP. Butler Letters, 1863, April 13 letter.

33 Alan A. Siegel, For the Glory of the Union: Myth. Reality, and the Media in Civil War New Jersey (Rutherford, Teaneck and Madison, NJ., 1984), 145. The account from the 14th Brooklyn soldier was dated April 10, 1863, published in the New York Times, April 13, 1863. Both accounts provided by John Hennessy.

State, and great and glorious country. They will do this through all hazards, though death and an unmarked and uncoffined grave should be their end and resting place."[34]

"Indiana" was not entirely grim. "McClellan stock is at a discount," he joked. "Hooker is at a high premium—as high as gold on Wall street . . . . [I]t is enough to say that he cares for his army and all its interests. And the army recognizes the directing mind and respect and admire him. He trusts his men and they in return trust him, waiting patiently, cheerfully, for the order to move, believing that 'Fighting Joe' will issue that order at the right time. The discipline and high tone prevailing in this army at this time has never been equaled on this continent."[35]

Friday the tenth saw Lincoln reviewing the XI and XII Corps. This time little Tad led the procession, followed by President and Mrs. Lincoln in a more-comfortable carriage, with Hooker and staff. To see them off on their day's work, an entire III Corps division lined the corduroyed road from Hooker's to Sickles' headquarters and cheered. From there, the party moved on a double-track, corduroyed road—also lined with troops—toward Stafford Court House. Arriving at Brooke, they took Howard's XI Corps salute—a force optimistically reported at 20,000 men. Vice-President Hannibal Hamlin reportedly joined them.

"Each regiment, its flag rippling gracefully as it bent to the wind, advanced in a double line, a quarter of a mile long!" enthused one soldier. "Bands played. Men cheered. The wide cove was black with soldiers. The hard damp earth throbbed with the pounding of their marching feet." General Hooker, mounted on a bay, sat next to the president. "He beamed with satisfaction and pride as our corps marched by," the soldier said. "His blue eyes sparkled with confidence. He held his chin up a little too high to suit me.[36] The parade lasted two and a half hours.

At about 3:00 p.m., Lincoln's group reviewed the 15,000-20,000-man XII Corps somewhere between Stafford Court House and Kane's Landing (off Aquia Creek). "Great preparations had been made. A field was cleared long enough for the whole corps to stand in line and wide enough for us to march in company front. . . ." enthused Rice Bull of the 123rd New York. "The troops were all in new uniforms. It was a spectacle not soon forgotten by those who were there. The music, the marching, the artillery salute, the splendid horsemen, were all very grand."[37]

Lincoln, on horseback, rode by the side of General Hooker. "There was contrast in the appearance of the two men," Bull noted. "Hooker was in full uniform, splendidly

34 "Indiana" letters, *Indianapolis Journal*, April 9, 1863.

35 Ibid.

36 BV 37, FSNMP. William B. Southerton, *Memoirs*, 2-3.

37 Rice Bull, 33.

mounted, and on this occasion at his best. The president was on a small horse and although a good rider presented a singular appearance . . . . He wore a tall stovepipe hat, which he had difficulty in keeping on his head."[38]

Youngsters Tad Lincoln and Gus Schurmann continued to enthrall the troops with their cavorting. There was a new diminutive element in this review: "Commodore" George Washington Nutt, the show-business colleague of "General" Tom Thumb in Barnum's New York establishment, was present. Against Lincoln's six foot, four inch height, Nutt's three foot, four inches must have seemed like a scene from Gulliver's Travels to the more literary observers.

The parades of men put into concrete view something already on the president's mind. One evening, while sitting in camp with Brooks, the President looked cautiously about, saw that they were alone, and in a half-jocular way took out from a pocket a small piece of paper and handed it to [him]," recounts Lincoln biographer Carl Sandburg. "On it were written the figures '216,718—146,000—169,000.' Brooks studied the three numbers. The president explained the first figure represented the sum total of the men on the army's rolls; the second was the actual available force; and the last was the numerical strength to which the force might be increased when the army should move." Problems determining the army's true manpower strength did not exclude the president. Lincoln allowed Brooks to send the numbers to his California paper, as they would not appear in the East for some time and, thus, he could avoid censure for releasing them.[39]

Lincoln also spent time with another important base during his visit: senior officers, who were no less politicized than their men. On the evening of the seventh, Lincoln made a point to visit Sickles' III Corps headquarters at "Boscobel." Lincoln's mood, given his difficult visits with so many sick and wounded, made him reflective and melancholy. Sickles, sensing this darker mood, persuaded a reluctant Princess Agnes Salm-Salm (wife of German Prince Felix, commander of the 8th New York Infantry) to cheer the commander-in-chief with a kiss. The five-foot-tall princess convinced Lincoln to bend over to hear a whispered message and then planted the ceremonial kiss. Apparently the tactic worked, as Lincoln and all present—except Mary Todd Lincoln— were cheerier.[40]

Lincoln also made a point to talk with II Corps commander Darius Couch, Hooker's de facto second in command by virtue of seniority. Lincoln had summoned

38 Ibid.

39 Jane Conner, *Lincoln in Stafford*, 67, 68.

40 Carl Sandburg, *Abraham Lincoln: The War Years*, 2 vols. (New York, NY., 1939), Vol. 2, 85-86.

Couch to Hooker's tent on the morning of April 10 for one final conference before leaving headquarters. "Gentlemen," the president advised, "in your next battle put in all your men." He believed the advice so strongly he repeated it again: "Put in all your men."[41]

Lincoln departed from the army late on April 10 after the reviews of the XI and XII Corps and a supper marked by "very good entertainment, cold meats, etc., "at Howard's XI Corps headquarters. The presidential party entrained at Brooke Station, and departed from Aquia Landing—again aboard the *Carrie Martin*.[42]

Soldiers reflected on the visit. "I for the first time saw the President," wrote Michigander Edgar Clark. "He is a young and better looking man than what I had formed an idea. He had a son, a little boy, who rode on a nice splendid horse by his side."[43] But while many soldiers shared Clark's sense of wonder at seeing the president, his opinion of the president's looks was definitely in the minority. "The honorable gentleman looked thin and careworn," one soldier wrote, expressing a more typical view. "Careworn" was the most common descriptor: "His thoughtful, honest, care-worn face" and "rather care-worn and anxious." "The poor man looked very wan and pale," one soldier empathized. "Abraham looks poorly . . . thin and in bad health . . . he is to all outward appearances much careworn, and anxiety is fast wearing him out, poor man; I could but pity as I looked at him, and remembered the weight of responsibility resting upon his burdened mind."[44]

On April 11, Hooker wrote President Lincoln from "Camp near Falmouth, Va." His letter confirms they had discussed campaign plans in some detail. "After giving the subject my best reflection," he revealed, "I have concluded that I will have more chance of inflicting a heavier blow upon the enemy by turning his position to my right, and, if practicable, to sever his communications with Richmond with my dragoon force and such light batteries as it may be deemed advisable to send with them." Hooker was apprehensive that Lee might "retire from before me the moment I should succeed in crossing the river, and over the shortest line to Richmond, and thus escape being seriously crippled." Hooker's cavalry would have to prevent Lee from such a move, he said. "I hope that when the cavalry have established themselves on the line between him and Richmond, they will be able to hold him and check his retreat until I can fall on his rear, or, if not that, I will compel him to fall back on Culpeper and Gordonsville, over a

---

41 Couch, "The Chancellorsville Campaign," 120. In his account of the meeting, Couch added: "Yet that is exactly what we did not do at Chancellorsville."

42 Jane Conner, *Lincoln in Stafford*, 68-70.

43 Edgar Clark, letter, April 9, 1863.

44 Jane Conner, *Lincoln in Stafford*, 39-70.

longer line than my own, with his supplies cut off." Hooker reckoned his cavalry would cross the "Aquia Railroad" near Hanover Court House after a fight near Culpeper. He announced he'd "given directions for the cavalry to be in readiness to commence the movement on Monday morning next [i.e., April 13th]." This would be complemented by infantry demonstrations along the river.

Hooker's plans seem well-thought-through. Clearly, he planned to use his new cavalry corps as a major maneuver element in the approaching offensive. Equally clearly, he wanted to trap Lee's army on its southward march and in the open. Lincoln probably worried about leaving a western opening to Washington. Perhaps harkening to the president's earlier 1862 experience with the Department of the Rappahannock's guarding Washington during the Peninsular Campaign, he gave his general a second bite at the apple.

Requesting approval for his plan, Hooker then ended his letter. "I sincerely trust that you reached home safely and in good time yesterday," he said. "We all look back to your visit with great satisfaction."[45]

The president, perhaps tired, responded less effusively on the twelfth: "Your letter, by the hand of General Butterfield, is received, and will be conformed to."[46]

*   *   *

Lincoln's time with the army had been immensely significant. It solidified his relationship with the soldiers. This was no doubt verified in thousands of positive homeward-bound letters. By visibly and tangibly contacting virtually every possible soldier, Lincoln forged an impenetrable bond. Those who loved him before loved him still; those on the fence moved in his direction; and those who hated him now hated him less.

Naturally, he did not win over every heart. A certain percentage would never moderate or change their views (the next two significant opportunities for them to change their minds came during the election of 1864 and after his 1865 assassination). "He has reviewed the army; let him review himself," one such detractor, an unidentified soldier, wrote. "Let his aims, his plans, his vacillating policy, his innumerable blunders, pass in review before him. Let him review the past two years."[47]

---

45 *OR*, 25, part II, 199-200.

46 Ibid.

47 Alan A. Siegel, *For the Glory of the Union: Myth. Reality, and the Media in Civil War New Jersey* (Rutherford, Teaneck and Madison, NJ., 1984), 145. Accounts provided by John Hennessy.

Soldier commentaries suggested mainly pro-Lincoln or neutral stances, though. A more sympathetic view was detectable in Lt. George Breck's commentary. "The President is probably one of the plainest appearing men in the country. He looks grave and worn, showing unmistakably the signs of vast care and responsibility that have so heavily borne and now rest upon him," Breck wrote. "We saw him when he passed through Rochester, during that eventful period before his inauguration, and he certainly seems a score of years older to-day than he did then. What a tempest of duties, what a terrible ordeal of labor of mind and body, what a conflict of the most important and difficult matters he has had to pass through since becoming an occupant of the White House." Whatever the President's strengths or faults, Breck concluded, and however he may have discharged the duties of his high office, "we must all admit he has been placed in the most trying and onerous position that ever befell the lot of a President of the United States. History will render an impartial verdict, either for or against him."[48]

Lincoln's visit "iced the cake" of Hooker's and Butterfield's reforms and validated the army's "Valley Forge" resurgence. He blessed the army's rebirth and launched its new course. Like Washington at Valley Forge, Lincoln's political best was revealed. Undeniably, he employed the common touch and meaningfully empathized with the army. His personal leadership blurred concerns over Emancipation's expanding war aims. He eradicated beliefs that the soldiers suffered beyond his cognizance. Combined with his exceptional ability to patiently explain, Abraham Lincoln set political standards for the ages. In the end, the army and Lincoln guarded each other's backs in their dual fighting against Confederates to their front and Copperheads to their rear. They needed each other, and both needed the support of the American people.

"One half ounce of lead with 60 grains of powder . . ."

"There is one thing that I wish could be understood by every wife, father, mother, brother, sister, and friend of soldiers: that they, in connection with the press, are the cause of the greater part of the dissatisfaction and demoralization in the army."

That angry screed came from "Com," a soldier with the 17th Maine. His letter in Lewiston, Maine's *The Daily Evening Journal* on April 6 excoriated Copperheads and accomplices alike. "That may look to you like a wild shot," he continued, but newspapers filled with "fault-finding and discouraging opinions and remarks about our government and our Generals" caused imaginations to soar and people to encourage "their dear ones in the army . . . to get out of the show." Then he went for the jugular:

---

48 Letter from Lt. George Breck, Battery L, 1st New York Artillery, from camp near Waugh Point, Va., April 10, 1863, to *Rochester Union and Advertiser*. Information provided by John Hennessy.

"There are those miserable, traitorous copperheads, crying 'peace, peace, when there is no peace,' and shrieking about this unrighteous war, this abolition war, and thousands of other like phrases." "Com" wanted those "aiding and assisting the rebels" to be thrown into Fort Lafayette prison "or some other like hotel." He pronounced it "every Union-loving person's duty, whether man or woman, to do everything within his power to crush this accursed rebellion, and finish the struggle." He wanted "friends at home" to "write, cheering, hopeful, and encouraging letters, urging us onward to the work of righteous justice. Let us know that their hearts are in the cause." With that, "this army would be an invincible host, that could not be conquered."[49]

A 140th Pennsylvania soldier now spoke for the vast majority of the army and placed things in an even harsher perspective: "If [the Copperheads] were only here to see the feeling the soldiers have for them and their policy of compromise, they would hide themselves. The soldiers are determined to conquer or paint this country with blood and they are the ones who have the hardships and danger to face. The Peace Democrats are not here and nothing but a draft will bring them here. I would be afraid to go into a camp here and talk compromise for I would get rough handled. That is the kind of feeling here and it is increasing every day." He added, "I believe Old Abe is the wisest man living for making that draft and not exempting the Quakers for, if he had, the Democrats would have all got wide brimmed hats and gone to peddling garden seeds."[50]

On April 10, a soldier wrote the Rochester *Democrat and American* registering yet another blow against the antiwar movement and Federal shirkers. More sardonic than most—an achievement—it hit at gut level. "An army sustained by proper home encouragement will never be demoralized," he argued. "Why does the Southerner, with long hair, sunken eyes, and sallow cheeks, still wear his greasy suit of grey, and fight triumphantly successive battles on scant rations and an abundance of rags and privations? Not because of conscription, but because his friends would blush to welcome him while the so-called confederacy was supposed to require his services." He then asked, "Why does the Unionist, warmly clad and abundantly fed, look with brighter anticipations toward the discharge of his troop than to the end of the war? Not so much from a lack of patriotism as because his release will give him the opportunity to again flourish in Blankville, and time to gain the hand of Sally, whose lover was stupid enough to enlist for three instead of two years."[51]

Milo Jones of the 1st Connecticut Heavy Artillery wrote more succinctly on April 13: "Newt Whitcomb and them other boys will see the day that they will repent for all

---

49 CHJHCF. Cites information given in text.

50 BV 112, part 13, FSNMP, letters of an unknown soldier in the 140th Pennsylvania Infantry.

51 CHJHCF. Cites "*Rochester Democrat and American*, April 15, 1863, 'Reynolds Batty'."

their doings. They must remember that [there] are hundreds of thousands in the field fighting to support the government and that some of them will return home after some time or another. We hate Copperheads worse than rebbles and if we ever return home they will not be forgotten by us."[52]

Lieutenant Thomas Connington of the 1st United States Sharpshooters, suggested a "prescription" for Copperhead ills at home: "one half ounce of lead with 60 grains of powder to make it easy to take." Connington's April 19 letter offered another theme common in soldier letters. "[I]t seems to me it must be our turn to win, after a while," he wrote almost plaintively, "for they [Confederates] have had it all their way for some time."[53]

Wilber Fisk of the 2nd Vermont Infantry, a soldier-correspondent whose letters kept Vermonters updated, called those losses to mind for his readers in an April 19 report. The army had been proud and confident during the 1862 Peninsular Campaign and laughed off Virginians' dire predictions of "certain defeat and probable destruction," he wrote. However, reverses brought reconsideration: "From being bold and confident, proudly conscious of our strength and prowess, we were humbled in great measure, and seriously distrusted our ability to cope with the enemy. We respected our enemies more and ourselves less. Demoralization was the certain consequence, desertions frequent."

Fisk fully blamed desertions on the Copperheads' influence: "Preach to [the army] the justice of the rebel course, dwell largely on their grievances, speak of the injustice and corruption of our own Government, and if soldiers will believe you, you have done more to demoralize the army than the enemy could by a thorough victory of their arms." "There are but few men in this regiment that desire peace on any terms short of entire submission on the part of the enemy," Fisk confidently added. "There may be some, there always is in every regiment some who care but little whether the North or South whips so long as they can have a jolly, easy time. A few days' hard marching with short allowances of hard tack and meat, is very apt to convert such soldiers into violent copperheads. But they are not the rule, they are exceptions, and there is hardly enough of them to make a decent exception."[54]

According to Charles S. Woodruff of the 26th New Jersey Infantry, a likely War Democrat, "The army are now in better spirits than they have been before since the war

---

52 CHJHCF. Cites: "April 13, 1863, letter from "near Falmouth" in Milo Jones Correspondence, Local History Room, Northern Illinois University; provided by Benton McAdams."

53 BV 106, part 17, FSNMP. Thomas Connington, per NPS/CWSSS, entered service in Company K (from Michigan), 1st USSS, as a first sergeant and mustered-out as first lieutenant. M1290 Roll 1.

54 CHJHCF. Cites: "Emil and Ruth Rosenblatt, *Hard Marching Every Day: The Civil War Letters of Private Wilber Fisk, 1861-1865* (Lawrence, KS, 1993), 68-69."

commenced, and great hopes are placed in Joe Hooker as a leader. He is idolized by the men. He seems to understand the responsibilities of his position, and he performs his duty in a praiseworthy manner." Woodruff praised the army as "well fed, well clothed, and well drilled, and in every respect qualified to cope with the rebels." They favored the draft and rejected Copperhead defeatism. Woodruff ended, "The army unite in saying that the 'Union must and shall be preserved'; and after making so many sacrifices, nothing will be listened to short of the 'Union as it was and the Constitution as it is'."[55]

Other April Activities

Army business and soldier life did not completely come to a halt just because of the president's April 4-10 visit and its aftermath. On April 6, Henry Ropes of the 20th Massachusetts asked for two baseballs for his company. On the same day, the U. S. Christian Commission in Falmouth reached men's hearts spiritually with daily prayer-meetings and weekly sermons.[56]

On April 7, Lt. Elisha Hunt Rhodes returned to the 2nd Rhode Island's camp and was surprised to find a promotion to captain waiting for him. "While I felt complimented by his kind appreciation of my services I declined the commission, because I did not care to step over the heads of ten First Lieutenants who are my seniors," he explained. The problem was quickly resolved, but it made Rhodes more aware of intra-army politics.

Rhodes had another surprise while on furlough at home. "I was surprised to find so little interest manifested in the war," he admitted. "The people seemed to take it as a matter of course, and hardly asked after the Army. The ladies however seem to be alive to the situation, and I hope their example will spur up the men to do all in their power to aid the armies in crushing the Rebellion." He had uncovered a sad reality: homefront war weariness and apathy were now even more prevalent and dangerous than Copperheadism.[57]

On April 8, the 1st Cavalry Brigade ordered Col. Clendenin of the 8th Illinois Cavalry to send a squadron on a two- to three-day scout to check picket reports of a Rebel cavalry company at Brentsville in Prince William County. Sadly insisting on command by "an energetic officer," the order gratuitously added that "it is about time

55 CHJHCF. Cites: "Alan A. Siegel, *For the Glory of the Union: Myth. Reality, and the Media in Civil War New Jersey*, (Rutherford, Teaneck and Madison, NJ: Fairleigh Dickinson University Press, 1984), 153."

56 Miller, *Harvard's Civil War*, 24.

57 Rhodes, ed., *All For the Union*, 94-96.

Stuart was making another raid." Security concerns over "purveyors" heightened, as well, and Lt. C. D. Mehaffey of the 1st U. S. Infantry, was detailed to Aquia Landing to inspect supplies coming through the Quartermaster's Department. Threats of confiscation; more systemic accountability; and anonymity for officers' packages embodied General Order No. 39, which concluded: "While the army remains in its present position, no passes for sutlers or purveyors to points beyond Aquia Creek will be granted, except by the provost-marshal-general."

On April 10, Hooker's headquarters replied to a request from the U. S. Christian Commission's leader, George H. Stuart, who asked the army to transport his delegates during the upcoming move. Although Hooker appreciated "the benevolent spirit which has brought here the gentlemen of your commission" and their "valuable services," he could not promise transportation or supplies.

Also on that date, high command evaluated intelligence reports that suggested Confederate forces were not greatly diminished. In fact, two of Longstreet's divisions had returned to Lee's army, and the Rapidan fords were being fortified. A spy named G. S. Smith reported that there were no Confederates troops or works along the railroad between Culpeper Courthouse and the capital at Richmond. Culpeper would not be held in strength, but the Rapidan and Fredericksburg line would be. Fortifications were going up in and around Richmond, but without extensive troop build-ups. Bread riots broke out in the Confederate capital. Northern men were arrested as spies. "[R]ebels are seizing all the able-bodied negroes north of the Rappahannock and taking them south," he added.

Also on April 10, Hooker's General Order No. 40 ordered more rapid information processing on deserters, contrabands, and prisoners. "The commanding general regrets that it has become necessary for him to reprimand, in general terms, officers who send incorrect information from the picket lines," he added. Threatening courts-martial to those providing inaccurate information, Hooker next railed against marcher straggling and threatened drum-head courts-martial for miscreants and relief for their officers. Lastly, he warned corps and division commanders and assistant inspectors-general against poor march discipline.[58]

Finally on that day, in the wake of Lincoln's departure, Hooker fired off a letter to the Army's Adjutant General, Brig. Gen. Lorenzo Thomas, that continued his ongoing feud with Halleck. The corps commanders had all submitted staff appointments, which Hooker was unable to consider "until the corps commanders themselves have been regularly designated by the President," Hooker explained. He respectfully requested

---

58 *OR*, 25, part II, 196-198. Smith, on loan to the army from Assistant Secretary of the War P. H. Watson, filed his report with cavalry general Alfred Pleasanton, who filed a report back to Watson.

"that the President will be pleased to confirm the . . . selections with as little delay as practicable." This was a bureaucratic masterstroke against Halleck, who had pointedly informed Hooker only the president could appoint corps commanders. Hooker's action rubbed Halleck's nose in the fact that it hadn't been accomplished. Hooker's timing could not have been more perfect, capitalizing as it did on Lincoln's recent visit. On April 15, War Department General Order No. 96 confirmed the names and grades of Hooker's corps commanders.[59]

On April 11, a Lincoln initiative, the Aeronautics Corps, lost more air. Captain Cyrus Comstock, the army's assistant chief engineer staff officer and the balloon corps' supervisor, informed Thaddeus Lowe he was going to regulate, reorganize, and revitalize the aeronauts in his own way—by firing Lowe's father and cutting pay. In true intelligence fashion, Lowe by-passed Comstock and ran to Butterfield, only to be trapped by a phalanx of adjutants-general. Rebuffed, Lowe was told to complain through Comstock, effectively dead-lining his rebuttal. The balloonists would not see effective use again. Hope did appeared briefly on April 22, though, when Lowe reported: "I examined the enemy's position more closely this p.m., between 4 and 6 o'clock, than I have had an opportunity for a number of days past." He estimated supports to Confederate batteries at about 10,000 men; a dense troop concentration at Hamilton's Station; and about 25,000 troops encamped. Lowe also concluded the enemy was reinforcing from Bowling Green. He may have misinformed Sedgwick by over-estimating the Confederate forces facing his forces. Ironically, the emerging campaign showed this intelligence source's first real viability.[60]

On April 14, while occupying the Pollock farm, Lt. Elisha Hunt Rhodes made note of more idiosyncrasies of "a great civil war." The Pollock family hosted a wounded, paroled Rebel cavalryman who, because he had lost his leg, attracted little Federal attention. Yank-Reb picket interactions on the Rappahannock also bothered him. Within view of 50 Confederates, he stopped a Rebel attempt to sail a crude boat across for New York newspapers or coffee. Amid verbal threats, he broke the boat to pieces. Rhodes next spotted a party of Confederate officers and ladies on far shore with none other than Lt. Gen. Thomas J. "Stonewall" Jackson leading the promenade. The Federals raised their hats in salute and the Southern ladies waved their handkerchiefs.[61]

---

59 *OR*, 25, part II, 194-195, 211-212.

60 Evans, *War of the Aeronauts*, 272-279. After additional observations during Chancellorsville-Second Fredericksburg, a disheartened Lowe resigned and moved to Washington. Comstock was promoted to captain on March 3, 1863.

61 Rhodes, ed., *All For the Union*, 94-96.

On April 19, Abel G. Peck of the 24th Michigan Infantry took pause from all the army hubbub around him and noted—with many others—that peach trees were blossoming in reputedly treeless Stafford. Discovering some local prehistory, he sent home several fossil sharks' teeth found along Potomac Creek to budding paleontologists on the home front.[62]

A Political Postscript

It didn't take long for Congress to provide a counterbalance to the positive energy created by Lincoln's visit. Whether timed intentionally or not, the Joint Congressional Committee on the Conduct of the War issued its first report on April 6. Volume one focused on the Army of the Potomac. The report opened with a lengthy section that pointedly outlined successes in other theaters of the war and "errors and reverses" in the Eastern Theater: "Had the success of the army of the Potomac during this period corresponded with the success of our arms in other parts of the country, there is reason to believe that the termination of the campaign of 1862 would have seen the rebellion well-nigh, if not entirely, overthrown." The report contained language that still attempted to sound dutifully patriotic.[63]

That didn't stop the Joint Committee from picking the Army of the Potomac's scabs and rubbing salt in the wounds. "Some of our points of attack have been so clearly indicated to the enemy beforehand," the committee criticized, "and our movements made with so much delay and hesitation, that he has been able to not only fortify his positions and concentrate his forces, but even to call into the field new armies to meet us. At such points we have failed." While such language might have referred to any number of engagements, soldiers sitting on the north banks of the Rappahannock, looking across at Marye's Heights, could not have helped but make direct comparisons to Fredericksburg's December battle.

But that army no longer existed except in-name. The "Valley Forge" winter had cauterized those wounds and transformed the Army of the Potomac into something far stronger. The men themselves certainly knew it and, despite the finger-pointing, the Joint Committee even recognized it. The committee's overly jingoistic tone and tendency to whistle past the graveyard made its sincerity difficult to discern: "The indications now clearly are that, both in the east and the west, the campaign of 1863 will give us brilliant achievements—decisive victories. Our generals in the field have the full

---

62 BV 212, part 4, FSNMP, letters of Abel G. Peck, 24th Michigan Infantry.

63 Volume 2 focused on "the [1861] disasters" at First Bull Run and Ball's Bluff, and Volume 3 on events in the Western Theater; Report of the Joint Committee on the Conduct of the War (Vol. I). http://archive.org/details/reportjointconduct01goverich (accessed June 12, 2014).

confidence of their soldiers and the people . . . . Never before did the world see such an army in the field; never before did generals lead such men to battle."[64]

"Everybody is reading the first report of the Congressional Committee on the Conduct of the War," said War Democrat Col. Charles Wainwright on April 12. "It is quite voluminous, and comes down to the close of last year. I am trying to get through it, but its unfairness, partiality, and in very many cases absolute falseness make me so nervous that I can make but little progress." This he blamed on the "radical party, who have complete control over the Cabinet and do pretty much what they please with our weak President." He complained of a War Department order dismissing "a volunteer lieutenant for . . . treasonable sentiments expressed in a private letter to his uncle in China!" Typical of the views of serving Democrats, Wainwright supported Union preservation while continuing to criticize the Administration and Emancipation.[65]

Congress, like the army, needed to achieve some level of team-work. Continuous political skirmishing among the War Democrats and Republicans of all stripes only aided the Copperheads and drove down soldier morale. Meddling was only legitimate if Congress accepted some measure of responsibility for its own failures—which it didn't seem to do. At least as far as the Joint Committee was concerned, though, the war of words was entirely within its purview, and "[a]s evidence of that," doubters could "refer to the large mass of testimony taken by them upon many subjects and herewith reported."[66]

The Finest Army?

Attorney General Edward Bates, returning from his trip with President Lincoln to the Army of the Potomac, was impressed by what he saw. "[Hooker] has renewed it, in courage, strength, spirit, confidence," he wrote to a former colleague. "He told me with emphasis that he had as many men as he wanted, & good men. . . . [S]eeing what Hooker has done in the rehabilitation of that army, I do not doubt that he will use it as effectively as he has reformed & inspired it."[67]

Hooker had no doubts, either, feeling so ebullient that he reportedly boasted that he and his army could "drive the Rebels to Hell or anywhere else." "The administration's plan doesn't involve so extensive a campaign," one observer wryly

64 Ibid.

65 Allan Nevins, ed., *A Diary of Battle: The Personal Journals of Colonel Charles S. Wainwright, 1861-1865* (Gettysburg, PA, 1996), 179.

66 Joint Committee report, 11.

67 BV 268, FSNMP. Edward Bates to James Eads, letter, April 1863.

noted, "only that we go as far as Richmond."[68] II Corps division commander Winfield Scott Hancock overheard Hooker make a similar boast to the commander-in-chief. "He . . . told Mr. Lincoln that he would either win a victory or be in hell," Hancock recalled. "The President told him to 'carry plenty of water along.'"[69]

"One of [Hooker's] most frequent expressions when talking with Lincoln was 'When I get to Richmond,' or 'After we have taken Richmond,'" remarked reporter Noah Brooks. At one point, the president asked whether Hooker meant "If." "Excuse me, Mr. President, but there is no 'if' in the case," Hooker corrected. "I am going straight to Richmond if I live." Later, the president confided to Brooks. "That is the most depressing thing about Hooker," Lincoln sighed. "It seems to me that he is overconfident."[70]

Perhaps he was. But, if Hooker didn't believe, who would? Amid many improvements, Hooker's behavior remained alarmingly the same. His earlier remarks to a party of officers on March 29 that "I have the finest army on the planet" revealed his continued pride and his ongoing arrogance. "My plans are perfect," he boasted, "and when I start to carry them out, may God have mercy on General Lee, for I will have none."[71]

---

68 Ibid, 71.

69 Almira R. Hancock, *Reminiscences of Winfield Scott Hancock, by his Wife* (New York: Charles Webster & Company, 1887), 94-5.

70 Noah Brooks, *Washington in Lincoln's Time*, 51-2; quoted in John Bigelow, *The Campaign of Chancellorsville: A Strategic and Tactical Study* (New Haven: Yale University Press, 1910), 130; Hebert, *Fighting Joe Hooker*, 182-3.

71 Bigelow, *The Campaign of Chancellorsville*, 108.

Chapter Nine |

The False Start

No sooner had President Lincoln left the Army of the Potomac than "Fighting Joe" Hooker turned his full attention to the Army of Northern Virginia. It was time to begin the spring offensive.

Hooker intended to kick off the campaign with a deep-envelopment cavalry raid from the Rappahannock River to Culpeper and then into Lee's rear area. The maneuver was designed to cut Confederate communications, supply lines, and routes of withdrawal. On April 11, 1863, Hooker ordered the army's Cavalry Corps to readiness for an April 13 move at daylight. "Let your watchword be fight," he impressed upon cavalry corps commander George Stoneman, "and let all your orders be fight, fight, fight, bearing in mind that time is as valuable to the general as the rebel carcasses."[1]

Hooker's faith was curious: the cavalry corps was still a classic one-trick pony and Stoneman's leadership —especially at Hartwood Church in February and on the perimeter—had thus far proven inadequate. And Hooker was deploying his new creation in an experimental and untested maneuver in a major offensive. Nevertheless, on April 12, Hooker's headquarters ordered Stoneman's entire force—with the exception of one brigade under Pleasonton, to be kept for use with the infantry— to march at 7 a.m. on the thirteenth "for the purpose of turning the enemy's position on his left, and of throwing your command between him and Richmond, and isolating him from his supplies, checking his retreat, and inflicting on him every possible injury."[2] Hooker's objectives—capture the R.F.&P. railroad and sever Lee's communications with Richmond—were clearly stated.

Hooker suggested multiple march routes to ensure security, and he recommended that small advance guards move well forward to clear away Confederate cavalry. He also

1   *OR*, 25, part I, 1066-1067.

2   Ibid.

Brigadier General George Stoneman actively supported the centralized use of cavalry for the Army of the Potomac —something the Confederates had long understood and had already used effectively. Union commanders had yet to grasp its full potential. Hooker, however, changed this by envisioning a much bolder use of his mounted wing, with General Stoneman at its head. *LOC*

suggested using a disinformation campaign by claiming that the Union cavalry was riding off to chase down "Jones' guerrillas" near Winchester in the Shenandoah Valley. Accompanying intelligence placed Fitz Lee's Brigade at Culpeper and "a small provost-guard of infantry" at Gordonsville.[3]

The Cavalry Corps' plan was simple enough. At around midnight on April 13/14, three squadrons of Davis' brigade would cross the North Fork of the Rappahannock southwest of Warrenton at White Sulphur Springs. They would follow the south bank, clearing any enemy to Freeman's Ford, then they would contact Davis, who would cross his brigade and open Beverly Ford for Averell's and Gregg's divisions. Buford would cross simultaneously with Averell at Rappahannock Station Bridge.

Once organized on the far shore, Averell would lead to Culpeper Court House on the right of the Orange and Alexandria Railroad line. Gregg would follow Averell. Buford would move ahead on Averell's left. If the enemy was contacted at Culpeper, Gregg was to move to Averell's right. This would secure their rear; then, per Hooker's plan, the command would march east to sever Lee's withdrawal route and lines to Richmond.

In preparation to support Stoneman's move, Hooker sent orders through V Corps for the infantry picket line commander to march his brigade on the morning of April 13 with five-days' rations to secure Banks's, U. S., and Kelly's Fords, thus protecting the cavalry's movement westward. The infantry was to prevent enemy crossings and communications, as well as cooperate with arriving cavalry. That brigade was also to protect returning cavalry wagons.

3   Ibid.

It was "show-time" for Hooker's new cavalry corps. "It devolves upon you, General, to take the initiative in the forward movement of this grand army," Hooker lectured, "and on you and your noble command must depend in a great measure the extent and brilliancy of our success. Bear in mind that celerity, audacity, and resolution are everything in war."

Actions by Stoneman's 9,000-plus cavalrymen had become an intentional campaign lynch-pin. Hooker was foregoing traditional cavalry roles and was making the corps a part of his maneuver plan. The question remained, though, whether the instrument was ready.

Bridges and Bayonets: Campaign Preparations

Impending campaigning did not preclude another petty Hooker-Halleck incident. On April 13, 1863 at 9:20 p.m., Hooker asked Halleck for a cavalry regiment from the Washington Defenses to patrol the now-abandoned Occoquan-Dumfries road and assure unimpeded telegraphic communications with Washington. Halleck's immediate response was predictably inept and snotty: "I do not think that the safety of Washington depends upon the maintenance of communication with your army, but I think it is your duty to maintain your communication with Washington." He then ordered Hooker to do so.

Unclear was whether Halleck actually knew or understood Hooker's plans. Either way, Halleck's response reflected poorly on him, concerned more with his own fiefdom than with facilitating the upcoming campaign. Hooker had no time to fool with him. On April 14 at 7:50 p.m., Secretary Stanton received copies of this exchange from Hooker requesting they "be laid before the President of the United States without delay." Whatever behind-the-scenes conversations took place from there, at 11 p.m., Halleck informed Hooker that a cavalry regiment was being dispatched by Gen. Heintzelman to scout from Occoquan to Dumfries. Hooker's assistant adjutant general (AAG), Seth Williams, notified Pleasonton, thus relieving him of that duty in order to participate in the plan's general maneuver. [4]

The exchange capped a day highlighted by other communication missteps. Given the army's November Fredericksburg pontoon disaster, the specific missteps seem incredible. That morning, Hooker sent two conflicting communications to Gen. Benham, the new engineer commander. The first said Hooker required only two pontoon trains to march with the army. Asserting it would "be a useless expenditure of the public means to have all the trains provided with teams with nothing to do," the

---

4 *OR*, 25, part II, 204-205, 209, 210, 213.

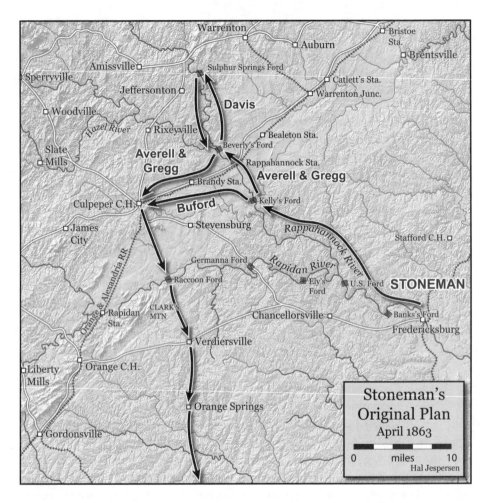

quartermaster would provide necessary animals when needed. The engineer commander was to keep his trains and men in good order and let army headquarters know if he was short men; if so, they would be detailed. That same day, Hooker's AAG wrote, "The commanding general directs me to say you will hold all your trains and entire command in readiness for a move in any direction on short notice." All of this certainly suggests that, although Hooker's general plans were sophisticated, little of his advanced planning was focused on the engineers. "I did not know any of his plans until I saw them being carried into operation," Maj. Gen. Gouverneur K. Warren later attested.[5]

---

5   Warren testimony, *Report of Joint Committee*, I (1863), 43.

Stoneman's Original Plan (April 1863). Stoneman's troopers would ride west of the Army of the Potomac to cross the Rappahannock at three points. Leaving Brig. Gen. John Buford's men at Kelly's Ford, the rest of the column would ride onward to Beverly's Ford, where another portion of the column would stop. Col. Benjamin Davis's men would then ride all the way to Sulphur Springs Ford and cross the river there. On the far side of the river, the troopers would retrace their direction south, clearing Beverly's Ford so Brig. Gen. William Averell and Brig. Gen. David McM. Gregg's men could cross. Buford, meanwhile, would cross back at Kelly's. The four elements would then converge on Culpepper Court House and stab southward into the Confederate rear. Historian Kristopher White assisted with the preparation of this map.

Nor did Hooker discuss options with his subordinates, no doubt due to his fixation on secrecy. His propensity to play things close to the vest applied even to his corps commanders (as will be seen).[6]

Hooker's army had given considerable thought to the important issues of what soldiers could carry: weapon, ammunition, clothing and equipment, and rations. A soldier writing to a Newark newspaper at April's end listed infantrymen's burdens: a packed knapsack (25 pounds); a haversack with eight days' rations (7 pounds); rifle and equipments (13 pounds); a filled canteen (4 pounds); and a filled cartridge box with 40 rounds (7 pounds). The total was 56 pounds—nearly 40 percent of the body weight of an average (143.5 pound) Union soldier. Despite proper motives and methodologies, this load was too great. The eternal question was how much equipment, food, and ammunition the men could carry and fight with?[7]

On March 9, a board of infantry officers had been convened to study reducing individual soldier loads to mission-essential items, eliminating excessive baggage trains, and keeping ammunition and other critical supplies as close as possible to the maneuvering units. Various combinations of soldier loads were considered and tested. Those investigations were summarized in an April 13 circular:

> The major-general commanding directs that your command have packed in their knapsacks by to-morrow (Tuesday) night five days' rations of hard bread, coffee, sugar and salt. That you have in readiness, so that it may be issued and cooked at short notice, three days' rations of pork or bacon, with hard bread, coffee, and sugar to be placed in the haversacks. That

6   OR, 25, part II, 202-203.

7   BV 193, part 2, FSNMP, newspaper articles from soldiers' letters. This letter was written from White Oak Church on April 28, 1863, and published in the Newark *Daily Advertiser* in its May 5, 1863, edition. As to leaving haversacks and knapsacks behind, see for example, BV 193, part 43, letter from the 43rd New York Infantry to the Albany *Evening Journal*, May 15, 1863. The reported action resulted in a lack of food for two days thereafter.

your command have drawn before Wednesday morning, and ready for the movement, five days' fresh beef on the hoof, making complete eight days' rations to be carried with the troops. That each officer, by use of his servant, and his haversack, provide himself with eight days' rations.[8]

Soldiers were ordered to each carry 60 rounds of ammunition and be equipped with a total of 150 rounds, with the balance carried in the pack train. Food and ammunition in these amounts simply added too much weight to the soldiers. "The supply trains will be in readiness for such movements as may be ordered," the circular forewarned. "Each teamster must have with him the forage for his own team." The same was true for artillery batteries, which had to carry "eight days' subsistence for the troops and their full capacity of forage, at least six days' grain, as much as possible on the guns."[9]

The general hospital for those unable to move was to be designated by the medical director, and the quartermaster's department was to supervise storage of "surplus clothing for the troops, beyond the extra shirt, pair of socks and drawers." Corps commanders were to require every serviceable man to march with the column, the order concluded.

Limited by available equipment, this sequence spoke well of military leadership, if not common sense. Persistent resupply problems had led to a reexamination of practices in an attempt to find the best possible solutions. Universal repetition of the base order in the records suggests army-wide compliance.

Stoneman's Raid Unravels

"This morning I can see nothing from the storm," wrote Joe Hooker on April 14 in a dispatch to Lincoln. "I am rejoiced that Stoneman had two good days to go up the river, and was enabled to cross it before it became too much swollen."[10]

In fact, to the best of the army commander's knowledge, everything upriver was going well for Stoneman. The Cavalry Corps set off at its appointed hour on April 13, and on April 14, Stoneman had sent word back to army headquarters that he would cross at three points above Rappahannock Station before daylight on the fifteenth. Per Hooker's orders, Stoneman was to issue supplies and send back his wagon trains prior to the crossing.[11]

---

8 *OR*, 25, part II, 203-204.

9 This circular was modified on April 14 to change the required 150 rounds to 140.

10 *OR*, 25, part II, 203-204, 213.

11 Ibid.

In passing this news on to Lincoln, Hooker added that he anticipated Stoneman would strike the R.F.& P. railroad between Lee's army and Richmond on the second day. In anticipation, Hooker planned to demonstrate opposite Fredericksburg and, if Lee's forces pulled back, cross and "pursue with all the vigor practicable." As of the night of April 14, Hooker believed the enemy had not reckoned his plans.[12]

But poor weather had settled over Stoneman's corps, triggering a series of foggy communications. Colonel Adolphus Buschbeck, commanding the XI Corps infantry brigade detailed at Kelly's Ford, informed his corps commander at 8 a.m. on April 15 that Stoneman had requested a demonstration at "early dawn." Stoneman had also wanted him to bring in a regiment from Rappahannock Station after the cavalry had crossed there and then demonstrate in such as a way as to make the enemy to believe Buschbeck was crossing at Kelly's. However, Stoneman's orderly carrying the message had lost his way, delaying the message. Buschbeck sent his adjutant to Stoneman's headquarters, then at Bealeton, requesting new instructions.

Next came heavy rain, and with that came the infernal mud. Stoneman's morning dispatches suggested that his artillery had bogged down. Hooker responded by saying that, if the artillery couldn't be managed, it should be sent back. Stoneman was also informed that, based on the cavalryman's input, Hooker had already reported a successful crossing to the president. "This army is now awaiting your movement," Hooker pointedly added.

Stoneman's movements that day, however, had done nothing but perplex Hooker. "[T]he commanding general desires me to call your attention to your letter of instructions," Butterfield pointed out in response to messages from Stoneman. "The tenor of your dispatches might indicate that you were maneuvering your whole force against the command of Fitz Lee, numbering not over 2,000 men. The commanding general does not expect, nor do your instructions indicate, that you are to act from any base or depot."

By 8:00 p.m. that night, April 15, Hooker was obviously disheartened. "Just heard from Stoneman," the army commander wrote to Lincoln. "His artillery has been brought to a halt by the mud, one division only having crossed the river. If practicable, he will proceed without it. All the streams are swimming."[13]

The presidential response, at 10:15 p.m., certainly was unnerving. "An hour ago I received your letter of this morning, and a few minutes later your dispatch of this evening," Lincoln wrote. "The latter gives me considerable uneasiness." Lincoln continued:

12 Ibid.

13 OR, 25, part II, 212-213, 214.

The rain and mud, of course, were to be calculated upon. General S. is not moving rapidly enough to make the expedition come to anything. He has now been out three days, two of which were unusually fair weather, and all three without hindrance from the enemy, and yet he is not 25 miles from where he started. To reach his point he still has 60 to go, another river (the Rapidan) to cross, and will be hindered by the enemy. By arithmetic, how many days will it take him to do it? I do not know that any better can be done, but I greatly fear it is another failure already.

A troubled President Lincoln closed his reply with a very simple request: "Write me often."[14]

Matters did not readily improve. Buschbeck's infantry brigade at Kelly's Ford suffered from Stoneman's delays. On the fifteenth, Buschbeck wrote to Howard that the early miscues had been fixed and that he had firm instructions to guard the river crossings and protect the wagon train at Morrisville once released by Stoneman. Unfortunately, dual command chains for cavalry-infantry operations now raised their ugly heads. Stoneman's weather delays exceeded the duration of planned cooperation, and Buschbeck was nearly out of provisions. "If we should remain here longer than to-morrow, I shall endeavor to draw rations and forage from the train at Morrisville," Buschbeck said. "Should I not succeed, I shall forage on the country." By doing so, though, he would be drawing rations earmarked for the extended cavalry raid.[15]

Word of Buschbeck's foraging worked its way up to army headquarters, which turned the situation on its ear. Hooker's staff messaged Howard on April 18 that they had been "unofficially informed that the brigade of your command [Buschbeck's] at Kelly's Ford has drawn supplies from General Stoneman. If true, this would interfere very seriously with the operation pending." The missive reminded Howard that he'd been told to resupply this force from his own resources, and as punishment—a pure Hookerism—Howard was instructed to replace Stoneman's provisions.[16]

Meanwhile, information about Stoneman's abortive operations continued to trickle in. On April 16, the cavalry commander wrote to Hooker from "Camp near Rappahannock Railroad Bridge, Va." His explanation was painful. Completely unable to move on the muddy roads and swim the raging river—one officer and two enlisted men had already been swept off—he worried the equally swollen Rapidan still lay ahead (and the swollen Rappahannock would, at that point, be behind him). He said the weather was "one of the most violent rain-storms I have ever been caught in."

14 Ibid.

15 Ibid, 215.

16 Ibid., 227-229.

Stoneman also answered Butterfield's earlier inquiries: he had not attacked Culpeper and Fitz Lee's command, noting that the enemy at Culpeper Court House had known about Federal movements by the morning of the fourteenth. Nor had he, as alleged, established a base to operate from. Least reassuring was Stoneman's strange, near-bizarre summary: "No command ever had higher hopes, or was more confident of success, though ignorant of what it was expected to perform; but the elements seem to have conspired to prevent the accomplishment of a brilliant cavalry operation."

On the morning of April 17, Hooker passed the bad news to Lincoln. He enclosed Stoneman's report, adding "His failure to accomplish speedily the object of his expedition is a source of deep regret to me, but I can find nothing in his conduct of it requiring my animadversion or censure. We cannot control the elements." Hooker, atypically backing up his subordinate, added he had ordered Stoneman to remain in place awaiting opportunity to move forward and that Stoneman had a week's provisions. "No one, Mr. President, can be more anxious than myself to relieve your cares and anxieties," Hooker wrote, "and you may be assured that I shall spare no labor and suffer no opportunity to pass unimproved for so doing. I have no reason to suppose that the enemy have any knowledge of the design of General Stoneman's movement."

Hooker didn't need to be relieving Lincoln's fears; he needed to be relieving his cavalry commander and rethinking and adjusting his plans. Stoneman had failed consistently since Hartwood Church, now two months distant. It had made no real sense to bank on his unproven ability to pull off such a complex and, for the Federals, unprecedented operation. Far too much was riding (pun intended) on this faltering cavalry operation.[17]

Hooker and Butterfield tried to keep the game going. They informed Stoneman at 1:30 p.m. on the seventeenth to keep up six days' provisions after he crossed the Rappahannock. As he had already been out four days and the army headquarters had received no logistical reports, they preemptively sent out a wagon train on the morning of the eighteenth with five days' provisions of hard bread, salt, sugar, and coffee, and one day's pork and four days' beef for 9,500 men, as well as five days' forage for their animals.

An accompanying message from Gen. Haupt informed Stoneman that the Bull Run Bridge had been destroyed by rain and high water and, thus, resupply via the Orange and Alexandria line was infeasible. Another message from army headquarters to Stoneman that day stated 300 wagonloads of grain (1,500 pound wagon loads) and 50,000 rations were headed his way. Confusion ensued whether Stoneman intended to take wagons on the expedition, contrary to Hooker's directions prescribing pack mules. Hooker also

17 Ibid., 220-223.

expressed worry about the artillery, which he believed would only cause problems for Stoneman because of the poor travel conditions.

Stoneman, meanwhile, continued to flail about. Exasperatingly, he ordered Gregg's cavalry division to send a squadron or more from the 1st Maryland Cavalry on a scout toward Warrenton—in the opposite direction he was supposed to be focused and moving—in response to "bushwhackers."

On April 18, Hooker's AAG tried to jump-start the action again with an 8 a.m. letter that gave the Cavalry Corps commander specific instructions to be ready to move quickly. Stoneman was to have six days' supplies and not to issue anything to another command. However, numbers again caused problems. "It was intended to forward you to-day five days' additional rations and forage," Williams related, "but if, as reported by your quartermaster, you have 12,000 men and 17,000 animals, it will fall short of that estimate." After questioning the accuracy of that number on Hooker's behalf, Williams added, "We must have positive and exact information on this subject."

Stoneman planned to take wagons and artillery—both contrary to Hooker's orders—and this rightly perplexed army headquarters. He was informed that no major shift of enemy forces toward the cavalry had been detected. Hooker now suggested Stoneman feed his command from alleged enemy stores and by-pass Culpeper or Gordonsville completely. If the enemy reinforced on the Rappahannock, Stoneman should engage them there. Additional intelligence sent on April 19 informed Stoneman the enemy force opposing him was "two small brigades of cavalry, numbering between 4,000 and 5,000 sabers"—almost certainly an overblown number—and they were "wretchedly mounted." That must have further confused Stoneman: could he allow a force of such size opportunity to harass his flanks and rear on an extended march?[18]

From top to bottom, it must have all felt like wheel-spinning—from Hooker and his staff, to Stoneman and his officers, to the cavalrymen themselves, their horses literally biting at their bits, starting and stalling, awaiting their opportunity to sally forth with firm purpose. "Time rolls away and is gathered among the shades of the past," one of the horsemen mused expansively; "men died, nations rise, flourish, and hasten to their decline, and yet no matter what has been preceding history, mankind never evinces so much surprise as at the nature of present passing events."[19]

Signed "Hoplite," the lyrical letter was penned by one of Stoneman's horse artillerymen, George Perkins of the 6th New York Independent Battery, from Camp Bramhall near Aquia Landing. Written April 19, it appeared in the April 25 edition of the

---

18 Ibid., 223, 227-229.

19 Richard N. Griffin, ed., *Three Years a Soldier: The Diary and Newspaper Correspondence of Private George Perkins, Sixth New York Independent Battery, 1861-1864* (Knoxville, TN, 2006).

Middlesex Journal. "No subject so convulses and occupies the general mind now as the progress of the great rebellion," Perkins wrote. He continued:

> At this point in our nation's history, while the din of battle is in our ears, and the groan of the wounded patriot assails us from the hospitals in our midst, while we see the battlefield and its concomitant horrors, while bereaved parents, silent, mourn their offspring, and broken-hearted wives mourn the wreck of their young happiness; while we experience at our very hearthstones all the dire evils of civil war, our attention is directed only to them.

Perkins brought his literary flair back to ground by closing out his letter with a progress report:

> "[O]ur [cavalry] forces are stretched along the river from Kelley's Ford to Rappahannock station, now and then shelling the rebs as they show themselves on the other side. Within a week something will probably be done. The infantry are in readiness to move with eight days' rations, 'Fighting Joe' evidently intends to push things through."[20]

Stoneman's Raid, Take Two

Stoneman's corps finally began to move on April 20. Colonel Buschbeck sardonically related, "[I]t appears that the cavalry are to leave this neighborhood." Buschbeck readied his position at Kelly's as Stoneman ordered his subordinates to action. He also ordered the commanding officer at Kelly's Ford to send 200 infantrymen to guard the railroad bridge and Beverly Ford.[21]

"This command will move at once," Stoneman announced. "Each commander will endeavor to mask his movements from the enemy as much as possible, both in advancing and encamping." Davis was to move to near the mouth of Carter's Run (Waterloo Bridge) and push patrols in the direction of the mountains and to his rear. Averell was to move to the vicinity of Sulphur Springs and connect with and picket up to Davis. Gregg would follow Averell, take a position on Averell's left, and picket down to Lawson's Ford near Foxville. Buford was to move to Lawson's Ford directly, relieving the pickets along the river as he advanced. When subordinates reached their assigned points, they were to send a staff officer to headquarters on the road from Sulphur Springs to Warrenton for further instructions.[22]

---

20 Ibid.

21 *OR*, 25, part II, 229-230.

22 Ibid.

"Everything not taken along, as per circular of yesterday, will be sent to the rear," Stoneman ordered. "The commanding general expects to be kept thoroughly informed in regard to everything that transpires by frequent messengers or dispatches."[23]

Hooker seemed hopeful. "General Stoneman seems to be warming up to his position," he wrote that day to Stanton.[24] Even Northern newspapers got in on the act as they began to excessively laud Stoneman's operations. Yet all this came even as Stoneman—against Hooker's hopes and the newspaper's plaudits—began dispersing his forces steadily to the west and northwest along the Rappahannock. It looked more like a defense of Warrenton than a raid toward Richmond.

Contemporary soldier letters held that Stoneman was successfully raiding. A typical (if more perceptive) letter was from Chaplain John R. Adams. "General Hooker, when he starts out, will make driving work somewhere.," he wrote. "The cavalry have already gone in force, and I fear the present storm will impede some of their plans. If the rain swells the streams so that they cannot advance, it is very certain that the enemy cannot follow them, for the same reason." Adams added: "Do not think that I am disheartened. I am not. I never felt more hopeful for the Army of the Potomac than at present. It is in good condition of health, of discipline, and of spirits. Give a chance, and something will be done; I have no doubt of it."[25]

Adams' forecast proved prescient. On the night of April 21, Hooker reported to the president: "Advices from Major-General Stoneman of today inform me that he has not been able to effect a passage of the river, from the depth of water at the fords." He put a bold face on it, but the news was devastating because of the continued delay it implied for Hooker's entire campaign.[26]

On April 22, Stoneman reported by telegraph from Warrenton Junction that Averell's division and Davis' brigade were on the railroad, halfway between Warrenton and the Junction. Gregg's division and Buford's brigade were at the Junction itself. He advised they wouldn't need wagons to transport supplies, and he was keeping on-hand "two days' rations of long, and six of short, forage, and eight of subsistence stores." The rest was flabbergasting: "I patrol the road to Bristoe Station, and have telegraphed the commanding officer of Alexandria of the fact, and requested at the force at Washington be sent out as far as Bristoe, where I will connect with it by patrols from Cedar Run. I am sorry to say that the horses have suffered considerably for want of forage and from exposure to rain and wind. A few days, I hope, will bring them up again. The railroad is

23 Ibid.

24 *OR*, 25, part II, 232-233.

25 BV 354, part 7, FSNMP, *Memorial and Letters of Rev. John R. Adams, D.D., Chaplain*, 104-105.

26 *OR*, 25, part II, 238.

in good order up to the Rappahannock railroad bridge and to Warrenton. The construction train is now at the bridge. Three trains have arrived with stores."

Hooker had to be beyond exasperation. Headquarters replied with restraint, acknowledging the good news that Stoneman was replenished. Williams, in Hooker's name, directed the cavalry to "proceed across the river to-morrow morning [23rd], if the fords are practicable," adding "The general does not look for one moment's delay in your advance from any cause that human effort can obviate, and directs me to add that this army is awaiting your movement."

A more lengthy message later that day better captured Hooker's actual mind-set: "The major-general commanding is of the opinion that you are encamped in the immediate vicinity of your depot of supplies, and that you will spare no labor to put your command in a state of the utmost efficiency, while you hold it in readiness to move at the earliest practicable moment." Hooker then cautioned Stoneman—now on the tenth operational day and not yet across the Rappahannock—to focus his attention on the condition of fords and to "mature" his plan "for an advance when the signal is given."

Hooker provided gratuitous instruction and, extending hope beyond evidence, informed Stoneman of the enemy situation at distant Gloucester Point. Continuing to dream on paper, he suggested that, once past the Rapidan, Stoneman should divide his force into two columns and move deeply into enemy territory. "You must move quickly and make long marches. The experience of your march up the river will, doubtless, satisfy you of what can be accomplished by celerity," Hooker said, waxing eloquent. "In marching, you must require your men to keep together as much as in Indian country. Send any officer to the rear who does not keep his command in hand. You will lose every man and horse who separates from his command." It was, unfortunately, as if Hooker was trying to wish forward movement and sweeping results where none existed or showed any promise of success.[27]

"The command is now separated by impassable streams," Stoneman lamented at noon on April 23, "and I am unable to communicate with the different portions of it, owing to the small streams being swimming. The pickets are cut off by high water." By the 25th, Stoneman lamely offered that he was ready to "move at any moment the commanding general might designate" and had received "horseshoes and cartridges (except pistol)."[28]

While his cavalry floundered, Hooker could only suffer and move on to things he could control. On April 25, following his earlier intentions for a demonstration on Lee's right flank, Hooker sent Col. J. P. Taylor on a raid from King George Court House into

27 Ibid., 242, 243, 244.

28 OR, 25, part II, 245.

the Northern Neck. Like previous sorties of this type, they were to capture prisoners, confiscate forage, break-up contraband activities, and arrest disloyal citizens. Army headquarters detached the Oneida Cavalry under Capt. Daniel P. Mann to reinforce Taylor. General Reynolds' I Corps cooperated by sending a small cavalry party to "seize a signal party supposed to be operating at that point, near Machodoc Creek."[29]

Sadly, this was about the best that the Army of the Potomac could manage. Stoneman's failure to cross the Rappahannock and Rapidan during the two days of good weather would be crucial to his overall failure in the Chancellorsville and Second Fredericksburg campaign. Hooker had clearly wanted the raid and envelopment to proceed in advance of the army's general maneuver so that it would distract Lee and cause disruption of Confederate options. Hooker had not planned for Stoneman to "make a demonstration" or "secure the flanks," but rather make a deep thrust into enemy country. By lethargy, Stoneman had squandered his opportunity to cross the rivers and apply operational pressure at Lee's rear. He also lacked sufficient leadership, forces, firepower, materiel, training, and expertise to make Hooker's wishes happen.

This raises the intriguing question: What if Stoneman's force had made it across the river before the heavy rains set in? With the storm-swollen Rapidan and Rappahannock both separating him from the rest of the Union army, and with innumerable storm-swollen creeks bisecting his path forward—not to mention the difficulty of traveling the mud-mired roads themselves—would Stoneman had been inclined or even able to press forward with his mission, deep into the heart of enemy territory, cut off from aid or escape? Judging by his lethargic slog under more-ideal conditions, it's hard to imagine a more vigorous prosecution of his mission under foul weather. Similarly, had Stoneman made it across the river in a timely fashion, Lee's more effective cavalry force might have made a counter-move.[30] Stoneman's best chance for penetration was that it was not expected (with good reason).

Paradoxically, Stoneman's failed operation gave heart to the army and home front —both ignorant of the actual facts. Beyond that, "Stoneman's Raid" fizzled into a non-decisive side-show.

Stoneman's Last Gasp

Although it would not become clear until after Chancellorsville, Stoneman's command would finally take part in Hooker's operation. On April 27, Stoneman would

---

29 Ibid., 249-250.

30 Any Confederate cavalry action might have been muted, however, by the reportedly "wretched" condition of their horses.

receive a telegram to report with his commanders and staff to Morrisville at 2 p.m. the following day. There, on the twenty-eighth, he would meet Hooker and his staff, who informed him of the pending infantry crossings at Kelly's Ford. Brushing aside the obvious historic question—why Hooker hadn't informed Stoneman earlier or gone there earlier—Stoneman would receive new instructions to maneuver along with the army.

Amazingly mal-deployed and -positioned, Stoneman would return to Warrenton Junction, 13 miles distant, to ready his command for action. During intense fog, with difficult roads due to rains, the cavalry gathered in their pickets and troops and moved to the river, arriving by 5 p.m. on April 29. Averell's division, Davis' brigade of Pleasonton's division, and Tidball's battery headed for Culpeper Court House. Stoneman, with Gregg's division, Buford's Reserve Brigade (now including Rush's Lancers), and Robert's battery moved to Stevensburg.

However, Averell moved only a short distance and encamped, initiating a sequence of events that was to cause severe operational distress. Averell, via aide Capt. Wesley Merritt, was instructed to move out, where they met the 13th Virginia Cavalry in several skirmishes. Skirmishing also took place with elements of the 9th and 10th Virginia Cavalry.

Gregg's division moved to Louisa Court House and elements went to Gordonsville while Stoneman pushed through, destroying facilities on the Virginia Central Railroad. They then moved to the James River at Goochland and the North Anna and South Anna Rivers. Part of Davis' command, the 12th Illinois Cavalry, moved against the R. F. & P. railroad at Ashland and Atlee's Station. Gregg pushed along the South Anna River, burning its bridges.

Thus, as the battle raged at Chancellorsville, Stoneman's command finally managed to cover the distances and perform the tasks they had been intended to cover before the battle ever opened. It was classically too little, too late, barely adding footnotes to the operational story. On the other hand, those results were better than nothing, and that apparently was the best that could be done.[31]

Clearly, all of this had overwhelmed the cavalry leadership, and Hooker's expectations exceeded their grasp and ability. More time and new leaders would be needed for the cavalry corps to realize its potential.

31 OR, 25, part I, 1057-1064.

Chapter Ten |

The End of the "Valley Forge"

"The past week the weather has been delightful," observed a Connecticut infantryman as the second week of April drew to a close, "just such weather, in fact, as brings General Hooker out of his tent in the morning and sets him running his sword into the ground to see how fast the mud is drying up."[1]

Everyone, from the commanding general on down to anonymous infantrymen, was trying to read the tea leaves and make their best guesses on when the army would rumble into action. "We are in more than usual uncertainty as to our destination as 'Old fightin' Joe' has remained mighty 'dark' in regard to any move," one soldier wrote.[2] Nonetheless—the false starts that would beset Stoneman notwithstanding—the looming campaign was obvious.

"The distant rumblings of the coming storm are everywhere heard—the herald of conflict and carnage, which to so many, must be the knell of parting—the grand finale in the great drama of life," remembered one Connecticut soldier of the 27th Connecticut Infantry who went by "D. S. T." The infantryman continued to provide New Haven with literate details. "But with composure the soldier dons his equipments, fills his cartridge box, and goes forth to meet it," he added. "He knows the dangers of the path, and he remembers the fate of comrades, and the bravest can not ban out speculations as to the future, which will flutter around his heart, and upon the Spring breezes will waft his thoughts to more peaceful scenes at home." He emphasized that the "soldier knows his duty, and whether it calls him on the fearful march or fatal field, his obligations to his

---

1   BV 311, part 82, FSNMP. Letter of "D.S.T." was published Tuesday, April 21, 1863.

2   CHJHCF. Cites: "Gilbert C. Moore Jr., editor, *Cornie: The Civil War Letters of Lt. Cornelius Moore*, n.p., 1989."

One soldier observing the commanding general's HQ quipped, "The past week the weather has been delightful—just such weather, in fact, as brings General Hooker out of his tent in the morning and sets him running his sword into the ground to see how fast the mud is drying up." *LOC*

oath and innate sense of honor alike compel obedience to law, and prompt exertions for principle."[3]

That obedience and discipline—so lacking in January—now served as firm glue holding the army together. "I have failed to notice any practical application of the moral suasion system in the service," D.S.T. noted, reconciling himself to his duty. "On the contrary, I have seen a good deal of the compulsory doctrine—so much of it, indeed, that I am forced to believe the doctrine popular, and that its principals form the great basis of obedience in the army," he observed. "I have never yet heard a general ask a regiment if it would please break up camp on a certain day, or, when upon the field if it would be kind enough to occupy such a position, and hold it until it heard from him again. I don't think such is the custom in war, and it is this knowledge that makes me think we will go when wanted, and keep going until ordered to stop."[4]

Henry Butler of the 16th Maine Infantry was likewise thinking about duty in a letter he wrote on April 13. "You say you do not want me to go into battle. You would not

3   Letter of "D.S.T."

4   Ibid.

want me called a coward. If I was well and should [skedaddle] from a fight, I should be called a coward forever, and that would be a disgrace to me. I do not feel anxious to go into battle. I come out here to fight for the Union and I shall have to do so. If I was born to be shot, I shall be." He added more positively, "But I hope I shall live through all the battles that I may be in. I want to see this rebellion put down and I want to see all the traitors in the north punished."[5]

Butler discussed reorganization in the 16th Maine necessitated by shortages of men. "The 10 companies in this regiment has got to be put into 5 companies," he explained. "Our company will be put with company I. They will be put together as the alphabet goes. Some of the captains will have to be mustered out. I hope we shall retain our captain. He is such a good man."[6]

Such last minute adjustments rippled through the army at all levels. "At last the long-looked for promotion has been made and [Samuel K.] Zook is no longer the colonel of the Fifty-seventh New York, but a full-fledged brigadier general," reported Lt. Josiah Favill on April 13. "His commission arrived in camp this morning, together with special orders, Headquarters, Army of the Potomac, No. 103, assigning him to the command of his old brigade." Favill reflected, "The general is popular, a magnificent drill officer, an excellent soldier, and richly deserves his promotion." He received hearty congratulations from division officers and was modest. General Hancock presented him with a pair of his own stars, which Zook proudly sewed on his coat.[7]

Sergeant John Cate of the 33rd Massachusetts Infantry shared similar news. "We have got a new Brigadier General, Barlow is his name," he reported. "The one we had, Gen. [sic] Smith, was only an acting Colonel and has now gone back to his regiment." Of Barlow, Cate inaccurately added, "It is said money and not merit brought his commission, although he was a Colonel on the Peninsula under McClellan."[8]

Inspection reports were wrapped-up. The VI Corps's Light Division at Belle Plain, inspected by Capt. Enoch Totten on April 26, proved typical. Its experience demonstrates the extent to which thorough inspections sharpened a unit's readiness. Commanded by Brig. Gen. Calvin E. Pratt, the division had four regiments—6th Maine,

5   CHJHCF. Letters of Henry Butler to his wife, 16th Maine Infantry, Castine Public Library, Castine, Maine, http://www.kalama.com/~mariner/front_butler.htm.

6   BV 316, part 8, FSNMP. Butler letters, 1863, April 15, 1863. Butler was originally a member of Company K, captained by Capt. Stephen C. Whitehouse of Newcastle. Whitehouse was killed on July 1, 1863, at Gettysburg; Butler was taken prisoner.

7   Favill, *The Diary of a Young Officer,* op. cit. in BV 196, part 1, FSNMP.

8   BV 183, part 4, FSNMP, letters of Sgt. John Cate, 33rd Massachusetts Infantry. Per NPS/ CWSSS, Cate was mustered into Company D (M544 Roll 6). Warner, *Generals in Blue,* 18-19.

61st Pennsylvania, 5th Wisconsin and 43rd New York—each of which was a three-years' outfit, and the 31st New York, a two-years' command.

The totals for the division "present and absent," were 39 field & staff officers, 132 company officers, 3,236 enlisted men, and "for duty" numbers included 33 field & staff officers, 106 company officers, and 2,355 enlisted men. Thus, the "Light Division" fielded 2,494 effectives.

The 31st New York was armed with .58 cal. U. S. Rifle Muskets in excellent condition; the 6th Maine and 61st Pennsylvania were armed with the same weapons and were rated good; the 43rd New York and 5th Wisconsin were armed with Austrian Rifles and were rated good. All regiments' men had the requisite ammunition of 60 rounds per man.

All regiments received good ratings for presence and condition of accouterments. Totten checked cartridge boxes, belts, cap pouches, slings, and bayonet scabbards. Clothing and equipment, as well as camp, were rated good. He checked overcoats, coats, and trousers, underclothing, shoes, stockings, blankets, haversacks, canteens, knapsacks, and shelter tents. Six weapons were deemed unserviceable.

The men were rated good in appearance and discipline and judged well acquainted with manual of arms, company drill, battalion drill, guard duty, picket duty, bayonet exercises, and target practice. The men were "indifferent" in judging distances in drill. Their system of military instruction was rated good.

Inspection ratings were: officers (efficient); commanding officers informed relating to the condition of their commands (well); regimental and company books and records (generally complete); company officers, quartermasters, commanders, etc. accounting for public property (regularly); wants of the command reasonably anticipated (they are); provision reports agreeing with morning reports (they do); orders (duly received and published); accommodations for sick (good); hospital department supplied (well); surgeons and assistant surgeons competent and assiduous (they are); camp police (thorough); kitchens and cooking (well arranged); corps, division and brigade commanders visiting and inspecting their commands (frequently); shelter tents (not as good as ought to be); and horses and mules (serviceable) and wagons (in good order).

The army's inspectors-general had done their best to judge the fighting readiness for the commanders. It was time for units to prove their worth in maneuver and battle.[9]

"We have five days rations of crackers, coffee, sugar and salt in our knapsacks," reported Emmet Irwin of the 82nd New York Infantry (2nd N.Y.S.M.) on April 25. "We sent our blankets and all except a change of clothing away about two weeks ago."

---

9 BV 191, part 10, FSNMP, inspector's report of the Light Division, VI AC. Per NPS/CWSSS, Capt. Enoch Totten was from 5th Wisconsin Infantry. Mustered in as a first lieutenant, he rose to major (M 559 Roll 30).

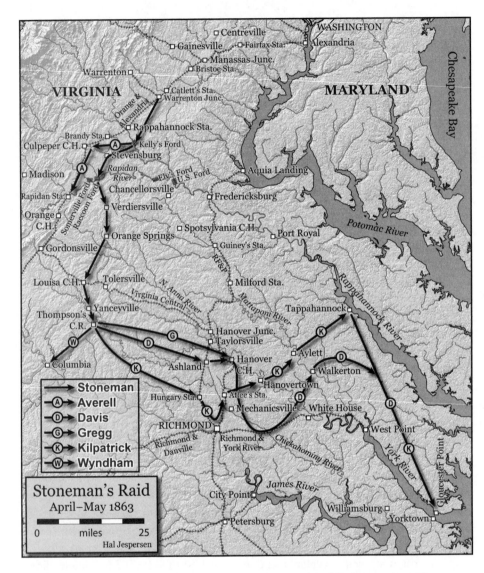

He added his take, typical now in the army, on Stoneman's failed operation: "Stoneman with about 20,000 cavalry has been out for the last two weeks but what he is doing is not know[n]. He crossed the river near Warrenton last Monday [April 20] his men and horses provided with 6 days forage since which time nothing has been heard of him, he sent all men and horses that were not reliable and able for a six days march to the rear."[10]

---

10 Author Collection, 4-page letter.

Stoneman's Raid (April-May 1863). After several false starts and weather-plagued movements, George Stoneman split his command into several smaller wings to inflict maximum damage on the enemy. The plan called for tying up resources in Lee's rear even as Hooker moved the rest of the army against General Lee's Army of Northern Virginia. Stoneman, rather inexplicably, set out at a snail's pace, doing little to distract or threaten Lee, despite the vast distance his troopers would eventually cover.

The infantry's time was coming soon enough. "I think for sure that we will march tomorrow or the next day," predicted Bay State Sgt. John Cate. Writing from "Camp Smith near Stafford Court House" on April 20, Cate seemed to suggest he was more in-the-know about the army's plans than most men in the lower echelons. "[E]verything is ready and we have our rations in our haversack for 8 days," he confided. "This makes a very heavy load, but we are obliged to carry it or go hungry. Part of the Corps have already moved. We shall be in the front, probably the advance of the Army. We shall cross the Rappahannock 12 miles above Fredericksburg at Kelly's Ford, 2 ½ days march. This is what things look like now but there may be different orders and we may be sent on a different course." He pronounced his health and spirits good, and noted he was acting orderly (first) sergeant ("a big opportunity for me"). "The general opinion among the troops is that the war will end this year," he concluded. "We all hope it will."[11]

Lieutenant Cornelius Moore reflected similar optimism in an April 14 letter. "If we can only make a triumphal march, we are all ready and willing to endure every hardship and danger," he enthused. "Oh! I hope we may be able, with the help of God and our own strong arms, to pull down this skeleton of a [Confederate] Government raised in rebellion to our own blessed institutions." Moore noticed the dramatically improved state of the army. "The troops were never in better 'fighting condition,'" he said and asked for home folks' prayers. "I may never see you again, but I have made up my mind to never flinch from the duty I have before me, and you may rest assured, should I fall, that it was while defending my country's honor."[12]

Two soldier letters to the *New York* (Sunday) *Mercury* on April 20 provided interesting views. "Empire Hose," writing from "White Oak Church, Va.," evidenced humor, indicating better morale:

11 Sgt. John Cate letter, BV 183, part 4, FSNMP.

12 CHJHCF. Cites: "Gilbert C. Moore Jr., ed., *Cornie: The Civil War Letters of Lt. Cornelius Moore*, n.p., 1989."

You are doubtless well aware, that, since the failure at Fredericksburg, we have occupied this portion of the sacred soil of Virginia as our winter quarters, with the exception of once (on or about the 20th Jan.) that we took a promenade for the purpose of trying how many inches we could sink in the mud, and then escape without the loss of our boots. Since the advent of Joseph [Hooker] into head-quarters, a new system has been adopted, to prevent the possibility of getting out of ammunition and supplies. We were to make a movement the other day, and each man was to carry 120 rounds of cartridge, and in place of clothing in our knapsacks, five days' rations of hard tack, etc., were to fill up the place—besides three days' provisions in our haversacks. Nobody can accuse us of being proud; for we do not rob our stomachs to cover our backs. But I do not approve of the plan; for Joseph will find, by the end of the summer, that however fast we may march and fight, we will be but slow coaches, in fact, only creeping.[13]

"[T]he papers saying that the best men [i.e., conscripts] are coming now," he added wryly. "Suppose we had all been best men and remained at home, enjoying the comforts and privileges that are denied us here, where would our capital have been. Long ere this it would have been numbered with the things that were; and perhaps the North would know by this time what war is." Now firmly on familiar ground, he added, "Do not let these Copperheads go too far. A coward is the only person who would speak of peace now. . . . Do not let us be called to the rear, to keep rebellion down at home; for our men think more of the full grown Rebel, who has the manliness to come out in the ranks and stand by his colors, than of those cowardly curs, who keep up a running fire in our rear. We would rather have them in front of us, across the Rappahannock; then we would know what their designs are."[14]

The second April 20 letter printed in the same paper originated with "J. J." of the 14th (Brooklyn) New York and was written from "Lower Belle Plain." The regiment had been brought up to strength, he recorded, and three balloons were aloft gathering intelligence. "Great preparations seem to be made preparatory for some kind of a movement," he predicted. "The officers' tents and superfluous baggage are all being turned in," he added, and "This depot is filled with all kinds of 'paraphernalia' of war." He also praised the new corps/division badges. "This badge is a good idea, and will enable commanders of regiments, brigades, etc., to assign soldiers to their respective commands, as well as enabling soldiers to know each other, and their whereabouts on the march."[15]

13 Styple, ed., *Writing and Fighting the Civil War,* 185-187.

14 Ibid.

15 Ibid.

"J. J." pronounced the army "ready to respond to the 'long-roll' and hoped that "when Gen. Hooker moves it will be at the right time." "General Hooker's 'orders' are to the point," he said. "Every soldier is expected to do his duty, and any lack of which (the offender) is to be severely punished."[16]

A Strategic Blunder or Duty Faithfully Performed?

On the eve of its major offensive campaign, with the war in the East in the balance, a colossal governmental mistake came to light, exposing a dumbfounding suspension of strategic focus. On April 20, Hooker provided Stanton with G. O. No. 44 issued that day. It dealt with the expiration of service terms for a substantial number of the army's units and soldiers. No explanation was included as to why or how this concern had surfaced so late, although it had been blatantly obvious to Chaplain John R. Adams and others earlier.[17]

The War Department at least had tried to address the issue as early as April 2 in General Order No. 85. It stated, where companies and regiments re-enlisted as a body, officers were to be retained. Furloughs were granted allowing units to proceed— under-arms, with their equipment, and at public expense—to their places of enrollment to be furloughed. If a unit declined to re-enlist as a body, the officers would be mustered-out, weapons and equipment turned-in, and transportation provided to return men to their enrollment places. If less than half of the men re-enlisted, then corps commanders would determine a proportional number of officers to retain. Special furloughs were provided for regiments enlisting for three more years or the war's duration. Three-year enlistees in two-year regiments were to be reassigned. If sufficient numbers remained in a given regiment, at the corps commander's discretion, they could be formed into battalions.[18]

The April 2 order also provided bounties to volunteer and militia re-enlistees: $50 for one year—half paid at re-enlistment and half on completion of term of service—and $100 for two years—of which $25 was paid immediately and the balance on service completion). Thirty-day furloughs were authorized, as well.[19]

Hooker ordered these instructions read to all two years' and nine months' regiments. Despite the inducements, he received the disappointing answer. Tallies

16 Ibid.

17 *OR*, 25, part II, 233.

18 Ibid., 234.

19 Ibid.

aggregated 16,480 two-years' men and 6,421 nine-months'—totaling 22,901—an entire corps equivalent of men unwilling to re-enlist.[20]

On the twenty-second, Hooker informed the War Department. "I have reason to believe but few, if any, will re-enlist at this time," he admitted. "They appear to be of the opinion that they will be under less restraint to retire from service before incurring new obligations, and that if they should conclude to return, they will be able to realize a larger bounty as substitutes for conscripts than is provided by law."[21]

Analyzing these results is problematic. Hooker and the War Department must have hoped for better responses. Some historians—especially those who have not experienced the impact of wounded-justice on field soldiers—might hold the thesis of this study hostage to these numbers and ask, "If the Army of the Potomac had indeed 'turned itself around,' wouldn't there have been more re-enlistments?"

The real issue was whether citizen-soldiers, after having already served their contracted service obligations, "owed" the country more service. They weren't being ordered or forced to reenlist; they were being asked—obviously from a weak position in crisis mode with a distinct smell of panic—to voluntarily reenlist. Faced with opportunity to remove themselves from privation, potential wounding or death, were they wrong or unpatriotic in seizing the moment?

A simpler question was simply "Had they done enough of their duty?" The lack of home front support and Copperhead subversion likely added to their personal burdens. This became a de facto plebiscite on their overall care by the army and War Department. Their reasoning was simple, direct, and compelling: we've done our part as volunteers; let the draftees and shirkers be herded at bayonet point to the front to do their bit for the country. We'll cheer that on. We volunteered to be here, did our duty without the home front support promised to us, and now it's our time to go.

The result at least was evident. Almost 23,000 men would be missing from the army at a critical start of a major campaign. America simply did not know how to raise and maintain an army during a long and brutal war. This strategic blunder was the fault of the Lincoln Administration, especially its War Department, and Congress for failing to anticipate and deal with it aggressively in February or March.

But this story was more layered and complex. Here it might be useful to examine a representative two-years' regiment, the 1st New York. Mustered-in at New York City on April 22, 1861—ten days after Sumter was attacked—it enlisted for two-years, believing that ample time to suppress the rebellion. They served at Fortress Monroe (May-July 1861); Newport News (July 1861-March 1862); and, from June 1862, in the

20 Ibid., 243.

21 Ibid.

III Corps. The 1st New York fought at Big Bethel; the Seven Days' battles (Peach Orchard, Glendale); Second Bull Run; Chantilly; and Fredericksburg, where they supported Franklin's attacks against Jackson. The 1st participated in the "Mud March" and suffered the privations of the "Valley-Forge."

Despite its scheduled service termination of April 22—the second anniversary of its mustering in—the 1st New York would go on to fight at Chancellorsville. On April 2, the regiment moved four miles closer to the Potomac Creek Bridge and established there "Camp Sickles." "Considerable effort" to induce re-enlistment failed and, on April 21 the War Department notified the men they "would be held in the service until the 7th of May"—the date on which its last company had been mustered-in. Outraged and feeling betrayed, on April 23 they put down their arms in a protest lasting several days. Despite this injustice, order returned and they left camp on April 28, crossed U. S. Ford on May 1 (held that day in reserve near Chancellorsville) and, on May 2 were engaged. At 11:00 p.m. they (together with the 1st and 3rd Brigades of their division) made a bayonet assault through dense woods to retake a road line. "The enemy were driven from two lines of rifle pits and breast-works, and pressed back to the road," one of them reported. Holding their position that night, they withdrew on May 3 to support the 4th U. S. Artillery under heavy fire and participated in another bayonet charge. The 1st then held its position until ordered across U. S. Ford on the 6th, returning to its Stafford camp.[22]

The 1st had shirked no action and fought a major battle after its service termination date. The regiment left Aquia Landing on May 8 and proceeded to New York via Washington, D. C. It arrived in New York on the tenth, and on the eleventh was honored with a grand military reception. On May 25, it was mustered-out. It had suffered 113 deaths (79 combat and 34 non-combat) during its two years' service. They had seen their share of combat; risked all in battle, camp, and on the march; and believed (correctly) their contracted term of service had ended on April 22. Their response on April 23 should have been a wake-up call—but wasn't—for the national government. Yet the regiment was persuaded by its officers to "stick"—and they did, as their Chancellorsville fighting attests.[23]

22 Frederick Phisterer, *New York in the War of the Rebellion*, (Albany, NY, 1912); *The Union Army: a History of Military Affairs in the Loyal States, 1861-65—Records of the Regiments in the Union Army— Cyclopedia of Battles—Memoirs of Commanders and Soldiers* (Madison, WI: Federal Pub. Co., 1908). New York, *Third Annual Report of the Bureau of Military Statistics* (Albany: The Bureau of Military Statistics, 1866), 40-46. All of these quotations are from the New York State Military Museum, New York State Unit History Project, found at that organization's website: www.dmna.state. ny.us/historic/reghist/reghistindex.htm (accessed July 30, 2009).

23 Ibid.

The 1st New York's soldiers were victims of a stupid policy. They were American citizen-soldiers, not Prussian drones or Hessian mercenaries. They had freely signed up for a specified period and were holding their government to that agreement.

Naturally, this caused resentment among the three years' troops. "It is now uncertain when we take up our line of march to victory, as the two years' troops are being mustered out," wrote "C. P. K." in the 140th New York to Rochester's *Democrat American*. His letters on April 27 and 28 appeared in the May 5 edition. "[T]hus causing brigades and consequently divisions to be broken, which will require some time before the men have been consolidated and again thoroughly organized." "Three years' men" in the departing regiments were now headed to new units.[24]

"I think that the Move Ment of this [Army?] has stopped now until the places of the 9 months and the two years mens places" were filled, suggested Isaac Hillyer of the 28th New Jersey. He noted the 4th New York had already departed and the 10th New York was leaving on the 28th. The 127th and 133rd Pennsylvania were also near departing. "I think no good generiel will Resk as important a battle as this would be while so Many Men whos time of servies is up," he predicted.[25]

Hooker was about to prove him wrong.

On to Chancellorsville and Second Fredericksburg

The good weather and high spirits of early and mid-April gave way to showers and gloom by the middle of the month, bogging down not only Stoneman's horsemen but the spirits of the infantrymen. "The wet and windy weather of April lingers with us like an unwelcome visitor, slow to take the hint that summer is almost here," gloomed New Yorker Emmet Irwin. "Peach and plum trees are in full blossom. One week of weather such as we might expect in this climate would bring what little there is left of oak, the king of the forrest, in its green mantle."[26]

Surgeon William Watson of the 105th Pennsylvania worried about the effects of the ongoing delay. "We have been prepared to move for several weeks but still we are here," he said on April 23. "A heavy rain set in last night and has continued incessantly ever since. The water is rapidly rising, rendering a big flood a sure thing. The roads will be so much impaired that it will be utterly impossible to move for one or two weeks. There is

---

24 BV 216, part 4, FSNMP. Left news column contains article beginning with "From the 140th Regiment. Camp of the 140th Regt. N.Y.S.V. Near Falmouth, April 27, 1863."

25 BV 33, part 24, Hillyer letters, FSNMP. Hillyer's April 26 letter also recounted the story of an acquaintance, Hank McGaw, who had tried to desert and was captured and court-martialed. McGaw, found guilty and sentenced to be shot, received a presidential pardon.

26 Author's Collection, 4-page letter.

something wrong." Mindful of improved Rebel fortifications and defenses, Watson also rightly worried about the impending loss of "some twenty or thirty thousand troops, the two year and nine month men." Perhaps the resultant shift of balance worried him.

"I am weary of this place and hence am anxious for a move," Watson admitted. "I know almost every acre of ground in Stafford County. When we came here it seemed but one immense forest. Now scarcely a tree is visible. If the former inhabitants are permitted to return they will be unable to find a single familiar landmark. You cannot conceive how a country is devastated by an invading army." He was grateful that "grim war is not desolating the fields and happy homes in the North."

Watson ended with a jab at the universal enemy. "How I despise those miserable traitors in the north who are aiding the rebels by calling every supporter of the administration Abolitionists," he sneered. "I would sooner be an abolitionist than a peace democrat—for the latter is the vilest thing on earth."[27]

Peace, believed Capt. Charles Bowers of the 32nd Massachusetts, was possible only through victory. "I am confident the only way to end the rebellion is to defeat the armies in the field, for although there may be no end to their resources of arms and food, there is to raising men," he contended, expressing wisdom beyond his years and rank. "Once we defeat or capture their great army in any field and it cannot be replenished."[28]

Bowers, like the vast majority of his comrades, felt hopeful. "I may be too sanguine," he admitted. "I know I have been again and again disappointed, but I certainly have never felt so confident . . . as I do now. I have seen defeats enough, I want to witness one good substantial victory."

"I yet think . . . we will whip them out of their boots," predicted Henry F. Young of the 7th Wisconsin Infantry. A fellow veteran from the western Iron Brigade weighed-in, an artilleryman in Battery B, commented more expansively. "The men reasoned that 'the old flag was still there,' and would be found there at the finish right side up and on top," he said, "and that . . . we are going to whip the Rebels and restore the Union some way, sometime, somehow in spite of poor commanders, silly editors, scheming politicians, and thieving contractors!"[29]

27 Fatout, ed., *Letters of a Civil War Surgeon*, 87-88.

28 Bowers Letters, Massachusetts Historical Society, Reel 16, Frames 1338-1341; Poirier, *By the Blood of Our Alumni: Norwich University Citizen Soldiers*, 88.

29 Alan T. Nolan, *The Iron Brigade: A Military History* (Bloomington, IN: Indiana University Press, 1994), 196. Nolan cites: "Young MSS; *The Cannoneer*, Augustus Buell, 49," referring to war letters of Henry F. Young in the Warner MSS, State Historical Society of Wisconsin. Buell's memoir was published in 1897 in Washington, D. C. by *The National Tribune*.

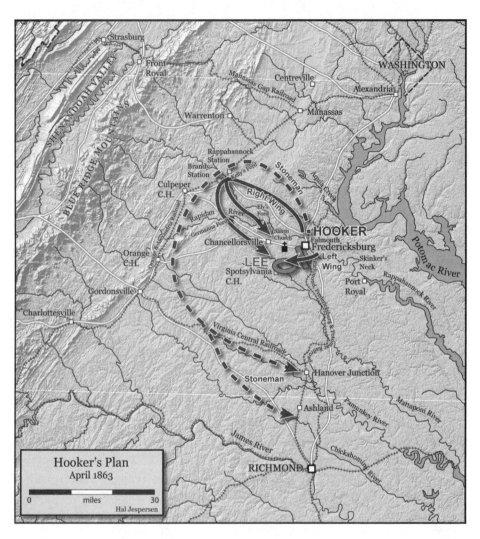

Hooker's Plan
April 1863

0   miles   30
Hal Jespersen

"When we do move it will be, undoubtedly, with much more rapidity than our armies have heretofore used in changing position," believed infantryman Gardner Stockman of the 5th Connecticut, describing the army's improved mobility in an April 26 letter. "No long lines of ambulances full of sick; no immense trains of wagons filled with superfluous tents and fixtures, nor loaded with officers' baggage, will block up the road for miles, or stick in the mud, to detain the whole army." Stockman was pleased that just "[a] few wagons, lightly loaded with necessary rations, will accompany us, but the main dependence will be upon our own 'muscle' and the 'pack mules,' a few of

Hooker's Plan (April 1863). Plans for Joe Hooker's spring offensive mirrored Ambrose Burnside's failed "Mud March," but with several key improvements. The most important was the dispatching of the newly reorganized Cavalry Corps under Brig. Gen. George Stoneman on a sweeping maneuver deep into the rear of the Army of Northern Virginia to wreak havoc on Confederate supply and communication lines and threaten Lee's line of retreat. As that chaos was unfolding, Hooker would use a portion of his army to hold Lee's attention in Fredericksburg while the bulk of the Federal army marched around Lee's left and into his rear. This move, thought Hooker, would either pin Lee against the Rappahannock River or force him out of his entrenchments and southward, where Stoneman's men were operating behind him. The two wings of Hooker's infantry would then converge on Lee and catch him in the open. (Historian Kristopher D. White assisted with the preparation of this map.)

which are furnished to each regiment, for the transportation of extra ammunition, and similar indispensables." The streamlining would allow them to now match "the hitherto proverbial speed of the rebel troops."[30]

At some point during that fourth week of April, Joe Hooker must have again come out from his tent and tested the ground with his sword, and he must have been satisfied with what he saw—because on April 25, he finally began to shift his army. Although it can certainly be argued that, under the urgency of secrecy, he provided his subordinates with insufficient planning time and consultation, the move began.

First, Hooker ordered Slocum to withdraw his infantry from Dumfries. The 1st Division of the XII Corps was ordered to full readiness and to march at daybreak on April 27th with eight days' rations. On the twenty-sixth, Hooker's headquarters queried Stoneman for information on routes to the interior from Rappahannock Station and enemy activity east of Gordonsville and Culpeper. Stoneman was to await movement orders.

Also on April 26, XI and XII Corps were instructed to march at sunrise on the twenty-seventh. The XI Corps was to march out first and reach Kelly's Ford without revealing itself to the enemy. The corps was to encamp on or before 4 p.m. on the twenty-eighth. The XII Corps was to follow. Both were to march with one artillery battery, two ambulances, and a pack train of small arms ammunition per division. Small numbers of wagons hauling forage would accompany them. The trains for the two corps would be initially positioned at Banks's Ford, off the road with intentions of crossing there. Later that day, Hooker confusingly ordered the XII Corps to take all trains with them. Destinations were considered confidential.[31]

---

30 BV 313, part 129, FSNMP, *The Waterbury American* on May 8, 1863.

31 *OR*, 25, part II, 250, 255-256.

Meade's V Corps was ordered out next, directed "to reach the vicinity of Kelly's Ford by Tuesday [April 28] at 4 p.m." Meade was advised Slocum's and Howard's corps would be on the same route, probably from Hartwood Church. He was told to leave behind men with expiring enlistments—as were the XI and XII Corps—and he was told to leave his trains near Stoneman's Switch. At 7 a.m., Meade acknowledged the orders and stated his intention to move to Hartwood, encamp there so as not to interfere with the XI or XII Corps, and await further orders. Some confusion in timing caused Williams to send another message to Meade confirming the commanding general's desire that V Corps move on the twenty-seventh.[32]

Couch's II Corps also received instructions on April 27. He had been told to replace one of Meade's regiments at Banks's Ford with one of his. The corps was to march at sunrise on the twenty-eighth and encamp two divisions near Banks's Ford (being careful to conceal their positions). Then, one battery and one brigade of a division were to move covertly to occupy a position near U. S. Ford. Couch was cautioned to have his ammunition and other supplies stockpiled and ready to advance, and he was told he could draw on the III Corps supplies, if necessary. A follow-up message ordered Couch not to construct bridges at Banks's Ford "until the night of the 29th." Finally, II Corps was to guard the river against potential Confederate crossings and to cooperate with Hunt's artillery in supporting or blocking crossings. Hooker and Butterfield apparently worried that extended deployments to the west left supply lines vulnerable.[33]

Orders to Sedgwick, Reynolds, and Sickles on April 27 laid foundations for "Second Fredericksburg." Sedgwick was to assume command of the army's left wing, initially comprised of three corps: the VI Corps was to cross at Franklin's Crossing; I Corps at Pollock's Mill Creek; and III Corps was to cross at either place. The VI and I Corps were to be in crossing position by 3:30 a.m. and the III Corps by 4 a.m. on the twenty-ninth, with two bridges at each crossing site. Ambulances and trains were to be concealed and ready to move one ridgeline at a time behind the corps. Artillery of the corps and the army's reserve artillery would support the crossing from Stafford Heights and along the river. Eight days' rations and forage were to be distributed with the troops and trains.[34]

Hooker called for Sedgwick to make a "demonstration in full force on Wednesday morning upon the enemy's defenses, with a view of securing the Telegraph road." He advised Sedgwick to sever the enemy's communications so that Confederates could not

---

32 Ibid., 262-263 for orders to Maj. Gen. G. G. Meade's V Corps.

33 Ibid., 266-267.

34 Ibid., 267-269.

detach any of their forces westward. If they did so, Sedgwick was pointedly to "attack and carry their works at all hazards." If the enemy fell back toward Richmond, Sedgwick was to pursue them and attack at every opportunity. Part of Sedgwick's force was to be placed on the Bowling Green Road to facilitate pursuit. Hooker closed with the inevitable gratuitous statement: "General Sedgwick will give such further instructions as may seem to him necessary to carry out the plans and wishes of the major-general commanding."[35]

"Today we got orders to be ready to move next morning," wrote Joseph Franklin Mancha of the 122nd Pennsylvania Infantry, part of the III Corps, on April 27. "The weather looks as though it was willing to favor us." Two days later, he added: "We expect to meet the enemy tomorrow when the ball will be opened & the Union army will show Jeff Davis that the last Fredericksburg battle did not in the least discourage our troops." Lieutenant Edward F. Hopkins of the 149th New York Infantry also wrote on that day: "Reg't left camp this morning 484 strong. 49 men in our company. eight days rations. Join the Corps at Stafford Court House. Camp about 12 miles from Brooks Station in the Direction of Kelleys ford. Never marched with such loads before. Men are cheerful. Not a man falls out."[36]

At the convergence of the XI, XII, and V Corps, infantryman "C. P. K." of the 140th New York took time to write on April 28. "Here we are with eight days' rations, awaiting the passing of a large number of troops coming from our right, and going ahead of us," he noted. "Orders for marching were given at reveille this morning, to be prepared to start at ten precisely. The day is warm, causing the men to relieve themselves of a part of their 'baggage.' The roads give indication of this. Overcoats and blankets cover the ground for miles in heaps of dozens. Cloth seems to be low in Virginia at present. I notice live beef is following us in droves."[37]

In the interest of secrecy, at least two of the corps wisely refrained from music or bugle calls. Another, equally wise, ordered only small cooking fires en route. Covert movements were essential. However, in another demonstration of inappropriate focus, army headquarters exerted undue consternation over news correspondents of the *New York Times* and *Philadelphia Inquirer* transmitting an account of compromised orders and

---

35 Ibid.

36 BV 152, Pennsylvania, part 2, FSNMP, Joseph Franklin Mancha Papers. BV 319, part 12, FSNMP. Diary of Lt. Edward F. Hopkins, Company F, 149th New York, entries for April 27, 1863 (quoted) and May 2 and May 22. The May 2 entry noted the men threw off their knapsacks before moving into the fight. The post-battle entry on May 22 noted, "Co drill in A.M. & target practice for the first time. 1st lesson consists of citing [sic] the piece."

37 BV 216, part 4, FSNMP. Left news column contains article beginning with "From the 140th Regiment. Camp of the 140th Regt. N.Y.S.V. Near Falmouth, April 27, 1863."

a Rebel "submarine cable" between Falmouth and Fredericksburg. Hooker, once again easily distracted at a critical moment, asked Secretary Stanton to have the papers' agents in Washington identify these correspondents by name. If these names were not supplied, wrote Hooker, he would ban the newspapers and their correspondents. His time might better have been used supervising any of the multiple actions he had ordered.[38]

One area he did pay attention to, though, demonstrated that he had learned at least one vital lesson from his predecessor, Ambrose Burnside: On April 27, he spent time directing—and in some cases, redirecting—his bridging components. Benham, commanding the army's engineers, received two messages on April 27. The first cautioned him to prepare to block any fires or wooden rafts floating downstream to damage pontoon bridges. The second instructed him to remove one of the three bridge trains from Franklin's Crossing and move it covertly up to the site below the Lacy House, Chatham, "to be used there when required."

Meanwhile, army engineer staff officer Cyrus Comstock was dispatched to supervise pontoon bridge laying at Kelly's Ford at or before daylight on Wednesday, April 29. To do so, he was to retrieve the bridge train and engineer detachment at Bealeton by 10:30 a.m. on Tuesday the twenty-eighth, drawing on Howard for additional support as necessary. Chief engineer G. K. Warren, meanwhile, analyzed the current status of a large number of bridging sites.

As Hooker's columns advanced, he stretched outward for information. An extensive reconnaissance report, sent by Stoneman—incredibly still at Warrenton Junction—responded to Hooker's request for information on roads, railroads, and the enemy situation around Culpeper and Gordonsville. "The inhabitants of Culpeper Court House have been leaving for the Shenandoah Valley," Stoneman concluded. "These fleeing inhabitants, as also the prisoners which have fallen into our hands, would lead us to suppose that the enemy expected an attack from this direction, but I am assured by yourself [Hooker] that such is not the case." Two interesting questions arise: Why would Stoneman, considering his own lack of success, be challenging Hooker's opinions? And why, after flailing around there for over two weeks, was he surprised the Confederates were expecting a movement?[39]

On April 28, Butterfield responded by sending Stoneman an intelligence report. "One of Colonel Sharpe's men just in from Kelly's Ford says in his opinion no large body of infantry there," the chief of staff said. "Held mostly by cavalry and artillery. Rebel sympathizers on this side believe enemy have fallen back beyond Rapidan,

38 *OR*, 25, part II, 269-270.

39 Ibid., 266, 265.

The army left behind a small makeshift city when it marched off to Chancellorsville. After the failed campaign, the men returned to the ghost towns of mud and timber they had left behind. *NPS*

meaning to make that their point of defense." Butterfield surmised that the enemy believed the cavalry move was a feint and that their main defense would be at U. S. Ford.[40]

And so the army moved, pulling out of Stafford, Falmouth, and White Oak and all the thousands of acres of Virginia countryside it had occupied for four and a half months, sliding westward, heading toward a date with destiny at a small crossroads in the heart of the Wilderness known at Chancellorsville. They left behind, as well, the poor morale, ill-discipline, lack of unity and pride, inefficient battle logistics, and poorly cared for men and animals with which they began their "Valley Forge." Whether they had improved enough was still at issue, but no one could deny that improvement was visible.

40 Ibid., 273.

"How does it look now?" an anxious President Lincoln asked his army commander on the afternoon of April 27.[41]

"I am not sufficiently advanced to give an opinion," Hooker replied at 5:00 p.m., just an hour and a half later. "We are busy. Will tell you all as soon as I can, and have it satisfactory."

41 Lincoln's note and General Hooker's response, OR, 25, part II, 263.

Chapter Eleven

After Chancellorsville

Nearly six decades after the Chancellorsville Campaign, Sgt. Wyman S. White of the 2nd U. S. Sharpshooters published his memoirs. Missing few particulars, White nailed Hooker's command tenure leading up to Chancellorsville, and it is worth quoting at length:

> But now Fighting Joe Hooker was in command and hope again hovered over that stricken army and all were ready for another trial. General Hooker at once set himself to work to organize the army. General McClellan had every brigade a unit. To each brigade of infantry was attached a squadron or more of cavalry and a battery of artillery. The transportation for quartermaster, commissary, and ammunition was also in very much the same broken condition.

> Now this manner of formation of a large army was disorganization rather than Organization. General Hooker remodeled the structure of the whole army in keeping with its proportions and requirements. The cavalry, which had been almost a pest, was consolidated into a corps by itself and in command of General Stoneman and were given to understand that in the future there must be some dead cavalrymen seen on the fields of battle; for up to that time it was a common expression in the army, "Who ever saw a dead cavalryman?"

> The artillery was put into a corps by itself, known as the reserve artillery and was in command of a competent officer and was an arm of the service that could be counted upon. The cavalry from that time advanced in efficiency and character until the world looked on with admiration. Commissary and quartermaster departments were consolidated, and the transportation consolidated in a proper manner, each department in a separate command.

> The quarters, the clothing, and the equipment were looked after. Drills and inspections were in order. Discipline was brought up to proper form and finally hope again came to cheer up the men of the Army of the Potomac and, although not led to victory by General Hooker, all felt and knew the Army of the Potomac was indeed a real army.

... On Monday[, April] the 27th, General Hooker reviewed our corps and I thought that he was pleased with our performance and I think that the organization, morale, discipline and efficiency of the Army of the Potomac had never been so good before and was never any better afterwards.

Hooker had taken command of a disheartened, disorganized, demoralized army. He first organized the troops he had in hand into an army-proper form, then with a master and brought discipline in place of demoralization and the men were quick to see their own improvement and took heart and were ready to do their duty and again battle for the Union.

General Hooker seemed to have satisfaction in what he had accomplished and no doubt felt his time would come when he, with his redeemed army would reap victory and it ought to have been so.[1]

"A Wonder in Its Way"

During one brief, shining hour, the "finest army on the planet"—as Hooker had called it—looked to justify the commander's praise.[2] In a series of maneuvers, Hooker fixed Lee's right flank at Fredericksburg and surprised him by putting three corps across at Kelly's Ford and sweeping down from the west. If the fates had smiled, Hooker would have had four corps—some 73,000 men—at Lee's rear and flanks and two corps —some 40,000 men—in his face. His cavalry corps would have swept into Lee's lines of communication and routes of withdrawal, wrecking havoc.[3]

A May 1 letter from Sgt. John Cate of the 33rd Massachusetts Infantry provided a soldier-level progress report:

Here we are, nearly (100,000) one hundred thousand of us in the rear of Fredericksburg. We have cut off the Rail Road communications from Richmond. We broke camp at Stafford Court House on Monday April 26th. We marched 17 miles in the boiling sun. We had 8 days rations and all the other things to carry. The second day we broke camp at 2 o'clock in the morning and marched 16 miles to Kelly's Ford on the Rappahannock. On this day our march was slow for there were so many troops, baggage trains, and ammunition trains that we had to halt quite often. About 6 o'clock we stopped and pitched tents, made coffee, and most of the men were asleep when the orders came to fall in. This was at 7 o'clock or a little later. We crossed the river on pontoon bridges, then marched about 2 miles and halted until morning. It was 1 o'clock when we stopped. The men were so tired many of them did not

---

1   BV 150, part 1, FSNMP, diary of Wyman S. White, 166-167.

2   3:00 p.m., April 29, 1863, to be exact.

3   *OR*, 25, parts I and II.

take off their equipments, but lay down on the ground with nothing over them and slept until morning.[4]

Sergeant Cate also mentioned the movement's secrecy and difficulty. "All this time the greatest secrecy was used, not a drum was beat or a bugle blast was heard, and the men were not allowed to holler or cheer," he wrote. "This was the severest marching I ever saw."

By all the laws and arts of war, Hooker's movement should have set up a true American Cannae on the Rappahannock and the last battle in the Eastern Theater. For 24 hours, it was the greatest maneuver in American military history.

And that would have remained the story but for one thing: the effective military partnership of Robert E. Lee, "Stonewall" Jackson, J. E. B. Stuart, and the Army of Northern Virginia. Lee, defying all conventions, did not fight a retrograde action or attack in one direction to escape encirclement. He split his force—outnumbered more than two to one—leaving a portion of his army in Fredericksburg to decoy the Federal forces that had supposedly fixed him in place. The rest of the army moved westward to face Hooker's flanking force.[5] Lee's total infantry forces disposed about 53,000 men. Stuart's cavalry forces added 6,500 men.

Had Federal cavalry operated more effectively, it's intriguing to ponder the effect they might have had countering Stuart's movements. As it was, Stuart's troopers harassed and otherwise impeded Slocum's and Howard's corps—the westernmost units of Hooker's army—and it supplied key intelligence about the Union flank on May 1. Reportedly, Howard's XI Corps was "in the air." That, in turn, laid the groundwork for Jackson's decisive flank assault on May 2.

"As I have written before our Brigade was out on a reconnaissance when the Rebels attacked," recounted Cate, who survived the fighting on May 2 and 3. "One Division of our corps fought well but there were so many gave way, it was madness for them to stand any longer." Cate listed all the equipment he lost as a result, quickly adding, "All these things are supplied by the Government free of charge. We were ordered to leave them by the General so that we could march more quickly."[6]

It would take a brutal third day of fighting on May 3—the second-bloodiest day of the Civil War—before Hooker's line finally collapsed. In the melee, Hooker himself was

---

4   BV 183, part 4, FSNMP, letters of Sgt. John Cate, 33rd Massachusetts Infantry.

5   Ibid. Keep in mind that General Lee had already split his army weeks earlier by sending a large portion of Lt. Gen. James Longstreet's First Corps—nearly one-quarter of his army—to southeastern Virginia on what would become a complex foraging mission with many conflicting objectives that we recognize today as the Suffolk Campaign.

6   Ibid.

knocked out of action by an artillery shell that exploded a portion of the porch he was standing on; a support column smashed into him, knocking him senseless. Dazed, he nonetheless refused to relinquish command at the very moment his army desperately needed firm, decisive leadership. It would fall to his under-informed corps commanders —particularly Couch and Slocum—to maintain an orderly withdrawal and prevent the collapse from turning into a rout.

Hooker ordered the army into a tighter defensive position closer to the Rappahannock and then hunkered down to await the outcome of fighting along the eastern front at Fredericksburg and, later, at Salem Church and Banks's Ford—but by the evening of May 4, Hooker had given up hope of victory. Despite a council of war with his corps commanders that recommended renewing the offensive, Hooker withdrew the army northward across U.S. Ford.

"To a military mind the nine days' campaign of the Army of the Potomac is most full of instruction," wrote an anonymous officer in the May 20 edition of a New Jersey newspaper. The critique of "Gen. Hooker's Campaign," attributed to "an officer of great experience and gallantry, who bore an active part in it," was a reasonably good contemporary assessment. "The plan, so far as revealed by the actual operations in the field of our army and that of the enemy, was fine up to the occupation of the Cross Roads at Chancellorsville, the evacuation of Fredericksburg by the Confederates in consequence of the endangering of their communications by Stoneman and Hooker, and the adoption of a line of battle by our forces. But here, the commencement of our general failure, I reluctantly admit."[7]

Complementing the article in that same edition of the paper—and also running in the *Newark Daily Advertiser*—was an assessment from a soldier from the 26th New Jersey. "Our late unsuccessful attempt to dislodge the rebels from Fredericksburg has neither destroyed the confidence of the army in itself nor in its commander," he wrote. "On the contrary a greater faith seems to pervade the troops in their ultimate success, than prior to the battle . . . . I feel, as the whole army seems to feel, that our cause will yet triumph. The Government should put forth at this critical period, a tremendous effort, and strike now while the iron is hot."

The soldier asked a question on the minds of many of his peers: "But if the Copperhead element can only be subdued in the North and the whole power of the nation be brought to the work, how can the rebellion last much longer? Our foes North do more harm than the whole Confederate army to our cause." He rejected downheartedness, adding: "This is not what is wanted. A confidence on the part of the people, is needed to support the Administration in its herculean task. Without that, the effort may as well be abandoned now."[8]

Sergeant John Cate, writing back to Massachusetts, was saying much the same thing in his letters. "You ask what seems to be the idea among the troops concerning the war," he wrote on May 25. "We think that the Rebels have got to give up the unequal contest for it is impossible for them to hold out."[9]

Cate's assessment reveals the true import of the "Valley Forge" winter: the Army of the Potomac once more sallied forth to battle and once more met defeat at the hands of the Army of Northern Virginia—yet Cate and tens of thousands of soldiers like him did not feel defeated as they had earlier. By any measure, including its top commander, the army had generally performed better than ever before. Although defeated at Chancellorsville and Salem Church, their confidence paradoxically grew, patriotism was reinforced, and faith held strong.[10]

The army demonstrated it was ready to turn the page. When they re-crossed the Rappahannock and returned to Stafford, the army's mood was predominantly disgust and anger mixed with a great deal of surprise. It was not, by comparison, the beaten, demoralized, and degraded force it had been after First Fredericksburg and following the "Mud March." At the beginning of the "Valley Forge," they knew they had been thoroughly beaten by the enemy, weather, and terrain in December 1862 and January 1863. After Chancellorsville, they were bitterly disappointed that they had not prevailed and had missed the opportunity to decisively defeat Lee's army.

Defeated but Not Whipped or Beaten

"This second movement back to our old camp is something which I cannot begin to comprehend," puzzled Corp. Uriah N. Parmelee of the 6th New York Cavalry, a highly commended orderly/courier for Caldwell's 1st Division. Writing from "Camp near Falmouth," he saw important distinctions as early as May 8. "The short campaign of ten days has been a wonder in its way," he wrote. "General Hooker has certainly acted with the greatest energy, secrecy & dispatch, besides displaying the enviable qualities of personal daring & coolness." A competent witness, Parmelee noted, "Our division has

---

8   Ibid.; Newark *Daily Advertiser*, May 26, 1863.

9   Newark *Daily Advertiser*, May 26, 1863.

10   The Second Battle of Fredericksburg, meanwhile, could without exaggeration be counted as an unqualified victory, albeit a slowly achieved one—"the only success obtained" in the campaign explained VI Corps commander John Sedgwick in a June 3, 1863, letter to his sister. For a deep and rich assessment, see Chris Mackowski and Kristopher White, *Chancellorsville's Forgotten Front: The Battles of Second Fredericksburg and Salem Church* (Savas Beatie, 2013).

been from first to last in the extreme front." Hooker, too, he asserted, "has always been in the front—the most conspicuous object on the field. He has spared himself no toil. His strategy was sublime. He has attended to everything in person. Even our little brigade went into battle under his immediate orders."[11]

Parmelee condemned the XI Corps's "Dutchmen," and blamed Sedgwick for the consequent need to hold back reinforcements, but then added: "I will not be too sweeping—the men have had much to discourage them, but the present campaign was most splendidly planned—Hooker completely surprised Lee and exceeded all my expectations—I admit now we have a general & that too in the face of a seeming defeat." Most significantly, he wrote, "I am more hopeful than ever before because I can see we are fighting for Liberty & believe that we will have a leader."[12]

Parmelee's spirits were widely reflected elsewhere. "Though the army has recrossed the river, we are not discouraged or down-hearted," reported Chaplain John R. Adams of the 5th Maine and 121st New York Infantry Regiments; "we are in good spirits, and the bands are not idle. Neither has the army lost confidence in General Hooker, but are ready to try it again if need be." His optimism did not prevent him from offering a realistic assessment of the situation, though. "The Rebels have superior generals, and interior railroads, to move troops rapidly. We have to march, and have had a violent rain-storm—one of the severest of the season—and now are in thick mud again," he had written on May 7, before they had returned to their old White Oak Church camp. "We have been through trying scenes."[13]

Some soldiers even refused to accept that they'd been defeated. "You are aware long before this that we have fought and you know the result better than I but I think it is far from a defeat," wrote Abel G. Peck of the 24th Michigan Infantry from "Camp Way, Near Fredericksburgh." Peck was allowing for the delay between letters and the stories that found their way into newspapers before letters found their way into mailboxes. "The troops are in good cheer. They feel as well as ever they did since I have been in the army."[14]

George B. Wolcott of the 44th New York Infantry held a similar opinion. "Another battle has been fought, another victory won and I am left to tell the tale unharmed and well," he wrote, "so you will please banish any fears that may have arisen in your mind concerning my welfare and safety." Wolcott described the fighting, their opponents' valor, and passed judgment on the army's leadership. "Gen. Hooker might be seen

11 BV 36, FSNMP. Uriah N. Parmelee letters.

12 Ibid.

13 BV 354, part 7, FSNMP, *Memorial and Letters of Rev. John R. Adams, D.D., Chaplain,* 108-109.

14 BV 212, part 4, FSNMP, letters of Abel G. Peck, 24th Michigan Infantry.

riding about on his gray steed at all times regardless of shot or shell," he recalled. "On Wednesday morning we were called up to pack our things and prepare to evacuate . . . . There was some disappointment manifested but it has long since worn away and the men have the most [unbounded?] faith in Gen. Hooker."[15]

Wolcott finally went on to qualify his opening statement. "I said another 'victory' has been 'won,' although many in the north do not see it in that light," he explained. "I think the result of good generalship which stole two days march upon the enemy, crossed the Rappahannock and Rapidan Rivers and succeeded in reaching Chancellorsville without losing any life with such an army was indeed a greater victory achieved than if we had fought to obtain it."[16]

U. S. Sanitary Commission official, "Earnest," wrote to the *Vermont Watchman and State Journal* on May 7th from Aquia Creek. After discussing care for the wounded, he urged readers: "Do not lose faith in our success. We shall be victorious. Unabated energy is every where apparent."[17] Another Vermonter wrote four days earlier, "This bitter alternative will cause the rebel army to fight desperately; but if Hooker only holds his own we win all."[18]

Probably most representative were sentiments expressed by Lt. Cornelius L. Moore of the 57th New York Infantry. "[B]y the tone of your letter, I see, you think I am nearly discouraged—low spirited. I am really sorry you have got this impression, for I was never more hopeful for the future, more confident of the abilities of my commanding general, or more anxious to again renew the contest with the Rebel host on the south bank of the Rappahannock . . ." he wrote from "Camp near Falmouth, Va." on May 15. "You know Adeline, there is nothing the American soldier dislikes so much as a backward step, and it was for this alone that I entertained, at the time, this petty feeling of dissatisfaction." Like so many others, "Cornie" Moore focused blame squarely on the XI Corps, adding: "We had been defeated, in strict compliance with the meaning of the word, it is useless to deny; for Hooker had planned a most brilliant campaign, but had failed to carry it out—had been defeated in his main object. But in another sence, I most emphatically deny that the army was whipped or beaten."[19]

---

15 BV 110, part 12, FSNMP; which contains a letter of May 13, 1863, from George B. Wolcott, 44th New York Infantry Regiment. He is listed as George B. Wolcott, a private in Company E, 44th New York, in the NPS/CWSSS (M551 Roll 155), which coincides with his letter.

16 Ibid.

17 BV 193, part 70, FSNMP, letters published in Northern newspapers. This letter from "Earnest" appeared in the May 15 edition.

18 BV 193, part 65, a letter written to the same paper, written four days' earlier.

19 BV 147, part 1, FSNMP, letters of Lt. Cornelius L. Moore, 57th New York Infantry.

Moore felt they had attacked the enemy; was gratified by Jackson's death; and pointed out the Union could withstand "a dozen such 'defeats'" while the South could not. "The Army of the Potomac has truly met with many reverses, severe enough to dishearten and demoralize a less determined noble souled body of men," he asserted on May 25. "And when I speak of the 'Army of the Potomac,' I have reference to the 'old Army' that first borne that name (this does not include the 11th and 12th Corps.) I cannot help but express a feeling of pride at the mention of its name, and the remembrance of its deeds."[20]

James H. Leonard of the 5th Wisconsin Infantry wrote on May 14 from "Camp near White Oak Church." "In the squad over which I have charge, there were eighteen previous to the crossing of the river and now there is only seven. Every American in it was either killed or wounded," he bemoaned. Unfortunately, Leonard's sympathies for "American" comrades did not extend to the "Germans of the 11th Corps," whom he blamed for the defeat. "With the exception of this sorrow for our fallen comrades," he continued, "those of us that are left are in good health and good spirits, and just as ready to meet the enemy now as ever we were. I never knew the boys to come out of a fight so little discouraged as at present, excepting after the battle of Williamsburg. The fact of the case is, though we did come back to this side of the river, we do not consider ourselves as whipped by a considerable."[21]

Similar sentiments expressing the common wisdom were rendered by Edward R. Geary, son of Gen. J. W. Geary and a member of Knap's Pennsylvania Battery. "We were not whipped, although we did retreat," he wrote on May 30, "and we should have been successful had it not been for the cowardly conduct of one of our corps which run at the first approach of the enemy."[22]

Bitter, often snide, remarks about the XI Corps made their way into letter after letter. However, soldiers also looked in other directions for factors that might have influenced their defeat. "[W]e felt almost discouraged for a day or two till we began to understand the real cause of the retreat," explained Thomas P. Beath of the 19th Maine Infantry on May 17. "I believe the failure is [owing] to the unforeseen element and not to any fault of Hookers. I think it would have been utterly impossible after the heavy rains that we had to get supplies to the army, for when we were on the roads guarding the [telegraph] line they were in wretched condition and after the rain they must have

---

20 Ibid.

21 BV 353, part 23, FSNMP, R. G. Plumb, ed., "Letters of a Fifth Wisconsin Volunteer" in *Wisconsin Magazine of History*, Volume 3 (September 1919 - June 1920), 72-73, pertaining to Lt. James H. Leonard, 5th Wisconsin Infantry. Leonard provided an interesting insight on relations between the armies.

22 BV 184, part 1, FSNMP, letter of Edw. R. Geary, Knap's Battery.

been awful." Most importantly, Beath said he hadn't lost faith in "old Joe" yet. "I believe his plans were good and that his next move will be more successful. All the troops seem to have great confidence in him, even the McClellan men have to admit that they think the plans were good."[23]

Lieutenant W. O. Blodget of the 151st Pennsylvania Infantry, at "Camp near FitzHugh Plantation, Va.," cast his blame a little eastward and northward. "Why was not Dix [Fortress Monroe area] or Heintzelman [Washington Defenses] sent to Hooker's assistance?" he pondered on May 10. "If Sedgewick could have been reinforced and sustained, the result would have been very different. It seems strange that so many men should be kept idle, but I do not presume to know." Blodget was positive about one thing, though: the condition of his comrades. "It certainly is a fact that the men of our [I] Corps at least are in no way discouraged or demoralized—neither do I believe those of the other Corps are."[24]

Sergeant Rollin L. Jones of the 29th Ohio Infantry, writing twelve days after Stonewall Jackson's death, ascribed some of the blame to the dead Confederate general. "I presume you have read the General Order published by Hooker on the 30th of April. He promised a good deal, but made a grand failure," he opined. "The success of his enterprise until the 2nd of May was all that could be wished. But Lee and Jackson were too much for him. But Jackson is out of the way, and hard work they will have to find a man to take his place. The rebels claim that he was killed by his own men by mistake. But it's enough for us to know that he was killed in battle." Jones was sharp to reckon Jackson's death alone compensated for "Lee's greatest victory."[25]

Warren Banister Persons of the 64th New York Infantry, fighting along the Chancellorsville defense line, survived his first battle thanks to a miraculously available shovel. He threw up enough of a dirt embankment to slow a rifle round which struck him painfully in the chest. Unwounded, he joined in his unit's stalwart defense. He was nevertheless disappointed as he wrote from "Camp near Falmouth" on May 30. "We failed to accomplish much this time, but we are bound to thrash the rebs, in the end," he said. "I am confident we shall ultimately win. We are vindicating the cause of the

23 BV 69, part 2, FSNMP, letter from T. P. Beath to Brother Ed, dated May 17, 1863. The 19th Maine was in 1-2-II Corps. Beath rose to the rank of captain prior to Appomattox. The NPS/CWSSS relates that Thomas P. Beath was mustered in as a corporal and out as a captain. M543 Roll 2.

24 BV 210, part 15, FSNMP. Letters of Lt. W. O. Blodget, Company F, 151st Pennsylvania Infantry.

25 "ALS, 6pp, 8vo." letter for sale by North Carolina Civil War documents dealers Brian and Maria Green, Vol. XVII, 2009, Fall, No. 66. The writer, identified as "R. S. Jones," is listed as Rollin L. Jones, Company C, 29th Ohio Infantry Regiment, in NPS/CWSSS (M552 Roll 56).

downtrodden and oppressed. We are fighting the battles of Freedom, of Justice and of Right and my assurance of our final success comes from my faith in the justice and omnipotence of God." Turning to the now familiar refrain, he said: "I do not think we have much to fear from copperheads. They will die of their own venom: We had Tories in the Revolution more numerous proportionately than copperheads are now, but the machinations of traitors can not avail anything against the decrees of Destiny."[26]

The Army of the Potomac still had its own internal machinations churning away, though, especially among lingering McClellanites. One was temporary captain of cavalry George Armstrong Custer. Custer, notoriously last to graduate in his hurried-up West Point class of June 1861, had gained fame as a reckless courier while serving on the staffs of Generals McClellan and Pleasonton. He also commanded a company of Regular U.S. Cavalry as Pleasonton's escort. On May 6, Custer wrote from division headquarters near the Lacy House to his old commander, McClellan. "I know you must be anxious to know how your army is, and has been, doing, particularly so if, as is reported here, the papers are prohibited from publishing the news," the cavalryman said, somewhat convolutedly. "I cannot give you any of the details, nor is it necessary, it is sufficient to know the general result, we are defeated, driven back on the left bank of the Rappahannock with a loss which I suppose will exceed our entire loss during the seven days battles." Custer proceeded almost gleefully to supply details of failures by Hooker, Stoneman, and Averell. "To say that everything is gloomy and discouraging does not express the state of affairs here," he said, and "the universal cry is 'Give us McClellan.'" Custer's delusion notwithstanding, by May 1863, there was actually a distinct dearth of cries for McClellan in the army. Only people with political axes to grind or military allegiances to uphold were singing that old song. It was not that Hooker was so much better; the majority had simply moved on.[27]

More disconcerting than Custer's was Gen. John Gibbon's May 18 letter to McClellan. A proven officer, Gibbon had been wounded at Fredericksburg while commanding the 2nd Division of the I Corps and returned to duty three months later. His II Corps division, held back initially, fought in the Second Fredericksburg assault under Sedgwick. His letter was, by definition, disloyal, but, it was—despite betraying intra-army factionalism—analytical, balanced, nuanced and apparently principled. "The army has all returned and now occupies pretty much its old ground," he wrote, "and there seems to be a prospect for a respite, that is if the enemy does not move, which it is

26 BV 73, part 7, FSNMP. Warren B. Persons enlisted as a private in August 1862 and was mustered-in to the 64th New York Infantry, in October 1862. (M551 Roll 110, NPS/CWSSS.)

27 BV 56, part 5, FSNMP, letter from Capt. G. A. Custer to Gen. G. B. McClellan in McClellan Papers, Library of Congress, Reel 35.

not by any means certain he will not do." Gibbon rightly worried that the pending discharge of two-year units and nine-months' units might embolden Lee.

"[T]here appears to be no doubt that our force was great enough and in a condition to have won a decisive battle," he wrote. "Hooker who is so well known to possess personal bravery seems to have yielded entirely to his nerves and to have shown a complete want of backbone at the wrong moment, to the surprise of every one." He offered tribalistic credit to the West Pointers who tried to shore Hooker up: "At the council Monday [May 4th] night every one of the West Point Corps Commanders urged Genl. Hooker to remain and fight." He singled-out Sickles's objections, dubbing him "a political Genl with no military experience and no character, public or private," because he urged "a retreat, contending with the old doctrines that the army occupied a political as well as a military position and that if it was destroyed Washington, that great bugbear, would be taken." Gibbon believed Hooker had succumbed to Sickles's and Butterfield's unmerited influence and both lacked "principle" (apparently meaning a West Point diploma). Hooker's injury was apparently unknown to Gibbon.

Gibbon admitted the army had begun the campaign "feeling every confidence in Hooker and his success," but he blamed Hooker's "congratulatory order on the operations of the 5th, 11th & 12th Corps" as "a great mistake and now after his failure no one can help referring to it." Finally came the gross disloyalty: "I do not believe [the West Pointers'] confidence in you is a particle less than it ever was, but if you cannot come back the Govt. had better take things in time & send either Franklin back, or appoint Meade in whom every one seems to have confidence."[28]

Gibbon's confidence in Meade was valid, but his prejudice against non-West Pointers as "men without character and without principle" betrayed an unconscionable level of professional snobbery. His insider's gossip also conveniently omitted mention of Hooker's West Point education (or Halleck's, for that matter).

The right principle—to use Gibbon's term if not his meaning—was that the army's generals and officers needed to concentrate on defeating Lee's army, eliminate endless factionalism, and pull together. That, after two years of war, good officers like Gibbon were so ignorant of this and so unknowledgeable of the men with whom they served confirms the assertion. If men at war distrust one another and fail to know one another, little success is possible, especially amid difficulty and adversity.

Chancellorsville's object lesson was the army had demonstrably improved. It now needed to execute its plans with single-minded purpose. The soldiers' correspondence points to the prevailing post-Chancellorsville attitude of frustrated anger rather than the

---

28 BV 56, part 6, FSNMP, letter from Gen. J. Gibbon to Gen. G. B. McClellan in McClellan Papers, Library of Congress, Reel 35.

hopeless despondency after Fredericksburg. The soldiers were rightly angry because they had allowed a victory to slip from their grasp.

"I hope people will be mild in their judgments of Hooker and above all I hope he will not be superseded," the pseudonymous "VT. SIXTH," wrote plaintively in a letter home. "I cannot believe it was a fault of his and he has shown his bravery and good generalship."[29]

New Eyes

Fresh to the post-Chancellorsville army was Maj. John Irwin Nevin, a former teacher who had served from the war's beginning. As a 28th Pennsylvania Infantry lieutenant he'd been held prisoner in Libby Prison from February through August, 1862. After October of that year, he raised and then commanded Independent Battery H, Pennsylvania Artillery, in the Washington Defenses. Resigning under a cloud in February 1863, on April 1st he was appointed major in the 93rd Pennsylvania Infantry, a unit in 3rd Brigade, 3rd Division, VI Corps, which was then without any field-grade officers. A dispassionate observer, Nevin arrived at Aquia Landing on May 5, just as the battles were concluding.[30]

Passing the night on dry straw in a quartermaster's shed, he joined his unit on May 6. His entry was illuminating. "Started at 8 o'clock on horseback for Falmouth. A rough road in places—knee deep mud—ugly gullies, swollen streams, and bridges torn away," he wrote. "Scenery monotonous on account of the desolation occasioned by army occupation, i.e., Army destruction. The road was almost anywhere one chose to go. So that he [the horse] kept a general southerly direction as the hills and valleys around were every where cut with deep wagon tracks."

At Falmouth, Nevin saw "mule teams, straggling parties of soldiers, trains of pack mules carrying ammunition," and III Corps returning in a "sad plodding, listless way in which they drag themselves along through the mud. A sad sight is a retreating army after a great defeat. I will not dwell on it." After interacting with the men, he concluded:

> I hope for happier times for the poor Army of the Potomac! The army is depressed but not demoralized; the feeling that prevails is not in the least fear, but an angry sadness, a

29 BV 193, part 74, FSNMP, a letter from the May 22, 1863, edition of the *Vermont Watchman and State Journal.*

30 Here and for subsequent paragraphs in this section, see Dana B. Shoaf, ed., "'On the March Again at Daybreak': The Gettysburg Diary of Major John I. Nevin, 93rd Pennsylvania Infantry," in *Civil War Regiments: A Journal of the American Civil War* (Mason City, IA, 1999), Volume Six, Number 3, 107-138.

reluctance to return from victory almost in our grasp to the tiresome, objectless camp life—and unwilling belief that the death of the Confederacy has been, for many months postponed.

Nevin noted that VI Corps men "as far as I have observed are not very much affected by the late reverse although scarcely a corps of the army has suffered as severely as they have. The men have the careless devil-may-care manner of taking any event that may happen as entirely a matter of course, a characteristic of the old soldier everywhere. They have become so used to the most tremendous excitements that they are (case) hardened, in fact seem to lose a goodly portion of their sensibility entirely."

"They talk with the most matter of fact tone in the world about fearful scenes and hairbreadth escapes sufficient to satisfy the demand of many sensations," he continued. "They joke about the bullet holes in each others clothes, talk with a shocking indifference about the loss of comrades struck dead at their sides. Truly this cruel war will demoralize the soldiers, patriots though they be, to a frightful extent." Perhaps most importantly he observed, "And patriots they are for I find not a single copperhead here—some may be tired of the war—of soldiering—wish they were home, but not a man but intends to fight it out to the last."

This was assuredly not the army of January 1863.

Old Eyes

Given his earlier brilliance, one might hope Rufus R. Dawes, now a lieutenant colonel, had provided similarly clear insights. If he did, they were omitted from his 1890 memoirs. Instead, Dawes reflected the men described by Maj. Nevin. "The reason General Hooker recrossed the river was because he was outgeneraled and defeated,—a humiliating confession, I own, but I believe true," he wrote on May 18, from camp. "I have taken up my work again . . . . The weather is fine and we are beautifully located in a grove near the White Oak Church. The church is mythical, but it is a pleasant name to mark a pleasant locality. Drilling, parading, reviewing and court martialing go on again as usual before the battle." If Dawes was looking for a cathedral in White Oak, he never noticed it: the frequently disrespected church was diminished even by those who recognized it; one soldier even compared it to his barn. More importantly, Dawes' post-Chancellorsville letters reflected increased unit pride, which was the nearest substitute for victory.[31]

That was another step in the right direction.

---

31 Dawes, *Service With The Sixth Wisconsin Volunteers*, 142, 150.

If anyone had reason to look for silver lining, it was XI Corps commander Maj. Gen. Oliver Otis Howard. Despite absorbing many criticisms for the army's defeat, he provided a good assessment of the "Valley Forge" and its battle connections. "My own feeling at that time [after Fredericksburg in II Corps] was that of a want of confidence in the army itself. The ending of the peninsular work, the confusion at the termination of the second battle of Bull Run, the incompleteness of Antietam, and the fatal consequences of Fredericksburg did not make the horizon of our dawning future very luminous. We had suffered desertions by the thousands," he summarized. "I brought two commissioned officers about that time to trial for disloyal language, directed against the President and the general commanding. Mouths were stopped, but discontent had taken deep root."

He then professionally assessed Hooker's role and reinforced this study's thesis:

> Hooker, however, by his prompt and energetic measures, soon changed the whole tone of the army for the better. Desertions were diminished, and outpost duty was systematized. The general showed himself frequently to his troops at reviews and inspections, and caused the construction of field works and entrenchments, which, with the drills, occupied the time and the minds of the soldiers. The cavalry became a corps, and Stoneman was put in command of it. The artillery reserve, given to General Hunt, was brought to a high degree of efficiency.

"In truth," he added, "during February, March, and April, the old cheerful, hopeful, trustful spirit which had carried us through so many dark days, through so many bloody fields and trying defeats, returned to the Army of the Potomac; and Hooker's success as a division and corps commander was kept constantly in mind as an earnest of a grand future."[32]

Fresh Eyes

The single most remarkable post-Chancellorsville document related to the "Valley Forge" appeared before the smoke had even cleared the battlefield in the May 5, 1863 *New York Times* from the pen of correspondent William Swinton. Written three days

---

32 Oliver Otis Howard, *Autobiography of Oliver Otis Howard, Major General, United States Army* (New York, NY, 1907). Memoirs quoted from: http://www.russscott.com/~rscott/26thwis /oohowmem.htm (accessed November 20, 2009). It is important to note that in July of 1864, Howard was promoted over Hooker for command of the Army of the Tennessee. By that time Hooker was already disgruntled with Howard and blamed him for the loss at Chancellorsville. That bad blood gave Howard every reason to withhold any generous assessment of Hooker's performance. Thus, it is of some note that Howard's memoirs treat Hooker as fairly as they do.

earlier on May 2, it reveals how the first historian of the army viewed his subject at the time.[33] Important is his direct testimony that he had been absent for the previous "couple of months," so Swinton was returning to the army with fresh eyes. "The army, in all its aspects is in splendid condition," he began. Swinton continued:

The army is larger than it was before materially. The health of the troops is better than it ever was before. From the first day General Hooker took command, it was felt that a directing brain animated the mass. Mens agitat molem. Great mobility has been secured by prodigiously cutting down the amount of transportation, and by employing pack mules, which go anywhere in all weathers, instead of our heavy wagons, which are always stuck in the mud. But two wagons are allowed to a regiment. The army is no longer encumbered with that ponderous impediment which used to be the marvel of all who beheld it. In fact, we now approximate the French standard, which enables an army to carry fourteen days' provisions without a wheel behind it.

The moral transformation is not less complete. It may be in the recollection of some of your readers that I had occasion two months ago to give a minute dissection of the condition of the Army of the Potomac as it was at the time of the last bungling campaign on the Rappahannock. I was accordingly much interested, after an absence of a couple of months, to make a comparative study of the internal change that had come over it in the interval under the new military regime. The metamorphosis could hardly have been more complete, and I have often had difficulty in convincing myself that that army, where general croaking, jealousies, disaffection, desertion and universal demoralization prevailed, is the same with this in which a new vitality animates the men. System, harmony and organization are seen, and a true military spirit pervades the troops.

Nothing in this line of phenomena struck me more than the admirable secrecy that existed in regard to the plans and movements of the opening campaign. It was a new and somewhat tantalizing sensation; for any one who has followed the movements of the army in the field will bear me out when I say that hitherto projected operations have always been known and discussed by nearly every body—even the negro servants in the camps—for days and weeks before they took place. In this case absolute ignorance prevailed. Not even corps commanders knew what was intended, and had only their specific individual order for the day.

Accordingly, early in the week every one was rubbing his eyes, and asking where is the army? No one could tell. There was a column moving up, another moving down, and the column that was up yesterday proves to be down today. I confess I was heartily glad of the general bewilderment, though it was rather puzzling for a correspondent to observe

33 Swinton's outstanding early history was entitled *Campaigns of the Army of the Potomac: A Critical History of Operations in Virginia Maryland and Pennsylvania from the Commencement to the Close of the War, 1861-1865* (New York, 1866).

movements along a line twenty-five to thirty miles in length. In this case it was the spectators of the great game of chess that were blindfolded. The master planner alone had his eyes open.

In the great game of war, time and space are the elements with which the General has to deal. Celerity (and for that purpose the greatest possible mobility) with secrecy are the indispensable conditions of all military combinations. The mind of General Hooker is one that will put forth all the resources of these elements.

Of significance from a historiographic perspective, Swinton—the first writer-observer to attempt to describe and analyze the Army of the Potomac's entire war service—was not present to witness its "Valley Forge." His extreme enthusiasm on May 2 was all the more revealing because he had not experienced firsthand the resurgence during the months leading up to Chancellorsville. Swinton's later history did not maintain that contemporaneous enthusiasm, his reaction dampened by the battle's outcome and the time to reflect on Hooker's performance. As the first of numerous army historians, Swinton's views indelibly affected subsequent analyses.[34]

Fittingly, Rufus Dawes of the Iron Brigade supplies us with a final significant observation comparable to the insight offered by newcomer Major Nevin or correspondent William Swinton. After Chancellorsville, Dawes' 6th Wisconsin experienced several minor skirmishes and numerous false starts. "I must brag a little about our regiment," Dawes wrote on June 10, reflecting on the entire post-battle period. "We have the healthiest regiment in the corps. We have a harmonious, quiet and satisfied set of officers. There is no intriguing, court-martialing or backbiting, which is common in the army. The arms, accoutrements and clothing are kept in excellent condition."[35]

---

34 *The New York Times*, May 5, 1863, 1, 8. Dispatch was written by William Swinton on May 2, 1863. A copy of Swinton's 1866 book *Campaigns of the Army of the Potomac* is located in the FSNMP Library. It contains a handwritten note by R. K. Gould (August 1964): "Swinton (William) and [L. L.] Crounse were two principal correspondents of *The N.Y. Times* with the Army of the Potomac—these two *Times* men were a study in contrasts: Swinton, tall and well-formed, with eyes large and luminous, and with a well modulated voice which failed to betray his Scottish birth; Crounse was small and dapper. Swinton had emigrated from Scotland to Canada with his family when he was ten, had prepared for Presbyterian ministry at Knox College in Toronto and at Amherst, had done some preaching and had then left the pulpit to teach languages in a female seminary in Greensboro, N. C. In 1858 he joined the staff of *The New York Times* probably with the help of his brother John, already an employee of the paper. Whereas Crounse was deliberate, cautious, and reliable, Swinton discussed military movements and criticized generals with such freedom that he was constantly in difficulties with the military authorities." See also Andrews, *The North Reports the Civil War*, 65; *Dictionary of American Biography*, Volume 18, 252-253; Grant, *Memoirs*, vol. 2, 145.

35 Dawes, *Service With The Sixth Wisconsin Volunteers*, 150.

Two days later, they began their long, arduous march to Gettysburg. Dawes and his men—and the rest of the army's combat troops—were now veteran soldiers who had learned everything they would ever need to know about army life, taken their own measure, recognized competent leadership, and understood the military character required of a good soldier. They had become Shakespeare's "band of brothers." These priceless lessons would play out on their next battlefield in Pennsylvania and for the remainder of their war.

Assessment

A century later, an interim judgment of history was passed on Joseph Hooker's performance at Chancellorsville, dispassionately pronounced by military professionals, predominantly veterans of a Second World War and Korea, at Hooker's alma mater:

> And then—with every opportunity at hand for a decisive victory—Hooker's courage failed. Over the indignant protests of his corps commanders, he ordered the troops back into their positions of the night before around Chancellorsville. Later, he countermanded this order, but by then his troops had withdrawn. Meanwhile, Sedgwick received several conflicting orders, and so did nothing aggressive. It is difficult to explain Hooker's unwarranted surrender of the initiative under such favorable circumstances. He was personally brave; he had built up a splendid army; and he had planned skillfully. It may have been that it was difficult for him to visualize and assess properly a military operation on such a large scale that many of its phases were beyond the range of his direct control. Possibly it was the inward knowledge of this inadequacy which, at a critical moment, weakened his determination. Later, as a corps commander in more restricted operations, he again proved to be a fine leader.[36]

The judgment of this study concurs with that assessment, but also believes Hooker lost his focus before and—through injury—during the operation. As importantly, Hooker did not demonstrate flexibility in readjusting his plans, given General Stoneman's failures and Lee's actions. But, critical to the outcome of the war, during their strategic pause in Stafford, Hooker's army turned around their fortunes with retrospectively masterful leadership actions and reforms during the core 93-day "Valley Forge."

For as much success as Hooker achieved during that difficult winter, more key reforms remained, particularly among the army's leadership. The reorganization and

36 Esposito, ed., *West Point Atlas*, Map 84.

reform of the cavalry corps, intelligence system, medical system, and tactical logistics—all spectacular—were not yet completed or perfected.

Had the Federals won, the army's complete resurrection could have been readily recognized at Chancellorsville/Second Fredericksburg. But, that slipped from its immediate grasp, and the true picture would not resolve until the army successfully defeated Lee's army at Gettysburg. What the army did demonstrate at Chancellorsville was that it could fight and defeat Lee militarily. At the end of the campaign, there was little doubt in the minds of intelligent contemporary observers that the corner had finally been turned.

If history were linear, the "Valley Forge" would have flowed neatly into victory at Chancellorsville; Lee would have surrendered or fallen back on Richmond; and, after a bitterly fought finale, victory parades would have commenced in 1863 or 1864. The Army of the Potomac, however, had more rivers to cross and battles to fight. No longer a beaten and discouraged army, they were ready to advance Hooker's and Butterfield's reforms and move on to fight again.

It remains to be seen whether history—that reality which Abraham Lincoln cautioned no administration, person, or group of persons could ultimately escape—will ever see the "Valley Forge" in the same way it is described in this work.

Epilogue

Hooker's army, now at least the second finest army on the planet, moved northward, shielded the capital—earning the "Thanks of Congress"—and shadowed Lee into Maryland and Pennsylvania. Amazingly, en route to Gettysburg and a higher destiny, Joseph Hooker fell into another interpersonal dust-up with the War Department.

"You have long been aware, Mr. President, that I have not enjoyed the confidence of the major-general commanding this army [Halleck]," Hooker wrote in a direct appeal to Lincoln, "and I can assure you so long as this continues, we may look in vain for success, especially as future operations will require our relations to be more dependent upon each other than heretofore."[1]

In the ensuing back and forth, Hooker requested control of the troops of the Washington Defenses at Harpers Ferry, commanded by Major General William H. French, as the army moved north. Halleck agreed—but with strings. Soon, Hooker found himself entwined inextricably. No doubt Halleck was supported by Stanton and Lincoln, probably on grounds that the forces were needed to protect Washington. However, it made military sense to unify command at that point, and Lincoln and Stanton probably erred.

The rashness Lincoln had warned Hooker about back in January now became Hooker's undoing. Disagreeing with Halleck's decision, Hooker threatened to resign over the matter—playing unwittingly into Halleck's plan. "My original instructions require me to cover Harper's Ferry and Washington," Hooker reminded them. "I have now imposed upon me, in addition, an enemy in my front more than my number."[2] If they wouldn't attach French's Harpers Ferry command to the army, he asked to be

---

1   OR, 25, part I, 45.

2   Ibid, 60.

relieved. Once again, Joseph Hooker approached the precipice of success only to throw himself over in a personality-flawed act.

Halleck's bland response must have belied his spiteful glee: "Your application to be relieved from your present command is received. As you were appointed to this command by the President, I have no power to relieve you. Your dispatch has been duly referred to Executive action."[3] Behind the scenes, the selection process for a successor rapidly commenced.

As with McClellan's firing, a trusted aide—Col. James Hardie, in this instance—was dispatched from Washington to inform V Corps commander Maj. Gen. George Gordon Meade of his new assignment. In violation of Army protocol—but again following the precedent set when McClellan was fired—Meade and Hardie went to inform Hooker. Not surprisingly, Hooker's response was described as "revulsion." Lincoln thanked Hooker for his service and quietly accepted his resignation on June 28. Ironically, the subject of his latest tiff—Harpers Ferry—ended up being the location where "Fighting Joe" resigned.[4]

Halleck's June 27 correspondence to Meade pretty much told the tale: it was unlike anything he was known to have communicated to Hooker. "I cannot doubt that you will justify the confidence which the Government has reposed in you," Halleck began. In direct opposition to his treatment of Hooker he added, "You will not be hampered by any minute instructions from these headquarters. Your army is free to act as you may deem proper under the circumstances as they arise." He finished with "you may rely on our full support."[5]

The battle at Gettysburg, three days after Hooker's replacement and unplanned by either side, was the post-"Valley Forge" meeting of the armies where the Army of the Potomac finally did defeat Robert E. Lee and his army. Hooker was not present and, no doubt significantly, neither was the incomparable team of Lee, Jackson, and Stuart. Jackson, the strong right arm, was gone and Jeb Stuart, regardless of subsequent explanations, failed in his basic responsibilities as cavalry commander. Even Lee, probably due to lingering heart angina and/or diarrhea, was not at his best at Gettysburg.

Although he played a positive role, Meade—appointed to command on the march and arriving on the battlefield after the first day's fighting to find that his subordinates held the dominant terrain—did not win the battle per se. It was the army en masse—the

---

3   Ibid.

4   Steven Trent Smith, "Firing Joe Hooker," *Civil War Times*, April 2014, 34-41 provides a rare focus on Hooker's relief and Meade's appointment.

5   *OR*, 27, part I, 61.

one Hooker and Butterfield had rebuilt—that achieved that victory.[6] Hooker, given the same events and circumstances, could have probably done as well. But Meade and his generals, colonels, captains, sergeants and soldiers held the army together for the next two crucial days, and Lee threw all that was left of the Army of Northern Virginia against both Federal flanks and then the Federal center. However, the tables of Fredericksburg were reversed: the Union troops held the defensible terrain and were defending their home territory against exposed Confederates advancing on their stone wall.

Yet, as the rains of July 4th, 1863, symbolically cleansed the bloody soil of the war's most significant battle in the East, it was the Army of the Potomac that prevailed. Demons exorcized, Gettysburg gave the resurgent army its first magnificent, if costly, victory. Meade, however, disappointed the president by failing to destroy Lee's retreating army. Perhaps Lincoln did not appreciate the Army of the Potomac's true situation. It fought at Gettysburg with 88,289 effectives—47,000 fewer men than at Fredericksburg and Chancellorsville. It suffered 23,049 casualties (26 percent: 3,155 dead; 14,529 wounded; and 5,365 missing). The Confederates, on the other hand, fought with 75,000 effectives—only 3,000 less than at First Fredericksburg, but 15,500 more than at Chancellorsville. Lee's army suffered 28,063 casualties (37 percent: 3,903 dead; 18,735 wounded; and 5,425 missing).[7]

Gettysburg was not the end, but it did turn out to be the Confederacy's last large-scale strategic offensive in the Eastern Theater. The argument holds that the "Valley Forge"— the true turning point—made Gettysburg possible, and Gettysburg made final victory possible. If the army's morale and combat effectiveness had been left to die in Stafford's mud, Lee's offensive might well have been successful and decisive.

As importantly, the turnaround of the "Valley Forge" and the victory at Gettysburg bolstered the vitally necessary will of the Northern people. The true victory in both events was defeating Copperhead antiwar momentum.

Confederate defeat in Pennsylvania suggested enormous new potentials—many unrealized by the North. Missed were the opportunities to pursue and destroy Lee's army away from its supply lines and to deliver a series of successive blows that could have ended war in that theater. As at Chancellorsville, Federal efforts fell short, and they did not rise during the Bristoe and Mine Run campaigns through December 1863. The army spent another winter in Virginia. But just as Chancellorsville had been a different kind of defeat from Fredericksburg, the winter of 1863-1864 would be a different kind of winter strategic pause. This time the army went into its winter encampment

---

6   Meade wisely retained Butterfield for continuity, though came to regret the decision.

7   Gettysburg statistics vary widely. These shown are representative and estimates.

"winning" and was confident of future success. The army could now, finally, look ahead to another spring campaign with greater potentials.

Lee could still exact an enormous price by tactical, even operational defensive successes, but he could draw no further strategic advantage from Federal shortfalls. At best, the Army of Northern Virginia could continue to defend, parry Federal blows while withdrawing, and make limited counterattacks.

Success for the Union ultimately came east with Grant, who permanently seized the strategic initiative during the Overland Campaign in the spring and summer of 1864. With Grant, the high command's missing link was secured and, at long last, the Union had a real general-in-chief coordinating offensives of several armies in the field.

The army still struggled with basic questions. "Orders have come down," said E. F. of the 14th Connecticut during that 1864 winter in Culpeper County, "that henceforth a five days' maximum of rations only shall be carried on the backs of the soldiers and only forty rounds of cartridges (what the cartridge boxes are made to hold). Whether to give the credit of this eminently sensible proceeding to Gen. Meade or the War Department, I do not know; but millions of soldiers' blessings will be on his head who ordered the curtailment."[8] Investigations on basic soldier loads, begun during the "Valley Forge," came finally to reasonable Civil War ends. Henceforth it was the task of the logistics specialists, using innovations begun by Hooker, Butterfield, and Ingalls, to move resupply food and ammunition forward to combat units by pack- and wagon-train.

* * *

In military historical analysis, post-mortems work best by examining the systems of war that comprise military forces:

Command, Control and Coordination
Organization
Communications
Personnel
Intelligence and Reconnaissance
Operations and Plans
Special Troops
Training and Education
Logistics
Medical

8 BV 311, part 5, FSNMP. *The Connecticut War Record*, January 1864, "Our Army Correspondence," 119-120. The identity of correspondent "E. F." remains a mystery.

Transportation
Civil-Military Relations and Operations
Weapons and Equipment
Morale and Recreation
Accountability, Discipline and Numbers
Army-Navy Cooperation

Command, Control and Coordination

The high command did not change during the "Valley Forge." Lincoln, as commander-in-chief, successfully performed the same functions he had from the war's outset, as did Secretaries Stanton (War) and Gideon Welles (Navy), Salmon P. Chase (Treasury) and William Seward (State). General-in-chief Halleck likewise retained his post despite proving ineffective in his duties.

The position of "commanding general of the Army of the Potomac" was somewhat diminished under Hooker compared to its larger sphere of responsibility under McClellan, when it encompassed the Washington Defenses and the Army of the Potomac. In that position, Hooker received his essential instructions directly from the president, occasionally transmitted through Stanton or Halleck, but by Lincoln-Hooker agreement, Halleck was largely pushed aside, creating a bureaucratic impediment and perpetual interpersonal thorn in Hooker's side. Cutting-out Halleck provided him ready excuses for non-involvement. Cutting him out, and occasionally Stanton, from information/decision processes negated or limited the War Department's strategic potential. Hooker's later endorsement of Stanton at least suggested they interacted favorably behind the scenes.

Essential strategic processes took place in the War Department: selecting key leaders; determining goals and objectives; allocating resources (forces and materiel); and assigning missions to the Army (and sometimes prioritizing them); and coordinating with the Navy. National command authorities monitored progress toward goals and objectives and adjusted resources. Although typical in political life, military-strategic "workarounds" were not acceptable. No one in that highest loop could be worked around without causing harm elsewhere. This shortfall fell directly on the president and Stanton. Lincoln's supreme political skills worked against him in this regard. His political success depended on convincing, cajoling, (gently) coercing, and compromising. Disposed to working with colleagues with different agendas, the commander-in-chief needed to insist on clear lines of authority and responsibility and to jump on failures. Lincoln had a good secretary of war, but poor generals-in-chief until Grant. Lincoln established good initial war aims: to defeat the rebellion and restore the Union and, after January 1863, emancipation. Stanton helped carry out those aims; and ensured organizational continuity and strategic materiel flow to multiple theaters. Halleck, despite alleged strategic knowledge, failed to translate war aims to operational goals in the various theaters of the war. He became an impediment and needed to be removed, not circumvented. Lincoln's selection of army-level commanders was arguably poor; but the nation had no institutionalized system to do better. In Hooker's case, his military administrative strengths during the "Valley Forge" and his indecisiveness on the field at Chancellorsville were both surprises. The Lincoln Administration failed to pick "the right man" because it failed to pick an effective general-in-chief who could have proposed effective field commanders. Thus, only trial and error reigned.

After Hooker's departure, the army's national command chain was changed to Lincoln (Stanton)-Grant (Halleck)-Meade. Strategically, despite adding more personalities, this was a better mix. One military commander now coordinated deployment of numerous field armies. Operating in the field, Grant was an operational-strategic commander and a modern chief of staff. He also represented the commander-in-chief at the front. Halleck became an administrative "chief of staff"— probably still a mistake, but at least it relieved Grant from some administrative burdens.

Hooker's command and control was generally limited to those operational aspects that the commander and his chief of staff could personally manage. Hooker's staff bore little resemblance to a modern general staff (administration and personnel; intelligence; operations and training; logistics; civil-military operations; etc.) or special staffs (representing the full range of special and technical services). His aides-de-camp, assistant adjutants-general and odd assortments of individual staff officers, all interacted directly and personally with Butterfield and/or Hooker. None were adequately educated and trained, and all lacked authority to act for the commander. They could only do the direct bidding of their respective commanders as "military helpers" and couriers. Headquarters command posts were not mobile, with no ability to split into forward and rear echelons. It was impossible to adequately inform subordinate commanders. When separated from headquarters, subordinate commanders could only be reached and commanded by direct message (couriers and occasionally field telegraph). Corps and divisions suffered from the same ills. Coordination of operational and logistical activities by headquarters was solely dependent on skills and initiative of commanders and key specialists. Even nineteenth-century, Napoleonic-styled armies were increasingly made up of individuals performing specialized functions. However, they lacked effective structures and doctrines to expand and extend a commander's reach and allow him sufficient time and space to direct operations and resupply, monitor current situations, think about all aspects of his command, and plan for follow-on operations. These deficiencies ultimately affected all other areas.

Organization

The Army of the Potomac suffered from organizational inadequacies (as did the Army as a whole). The ridiculously small antebellum Regular U. S. Army necessitated radical wartime expansion incorporating vast numbers of militia and volunteers. The lack of mobilization and strategic deployment readiness inhibited the Union Army's swiftly suppressing the rebellion. In the 1920s-1940s, military historian John McAuley Palmer made the case that the Swiss-model defense system, conceptualized but not implemented by President Washington, might have dissuaded the South from secession and/or restored the Union rapidly.[9]

Washington's vision called for rapid deployment of the best-trained and most efficient units, followed by an orderly progression of less-trained formations. That speed, which the South would also have had, would be supplemented by the North's superior numbers and industrial capacity to end the Civil War. As a consequence of the lack of systematic mobilization, though, former captains and lieutenants of the Regular Army, militia and volunteer veterans of the Mexican War, and an uneven host of new political appointees to military commands were suddenly commanding armies, corps, divisions and brigades.

The army's Civil War organizational evolution, as described by William Swinton, was originally cobbled from the "force around Washington" by McClellan, a 35 year-old erstwhile Regular Army captain, Mexican War veteran, Crimean War observer, and railroad president. He was undeniably bright; but, in July 1861, the expanded army consisted of some 50,000 men, less than 1,000 cavalrymen, and 650 artillerymen in nine incomplete batteries—a semi-trained, armed mob with "an utter want of discipline and organization." The division of two or more brigades was considered a permanent unit. McClellan organized brigades of four regiments. Once brigades were "somewhat disciplined and instructed," he created divisions of three brigades each. Army corps ("corps de armee") of two or more divisions, on the Napoleonic model, were planned and organized once divisional commanders had "mastered" their trade.[10]

Burnside originated "grand divisions," each with two corps. They reduced the army commander's span of control from eight corps to four grand divisions; however, that denied the corps commanders direct access to the army commander, adding another layer of military intrigue and bureaucracy. If continued, grand divisions might have

9   Brigadier General John McAuley Palmer, U. S. A. (Retired), *America in Arms: The Experience of the United States with Military Organization* (New Haven, CT, 1941).

10 Swinton, *Campaigns of the Army of the Potomac.*

added value by permitting the ponderous army to be split or broken into smaller formations for independent operations.

By 1863, the Union's basic maneuver unit was the corps. Hooker, by dispensing with grand divisions, increased his span of control beyond his grasp. In early February 1863, the army reorganized into seven corps, and one independent cavalry corps, all with their own artillery. Hooker's restructuring of the army's artillery mistakenly returned to earlier organizational and tactical approaches. Removing reserve artillery as an independent command under the army's artillery chief was a mistake and backward step, soon evident at Chancellorsville (and quickly fixed thereafter).

Less obvious was the extent to which the army, corps, and divisions were "task organized" and "tailored" to the operational methods and preferences of their commanders. As evidenced by the periodic orders-of-battle in the Official Records, these commanders exercised considerable latitude in organizing their commands. Numbers of divisions and brigades were mainly reflections of the army's and corps' resource allocations; but, some formations were built for specific missions (e.g., a light division and an independent artillery assault unit). When commanders were actively engaged in the process, this suggested organizational flexibility.[11]

Hooker's major organizational success was his creation of the independent cavalry corps. However, Hooker's inability to place the right commander(s) and provide command direction slowed progress and diluted the achievement. Nevertheless, this would become one of the army's greatest longterm organizational successes.

In staff and operational contexts, Hooker's and Butterfield's second best organizational work was the Bureau of Military Information. This gave meaning and integration to the army's operational and tactical intelligence work. It gave greater purpose to the units and organizations capable of gaining and reporting enemy information. Medical, ordnance, tactical logistics, and provost-marshal activities saw similar restructuring to good effect. However, staff reforms were not implemented or apparently considered.

Communications

The establishment of the U. S. Military Telegraph Corps (U. S. M. T. C.) resulted in some 15,000 miles of military-controlled telegraph lines nationally. Initially the U. S. M. T. C. was under the Army's Quartermaster's Department. After January 1862, it was directly subordinated to the War Department. Its central office was at what is now the

---

11 See O'Reilly, *Fredericksburg Campaign* (appendix in soft-bound editions only), and the Appendix Order of Battle at the end of this study.

Executive Office Building next to the White House. The system was dependent on civilian expertise and innovation.[12]

Using existing telegraph networks and field-deployed systems, the army communicated back and forth with national authorities, and it kept its major headquarters interconnected—army headquarters to the corps headquarters and, when needed, down to the division level. Field telegraph lines were also employed using spooled-out, rubber-coated, twisted-metal wire land-lines connecting the various headquarters. Telegraphic communications thus stretched from division to Washington and included even naval and reconnaissance balloon access. Thus personnel, intelligence, operational, and logistical information could be reported—and encrypted when desired—though seldom disseminated or shared.

Absence of standardized messages or precise terminology led to ambiguous and confusing orders. Union signal corps units could also intercept Confederate signals and send disinformation via signals. A major shortfall was a distinct lack of clarity in messaging.

Personnel

The wartime personnel system of the Army of the Potomac and the Union Army was so arcane and complex that it is unlikely any single person or group of persons could explain the actual rankings of generals and brevet generals and officers and brevet officers. Distinctly different appointment and promotion systems by Federal and state authorities and rankings among Regular Army, volunteers, and militia officers left hopeless confusion and impossible record keeping. Effectively tracking unit musters, leaves of absences and absences-without-leave, re-enlistments, hospitalizations, and recognition for service or valor bogged down the army's administrators. Personnel accountability devolved literally to periodic "nose counts."

The "system" for picking men to command units and formations or to serve on staffs was byzantine: nepotism, factionalism and cronyism reigned, and national, state, ethnic groups, and Army political operatives ran amok in the process. The army's saving grace was that, by 1863, a limited military Darwinism had surfaced. Previously, every military appointment traced to some personal, political, or professional exertion by ambitious men, their proxies, or their sponsors. By 1863, the unqualified and grossly incompetent had largely been self- or command-selected out. Survivors were those of passable military abilities with the good fortunes of war not to have been pegged as incompetent by circumstances. This led to a sort of meritocracy with officers rising

12 Donald E. Markle, ed., *The Telegraph Goes to War: The Personnel Diary of David Homer Bates, Lincoln's Telegraph Operator* (Hamilton, NY: Edmonston Publishing, 2003).

successively and gaining experience through command and staff positions. It became increasingly difficult to deny advancement to proven officers. Retrospectively, the best were those who started as lieutenants and captains and advanced up the chain of command into field-grades or even general officer ranks. Of particular note were the numbers of merited non-commissioned officers rising in rank. Although not systematized, and uneven in application, the better regiments facilitated advancement of proven fighters and leaders.

Command selection was negatively affected by careerism and cronyism. Commanding generals should have been able to select key subordinates; after all, no commander—whose own success was tied to their performance—would intentionally select incompetents. However, just as few men were capable of commanding large units in combat, equally few were capable of making uniformly wise command/staff selections. Good commanders had to be good judges of subordinates and/or rely on good judgments by others. The worst alternative was when someone was imposed on a commander by another authority, with no direct stake in the outcome. Old Army, national, state, or political cronyism often led to selection errors.

Further, no effective system existed, except through uneven state initiatives, for replacement of the dead, wounded, and mustered-out soldiers. Thus, regiments of 800-1,000 men in 1861 were whittled down to 200-400 by the beginning of 1863. The 100-man companies of 1861 were down to 20 or 30 men by the beginning of 1863. Few regiments received replacements through state auspices. Governors were more likely to create new regiments than to replace individuals in older units because the number of regiments a state provided represented a kind of bragging rights.

This system, if it merited that term, overworked existing regiments and left them less able to accomplish characteristic missions. Combat units generally fulfilled assigned missions with about 60 percent of their complement; below that level, everything suffered. From unit and ordnance returns, it is clear that regiments redistributed men to achieve uniformity of company size. They also put more regiments into brigades to achieve a reasonable size for those formations.

As an unintended consequence of the poor replacement processes, the survivors in those undermanned regiments possessed extraordinary cohesion. Accepting and integrating replacements was haphazard (and the army was equally weak in welcoming new units, too). Too many "vacant chairs" existed in fighting regiments. Remaining soldiers were thus forced to pull too-heavy loads of guard, picket, outpost, and work duties without relief. As a result, they pragmatically welcomed conscription and desertion forgiveness.

Hooker drew on established military academies as sources for officers. West Point provided the bulk of the higher-level commanders for the North. Besides the national military academy, only Norwich University provided the Union with senior, military-trained officers and many mid- and lower-level officers (and enlisted men).[13]

Intelligence and Reconnaissance

Second only to medical reforms before and during the "Valley Forge," the army's reformed military intelligence and reconnaissance system contributed most in scope and value. The ability to task, collect, analyze, and evaluate information gleaned from cavalry, infantry, artillery, engineer, signal, military scout and agent networks, balloon units, open-source information (newspapers), and rear-area security organizations, and connect it with information/intelligence from Washington and other commands, were true military innovations absolutely needed by the army.

It was the first time in American military history that a field army employed a wide range of intelligence and reconnaissance assets with any hope of making sense of them. The enemy picture started to come into focus. While relative progress was astronomical, absolute progress was still retarded by a lack of sophistication and specialist development. Most needed was development of soldiers with adequate training and experience to glean the meaning of the disparate data and communicate it effectively to senior officers.

The greatest area of weakness remained: Hooker and his intelligence staff did not develop effective systems to disseminate intelligence to subordinates. Corps commanders attempted to run their own intelligence services and were often pitifully under- or mis-informed. This often negated any planning efforts below the army level.

Operations and Plans

The post-"Valley Forge" army was far superior in its capabilities for maneuver than ever before. Prior to Fredericksburg, its maneuvers had all been lethargic, and even its initial quick march to the banks of the Rappahannock under Burnside was hampered by a lack of logistical support that ultimately stranded the army on the north bank.

The Chancellorsville plan featured long, sweeping marches and deep envelopments by cavalry and infantry; multiple river crossings; demonstrations and feints; and "movements to contact" in which units sought out enemy formations. These demonstrated good planning with the desirable effect of concentric attack. This was

---

13 Palmer, *America in Arms*; Poirier, *By the Blood of Our Alumni.*

followed by impressive maneuvering. The army achieved greater march speed, as well (although neither Union nor even Confederate infantry ever achieved the maneuver speed of "Stonewall" Jackson's 1862 "foot cavalry").

The army's fire-support capabilities—the use of artillery to support the infantry and suppress enemy artillery—had demonstrably improved by the Fredericksburg battle, and they continued to excel in positioning their guns. Its numerical and qualitative superiority over Lee's artillerists had been too long in coming, though. At Fredericksburg, the Federals used reserve artillery in an independent command, which was a distinct qualitative improvement. Yet the use of organic artillery—artillery at the corps and division level—was less impressive. The army's fire support did not effectively maneuver across the river and find effective firing positions. Thus the Federals could not effectively employ more than half of their artillery to suppress Confederate defenses with fragmentation fires during assaults.

Hooker's "Valley Forge" artillery reorganization was not a success: most critics validly rate it a step backward. However, the army's artillery resumed positive development during and after Chancellorsville. Superior performance at Gettysburg attested to that. Planning for Tyler's independent artillery assault unit revealed an evolved organizational sophistication, as well.

Although needed details are lacking, Hooker's—and/or Butterfield's—planning for Chancellorsville markedly improved. Certainly army planning improved beyond what Burnside had managed at Fredericksburg and during the "Mud March." Cavalry-infantry schemes of maneuver; effective and rapid river-crossings; and operational-tactical resupply were effectively planned. A distinct question remains concerning planned engineer support, however. Because little planning or consultation time was allowed at the corps and lower levels, the larger planning and execution processes suffered egregiously. Stoneman's crucial failure to rapidly cross the river and raid deeply into Lee's rear area prior to the battle serves as the perfect illustration. Although on a smaller scale, Hooker's and Butterfield's February contingency planning for the defense of Stafford Court House and Aquia Landing merits further analysis.

This demonstrated sound planning throughout the winter beyond the immediate defensive mission. In the end, though, Federal planning was limited by a lack of standardization, coordination, and rehearsal. Assembling known information for command decision was too slow and dependent on the army commander's and chief of staff's personal skills. Successful contingency planning demonstrated higher levels of military art; however, adequately disseminating those plans to subordinate units did not occur.

In short, planning, fire-support, and maneuver in Hooker's army all progressed, but still fell short during execution. Hooker at least set the army on a better path and raised the qualitative bar.

Special Troops

Engineers—including those who constructed and operated the railroad—and the Signal Corps were the army's main special troops. Progress made through Fredericksburg saw further improvements during the "Valley Forge." Pontoon bridging steadily advanced in speed, quality, and quantity—these were and would continue to be critical given the numerous east-west oriented rivers and creeks lying ahead toward Richmond. Even wide rivers no longer blocked passage. In railroad construction, an increasingly effective construction corps—armed with increasingly innovative railroad bridging and track construction equipment and methods—followed the army. Combat units were called upon less frequently to construct bridges, but they continued to adeptly construct roads, especially corduroyed roads. As the army moved southward, it could count on greater use of naval combat and cargo vessels operating from the Chesapeake and its tributaries.

Topographic engineers, an established military elite, drew the best and brightest of West Point's graduates. Some of the best generals—such as Lee and Meade, with solid military-geographic and -geospatial skills—were developed in that corps. Engineer staff officers visualized the deployment of infantry, cavalry, and artillery and linked them to key terrain, logistics centers, and transportation nodes. Hooker's army benefited from such officers and their maps, although topographic engineers suffered from a lack of local familiarity and reference materials. No evidence of improved awareness of trafficability constraints—soils and weather—was evident, however.

Signal troops made more effective use of field telegraphs. Field lines increasingly supplemented or replaced existing telegraph lines within the army's zones of action. Telegraphic teams proliferated within corps and divisions. Semaphore and heliographic systems (sending visual flag and light Morse signals), and collocated observation posts (reporting enemy movements and activity) became increasingly effective. Message encryption in both telegraph and visual signals also became more sophisticated.

Although not specified as special troops per se, provost-marshal units became more professional and more knowledgeable in rear-area control and operational security. They played increasing roles in straggler and deserter control; ferreted out spies and saboteurs; reacted to rear area incursions by cavalry and partisans; and controlled prisoners, civilians, and freed-slaves. They also censored newspapers, limited access of reporters, and inspected incoming packages.

Training and Education

Self-education remained the mainstay of self-improvement. Those with initiative and ability studied the available military works. There was evidence of some self-initiated subordinate training within units. Unfortunately, only hard knocks on the battlefield provided officer and NCO training for most soldiers. Despite ample opportunities in winter camps to do so, the army did not develop officer and NCO training sufficiently to share knowledge and wartime experiences ("lessons learned").

Logistics

Officers responsible for the supply and resupply of the commissary (food), quartermaster (clothing, equipment and forage), and ordnance (artillery and small arms weapons and ammunition) operated within separate "stove-piped" systems. Their only common ground was competing for railroad and road transportation assets. Coordination between these and operational elements was by established peacetime practice and local agreements.

None of these systems seamlessly moved supplies, other materiel, or equipment from production to storage and handling facilities in the strategic rear area in the Washington Defenses or to the field army. Prevalent supply/resupply systems involved transporting supplies from Northern production sites to arsenals, bases, and depots, where they could be requisitioned and drawn on by supply and transportation organizations. Because it was perishable, food moved most rapidly to the army.

Thanks to Brig. Gen. Herman Haupt's crucial and numerous improved rail-ship-rail-road handling innovations, supplies were moved to the army by steamboats and barges from Washington and, in Stafford, by rail and road. These innovations saved time and energy and were truly a revolutionary dimension in warfare.

Within the army, field depots were established at Aquia Landing and Belle Plain and at other points in the rear area (e.g., Brooke, Stoneman's Switch, Falmouth, etc.). However, mobile reserve supplies were not created to facilitate forward distribution to subordinate units. Supplies were almost exclusively drawn by units from specialized depots (food, clothing, equipment, munitions/ammunition, forage)—as opposed to being pushed forward to them by the army supply and transportation system. No one considered the efficiency of regularly forwarding preset amounts to units based on consumption norms.

Nonetheless, Hooker's and Butterfield's tactical logistics reforms were worthy of recognition. The army effectively established, improved, maintained, and protected its interior lines of communication and supply. Determining soldiers' basic food, ammunition, and equipment combat loads was laudable. By systematizing and standardizing loads for individuals and units, reforms facilitated more sensible accounting, allocation, and transportation. Unfortunately these improvements had to work with cumbersome leather and treated-canvas knapsacks and haversacks and heavy ammunition and ration loads, essentially denying use of all other items. Rapid movements in combat required abandoning heavy knapsacks. Despite these shortcomings, improvements occurred.

The use of pack-saddles to create and carry mobile tactical ammunition and food reserves for immediate resupply was a brilliant innovation for cavalry on extended scouts and raids and for engaged infantry regiments. However, reliance on untrained pack mules and horses proved difficult and, at times, disastrous. Those animals unwilling to perform such roles found ways to divest their loads.

Another significant innovation was identifying ammunition resupply wagons by corps/unit and color-coded (artillery-, cavalry- and infantry-) markings for rapid identification. This precluded endless searches in unmarked wagon trains for resupply sources.

Hooker's emphasis on improved troop rations demonstrated the eternal value of a commanders' intensive management of food quantity and quality, and it realized positive morale effects. Ammunition, food, and water became synonymous with a soldier's and a unit's basic combat capabilities. These all pointed to the army's thinking ahead about logistics requirements, stockpiling them, and protecting the stockpiles. The Federals thus systematized supply and resupply. Unfortunately, these changes were innovated and implemented at army level, and the corps and divisions did not uniformly seek better ways to expedite distribution within their commands.

Medical

Medical troops and organizations made dramatic wartime progress. Reforms immediately before, during, and after the "Valley Forge" were substantial and deserve great credit as first steps toward modern military medicine.

After April 1862, Surgeon General William Hammond created a better medical service. The medical director of the Army of the Potomac, Surgeon Jonathan Letterman, implemented reforms at the army level. First evident at Antietam, those reforms continued at Fredericksburg, during the "Valley Forge," and at Chancellorsville. They included an emphasis on forward screening and treatment and battlefield evacuation, which were crucial to saving lives.

Expeditious evacuation to care became a saving grace of the medical service. Development of the Ambulance Corps—initiated in August 1862 and ultimately 1,000 vehicles strong—moved the wounded and expedited evacuation to field and general hospitals via road, rail, and steamboat respectively. General hospitals afforded the best possible convalescent care. Although existent medical knowledge was far below required levels, army medical staff made undeniable and scientific progress. Unlike their command and staff comrades, medical staff made concerted efforts to study, evaluate, and disseminate wartime lessons to improve performance. The army benefited from the fact that it was predominantly composed of tough, healthy American farm boys. Many a hardy lad survived appalling wounds and "toughed-out" recovery and side-effects. A sad corollary was that disease and sickness, the primary causes of Civil War death, attacked the uninured immune systems of those same farm boys with a vengeance. Ironically, those mainly immigrant and city poor coming to the army from over-crowded slums had developed life-saving immunities. Infection, exposure, weakness from wounds, and lack of useful medicines all contributed to the grim statistic that two-thirds of deaths derived from sickness and disease. Improved field sanitation and hospital/camp feeding helped as much as any other remedy.

Sadly, 1863 saw critical medical research advances. Too late to help "Valley Forge" soldiers, an obscure French researcher, Casimir-Joseph Davaine, determined microorganisms or "little rod-like germs" existed, which he named "bacteria." Davaine's research, unfortunately based on 14-year-old investigations by Franz Alois Antonin Pollender, did not save the innumerable lives it could have if more timely medical research and information dissemination took place. Medical knowledge shortfalls greatly assisted the germ in its deadly work.[14]

Transportation

War in the East attained its highest levels of transportation effectiveness during and after the "Valley Forge." Forces and materiel moved to and from logistics centers, such as Aquia Landing and Belle Plain, by steamboat—also employing towed barges and rail cars mounted on barges—and to troops via rail, and road. Sailboats were also drawn into logistical service. Thousands of railcars and wagons carried materiel to the army's depots and distribution points and returned with wounded, sick and prisoners. Adequate (corduroyed) roads from landings to depots to units aided corps, division, brigade and regiment transport. Although dependent on supply pickup from fixed depots, they could expeditiously bring food, weapons and munitions, clothing, equipment, and animal fodder to units. Resupply efforts, organized by appropriate staff officers controlling lines of supply, were naturally uneven. Accountability, achieved by maintaining receipts and requisition copies at the various staff levels, often overwhelmed single staff officers. At least one regimental quartermaster kept his cumulative receipts in a barrel; when he received inquiries, he delved into the appropriate "geological" level looking for the particular document.

Civil-Military Relations and Operations

During the "Valley Forge," civil-military relations in Stafford were reasonably respectful. Cordiality varied, however. Generally, they were reciprocal and, when people

---

14 Glenn Tucker, "Year of Decision," in *Civil War Times Illustrated*, 6-9, 28-30.

of good will met, results were usually satisfactory. Naturally, distrust persisted and Federals suspected, with good reason, most of the Staffordians were either spying for the Confederacy or providing the Rebels aid and assistance. Staffordians believed, equally correctly, the Yankees held the upper hand and would club them with it if provoked. Occasionally, barriers were toppled by well-meaning people or even good old-fashioned romance.

For all the resident mythology about evil Yankee occupiers, there was no substantial evidence of systemic abuses beyond confiscations and episodic vandalism. Military officers probably treated people better than they deserved, considering an armed rebellion was in-progress. Federal military and civilian lawbreakers who surfaced were punished when transgressions were proved. As with McDowell's earlier occupation from April through September of 1862, Hooker did not devastate old Stafford any more than had the Confederates of April 1861-April 1862. There were just more Federals. Hooker's officers confiscated horses and mules, especially when they were being used for disloyal purposes; but, he also ordered his men—to the army's detriment—to desist from confiscating fodder and insisted on proper payment to those from whom it was acquired. Hooker's orders, when carried out, were positives in civil-military relations.

Provost Marshal Marsena Patrick maintained generally friendly relations with Stafford citizens, even going so far as to show kindly dispositions to ladies he suspected of espionage. If he caught them in the act—which he apparently never did—they likely would have been prosecuted. Suspected disloyal citizens were arrested and shipped to Old Capitol Prison in Washington. Interrogators there attempted to find holes in often half-baked stories. Dossiers were prepared outlining interrogations. However, as no reliable system existed for simply establishing one's true identity, these incarcerations and interrogations were not productive. After a few hours or a few days—depending on prison populations—suspects not confessing were given oaths of allegiance and released. Inconvenienced they may have been, but their treatment was far from oppressive.

That is not to say that Stafford's residents and land did not suffer wide-spread physical devastation. A nineteenth century army, living close to the land, "traveling on their stomachs," was especially destructive. Whole forests became barren ground, and rains eroded remnants into alternating muddy bogs and dust bowls. Bridges, railroads, and corduroyed roads devoured trees. Some 30,000 or more shelters and hundreds of warehouses, shop buildings, landings, hospital buildings and signal towers required huge amounts of lumber. Endless fires, cooking three meals daily and warming sentinels for seven months, further consumed trees, rail-fences, wood panels, and furniture. Civilians watched their modest world as it deconstructed. As predominantly Confederate supporters, they could not—and should not—have been entitled to Federal damage compensation. Those who could present unchallenged claims of

Unionist loyalties later received compensation. Curiously, despite supporting and voting for revolution or rebellion, Stafford's civilians expected their full American rights.

Operational Security

Hooker's army grasped the need to secure rear and flank areas against spying and information leakage. Controls over sutlers and "newsboys"—reporters and purveyors of newspapers—contributed to better security, as did controls over contractors, although virtually none of them were ever fully investigated. Denying local citizens' access to camps was prudent, as well. However, it is clear that family members—wives and male relations—and "home friends" commonly entered and stayed in the camps. Others—"camp followers," one might say—were alluded to as visitors. These non-military interlopers contributed to poorer military security. Occasional military crackdowns sometimes resulted in innocents suffering. For example, civilian male and female hospital volunteers were summarily ejected at one point. Little was known systemically about the various and sundry activities of the Confederate Signal Corps and Secret Service or partisan intrusions. Therefore, the "Secret Line" from Aquia Creek and Potomac Creek into southern Maryland was apparently never uncovered by the Federal Army or Navy.

Weapons and Equipment

Improved weaponry added to the army's turnaround, although the standard weapons of 1861-1863 still predominated. However, increasing numbers of breech-loading carbines and rifles stiffened Federal defenses and made the Cavalry Corps more formidable. Repeating carbines were on the horizon, but did not enter service until after the "Valley Forge."

Just as importantly, infantry had more opportunity to become familiar with whatever armaments they had available to them, increasing the efficiency of both men and weapon. This was offset, though, by large turnovers in men and units in 1863; even as men became more proficient with their weapons, many of them mustered out of service. Archaeological evidence points to extensive marksmanship practice within the army. Correlating that data with diaries and letters suggests the main activity took place after Chancellorsville and before the army's departure for Pennsylvania. This "picking oneself up by the bootstraps"—or cartridge boxes, as the case may be—suggests a gritty determination to continue improving in preparation for the next fight, rather than the kind of demoralized defeatism prevalent after the loss at Fredericksburg.

Artillery technologies did not advance significantly, but the quality of artillery use and the accuracy of fire likewise continued to improve with experience.

Morale and Recreation

Little understood and less appreciated was the improvement to troop morale through rest and recreation. Combat troops' expectations for such benefits were decidedly low.

At the base level, regular, good, fresh food was a primary morale builder; however, once such problems were addressed and resolved, the bar raised quickly. Soldiers' greatest morale needs were satisfied when the army "worked"—meaning it operated as intended with strict, fair leadership. Fairness and justice prevailed when discipline was tight. It sometimes seemed draconian, but it had to be scrupulously fair. Leaves and furloughs needed to be dispensed fairly and consistently. Pay needed to be distributed on-time. (The army's pay system, never effective, requires additional research. It appears the Army lacked sufficient funds to pay everyone at once and on-time. Known Federal appropriations, such as $10,000,000 on January 19, 1863, were definitely large, but still less than needed.) Soldiers needed to be treated with dignity and respect in camp, in hospital, in cemeteries, on work details, on the march, and in battle. Like food services, once fairness and discipline were addressed and set on a good course, the bar was reset higher.

Stand-downs for recreation were necessary. However, stand-downs without active recreation created problems. Celebrations; games and races in March 1863; snowball fights; baseball games; and even unit meetings to address common grievances all had positive effects. Mail service aided troop morale, although the army still struggled to always ensure prompt and efficient distribution. The military was further hampered by the uneven civilian mail system operating throughout the Northern states. Spiritual materials, clergy talks, and comfort items (including stationary) from the Christian and Sanitary Commissions also improved morale. A clean shirt or a beefsteak was as good as a sermon in nurturing spirituality. Soldiers required little, but what they received went a long way.

No one expected such services to continue on active campaign, but camp opportunities surfaced and required action. In the end, morale issues were deceptively simple: commanders needed to make the systems, and those who operated them, work for the benefit of the soldiers carrying the heaviest burdens.

The army did not completely achieve all these things at any one time. Because armies were hierarchical, the natural tendency was to skew morale improvement and recreational opportunities to higher ranking and more accessible (rear-area) individuals. Success was easily tested: they worked when programs reached the lowest ranking soldiers and those in the most remote assignments.

Accountability, Discipline, and Numbers

The Compte de Paris, as reported by historian Ella Lonn, asserted: "More than any one preceding him, General Hooker . . . brought the officers to a sense of their duty and of the respect due their chiefs by few sharp examples." Despite credits to Hooker and his own assertions, Lonn's study concludes that the army did not completely end desertion. Hooker dramatically slowed and dealt with it, however. Courts-martial and non-judicial punishments assisted, as well.[15] Mere word of such actions took effect on the discipline of others.

Accountability in the army appears to have modestly improved during the "Valley Forge." However, simply ascertaining the correct numbers of soldiers in the army remained elusive. Equipment accountability, simpler and easier to check through inspections, was effective.

Army-Navy Cooperation

The Federal Army and Navy, as wholly separate departments, certainly interacted and cooperated. The Navy Department promptly responded to every known request for gunboats or operations to check-out suspected enemy activities. They maneuvered ships along the army's riverine flanks to meet Army needs. However, there was clearly nothing like effective joint strategic and operational relationships between the services. Each performed its characteristic missions and tasks and treated inter-service cooperation as a sideline. This was particularly evident in naval disconnects stopping the flow of deserters across the Potomac into southern Maryland. Considered crucial by the Army, the Navy consistently focused on "smuggling"—itself a lack of systemic recognition of trans-river Confederate Secret Service activities. Stopping the hemorrhaging deserters could have been achieved by operating north of and opposite the Army of the Potomac's sector. Instead, the Potomac Flotilla habitually operated below that area and missed interdiction opportunities. The Army of the Potomac, for its part, failed to articulate its specific needs to naval counterparts. On the positive side, the Potomac Flotilla performed its "brown water" functions with regularity and energy. Accounts of flotilla vessels stopping vessels on the Potomac and Rappahannock Rivers and frequently sending armed patrols ashore certainly mitigate naval shortfalls. One can only speculate how much more effective cooperation might have been if there was a dedicated squadron of appropriate vessels with squads of marines and sailors patrolling ashore which answered directly to army headquarters.

15 Ella Lonn, *Desertion During the Civil War* (Lincoln, NE, 1998), 167. Lonn also cites Compte de Paris, *History of the Civil War in America*, Volume III, 4.

"The stone the builders rejected has become the capstone":
A General Assessment[16]

The true culprits in the army's systemic failures were the American people and, most of all, their elected representatives after George Washington. Our first constitutional president had laid out a military defense system and establishment for America which, if followed, could have negated a civil war or at least would have shortened its duration and attenuated its effects. President Washington had designed a conceptual military establishment responsive to the founding fathers' dislike of large standing armies.[17] Congress had faithfully ignored prudent preparations.

Historians J. G. Randall and David Donald detailed unpreparedness issues in creating and sustaining the Union Army. Early War Department policy allowed private citizens to compete with state governments in forming volunteer units, resulting in too many partially filled-out units and a maldistribution of capable officers. The Union failed to make effective use of its Regular U. S. Army because the nation had no systematic way to select and move professional officers into wartime command of volunteers. Randall and Donald also blame the election of officers in the line units. Although replaced in the Federal army as early as August 1861, this mobilization method, combined with the other approaches, left lasting harmful effects (Hooker was still alluding to this systemic error in 1879).

Lack of strategic preparedness forced materiel procurement systems of the United States into emergency modes and led to price surges and substandard food and clothing (the word "shoddy" putatively arose from such practices). Lack of preparation in ordnance production and procurement resulted in unnecessarily large numbers and types of weapons and munitions from numerous producers.

Recruiting was another shortfall as conscripts were allowed to avoid service by furnishing substitutes and unscrupulous substitutes enriched themselves by "jumping bounties"—the enlistment bonuses they'd been paid to sign up—and repetitively reenlisting. Nothing was worse than varied enlistment terms of service with regiments. As few states had anything remotely approximating replacement systems, regiments

---

16 During the Civil War, this phrase was as expressed as in *The Holy Bible* (New York, NY: American Bible Society, 1857), Psalm 118: 22, "The stone *which* the builders refused is become the head *stone* of the corner." *The Holy Bible: Revised Standard Version* (New York, NY: Thomas Nelson and Sons, 1952) expresses it thusly: "The stone which the builders rejected has become the chief cornerstone." *The Holy Bible: New International Version* [Study Bible] (Grand Rapids, MI: Zondervan, 2002), expresses it as "The stone the builders rejected has become the capstone."

17 Palmer, *America in Arms*. The case, elegantly made by Palmer for the period 1920s-1940s, was ignored in spectacular fashion by the U. S. Congress and military leaders before, during, and after WWII.

were attrited nearly out of existence and beyond reasonable combat effectiveness expectations. Thus, units terminated their service periods at critical war junctures, such as May 1863, with departures of two years' and nine months' regiments. All of these measures led to war weariness on the part of soldiers and populace; lack of confidence in political and military leaders; and general discouragement. All were completely avoidable.[18]

Turnaround in the army's military fortunes did not bring forth immediate victory, but it did set the army on the surer path. In military affairs, nothing "just happens." Correct leadership, effective operations and plans, and systematic support work best when prepared in advance and when men and systems have been trained and prepared before a war. That failure forced the army to develop during the war at enormous cost in lives, blood, time, and treasure.

Hooker's and Butterfield's leadership brought a reinvigoration of the army's fighting spirit and a revitalization of its fighting capabilities. Specialized accounts have detailed the reorganization of the cavalry and creation of the Bureau of Military Information. Most historical accounts have focused on improved food and pay for the troops and systematic furloughs and leaves. Many mention positive morale effects of the corps and division badge system. A few mention reforms of the army's operational (rear area) security, commissary and quartermaster services, sutlers and other means of direct supply, camp and field sanitation, field fortifications, basic discipline and straggler/deserter control, active patrolling and rigorous picketing and outpost duty. None have discussed improved care of horses and mules, and a wide range of field ordnance, logistics and transportation reforms. Most significantly, none have detailed all of these things, let alone in a systematic way with a holistic perspective. Instead, these measures have generally been described at the level of "just happening" or as part of an evolving process rather than through conscious and vigorous leadership.

The end product was a veteran army ready to engage and defeat a formidable foe and an army capable of supporting itself with a full range of combat, combat support and service support functions.

The Army of the Potomac had evolved from "rejected stone" to become "the capstone" of the Union's future military success in the East.

We the People, We the Army

On May 23, 1865, the Army of the Potomac finally received that one bright and sunny day for which the soldiers had so often prayed and hoped. Two prior days of

---

18 N. J. G. Randall and David Donald, *The Civil War and Reconstruction* (Boston, MA, 1961), Chapter 18, "Army Administration," 325-339.

heavy rain no doubt revived old memories. Now, with dust suppressed, they had their day in the sun in a final grand review in the national capital. President Andrew Johnson and Generals Grant and Sherman had not endured the "Valley Forge," but they substituted in the reviewing stand on Pennsylvania Avenue for the fallen president who had reviewed the army two years earlier on Stafford's plains. General Meade, alone perhaps, knew just how far this army had progressed. Symbolically, the Cavalry Corps—which had jts beginnings in the Stafford "Valley Forge" and later emerged as a decisive force—led the way.[19]

After the Cavalry Corps and provost and engineer brigades, came the long procession of army corps. The IX, V (including elements of I), and II (including elements of III) Corps were all that remained of the vast army that had spread across Stafford's hills and plains. The VI Corps was still in the field, and XI and XII Corps had been consolidated into the XX Corps of Sherman's western army and would march with them the following day.

Correspondent-turned-historian William Swinton, whose history of the Army of the Potomac would appear within a year, pronounced the army "that mighty creation of the patriotism of a free people" that "never gave up, but made a good fight, and finally reached the goal. For that it should be accorded history's due."

This same sentiment weighed on the soldiers' minds. "It is actually wonderful how the Army of the Potomac stand the deprivations, trials & reverses that have been heaped on them without stint or mercy to meet the foe with undaunted spirits," wrote Charles Bowen of the 12th U. S. Infantry. "I do not believe there ever was an army in any country that would endure the treatment this army has & yet be ready to fight as good a battle, & perhaps a better one than they could when they first came out. Although we have been deprived of winning any lasting victories, it has not been our fault, as history in future days will show. I look forward to the time when a man can say with pride, 'I belonged to the Army of the Potomac.' We look to history to give us our just due & to place all the blame where it belongs."[20]

That history, even then, was in progress. While the Army of the Potomac's official history ended on June 28, 1865—the result of General Order No. 35—the army's place in history continues to be discussed and debated. "The Army of the Potomac remains one of the most famous armies in American military history," concludes historian Stephen Taaffe. "Despite its numerical and materiel advantages, it lost more battles than

---

19 Historian Jeffry D. Wert, in *The Sword of Lincoln: The Army of the Potomac* (New York, NY, 2005), 411, contended, "By war's end, there were few, if any, better fighters in the Union armies" than the cavalrymen.

20 Wert, *The Sword of Lincoln*, 411-416. See also, BV 123-06, FSNMP, letters of Corporal L. E. Davis, 1st New York Artillery.

it won and sustained more casualties than it inflicted before it finally fulfilled its mission." Taaffe further asserts that while the army's officers and men never lacked courage, they were notably hampered by "dissension, political intrigue, backbiting and cliquishness."[21]

By way of a military benediction, the Army of the Potomac beat the Army of Northern Virginia when it stopped beating itself. The army came out of Stafford in June 1863 and defeated the Army of Northern Virginia at Gettysburg, and regularly thereafter in what was perceived as the main theater of operations. Even when it didn't win, the army asserted strategic initiative and gained momentum by exacting unacceptably heavy prices from the Confederates. Its sustained blows wore down the Confederacy's ability to parry, finally bludgeoning the Army of Northern Virginia into submission and surrender.

In doing so, the army also destroyed Virginia's pivotal role sustaining the Confederacy, effectively ending efforts to establish a separate Southern nation. The army saved the Union; freed enslaved Americans; and liberated its own immigrants into the American political mainstream. Paradoxically, it also gave birth to a "New South" in what became a reunited and reconciled nation, "conceived in liberty and dedicated to the proposition that all men are created equal."

The Army of the Potomac saved the America that emerged from civil war. It facilitated "a new birth of freedom" and established a new "government of the people, by the people, and for the people"—the goals of Lincoln's "second American constitution," the Gettysburg Address. Its victory laid foundations for further progress. Its veterans led the ascendancy toward an "American Century," the twentieth. Through joint reunions, veterans—not political leaders—led the way to sectional reconciliation. The army in memory provided the role models for American youths through at least the Spanish-American War and two World Wars.

They set the standard for a citizen-army. "The private soldier is the basis of our army, the pillar of our country's defense," wrote "E.F.," the unidentified soldier from the 14th Connecticut. Stating what might be considered obvious, his was perhaps the most vital observation of all. In doing so, he put "Valley Forge" lessons into profound perspective. "God bless every man that seeks to make his burdens less, every officer, high and low, who gives his first and chiefest attention to make those under his command as comfortable as possible. If there is any man in this world whom I respect, whom I especially honor, for whose patriotism I have a sincere reverence, it is the man who, from a simple sense of duty, without the inducement of the dignity and

---

21 Taaffe, *Commanding the Army of the Potomac*, especially "Conclusions," 208-218.

emoluments of office, has subjected himself to the hardships and dangers of a private soldier's life, and done his duty in the ranks in his country's defense."

This uncovered a vital truth: experienced citizen-soldiers—rising from a sense of duty, doggedly holding on with patriotism and faith, and persevering to the bitter end—brought victory. Those soldiers came from and were inextricably connected to the American people, by which E.F. meant those of the people who contributed positively to the war-effort. "The people, the sturdy, liberty-loving common people of these Northern States, saw the great meaning of this great rebellion against our Democratic government (the people's government) and rose in their might to put it down, and defend the institutions that were most emphatically their own," E. F. added:

> And it is the people rushing to arms and bravely fighting in the ranks who have brought us such a measure of success in the field, bearing all the losses and waste resulting from blunders of incompetent commanders, persevering against every discouragement, never wavering in the great object set before them. And it is the people, bearing every burden of taxation and the loss of productive labor, the common people of our land, undismayed by the cost of the war in treasure and the blood of their sons (no house from which there is not one dead) who, in the recent elections and every way in which their will can be made known, are still showing themselves resolute as ever to finish up the work they set before them, and bring our government and free institutions unscathed out of their fiery trial . . . . Against traitors South and traitors North, disregarding sneers and evil prophesies, and threats of intervention abroad, through severe defeats and disappointments, against all manner of trickery and coalitions, the will of the American people and their good right hands, the valor of the men and patient self-sacrifice of the women, the steady, persevering, irresistible determination of the people, has carried on this war, and it is going to finish it honorably and successfully, and woe to him who this gainsays.[22]

Whoever he was, E. F. accurately perceived the past, present, and future of America's military. Whatever linked the army and the people was positive; whatever drove a wedge between them was destructive. If learned, no greater lesson could be derived from the war's enormous suffering, blood, death, and destruction: success ultimately depended on the combat soldier, his effective leadership, and his support from the people.[23]

22 Ibid.

23 Ibid.

Posterity and Commemoration

Like much of north-central Virginia along the I-95 corridor, Stafford County's housing market exploded in the early 2000s. Where once the Army of the Potomac had built crude log huts, homes worth hundreds of thousands of dollars began to checker the landscape. In the rush to build, developers began to clear away some of the last traces of the Army of the Potomac's stay in Stafford County.

For Glenn Trimmer, the last straw came in 2005 when a massive Union redoubt went under the plow. With sides 80 to 100 feet long, rising 10 feet from the bottoms of their ditches to the tops of their parapets, the redoubt had been well-known to some locals, but it went unprotected by any official agency. "They were really significant remains," Trimmer says.[1] He realized any preservation efforts for remaining sites would have to come from citizens and private grassroots groups, and not from government. At the same time, governmental assistance to undertake longterm operations would ultimately be critical.

It soon became clear, though, that no one quite knew what might still be hidden out in Stafford's undeveloped-but-threatened landscapes. So Trimmer, a retired Air Force colonel in his early fifties, took to the woods with his friend, D. P. Newton, owner of the White Oak Civil War Museum. Their quest was to identify the remaining earthworks in eastern Stafford County, with an eye on preserving as many of them as possible. Trimmer envisioned a park, perhaps maintained by the county, to protect and interpret the works.

Enter Bill Shelton and his father, Bill, Sr. The Sheltons had spent much of their lives hunting in the woods of Stafford, and as a Civil War enthusiast, the younger Bill had mapped earthworks during his woodland sojourns. He provided Trimmer, who'd begun

---

1   Quotes in this Postscript are from a November 7, 2013, interview with Chris Mackowski.

to compile his findings for local officials, with a full set of GPS coordinates for most of the former Civil War earthworks.

On one particular plot, where the Federal XI Corps had spent the winter before marching off to Chancellorsville, Trimmer and Newton found encampment remains, original corduroy roads built by the army, and a number of artillery and infantry earthworks, along with some earlier artifact sites. The property, on the backside of the county landfill, was actually jointly owned by Stafford County and the city of Fredericksburg. "D. P. and I were out there one day, and we found a stake in the ground that had some flagging tape on it," Trimmer said. "We didn't even know what it was for at the time—we assumed it was a surveying stake—but we knew it was a sign that we were running out of time."

Soon afterward, they approached the county about the possibility of establishing a Civil War park. While the county had no available money for the project, they committed to preserving the land if local preservationists could raise the money and resources to build it. The county provided engineering support and, in exchange for a financial grant, they promised the Civil War Trust they would secure a permanent land easement with the Land Trust of Virginia. For six years, Trimmer, Newton, the Sheltons, and others—eventually coalescing into the Friends of Stafford Civil War Sites (FSCWS)—raised the donations of money, materials, and labor to make the park a reality. Vulcan Materials Corporation provided the essential rock and gravel underpinnings for the substantial road network, and engineer units of the Virginia Army and Air National Guards—using the opportunity to give guardsmen active-duty training—cleared the roadways and view-sheds, and built the roads with modern equipment where, once, thousands of their nineteenth-century comrades had worked with axes, picks, and shovels.

On April 27, 2013—one-hundred and fifty years to the day that the XI Corps marched out of the area on the road to Chancellorsville—Stafford County's Civil War Park opened to the public.

"While it could represent any of the Union Corps around Stafford during this period, this was specifically an XI Corps area," Trimmer says of the 41-acre park, located off Mount Hope Church Road. Some seven- to eight-thousand men of the first and third divisions made their home there during the "Valley Forge," he estimates. These defenses were part of the network of fortifications planned by Hooker and Butterfield to secure Stafford Courthouse and Aquia Landing against a potential Confederate attack from the southwest and discussed extensively in this study.

The Stafford Civil War Park, like so many other preservation efforts in the Rappahannock Valley, represents an important grassroots victory. But unlike the higher-profile efforts to save the Slaughter Pen Farm at Fredericksburg or the Day One battlefield at Chancellorsville, the effort to establish the Stafford park is especially noteworthy because it is the only piece of the "Valley Forge" story to be intentionally preserved for interpretation—and, currently, the only such piece.

Fortunately, other places, including standing private houses, bridge sites, fortifications, hospital sites, artillery positions, camp sites, period churches, skirmish sites, and Aquia Landing still survive and can now be added to the story. The park fits nicely with the interpretive themes of Stafford's privately-owned, award-winning White Oak Civil War Museum and the planned Stafford Museum. Another encouraging fact is that the park was brought to fruition mostly by people with roots in Stafford and Virginia. The acceptance of the "Valley Forge" as a truly Virginian and American story, along with its complementary tribute to the common soldiers of the war, may now be possible.

Lost to History?

There is also an interesting historiographic question: Why did the "Valley Forge" winter remain forgotten for so long, especially when the historical pieces of this story lay hidden in plain view in Official Records, unit histories, memoirs, diaries, and letters? Historians occasionally rummaged through the bits and pieces scattered throughout those proverbial dusty recesses, but they never focused wider attention on it, stranding the story in the temporal space between Fredericksburg and Chancellorsville. Suspended in time between two dramatic battles, the so-called "winter encampment" could be easily dismissed or overlooked.

If there's a starting point for this ongoing historiographic failure, it rests, through no fault of his own, with journalist William Swinton. His previously quoted May 2 report in the May 5 edition of The *New York Times* serves as a true "smoking gun" document that explains best how the "Valley Forge" was initially overlooked. Swinton wrote that he had been missing from the army for several months and did not personally witness the events described over that bleak midwinter. On his return, however, as he witnessed the resurgent army deploying for Chancellorsville, he was clearly struck by the army's transformation, and he described the results in considerable detail. His later book, 1866's *Campaigns of the Army of the Potomac,* touched only on the basics: "Driven hither and thither by continual buffets of fortune; losing its strength in unavailing efforts; changing its leaders, and yet finding no deliverance; misunderstood and unappreciated by the people whose battles it was fighting—it was not wonderful that it had sunk in energy."[2]

---

2   Swinton, *Campaigns of the Army of the Potomac,* 267.

In his battlefield dispatch of May 2, however, Swinton praised the triumphant-looking army as it marched off to battle and its obviously reformed leadership, secrecy, maneuvering, logistics, and transportation. With the army's loss on the battlefield and Swinton's inability to observe the subsequent fighting, that euphoric moment passed, and the correspondent returned to his normal skeptical self. Hooker's failure, his post-Chancellorsville squabbles with Washington, and his eventual resignation and departure from the army in June 1863, tempered Swinton's exuberance.

With Hooker out of the picture, there was no obvious "cause and effect" in the Gettysburg victory that could be traced to the previous winter in Stafford. Thus, as the war ground on, Swinton felt no call to revisit the un-witnessed "Valley Forge" resurgence that, although obvious on his return, had not produced a Chancellorsville victory. His 1866 history on the Army of the Potomac made only passing reference to Hooker's reforms, which were, he said, "judicious":

> [Hooker] cut away the root of many evils; stopped desertion and its causes; did away with the nuisance of the 'Grand Division' organization; infused vitality through the staff and administrative service; gave distinctive badges to the different corps; instituted a system of furloughs; consolidated the cavalry under able leaders, and soon enabled it not only to stand upon an equality with, but to assert its superiority over, the Virginia horsemen of Stuart.[3]

From there, Swinton focused on chronicling the army's battles and campaigns—significantly, a practice followed by others. In that way, not feeling a compulsion to ferret out a turning point, Swinton inadvertently buried the story and influenced subsequent scholarship.

About the same time, however, historian Frank Moore made three allusions to the 1863 "Valley Forge" in his 1866 work *Women of the War*. Moore was apparently the earliest historian to make a direct connection between the Revolutionary and Civil War events. Moore had authored *Songs and Ballads of the American Revolution* (1856) and the two-volume study *Diary of the American Revolution* in 1860, so perhaps he was more sensitive to those connections than his contemporaries. Curiously, Volume VI of Moore's *The Rebellion Record* does not reference the "Valley Forge" connection. He presumably drew that conclusion around 1864 or 1865.[4]

Otherwise, the "Valley Forge" winter, except in Union regimental histories and tangentially in general histories, remained nearly forgotten for almost a century.

---

3   Ibid, 268.

4   Frank Moore, *Women of the War: Heroism and Self-sacrifice* (Hartford, CT, 1867). *The Rebellion Record*, a 12-volume war document collection, covers items published between 1861-1868; Volume VI covers the October 1862-June 1863 period.

Slow Awakening

In 1952, journalist-historian Bruce Catton finally encouraged the "Valley Forge" historiography in the right direction. His widely read *The Army of the Potomac: Glory Road* devoted two large chapters, "All Played Out" (pages 63-110) and "Revival" (pages 111-170), to the period between Fredericksburg and Chancellorsville. Catton described the period in precise terms and incisively analyzes many aspects of events, but he did not attribute wider meaning to those events except to say:

> There exists an informal history of one of the New York regiments in this army, a book in which the military career of every member of the regiment is briefly summarized. The regiment had an eventful career and suffered numerous losses, and after many of the names in its roster are entries like 'Killed in the Wilderness,' 'Died in Andersonville Prison,' and so on. But the commonest one of the lot is the simple 'Died at Falmouth.' The Wisconsin officer who said that this winter was the army's Valley Forge was hardly exaggerating.[5]

Similarly, Allan Nevins's 1960 work *The War for the Union: War Becomes Revolution 1862-1863*, bemoaned the army's situation in a key paragraph in the chapter "Fredericksburg and Government Crisis," alluding to the army's morale nadir: "People said later that this was the Valley Forge winter of the war."[6]

Not until historians began looking at specialized aspects of the war—e.g., cavalry, artillery, common soldiers, camp life, etc.—did the winter of 1863 start to get more attention. Those historians include Alan T. Nolan's *The Iron Brigade: A Military History* (1983), which quotes Dawes' "Valley Forge" allusion, but goes on to state this "was perhaps exaggerated" (due to Dawes' subsequent remark about no increase in courts-martial compared with the previous year); William K. Goolrick, in *Rebels Resurgent: Fredericksburg to Chancellorsville* (1985) brilliantly traces the combat and logistical aspects of the battles and describes the "Valley Forge"; and John Hennessy's 1996 insightful essay on the army on the eve of the Chancellorsville Campaign, "We Shall Make Richmond Howl" in *Chancellorsville: The Battle and its Aftermath.*[7]

---

5   Catton, *Glory Road*, 93.

6   Allan Nevins, *The War for the Union: War Becomes Revolution, 1862-1863* (New York, NY, 1960), Volume II, "War Becomes Revolution," 367.

7   Catton, *Glory Road*. Alan Nolan, *The Iron Brigade: A Military History*. William K. Goolrick, *Rebels Resurgent: Fredericksburg to Chancellorsville* (Alexandria, VA, 1985), 122 (see, in particular, Chapter 4, 92-117, including the sidebar "Rebirth of a Beaten Army"); John Hennessy, "We Shall Make Richmond Howl," *Chancellorsville: The Battle and its Aftermath*, 1-35.

Later historians came even closer to broader conclusions. Eric J. Wittenberg, in his *The Union Cavalry Comes of Age: Hartwood Church to Brandy Station, 1863*, summarized as follows:

> Bloodied and discouraged after the disaster at Fredericksburg, the Army of the Potomac went into winter quarters near the town of Falmouth, Virginia, across the Rappahannock from the scene of their December defeat. There a remarkable transformation took place. During the long lull in the fighting, the demoralized army, rife with desertions and disease, again became a powerful, confident force. Much of the credit went to a new commander, Major General Joseph Hooker, who improved rations and medical care. But the men and their officers, with the timeless ingenuity of troops in the field, helped ease their own lot.

Wittenberg goes on to describe the encampment and recreational events in February and March, adding, "By the time Hooker's forces broke camp in late April, a veteran recalled, 'the discipline and morale of the army were about perfect.' The troops, one soldier reported, 'were once more ready to fight.'"[8]

Jeffry D. Wert, in *The Sword of Lincoln*, also outlines the basic elements "The weeks after Fredericksburg had marked the nadir of the army's morale. It had boiled to the surface in the despair found in their letters and diaries, acts of insubordination, and the rampant desertion," he writes. "Beneath the evident demoralization, however, lay one of the army's defining characteristics, resiliency. They had passed through Fredericksburg's slaughter, endured serious shortages of food and clothing, and witnessed a reshaping of Union war aims with the Emancipation Proclamation." Wert continues: "They had clamored for a change in commanders and fled the ranks by thousands. But the majority stayed, steeled by a belief in a cause that transcended their sufferings and defeats and by a commitment to duty and to each other."[9]

The approach taken by Catton and others—describing but not ascribing larger significance to the "Valley Forge" period—has been followed by other historians who've either focused on Fredericksburg and its aftermath or the build-up to Chancellorsville. Mainly, their accounts use the space between as a way to set the context for the battles rather than focus on the period as having its own military-historical significance.

Thus, the difference between the Union Army's "Valley Forge" or "Winter Encampment" or "Winter Quarters" or "Winter of Transition"—or, for that matter, between Seizing Destiny or "All Played Out" or "Revival"—becomes a crucial matter of degree. Regardless of this study's success or failure, it must recalled that qualitative

---

8 Wittenberg, *The Union Cavalry Comes of Age.*

9 Wert, *The Sword of Lincoln: The Army of the Potomac.*

and quantitative differences between history and memory are primarily matters of emphasis, making judgments, ascribing significance, and providing tones and shades to existent facts. Put another way, all history and memory are enduring arguments.

But what has been missing from the argument at all, until now, has been any overarching conclusion as to what that winter of 1863 meant.

With specific regard to the period, at the strategic level, the Army of the Potomac undeniably reached its wartime lows in morale and effectiveness in January 1863. With the possible exception of Antietam's Pyrrhic result, the army had lost all of its battles before the "Valley Forge" and, despite a setback at Chancellorsville, won at Gettysburg and in nearly all of them afterward. That alone suggests a non-battle turning point. Beyond that, detailed accounts and analysis of the precise progress made in restructuring and revitalizing the army add necessary weight to the argument. Another critical dimension not covered in existing histories is that the army's soldiers, from their Stafford camps, demanded their nation's vital homefront support and attacked the antiwar movement—the only such effort by a deployed force in American military history. The soldiers also assumed the military responsibility for the outcome of the War in the East. This alone commands greater attention and likewise presents new evidence of the period's historic significance.

With general regard to Civil War historiography and scholarship, it should also be mentioned that to this point there is a definite shortfall in dealing with the non-battle operational art (military activities of national authorities, field armies and corps) in the war. This book, it should be further noted, essentially covers a seven month period of the war and deals with the inner workings of military leadership at the operational level in about the same space normally covering a typical five-day battle with its prelude and aftermath. Similar research, focusing on the operational-strategic interactions of national command authorities and field commands, as well as the internal activities of operational forces, needs to emerge from America's capable military historians in the future.

Commemoration and Legacy

In 1900—thirty-five years after their war—a transformative event took place in Fredericksburg: The Society of the Army of the Potomac held its first reunion below the Potomac River. Memories of battles fought and privations suffered returned to the old veterans. As Joseph Hooker had been the improbable leader of the army's 1863 renaissance, Daniel E. Sickles now became its improbable twentieth-century spokesman. He spoke of past scenes, reconciliation, and a "New South." Reflecting on the recent Spanish-American War and postwar rise in Southern economics, education and industrialization, he equally praised Lincoln and Lee, and spoke with hope for

African Americans. He spoke with unbridled Gilded Age excitement of the growing shared wealth, power, and influence of North and South.

As part of his comments, Sickles proposed creating a national military park in the Fredericksburg area:

> Our battle-field parks are an American institution. . . . . They hand down our military traditions to succeeding generations. They keep alive the martial character of our people. They teach the American boy that he belongs to his country and that his country belongs to him. Here, in the National Military Park of Fredericksburg, let all the heroic dead, on both sides, who fell in those memorable struggles, be gathered in one common cemetery, where they may lie forever in peaceful slumber, honored by the citizens of a common country, now happily reunited and inseparable, as a memorial of a reconciliation which has made us one people—under one flag—under one constitution—and under one God.[10]

Sickles saw clearly the direction of America's future, if not its timing, pace, or scope. While the "common cemetery" for Union and Confederate alike never happened, the national park came along a quarter-century later. Encompassing four major Civil War battlefields (the eclectic grouping of Fredericksburg, Chancellorsville, and The Wilderness and Spotsylvania Courthouse), the Fredericksburg and Spotsylvania National Military Park is currently the second-largest military park in the world. The park's headquarters, "Chatham Manor," which played a role in the "Valley Forge" and so much more of America's history, stands in Stafford County.

The national miliary park has been a work in progress since its founding, growing as land has become available and as understanding and interpretation of the battles has evolved.[11] None of that translated to the commemoration of the 1863 "Valley Forge," primarily because it faced the perfect storm of local indifference, the always "dollar-able" value of the land on which it took place, and the abject failure of historians to plumb the depths of the story or even correctly define or acknowledge the place where it happened. The national military park Sickles had once dreamed of—originally created to preserve the fortifications and earthworks of the battlefields in public

---

10 BV 52, part 9, FSNMP. Sickles' speech to the Society of the Army of the Potomac at Fredericksburg, 25.

11 The Slaughter Pen Farm at the south end of the Fredericksburg battlefield offers a good example. Mostly ignored for 135 years, the property finally garnered the interest of preservationists after historian Frank O'Reilly's groundbreaking research revealed that Burnside's main attack was to have crossed that part of the field. This contradicted an earlier understanding of the battle, which placed the focus on the action at Marye's Heights farther north. The shift in understanding triggered the involvement of the Civil War Trust, which purchased the land after conducting the largest fund-raising initiative in its history to date.

memory—adjoins the original area of the "Valley Forge." Yet, not one square inch of the "Valley Forge" was intentionally conserved by the nation. That happened only through the efforts of the local FSCWS private preservation group and Stafford County government, with critical support by the Virginia Army and Air National Guards and local businesses and donors/supporters.

*   *   *

If the Union Army's 1863 "Valley Forge" was as significant as the evidence suggests, and if these events were, indeed, ninety-three days that saved the Union, then what might have happened differently if posterity had previously understood this story?

It is intriguing to ponder what might have happened during the Vietnam and Iraq wars when they became politically unpopular and were opposed by analogous home front antiwar factions? We suggest that, if Americans had been armed with a common knowledge and precedent of the Army of the Potomac's confrontation of the home front population, demanding their support and loyalty in 1863 and 1864, American soldiers of 1968 or 2005 might have acted and demanded something similar and better.

It might be argued the citizen-army of 1863 was somehow different from the forces of Vietnam (greater regular force leadership of conscripted and volunteer troops) or Iraq (an all-volunteer, professional force). If those differences mean anything, then modern armies in the field could not legitimately demand the support of their fellow citizens. However, if that is so—and presumably all would now agree that saving America in 1861-1865 was the historically right thing to do—why did we drift so far from our citizen-army roots in forming an all-volunteer force? The armies we send forth were and remain citizen-soldiers in citizen-armies—men and women tied in every respect to the American people. Only the Army's organizational forms have changed.

We can return the discussion to a poor understanding of the history itself. There are many direct lessons of value from the "Valley Forge"—lessons related to strategic policy and action, mobilization, staffing, intelligence, training, logistics, civil-military relations, and special operations. However, if America failed to grasp the significance of this (or any) period or sequence of historical events, it could not help but fail to learn and apply these lessons. That, in turn, would be a colossal object lesson of its own.

To be true to the Army of the Potomac's history and memory, Americans must forever understand that, once an army is committed by the nation to war, anything less than full support and all-out effort is inexcusable. It is not possible to "support the troops" and simultaneously oppose what they do. The armies draw their ultimate strength from the sincere support of the people through the government that represents them, and the patriotism and faith of the soldiers themselves. That is the "Valley Forge" army's ultimate legacy—if America will only hear what those men are shouting to us from their Stafford, Virginia, camps of 150 years ago.

Appendix 1

After the Army of the Potomac's "Valley Forge"

The "Valley Forge" actors left distinct legacies, good and bad, for posterity:

Abraham Lincoln, the leading actor, persevered and conquered most of his early-1863 concerns with the army. His best wartime strategic direction and political leadership were demonstrated when he expanded war's aims to include emancipation, absorbed the political backlash, bonded with his troops, and moved into the war's next strategic phase. By joining his fate with the Army of the Potomac's, in particular, and winning their support, he accomplished some of his finest political work. Together, they then won battles (military and political), and demanded and retained popular support.

Lincoln's "Valley Forge" actions and his Stafford visits in April 1863 achieved those things, especially in his interactions with army's rank and file. Lincoln and the army finally found common ground in defeating the antiwar movement. The army's renewed fighting spirit—based on patriotism, religious and political faith, and a more mature understanding of what was needed to win the war—progressed steadily from their time in Stafford. The army and Lincoln, once joined, never severed intellectually or emotionally. Whether by conviction, pragmatism, expediency, or a combination, new unity and common purpose emerged. For Lincoln, as with the army, the strategic corner was turned.

Lincoln had never done better service for the country than among his Federal troops in the Stafford spring of 1863. Their allegiance and political conversion, and their advocacy, secured necessary support among the Northerners for Lincoln's re-nomination and re-election in 1864. And they aided immeasurably to concluding the war victoriously.

Lincoln fell to an assassin's bullet on April 14, 1865, and died the next day—just two years and a few days after he had reviewed the army in Stafford near the end of their "Valley Forge." He rests in Springfield, Illinois, and his monument in Washington, D.C., stands, as it should, equal to George Washington's: Washington did more than anyone to create the nation, and Lincoln did more than anyone to save it.

Edwin McMasters Stanton reformed the "War Department at War": personnel administration; fiscal management; contracting; and general efficiency. He was rightly credited with conducting war on a "new basis" of material superiority. Stanton reshaped the department and improved national resupply and manpower replacement. He tightened security, improved communications, and censored the press with a sufficiently iron hand to prompt cries of "tyranny." But even Stanton's fiercest political enemies—and they were numerous—would not have argued against his preeminence as an effective "war minister" and master political operative.

After Lincoln's death, Stanton's heavy-handed manner and political intrigues with Radical Republicans—an odd outcome of war—soon ended his usefulness to President Andrew Johnson. In fact, Stanton's firing precipitated Johnson's impeachment. After those efforts failed, in May 1868, Stanton resigned. In ill-health, he died before being seated on the U. S. Supreme Court, to which he had been appointed by President Grant on December 20, 1869. Stanton died on Christmas Eve, December 24—seven years to the day after Rufus Dawes made his Fredericksburg pronouncement about the "Valley Forge" of the war.

Henry Wager Halleck, by any measure, must number among Lincoln's greatest military failures, and he certainly impeded resurgence during Hooker's tenure and the "Valley Forge." Propelled to prominence by Grant's victories while under his command, Halleck was finally undone—ironically—when Grant came east in 1864. As general-in-chief commanding and coordinating all the Union's armies from the field, Grant relegated Halleck to "Chief of Staff," effectively demoting him.

The end of **Joseph Hooker** as an army commander came at Harpers Ferry, when he handed a loaded bureaucratic pistol to Halleck; Hooker's personal self-destructiveness took care of the rest. Resigning three days before Gettysburg, he transferred army command— and the subsequent redeeming victory—to Meade. By war's end, Hooker ultimately crossed personalities with Scott, Halleck, Burnside, Grant, Sherman, and virtually everyone in the Army hierarchy who might cast pity on his declining career.

Reportedly affected by Lincoln's death and because interment took place in his Northern Department, Hooker presided over the ceremony to bid Lincoln farewell at his commander-in-chief's gravesite. On horseback, "Fighting Joe" personally led the procession to the Oak Ridge Cemetery and sat "stiffly in his saddle as the closing prayer was offered." Lincoln had been his best friend among the mighty—and, characteristically, Hooker failed to publicly acknowledge Lincoln's greatness or kindnesses.

Officially cleared in May 1865 by his old comrades in the Radical Republican-dominated Joint Committee on the Conduct of the War of fault at Chancellorsville, what mattered most to him were reunions with "his" soldiers. In declining health, he at least found love, marrying Olivia Groesbeck in Cincinnati in October 1865. Soon after—attributed to the Chancellorsville head injury some deemed "minor"—Hooker suffered stroke and paralysis. To his further sorrow, his wife passed away in July 1868, only three months after his retirement.[1]

Arguably, Hooker redeemed the "fatherly" letter the president had given him in January 1863. Together they restored the army's fighting spirit and, consequently, the nation's hopes for victory in the East. His wartime testimony certainly suggested his time in Stafford County was significant: "I am, and have been, censured for that which I consider as the most meritorious of my military service . . ." he said. "[I]f my services have not been such as to merit reward, they should shield me from punishment."

His service from January 25 to April 27 in 1863 was—unquestionably—Hooker's highest wartime contribution. In its darkest hour, "Fighting Joe" provided the army essential military leadership and administrative, logistical, and organizational reforms. His administrative skill, soldier-oriented leadership and organizational abilities as army commander during that crucial period ultimately did more to win the war than all of his battles combined. Historical justice for Joseph

---

1   Hebert, *Fighting Joe Hooker*, Chapter XXI, "Later Life," 288-296.

Hooker demands such a judgment. His supporters always said so, and even his detractors said as much. "The Army of the Potomac never spent three months to better advantage," wrote one of the latter, Francis A. Walker of the II Corps. Even one of his greatest detractors, Darius Couch, later wrote: "I have never known men to change from a condition of lowest depression to that of a healthy fighting state in so short a time." Wartime military leadership not only leads men into battle, it also prepares them for battle and ultimate victory. Joseph Hooker and Daniel Butterfield accomplished that at the army's helm, and their work deserved this and further research.[2]

Hooker's later pronouncements shed further light. Writing to Samuel P. Bates between 1876 and his death in October 1879, Hooker was of course self-laudatory and denigrating of others, but his writings nonetheless constitute his summation to the historical jury.[3] In December 1876, he sent his key orders, boasting that they were used as models in other armies. He emphasized the order granting leaves of absence and furloughs. "Presdt. Lincoln telegraphed me to come to Washington," he recounted, "he said that I had ruined my army —that when the men left I would never get them back, when I begged him to let the order work three weeks before countermanding it and then if unsuccessful do as he liked." He next referred to the March 21, 1863, circular on corps/division badges, adding it was "adopted by the Armies in the West as well as in the East and had a magical effect on the discipline and conduct of our troops ever after." Hooker accurately stated, "The badge became very precious in the estimation of the soldier, and to this day they value them more than anything." These Hooker-selected highlights comprised what he termed, "[T]he secret of how I built up the Army of the Potomac to accomplish the great achievement it was expected and destined to make."

He asserted that Chancellorsville was not a demoralizing defeat. "In but little more than a month after our return to camp, [the army] embarked in the campaign of Gettysburg and fought a great battle there," he pointed out. "I think no appearance of demoralization can anywhere be found in these events." Hooker emphasized Meade had changed none of his orders after the change in command.

Of Gettysburg he emphasized, "you will be able to appreciate its [i.e., the army's] true condition, for it really won the great battle of Gettysburg without a commander. Hancock was grand, and so were Reynolds and Buford, and a host of others. When you re-write Gettysburg I beg you will not fail to render unto Caesar the things that are Caesar's"—by which, he naturally meant Hooker's.

In 1879, he expounded upon some of those ideas in a passage that well could have been his own military epitaph:

> But I have since consoled myself with the conviction that the time had not yet arrived [at Chancellorsville] in the mind of the supreme Ruler of the universe for giving the Rebellion its coup de grace, and to suppose under these circumstances that I would do it, would be supposing that I was stronger than fate itself. Had the war ended at Chancellorsville we doubtless would have had another before this . . . . No Army ever entered upon a campaign with more confidence and resolution than was shown by the Army of the Potomac in its advance on Gettysburg, and long before that battle was ended

2 BV 406, part 2, FSNMP. Pennsylvania Historical and Museum Commission. Bates Collection. Division of Public Records, Folder C. Joseph Hooker to Samuel P. Bates 1875-1879.

3 BV 406, part 2, FSNMP. Pennsylvania Historical and Museum Commission. Bates Collection. Division of Public Records, Folder C. Joe Hooker to Samuel P. Bates 1875- 1879.

no doubt their enemy fully realized the serious mistake they had made in representing it to have been in a forlorn, demoralized condition.

Throughout his correspondence with Bates, Hooker remained classic Hooker: he denigrated Meade, Hunt, and Stoneman, and attacked—primarily for his 1866 army history —correspondent William Swinton, who had extolled Hooker on May 2, but had later reined-in his enthusiasm. Hooker offered enthusiastic endorsement of Rufus Ingalls: "I doubt if any Army ever had his superior in technical and profound knowledge of his profession, and in administrative ability and devotion." This apparently confirmed Ingalls' role in Hooker's logistical reforms and innovations. His views on Hunt mellowed a bit, stating he "was opinionated, but able."

Hooker passed on a vital lesson: he credited "The rank and file of the Army, which determines all battles." He took care of his men with improved provisioning and took concrete military steps, namely reorganizing the cavalry and military intelligence, and reforming tactical ordnance and logistics. These improved the army's combat performance and, although all reforms did not provide immediate dividends, they ultimately aided the army's ability to maneuver and defeat the Confederate forces. Hooker's main failures were in personal and military character and in putting the wrong men into positions to make the cavalry reorganizations immediately fulfill their promise. Like Hooker, his subordinates generally lacked the ability to work together. Hooker hadn't created that poisonous atmosphere of intriguing and backbiting, but he certainly contributed to it.[4]

Daniel Butterfield was legitimately described as "the brains of the outfit." Perhaps reflective of that, he continued as the army's chief of staff after Hooker's resignation. After Gettysburg, where he was severely wounded, he clashed with Meade over a battle order. When displaced, Butterfield rejoined Hooker in the Western Theater in October 1863 before succumbing to illness.

Butterfield returned to Fredericksburg on May 30, 1901, and dedicated a V Corps monument in the National Cemetery. He died only a few weeks later, on July 17, 1901, in Cold Spring, New York, and was buried at West Point—a special tribute for a citizen-soldier. "Taps" was played at his funeral.

All known historians who have seriously looked at Butterfield's wartime contributions feel that he had played a greater role than has been credited to him. If the history of the "Valley Forge" achieves wider recognition, then Butterfield should gain greater respect. His close associations with Hooker did not help his case. Butterfield at a minimum deserves a more definitive and thorough biography.[5]

George Gordon Meade, commander of V Corps during the "Valley Forge," commanded the army at Gettysburg. He might have been a better choice than Hooker in the first place, but it could be

---

4   William P. Styple, ed., *Generals in Bronze: Interviewing the Commanders of the Civil War* (Kearny, NJ, 2005), 40-44; Ibid. James Kelly (1855-1933) conversed with his subjects about their postwar reflections. More remarkably, 27 boxes of Kelly's notes survive in the New York Historical Society.

5   Warner, *Generals in Blue*, 62-63. Styple, ed., *Generals in Bronze*, 71-72. www.west-point. Org/taps/Taps.html (accessed on May 28, 2009) provides a balanced discussion from an article by Civil War musical historian Jari A. Villanueva, entitled "24 Notes that Tap Deep Emotions." The article concludes Butterfield certainly had a hand in the process, but may have modified a call dubbed "Scott's Tattoo." BV 220, part 1, FSNMP. Gareth O'Bannon, "Taking the Hill: A History of the Fredericksburg National Cemetery."

argued that the army at that time needed Hooker's assertiveness and self-confidence. The humbler Meade might have been unable to make such rapid exertions, as evidenced by the order he issued when he first assumed command on June 28, 1863 (General Order No. 67): "By direction of the President of the United States, I hereby assume command of the Army of the Potomac . . . . As a soldier in obeying this order—an order totally unexpected and unsolicited—I have no promises or pledges to make." His next statement might well have been written by Lee or Jackson: "The country looks to this army to relieve it from the devastation and disgrace of foreign invasion. Whatever fatigues and sacrifices we may be called upon to undergo, let us have in view constantly the magnitude of the interests involved and let each man determine to do his duty, leaving to an all-controlling Providence the decision of the contest."

George Stoneman, who had rendered valuable service as an infantry division and III Corps commander, was badly miscast as Cavalry Corps commander. Comparison with J. E. B. Stuart left much to be desired, as amply revealed during "Stoneman's Raid" and Chancellorsville. Stoneman, replaced by the equally dubious Alfred Pleasonton after Chancellorsville, was "kicked upstairs" as chief of the new (July 1863) cavalry bureau in Washington. There, paradoxically, his considerable administrative talents and practical horse-logistics experience were used to better effect. He finished the war in various field commands related to the Western armies.[6]

William Woods Averell, briefly a rising cavalry star before and after his Kelly's Ford raid, saw his military fortunes precipitously decline. Within two months, his under-performance on "Stoneman's Raid" and during Chancellorsville left Hooker with a deep enmity. Averell's military banishment followed, and he led a series of minor raids in western Virginia. Sheridan's coming east ended chances for Averell's return. Younger (and better) rising cavalry generals also hurt his case. In many respects, Averell seemed to have the "right stuff" but was a likely victim of the hurried development of the Cavalry Corps. His rapid rise worked against him, and he probably would have been better-served with a more gradual ascent.[7]

Alfred Pleasonton rightly garnered no admirers at Hooker's headquarters for his lethargy during the Hartwood Church raid. His Chancellorsville service merely helped him escape retribution. Yet, he replaced Stoneman on June 7, and a few days later, surprised Stuart at Brandy Station. He returned to good repute for his success in what turned out to be the largest cavalry battle of the war. The corps was beginning to show progress as an independent force.

Pleasonton's Gettysburg performance was deemed undistinguished, though. He showed himself to be a better thinker than commander—many of his earlier ideas were incorporated in the Cavalry Corps reorganization. Rising cavalrymen (e.g., Merritt, Custer, and Mackenzie) carried Pleasonton for a bit and, to his credit, he mentored their ascendance. When Grant came east, the new Commanding General of the Armies brought Maj. Gen. Philip H. Sheridan, who replaced Pleasonton on March 25, 1864, and perfected the Cavalry Corps's development.[8]

Marsena R. Patrick served as the Army of the Potomac's provost-marshal-general for the rest of the war and gave effective and loyal service to all of his commanders. A Democrat, he ran afoul of

6   Warner, *Generals in Blue*, 481-482.

7   Ibid., 12-13.

8   Ibid., 373-374.

Republicans in the elections of 1864 and was estranged politically within upper military circles. Nevertheless, he was at Grant's side coordinating the provost duties of all the Union armies and was rewarded with a brevet major generalcy on March 13, 1865.[9]

Rufus Ingalls, argued historian Ezra Warner, was "perhaps the only officer in a position of great responsibility who gave satisfaction to every commander of the Army of the Potomac from first to last." His reward for success was becoming permanently typecast and remaining in the quartermaster service for the rest of his 40-year career.[10]

Colonel George H. Sharpe, chief of the Bureau of Military Information and Marsena Patrick's deputy provost-marshal-general, continued in that capacity under Meade and, finally, in Grant's headquarters. He has been rightly included among the pioneers of American intelligence. In a January 1876 speech, per the *New York Times*, he gave fitting benedictions to both the army and its Southern enemy: "[Sharpe] concluded with an eloquent tribute to the Army of the Potomac, the breastplate of the nation, which had stood through all the trials and struggles of the war, the army which was often complained of for not moving enough, but never for not dying enough, and whose heroic labors were finally crowned by the surrender of the bravest and most successful of the Confederate forces— the Army of Northern Virginia."[11]

Elisha Hunt Rhodes, a colonel by the time the 2nd Rhode Island Infantry mustered out in July 28, 1865, penned an elegant final diary entry: "No more suffering, no more scenes of death. Thank God it is over and that the Union is restored. And so at last I am a simple citizen. Well, I am content, but should my country call again I am ready to respond. The Governor has given me a commission as Colonel for gallant conduct during the war. But what are honors now, compared to the delights of peace and home."[12]

In 1890, **Rufus Dawes** he published Service with the Sixth Wisconsin Volunteers. The man who had pronounced the commencement of the "Valley Forge" left behind an indelible record. In life's twilight, Dawes focused on veteran survivors: "To my living comrades this book will be my greeting

9   Ibid., 361-362. Internet web-sites, including: http://en.wikipedia.org/wiki/Marsena_ R._ Patrick; an interesting article by Benjamin P. Thomas and Harold M. Hyman at http://adena. com/adena/usa/cw/cw148.htm, which addresses election and electioneering issues in the 1864 army (all accessed on April 28, 2009); David S. Sparks, ed., *Inside Lincoln's Army: The Diary of Marsena Rudolph Patrick, Provost Marshal General, Army of the Potomac* (New York, NY., 1964).

10 Warner, *Generals in Blue*, 245-246.

11 Several Internet web-sites provide information on Sharpe's postwar life; these include: http://en.wikipedia.org/wiki/George_H._Sharpe; Dr. Dennis Casey, "George Sharpe: American Intelligence Pioneer," atwww.fas.org/irp/agency/aia/cyberspokesman/99-09/ history1.htm; http://localhistory.morrisville.edu/sites/unitinfo/sharpe-120.html. Sharpe's obituary can found in the *New York Times*, dated January 15, 1900: query. Nytimes.com/ gst/abstract.html?res=F2091EF93D5D147B93C3AB178AD85F428784F9. This concerns the January 1876 speech he gave on the last days of Lee's army at Harlem Congregational Church. (All accessed on April 28, 2009.) Sharpe's date-of-rank as brevet brigadier general was March 13, 1865, per Phisterer; other, apparently incorrect accounts list him as receiving brevets to brigadier general in 1864 and major general in 1865.

12 Rhodes, ed., *All For the Union*; Farewell address provided by Gregg A. Mierka: http://www. angelfire.com/ri2/GARvets/2ndRIphotoAlbum.html (accessed on May 8, 2009).

and farewell." He regretted overlooking "many noble deeds and some brave men," adding, "But remember I was not then a historian. I was then only writing to my family, friends and M.B.G., (my best girl) [also Mary Beman Gates], who were personally strangers to you all." Dawes wanted to show "the generations yet to come that our band was the finest quality of heroic mettle, and 'equal,' as Gen. McClellan wrote, 'to the best troops in any army in the world.'" He poignantly added:

> The shadows of age are rapidly stealing upon us. Our burdens are like the loaded knapsack on the evening of a long and weary march, growing heavier at every pace. The severing of the links to a heroic and noble young manhood, when generous courage was spurred by ambitious hope, goes on, but you have lived to see spring up as the result of your suffering toil, and victory the most powerful nation of history and the most beneficent government ever established.

Despite all the dangers that seem to doom good soldiers, **Thomas White Stephens** survived the war. He went on to fight at Chancellorsville, Gettysburg, the Overland Campaign and Petersburg before mustering out in August 1864. Without denigrating those who prayed and died, his frequent "seasons of prayer" during the "Valley Forge" *may* have saved him, as a later biographic sketch related: "he was four times slightly wounded, being protected from serious wounds by his cartridge box and knapsack, once by a book inside his clothing, a Bible taken from Chancellorsville battle field." His rifle was also shattered deflecting an artillery round. No doubt thankful for his blessings, he remained a faithful Methodist for the rest of his days.[13]

In final victory was redemption for certain units and soldiers. **Sergeant Henry C. Morhaus** of the 123rd New York Infantry Regiment provided an interesting finale for the much maligned XI and XII Corps in an 1879 memoir. Consolidated into Sherman's forces, they moved north for the Washington victory parade after Confederates surrendered in North Carolina. En route, they passed through the Rappahannock Valley. "At about noon [May 15, 1865] the Regiment reached the old Chancellorsville battle field, the scene of their first terrible conflict over two years before," Morhaus related. "Here they halted two hours, and visited the spot where so many of their comrades had fallen, and a prayer of thanksgiving went up from many a heart that day, that God in his great goodness had seen fit to spare them." They walked the field and recalled "that terrible 3d day of May, 1863." Visiting graves of fallen comrades "scarcely covered with earth by the Rebels," they improved them with shovels and identified the still identifiable. "Soon the bugle sounds to 'fall in,'" Morhaus recalled,

> and with one more look at the graves of fallen comrades they hasten into line, and are soon on the march, taking the same road to United States Ford they did two years before, but under what different circumstances! Then they had been defeated and falling back to their old camp at Stafford Court House; now they were on their way home after having helped conquer the Rebels. Moving down on the flat by

---

13 Phisterer's 1883 Statistical Record of the Armies of the United States, 312, probably a clerical error, lists Dawes' brevet rank date as March 18, 1865. Se his Congressional biography at: http://bioguide.congress.gov/scripts/biodisplay.pl?index=D000149 (accessed April 23, 2009); BV 106, part 3, FSNMP. Paul E. Wilson and Harriet Stephens Wilson, eds., "The Civil War Diary of Thomas White Stephens, Sergeant, Company K, 20th Regiment of Indiana Volunteers," biographic: http://www.kancoll.org/books/cutler/shawnee/ shawnee-co-p41. html (accessed July 13, 2009). William G. Cutler, History of the State of Kansas.

the Ford they camped for the night, feeling that they had passed through an eventful day—a day in which scenes of other days had been brought fresh to their memories. May 16th the boys were up early, and after a breakfast of coffee and hard-tack, pushed on across the Rappahannock river at United States Ford, and soon afterward reached Hartwood church. . . .[14]

Many Union soldiers never left the Rappahannock Valley. A September 1872 reunion of the 107th New York Infantry Regiment recalled Stafford scenes. An elaborate graveyard, unfortunately atypical, had been left by the 107th to dignify the graves at "Camp Valley Forge":

The grave yard of the regiment was in a beautiful place [Hope Landing]. It was on a knoll close to the [Aquia Creek] bank, and was shaded by two great trees. A neat stone, bearing a suitable inscription marked each soldier's resting place. The graves were all in exact rows, and in the center of the ground was an extra stone, upon which Lieut. Dennison, with exquisite taste, had placed simply the words, "107 N.Y.V., In Place Rest"

"In Place Rest!" Is a command frequently given to the men "wearied with their drill," the writer recalled. "[T]hey could rest themselves in any position merely keeping in line, so that when they heard the bugle call, 'Attention' they might spring promptly to their places. So we laid in ranks and lines, our comrades tired with life's battles inscribed above them the order, 'In Place Rest,' and left them waiting for the one great bugle note which in some coming time shall sound throughout the world." The bodies were later disinterred and moved to the new Fredericksburg National Cemetery joining 15,000 burials there from battles in the Rappahannock Valley—85 percent of whom are "unknown."

David B. Tappen of the 1st New Jersey Infantry, who had found his faith in the army and rejoiced in his brother's conversion in April, died in action in May at Chancellorsville. Missing after a bayonet charge, comrades Edward W. H. Graham and Stacy L. Disbrow wrote to Tappen's family sharing what little they knew.

An enemy soldier's letter of May 12, 1863, from "Rebel Camp 11th Ala. Regt., Fredericksburg, Va." completed the story. "I found on the person of David B. Tappen a Memorandum Book with a piece written in requesting anyone who chances to find it if he was killed to write to his friends," the letter said. "He had nothing valuable about him that I saw. He was killed in battle on Sunday evening the 3rd of May in front of my Regt." The writer, J. J. Cook, related the ball that killed David hit him in the breast. He was buried "near the place where he fell near Salem's Church about 3 ½ miles from Fredericksburg on the plank road." Cook added, "Many of his comrades lie close by his side. I am in hopes that you will get this as the deceased desired his friends to know what became of him. I also enclose the piece he left written on an envelope. "I will close by saying I am in hopes that the Northern States will soon see their error and let the South depart in peace."

This simple "From a Rebel" letter offers a simple testament to American decency in the midst of its cruelest war.[15]

---

14 BV 319, part 8, FSNMP, published work, Sgt. Henry C. Morhaus, *Reminiscences of the 123d Regiment, N. Y. S. V.* (Greenwich, NY: People's Journal Book and Job Office, 1879), 186-187. Morhaus or the type-setter misspelled Hartwood as "Hastwood."

15 BV 213, part 2, FSNMP, letters of David B. Tappen.

The Union Women of "Valley Forge"

There was a female element of the Union "Valley Forge." Like the men of the Army of the Potomac, these women served their country well, and represent some of the best of the women of that Civil War era. Their faith in God and country sustained their extraordinary service. Like the soldiers of the eastern army, they risked everything and paid the price in many ways, including damaged health. Some paid with their lives.

It has become commonplace for modern historians to assume gender bias in records and to refer to "untold stories" of Civil War women. What is not widely known is that Union women have been documented in two 500-page books published within two years of the war's termination. It is fair to state, however, that they were subsequently forgotten and their known stories were relegated to the "dusty recesses of history."

A brief summary of their lives and work complements the known record of the "Valley Forge" period and provides another dimension to this book's thesis. Each was associated with the U. S. Christian and Sanitary Commissions, as well as ladies', soldiers', or state aid societies. Each woman came to Stafford on her own initiative as a volunteer.

In 1866, just a year after the end of the war, Frank Moore wrote *Women of the War: Their Heroism and Self-Sacrifice*. He identified seven women with the "Valley Forge of the War": The married Mary A. Brady, Isabella Fogg, Mary W. Lee, Ellen Matilda Orbison, Charlotte E. McKay, Mary Morris Husband, and Miss Amy M. Bradley. Curiously, he omitted well-known women like Clara Barton, Dr. Mary Walker, and Dorothea Dix, who I included here. Moore used the phrase "Valley Forge" throughout his book, which was published 20 years before Rufus Dawes' December 1862 letter was made public.

The following is a brief biographic summary of these ladies, emphasizing their wartime service before, during, and after the Union "Valley Forge."[1]

Mary A. Brady, born in Ireland in 1821, had married an English lawyer in 1846; they lived in America before the war. During the war, after some preliminary hospital work at Satterlee Hospital in West Philadelphia, she served by drawing supplies from the Fifth Street Depot and distributing them to the hospitalized men, mostly from the Peninsula fighting. Concerned that supplies shipped to Virginia were not reaching their intended destinations, Mrs. Brady left home and family (five children) to work at the front, where she served until 1864, excepting brief visits home. Traveling from

---

1 Moore, *Women of the War; Their Heroism and Self-Sacrifice*. "Valley Forge" references are on 44, 195, 319. Moore served as assistant secretary of legation in Paris (1869-1872) and died in 1904.

Alexandria and Fairfax, she joined the army in Stafford. An early connection came in a January 19, 1863, letter from Joseph A. Winters of the 7th Pennsylvania Infantry from "Camp near Belle Plain, Va." asking her to visit a comrade, Henry Griffin, in Ward H.

As Moore related, "The army was greatly used up and demoralized, and the sick list was fearful." Brady conveyed 60 boxes of food and supplies from Philadelphia, although some were distributed in Washington hospitals. She also reported working in a convalescent hospital of 12,600 patients between Alexandria and Falmouth. A month later, she returned with another 60 boxes, which were distributed within the army's perimeter. Brady took a four-mule wagon and stopped at every tent where a "little red flag, indicated a sick tent."

She went home in April for more supplies and returned with 45 boxes and two cooking stoves for the Chancellorsville battles. Working at the VI Corps hospital, she provided the wounded with food supplements. Sparing no expense or effort for the hospital's needs, she requested Philadelphia for "fifty dozen cans of condensed milk, a hundred dozen fresh eggs, thirty boxes of lemons, ten boxes of oranges, one and fifty pounds of white sugar, two hundred jars of jelly, and twelve dozen of sherry," urgently adding, "Everything is wanted." Mary cooked all day, and visited the sick and wounded at night. At 5 a.m., she started her cook fires again for the next day's work. Following that routine until June, she went with the army to Gettysburg and worked in hospitals there until August.

Returning to Philadelphia, she renewed her hospital work and began fund raising. An incident that must have convinced Brady that her duty had been faithfully performed:

> [A]s she entered a [crowded] street car . . . she noticed that a soldier was looking very steadily at her face. His sleeve was empty. Presently the maimed warrior called out, with some emotion, "Don't you know me, Mrs. Brady?" "Really," she replied, "I can't quite recollect you, I see so many of Uncle Sam's brave boys." "Not recollect me, Mrs. Brady?" said the soldier, his eyes now filling with tears: "don't you remember the day you held my hand while the doctors cut my arm off? You told me to put my trust in God, and that I should get well over it. You said I was sure to recover; and here I am, dear madam, thank God!"

Brady returned to the army in the winter of 1864 for the Overland Campaign. By April and May, the hard winter had taken its toll and she was suffering from some heart ailment. On May 27, 1864, she died, not yet reaching her forty-second birthday. No less so than the soldiers she had served, Mary Brady had died on the field of honor.[2]

Isabella Morrison Fogg entered the war when her son enlisted. Volunteering her services to Maine's governor and state surgeon-general, she accumulated medical stores and supplies. She left the Pine Tree State in 1861 with a regiment and went to Annapolis, Maryland, where she worked for some months in a general hospital's fever ward; in spring of 1862, she joined the Sanitary Commission and went to the Peninsula. Fogg aided in transporting wounded, and then went to Antietam.

---

2   Moore, *Women of the War*, 36-53.

In December 1862, Fogg joined the army in Stafford, serving with hospitals that served Maine units. That month, she and Mrs. Harriet Eaton shared dinner on tin plates with Lt. Col. Joshua Lawrence Chamberlain of the 20th Maine.[3]

Moore recorded Fogg's daily diary entry for a typical day during the "Valley Forge":

Started with ambulance filled with necessary stores of all kinds, such as bread, soft crackers, canned chicken, oysters, dried fruit, preserves, condensed milk, dried fish, pickles, butter, eggs, white sugar, green tea, cocoa, broma, apples, oranges, lemons, cordials, wines, woolen underwear, towels, quilts, feather pillows, all invaluable among so many sufferers so far from home and its comforts. My first visit was directed to those regiments where the wants were most pressing; but my special mission was to those who languished under bare shelter tents, they being entirely dependent on their ration, and seldom or never reached by sanitary and hospital stores. In company with the surgeons, who always welcomed us, we made the tour of the camp, going from tent to tent, finding from one to three in each of those miserable quarters, suffering from camp diseases of every form, distributing our stores at the surgeons' suggestion. We left reading matter generally in each tent. Then we would hasten away to the General Hospital, and pass the latter part of the day in reading the Bible to some dying soldier, or write out his words of final and touching farewell to the loved ones at home, then battle fevered brows, moisten with water and refresh with cordials mouths parched with fever, and, adjusting pillows under aching heads, bid our patients farewell. Weary, but glad at heart for having put it in our power to do so much for our boys, we sought our tents, which scarce protected us from snow and rain, but we were happy in a sense of duty discharged, and enjoying the grateful love of our sacrificing heroes.

Fogg returned to Washington periodically, picking up supplies "regularly shipped from Portland and other places in Maine" to the camps. She contracted pneumonia and did not recover till spring. During Chancellorsville, she and Eaton spent five days at U. S. Ford dispensing food to the wounded. On May 4, they came under artillery fire.

In the spring 1864 she was back for the Overland Campaign and worked in Fredericksburg hospitals. However, the war had taken its toll. "The close of the war found her a permanent invalid among strangers," Moore wrote. "But this affliction was as nothing in her estimation. Her son was a cripple for life. She would never enjoy health again. But, to use the language of her diary, she is daily solaced and penetrated with deep gratitude to God that he so long preserved her in health and strength, to witness the triumph of the right, and the dawn of peace, and the days when the patriot, no longer languishing in camp nor agonizing in the field, will not suffer for what woman, in her tenderness, can do for him." No less than the soldiers, Isabella Fogg had given everything for her country.[4]

A modern account provides supplemental information on Isabella Fogg. She was from Calais, Maine—one of the most remote areas of coastal "Downeast." Her son, Hugh, was in the 6th Maine Infantry, and she began her volunteer work in Washington for the Maine Camp and Hospital Association of Portland. She assisted in the Annapolis hospital during an outbreak of spotted typhus fever in September 1861. That work lasted until spring 1862, when she joined the Hospital Transport

---

3   Chamberlain documented this meeting in a December 2, 1862 letter.

4   Moore, *Women of the War*, 113-126.

Service under the U. S. Sanitary Commission in the Virginia Peninsula. Afterward she returned to Washington, working for the Maine Camp and Hospital Association and the Maine Soldiers' Relief Agency, headquartered there. That led her to the Antietam/Sharpsburg battle area in November 1862, where she and others assisted the wounded from the September battle. Working with Harriet (Mrs. J. S.) Eaton and Charles C. Hayes, they were "horrified to find sick and wounded soldiers, supposedly long since removed, still languishing all over the area."

On November 10, Fogg described the Smoketown Hospital, where she had found 30 Maine soldiers. "This place is in the most miserable condition," she wrote. "[T]he men complain very much. The effluvia arising from the condition of these grounds is intolerable, quite enough to make a man in perfect health sick, and how men can recover in such a place is a mystery to me." They dispensed their supplies and went to Bakersville by wagon, found 20 wounded from the 5th Maine, and continued on to hospitals at Sharpsburg, Berlin (Brunswick), Harpers Ferry, Keedysville, and Hagerstown. Returning to Washington, they replenished and returned to disperse supplies at those hospitals.

Fogg and Eaton went to Stafford and cared for Maine and other soldiers. Isabella also served at Gettysburg, the Bristoe and Mine Run campaigns, and during the Overland Campaign at Belle Plain and Fredericksburg). During the winter of 1864, while visiting home, she received "a sizeable sum of money to be placed at her disposal by the [Maine] Legislature, to be spent at her discretion for the comfort and care of Maine soldiers."

Previously, during the fall of 1864, she had received word that her son had been "mortally" wounded at Cedar Creek. Quickly going to Martinsburg, West Virginia, she discovered Hugh had been wounded and his leg amputated. He was evacuated to Baltimore. While tending him there, Fogg's health broke down and she went home to recover. By November of 1864, she was back in Washington, where she joined the U. S. Christian Commission's "Special Diet Kitchens in Hospitals" unit under Mrs. Annie Wittenmyer. Mrs. Fogg, assigned to duty on the hospital ship Jacob Strader on the Ohio River, operated the ship's special diet kitchen. She accidentally fell through an open hatch and severely injured her spine; she remained an invalid thereafter. Generals Chamberlain, Meade, and Grant aided in securing her a pension.[5]

Mary W. Lee, a child immigrant from Great Britain, was led by patriotic zeal to war work, starting in Philadelphia's Union Refreshment Saloon. After a year she joined Ellen Harris and others in caring for the transported wounded and sick from Virginia. She served at Antietam in field hospitals of Sedgwick's division and was a mainstay of the Smoketown Hospital. Lee moved with the army to Stafford in November 1862 and participated in its "Valley Forge" with only a brief respite to nurse her sick son at home in March. During Chancellorsville, she worked at the Lacy House (Chatham), where she and others witnessed the VI Corps's assault on Marye's Heights. As Moore related:

> When that fierce engagement was at its height, the men that had been wounded in the skirmishes of the days previous, all dragged themselves to the galleries and terraces of the house, Mrs. Lee helping them, and watched the conflict with eager forgetfulness of their own sufferings. When at length Sedgwick, and the brave Sixth corps, after two repulses, made the final and triumphant charge, sweeping over the battlements from which Burnside had been so terribly repulsed in December, everybody that had a well arm raised it, with ringing cheers, over his head, and shouted, till their brave companions on the other

5 http://www.civilwarwomenblog.com/2008/08/isabella-morrison-fogg.html.

side heard and answered back their triumph. Mrs. Lee stood by her little cooking tent, whipping dishes, and joined in the general delight by waving her towel, as a flag, and shouting with the rest. She did more than this. She fell upon her knees, and thanked God that those formidable lines, from which the Union forces had been so often repulsed with frightful carnage, were at last carried, and the national flag waved in triumph over them.

The triumph may have been complete, but the butcher's bill was due. Some 8,000 wounded were carried across the river to the Stafford hospitals. Lee worked at Chatham and followed the army to Gettysburg. Forced to interrupt her service and remain at home with sick family in the winter of 1863-1864, she rejoined the army in 1864 at Brandy Station and followed it on the Overland Campaign (where she again worked in Fredericksburg). Lee continued serving until the war's end, which found her in Richmond hospitals a month after the Army of Northern Virginia's surrender. There, she met President Lincoln, who went through the wards and talked and shook hands with each man.

"Then," Moore added, "when there were no more homeless and suffering patriots; no more wounds to be stanched; no more long trains of ambulances, with their groaning and bleeding freightage; no more caldrons of gruel and mutton soup to be cooked for great wards full of half-famished boys, Mrs. Lee went home, and slipped into the happy routine of domestic usefulness." She had given her all: three long years of patriotic duty.[6]

Ellen Matilda Orbison (Mrs. John) **Harris** began her war work in Philadelphia as a member of a ladies charitable group at "the [10th Presbyterian] church of the Rev. Dr. Boardman." The group's secretary, she was mistakenly described as "one of those delicate, fragile, and feeble-looking ladies who are apparently condemned to lives of patient suffering and inactivity by constitutional defect of physical vigor." When the war began, she buried that description when she "entered upon a self-imposed and self-directed career of Christian and sanitary labors, more extended, more arduous, and more potent for good, than any other that can be found in American annals." Moore added: "If there were any such vain decorations of human approbation as a crown, or a wreath, or a star for her, who in our late war has done the most, and labored the longest, who visited the greatest number of hospitals, prayed with the greatest number of suffering and dying soldiers, penetrated nearest to the front, and underwent the greatest amount of fatigue and exposure for the soldier—that crown or that star would rightly be given to Mrs. John Harris, of Philadelphia." Amid such breathtaking praise, though, she remarked: "[N]ot one in all the noble sisterhood is more indifferent than she to all human applause."

Harris soon aspired to do more than the Ladies' Aid Society could require of her. She went to Washington after First Manassas, making delivery trips to the quickly expanding hospitals. By spring of 1862, she had visited more than a hundred hospitals, distributing donations from the society.

After extensive visits to Fairfax and Arlington, she served in the Peninsula Campaign. She reported back to her society regularly—a thorough, if self-effacing, record. First, she worked at Fortress Monroe and then with McClellan's army. It was exhausting, but she took time to marvel at the peculiar reality of wounded and sick boys from both sides—Alabama, the Carolinas, and Massachusetts—lying side-by-side in the hospitals. She divided her efforts and supplies between those

6 Moore, *Women of the War*, 148-169.

Ellen Matilda Orbison (Mrs. John) Harris.
LOC

transported up the Chesapeake and others who remained in army hospitals. Philadelphians met her requests for more of everything.

Harris worked on ships and in field hospitals with equal vigor. Her drive and energy occasionally put her at cross purposes with a lazy chaplain or recalcitrant surgeon, but in the main she garnered the respect of all, especially the soldiers. She rendered valuable service at Harrison's Landing and at hospitals on the James River.

The supplies flowed in and included ascorbic foods so critical for health and recovery (then missing from routine army fare). During the final two weeks of August 1862 alone, she distributed 100 baskets, 72 barrels, five bags, and five boxes of onions; eight barrels of apples; three barrels of beets; three barrels of squashes; 18 bushels of tomatoes; five barrels of pickles; one barrel of molasses; two kegs of butter; six kegs of dry rusk and crackers; 80 pounds of cheese; and large quantities of farina, milk, wine and cocoa to the men. Harris moved to Maryland with the army and, at Antietam, she again rendered invaluable service.[7]

During the war's bloodiest day, she found herself leading prayers as much as cooking and feeding the wounded. Amid the dead, wounded, sick, and dying, the women distributed the supplies they had, comforted the men, and sang (she noted "Miss G's [Helen Gilson] loud, clear voice leading"). They worked at French's division hospital, and Bolivar and Smoketown hospitals, caring for "a thousand of our wounded, and a number of Confederates." Her letters from the Peninsula were published and distributed in the North, triggering an extensive flood of supplies, all forwarded directly to her.

With the army's movement to Stafford, she became identified with what transpired in the "Valley Forge" period. Moore explained:

> During the period from October, 1862, to May, 1863, although but one great battle took place in Virginia, Mrs. Harris continued her hospital labors with unabated zeal and devotion. At no time in the long struggle was sanitary service more needed; for the winter of 1862-3 was in the war what that of 1777-8 was to the Continental army under Washington. The troops had been worn down by the unexampled fatigues of the fall campaign, and when the cold weather set in, sickness multiplied at a rate so alarming, as to threaten, at one time, the very organization of the army.

7   Moore, *Women of the War*, 176-212.

Moore estimated the number of sick and convalescents in camps between the Rappahannock and Potomac at 30,000-40,000. The wounded and more seriously ill in Washington numbered another 30,000. In November and December, she challenged Philadelphians to send more supplies, and that continued throughout the winter. Picket duty in adverse weather was a heavy burden. "Mrs. Harris," Moore continued, "was for many weeks established at the Lacey [sic] House, where her self-imposed duties were onerous and varied." Probably operating out of the kitchen out-building, her stove provided endless rations of "Ginger panada" or "bully soup" (compounded corn-meal, ground ginger, wine, and crackers) to the interminable picket shifts numbed by cold and exposure. Her reports included a vivid description of a Sunday at Lacy House:

> Could you have looked in upon us at breakfast time this day of sacred rest, your eye would have fallen on scenes and groupings all out of harmony with its holy uses. One cooking-stove pushed to its utmost capacity, groaning beneath the weight of gruel, coffee, and tea, around it clustered soldiers, shivering, drenched to the skin, here and there a poor fellow coiled upon the floor, too full of pain and weariness to bear his own weight. Seated along the table, as closely as possible, were others, whose expressions of thanks told how grateful the simple repast was—bread, stewed fruit, and coffee. All alike were wet and cold, having been exposed throughout the night to the driving snow and rain, the most uncomfortable one of the season.

She recalled 72 haggard men awaiting food in the March 1863 winds. With icicles on their wet blankets, they bolstered themselves for a three- to five-mile march in cold mud after 42 hours of sleepless duty. "Simple as it was," she reported, "you would feel that God's own day was honored." After Chancellorsville, Mrs. Harris reported (May 18):

> After seeing Mrs. B. [Brady] and Mrs. L. [Lee] off, we filled two ambulances with bread and butter, prepared stewed fruit, egg-nog, lemons, oranges, cheese shirts, drawers, stockings, and handkerchiefs, and went out to meet a train of ambulances bearing the wounded from United States Ford. Reaching Stoneman's Station, where we expected to meet the [ambulance] train, we learned we were a half an hour too late, but could overtake them; so we pressed forward, and found ourselves in the rear of a long procession of one hundred and two ambulances. The road being narrow, steep, and most difficult, we could not pass, and were obliged to follow, feeling every jolt and jar for our poor suffering ones, whose wounds had just reached that point when the slightest motion is agony . . . . When this sad procession halted near the hospital of the Sixth army corps, we prepared to minister to the sufferers. Some gentlemen of the Christian Commission were there to assist us. No pen can describe the scene. Most of these sufferers had been wounded on the 3d instant.

Amputations were rampant, she wrote, and many had to be left with the enemy who were overtaxed caring for their own wounded. "By day and by night I see their poor mutilated limbs, red with inflammation, bones protruding, worms rioting as they were held over the sides of the ambulance to catch the cooling breeze!" she lamented. "Those anguished faces—what untold suffering they bespoke! Many a lip quivered, and eye filled with tears, when approached with words of sympathy; and not a few told how they had prayed for death to end their sufferings, as they were dashed from side to side, often rolling, in their helplessness, over each other, as they were driven those 20 weary miles."

The Philadelphians sent supplies, Ellen noted, to Mrs. Husband and Mrs. McKay. She also mentioned that Miss Dorothea Dix, superintendent of Army nurses, was present and asked her to distribute other supplies to the two ladies. Of critical need was the nourishing food. Each day for a week, Ellen related, they cooked up five gallons of custard, using six dozen eggs each time, and about eight gallons of pudding for the sick and wounded.

In addition to cooking, she conducted prayer meetings. Attendance grew to the point where the meeting had to be held in the main house at Lacy House. "Mrs. Harris assumed the whole responsibility," Moore explained, "occasionally calling upon clergymen and others, whom she knew, to lead the devotions of the audience." Harris's efforts continued until the army left for Pennsylvania. Ellen Harris continued her service at Gettysburg in her own state. After the victory, when she could have easily returned to her home, she resolutely stayed with the army as it returned to Virginia for fall campaigning. In October she returned to Philadelphia. Again, she could have easily retired from her strenuous service; but, instead, she decided to go to the Western Theater and serve there! Her subsequent wartime service took her to Tennessee and Georgia, working with the sick and wounded soldiers, as well as with poor white refugees displaced from their meager farms by war and destroyed economy. Though in broken health, she returned to the Army of the Potomac for the campaigning of 1864 and 1865. Not surprisingly, after Lee's surrender she finished the war in the Carolinas. She had served through late April "as apothecary, sometimes as physician, constantly as nurse and Christian friend." Grossly miscast as "delicate, fragile, and feeble-looking" in 1861, Ellen survived until 1902 and died in Florence, Italy.[8]

Charlotte E. McKay of Massachusetts, after suffering the 1862 deaths of her husband and only child, joined the army in spring 1862 at Frederick, Maryland. There she cared for the wounded from the latest fight at Winchester, and she had the unusual experience of face-to-face contact with the Confederates. The Federals, thinking their hospitals safely tucked behind friendly lines, left them behind as "Stonewall" Jackson's troops advanced from Harpers Ferry into Maryland in September 1862. Charlotte chose to remain with her charges when home guards faded away and the advancing Rebels swept into the town, taking possession of the hospital and its Federal patients, nurses, and surgeons. What passed between the opposing forces afterward was spirited banter, in which Charlotte took an active part. The Confederates felt unbeatable at that point, but the Federals cordially predicted their demise. Soon South Mountain and Antietam occupied everyone's attention, and the Rebels returned on their way to Virginia. Mrs. McKay remained at Antietam until the army moved to Falmouth in November 1862.

Initially going to Washington, she nursed there before securing—"after much difficulty"—a pass to Falmouth, where she visited her brother and friends in the 17th Maine and took up duties in the III Corps hospital in January 1863. During the "Valley Forge," she cared for the sick and wounded and prepared meals for hospitalized soldiers. Assisted by Mrs. Birney, the wife of Gen. David Birney, they labored to make the men more comfortable and supplied them from the U. S. Sanitary Commission's and other stocks.

Most probably she was the "Mrs. McK" described in a March 24, 1863, letter to the Lewiston, Maine *Daily Evening Journal* as escorting a group of visiting Maine people to the headquarters of General

8 Ibid.

Howard—then stationed with the 2nd Division of the II Corps— near Stoneman's Station in an ambulance driven by an orderly from the 17th Maine camp.[9]

In mid-April 1863, McKay was located at Potomac Creek with the new hospital of the 1st Division, III Corps. When the corps deployed, Charlotte took an ambulance with supplies and followed them over a pontoon bridge to Chancellorsville and "established herself at a large brick house, two or three miles from the front line of battle." While there, she treated the wounded even as she received the news that her brother had been killed. Perhaps as bad, when the army was ordered to withdraw across the river at U. S. Ford, they knew that they were abandoning many wounded soldiers still on the battlefield.

Charlotte went to Washington while the army deployed toward Pennsylvania in June 1863. The news of Gettysburg came too late for her to move there, so she went to Baltimore, where she found the hospitals were still operative after the Gettysburg battle. She left, arriving in time to work there through August. She rejoined the army in the Bristoe, Mine Run, and Overland Campaigns. During the latter, she served in Fredericksburg.

McKay joined the hospital of the Cavalry Corps and took charge of its special diet department. On December 24, 1864, she was presented with a gold badge by the Cavalry Corps. A few months earlier, she had received the Kearney Medal by the officers of the 17th Maine Infantry.[10] Her army service ceased by March 1865. She remained in Virginia, however, for another year, "engaged with the freedmen; nursing the sick, taking care of those who were unable to care for themselves, listening to many a weird tale of cruelty and injustice in the old days of bondage, and giving the rudiments of education to minds that were sitting in darkness."[11]

Mary Morris Husband, a granddaughter of Robert Morris, one of the Founding Fathers, was the wife of Philadelphia attorney J. J. Husband, a man of deep pockets whose was prominent in the community. Mrs. Husband began her Civil War service in 1861 with hospital visitations and library work at the hospital at 22nd and Wood Streets in Philadelphia. In July 1862, she joined the transport nursing group in the Virginia Peninsula at Harrison's Landing. After three trips with wounded and sick soldiers, she assumed a leading role at the National Hospital at Baltimore in August of 1862, engaged with handling wounded from Second Manassas, Chantilly, Harpers Ferry, and South Mountain. She went to the Smoketown Hospital near Antietam Creek and worked there during and, for two months after that battle, cared for the wounded and sick.

Husband's "Valley Forge"-period service consisted of spending the entire winter as matron of the V Corps's 3rd-Division hospital. During Chancellorsville, she shifted to the hospital of the III Corps's 3rd Division. As the army moved toward Pennsylvania in June 1863, Husband briefly served in Alexandria and Washington before moving on to Gettysburg, where she remained until December 1863 taking care of "her boys."

As a unique sideline, she vigorously advocated appeals of convicted deserters. Usually successful, some of her appeals were personally taken to Secretary of War Stanton and to President Lincoln.

---

9   See Chapter 6, 172.

10   Moore erroneously referred to this as another medal (the Kearney Cross).

11   Moore, *Women of the War*, 278-297.

Noted for her advocacy for guard-house prisoners, as well, Husband remained with the army through April 1864 when General Grant's order expelling all women from the army provided her an opportunity for home-rest. Returning after several weeks, she went to Fredericksburg hospitals to resume duty. She ended the war in Richmond where, during an impromptu review of the victorious Union forces, "Mother Husband" was cheered.

Exceptionally large numbers of soldier testimonials were prominent in Moore's work. No less than the soldiers, she had labored long and hard, with great effectiveness in their behalf.[12] A modern summary of Husband's wartime service adds one final colorful detail: "She was known as the nurse with the apron of miracle pockets, because her deep, wide pockets carried games and reading material that entertained and filled the soldiers' long hours of recovery."[13]

Amy Morris Bradley of East Cambridge, Massachusetts, was a Mainer by birth, born in East Vassalboro in 1823. She commenced her service to the Union shortly after First Manassas. Traveling to Washington in August 1861 with the 3rd Maine Infantry of Colonel O. O. Howard, she took charge of the sick in makeshift hospitals in Powell House and The Octagon House for General Slocum's brigade. In that capacity, she connected with the U. S. Sanitary Commission, from which she drew supplies. In April 1862, she went with the division to Warrenton Junction and, in May, to the Peninsula. Sharing workloads with several women, Bradley was mildly censured for spending too much time caring for a wounded Confederate, William A. Sewell of the 8th Alabama Infantry. "Doctor," she replied, "I profess to be a Christian, and my Bible teaches me, if my enemy hungers, to feed him; if he is thirsty, to give him drink; that poor boy is wounded, and suffering intensely; he was my enemy, but now he needs my aid. If I obey not the teachings of my Saviour, I am not a true disciple." It was an eloquent demonstration of the caliber of all the "Women of the 'Valley Forge.'"

After the Peninsula Campaign, during which she transported wounded and sick to Philadelphia, Amy went with the army to Aquia Creek, then transited to Manassas. Afterward, she cared for the sick at the Washington Soldiers' Home. Bradley joined the army under the auspices of the Sanitary Commission in December 1862 and served during the "Valley Forge" as a "special relief agent." This involved shuttling supplies from Washington and Maryland to the army and giving them to proper agents for distribution.[14]

A modern account by Maggie Maclean provides details about Bradley's postwar career. In January 1865, the Soldiers' Memorial Society, formed by Boston Unitarians, was formed. After the war she went under their auspices to Wilmington, North Carolina. During Christmas 1866, she opened a school in cooperation with other vestiges of the war—the American Missionary Society founded by New Englander Rev. S. S. Ashley, and the General O. O. Howard's Freedmen, Refugees, and Abandoned Lands Bureau. After January 1867, initially with three pupils, Bradley operated the Dry Pond Union Schoolhouse, which had been abandoned since 1862. Despite social ostracism from some Wilmington ladies, the school caught on. She did not receive rave reviews from unreconstructed Southerners, but financial support from concerned Wilmington citizens and Northern philanthropists

---

12 Moore, *Women of the War*, 313-332.

13 www.civilwarwomenblog.com/2008/05/mary-morris-husband.html, accessed on March 6, 2010.

14 Moore, *Women of the War*, 415-452.

rolled in. After her death, she was buried in Wilmington's Oakdale Cemetery; her headstone reads, "Our School Mother."[15]

Although not included in Frank Moore's work, **Clarissa Harlowe "Clara" Barton** was the most famous of the women who worked with the Union Army. The most enduring "human face" personifying the work done in Stafford during the war, Barton also illustrates the "Union Women of 'Valley Forge.'" Historian Stephen B. Oates tells Clara's story in some detail and provides tangential information on other women.

Barton, through her postwar lectures across America, brought home the vital role women played in humanitarian efforts supporting the war. Reminiscing about her wartime experiences—particularly her 1862 activities at the Lacy House in Falmouth and in the Fredericksburg churches, and her 1864 activities at Belle Plain and in Fredericksburg— she drew national attention to all of the women.

Oates relates women manned the homefront (running farms, businesses and industries); filled in for government service and war industries; replaced male teachers; and fought (he estimates that 400 Union women served disguised as men). He quotes Jane E. Schultz that more than 18,200 women had worked in Northern hospitals as matrons, nurses, laundresses, and cooks (about 3,214 women had served in Dorothea Dix's department alone). That figure includes some 2,000 black laundresses and cooks, many of them freed slaves. Like Clara Barton, another 2,000 women worked as unpaid volunteers in hospitals. In all, about 20,000 contributed to the medical side of the war effort. Beyond that, virtually all of the money that was raised (estimated elsewhere at $6 million) and private supplies that were collected was accomplished by women through a myriad of aid groups and events.[16]

Barton herself could be assertive and self-serving, but her lifetime humanitarian contributions were exceptional by any measure. She came to Stafford four times during the war. She was present during the first Federal occupation of Falmouth, which began on April 18, 1862. She landed at Aquia and, after spending the night, made her way to Falmouth Station and checked in with King's headquarters at Chatham. Crossing over to Fredericksburg, occupied since May 2, she witnessed her first amputation. She observed the arrival of Burnside's troops on August 4, and she then distributed supplies to her "pet" 21st Massachusetts Infantry, before returning to Washington. Accumulating more supplies, she went out to Culpeper and the Cedar Mountain battle area.

She was back in Washington when she received news of the Second Manassas battles. She went to Fairfax Station, off-loaded her supplies, and she and her two compatriots pitched in as nurses. This was Clara's first wartime nursing stint. She next served at South Mountain and Antietam Creek in September. Along with some of the other women in this group, Antietam was where they began to understand what could and could not be accomplished by women volunteers.[17]

Historian Jane Conner provides additional details. Born on Christmas Day, 1821, Barton lived on a farm in Oxford, Massachusetts. She worked as a teacher for two decades in Oxford and in Bordentown, New Jersey, before receiving an appointment as a U. S. Patent Office clerk in

---

15 www.civilwarwomenblog.com/2006/10/amy-morris-bradley.html; accessed on March 6, 2010.

16 Stephen B. Oates, *A Woman of Valor: Clara Barton and the Civil War* (New York: The Free Press, 1994).

17 Ibid.

Clarissa Harlowe "Clara" Barton. LOC

Washington. Rising to supervisory clerk for a period, she became the highest-ranking woman in the Federal government. At the beginning of the war, she reconnected with Massachusetts friends in units stationed in the U. S. Capitol, and arranged for items to be sent to her and passed out to these men. In December 1861, the Ladies Relief Committee of Worcester, Massachusetts, to whom she had written asking for help, petitioned her to become their distribution agent. She became adept at soliciting, receiving, storing (stockpiling), and distributing supplies.[18]

Barton interrupted her work in February 1862 to nurse her dying father. She returned to Washington in July and made frequent sorties with aid for her chosen units. She wanted to provide support in the battle areas and traveled to Falmouth for one of her first such missions. She expanded supply distribution to the 8th and 11th Connecticut regiments. Her next service in Culpeper required five days of work on three hours' sleep as she cared for almost 1,500 wounded soldiers. She followed the army (her new motto was "Follow the Cannon") to Second Manassas, Chantilly, and Harpers Ferry, followed by service at Antietam in the Maryland Campaign of September 1862.

She had learned she needed more logistical support, which was accomplished with eight to ten men detailed to help her, plus a small crew of male and female followers. Barton stored supplies in advance, expended them, and drew on army and U. S. Sanitary Commission resources thereafter. Working in harness with army surgeons and the commissions they would allow her, she did all she could for her "beloved boys." Barton was particularly adept at developing sponsors and supporters within the government (e.g., Sen. Henry Wilson) and the army (e.g., Generals Burnside and Sturgis).

During Fredericksburg, Barton and her crew operated from both the Sthreshley (pronounced without the "S") and Lacy Houses. She nursed and looked to the general comfort of the wounded and recorded as many names as possible. This accounting, lacking in the military medical system, evolved by war's end into Barton's primary role. From Chatham, she observed on December 11 the first American combat river-crossing by Hall's brigade. She also nursed the wounded from that assault. Inside Chatham and its outbuildings, she and the other ladies—mostly from the U. S. Christian Commission— cared for the wounded and dying. She remained there until December 25 and celebrated both the final evacuation of the wounded and her 41st birthday.

18 Jane Hollenbeck Conner, *Sinners, Saints and Soldiers in Civil War Stafford* (Stafford, VA:, Parker Publishing LLC, 2009).

Unlike the other women of the "Valley Forge," Barton did not fade into domestic obscurity at the end of the war or during Reconstruction. She lectured throughout America about her wartime experiences; this obviously drew attention and allowed her to build up a reserve of funds to undertake new projects. For instance, Barton was involved with the International Red Cross in the Franco-Prussian War of 1870. After a physical breakdown requiring rehabilitation, she formed the American Red Cross and succeeded in persuading America to subscribe to the Geneva Convention. Her organizations fought forest fires in Michigan, floods in Ohio, droughts in Texas, tornadoes in Illinois, and yellow fever epidemics in Florida. Internationally, they helped with a Russian famine and starvation in Armenia.

In 1884 and in 1902, Barton led the U. S. delegations to the Geneva Convention Conferences in Geneva and St. Petersburg, respectively. She led relief efforts following the Johnstown Flood in 1889, and in 1898, at age 78, she was again with "her boys" in the Spanish-American War.

At 82, Barton finally retired and lived at Glen Echo, Maryland, until her death in 1912. Buried in North Oxford, Massachusetts in the family plot, she had finally gone home. A eulogy by her cousin, Rev. William Barton, was on the mark: "No American woman received more honor while she lived either at home or abroad, and how worthily she bore those honors those know best who know her best."[19]

Several other Civil War women of note were also in Stafford during the Union "Valley Forge" and not featured in Moore's 1866 work including **Dorothea Lynde Dix**, one of the more famous women in the war. Widely known before the war as a social reformer, she had worked tirelessly for better treatment for the mentally ill and women in prison.

Dix was born in 1802 in Hampden, Maine. She overcame a difficult dysfunctional family and frustrated romantic relationship to head several schools in Massachusetts, investigate mental health and female prison issues of her day, and help establish two state hospitals. At age 59, with the start of the Civil War she volunteered her services and became the Superintendent of Female Nurses for the Union Army. In that capacity she organized the women, placed them in hospitals, and inspected the facilities regularly. Dix also raised money for medical supplies.

Famously known as "Dragon Dix" for her formidable and brusque sternness, she certainly ran a tight ship. She outlawed hiring young and attractive women on the grounds that they would dwell too much on romantic and marriage possibilities. She dressed them in drab black or brown and forbade ringlets, hoops, or jewelry. Despite such draconian measures, Dix managed to assemble a nursing force of more than 3,000 women, who worked predominantly in the wartime general hospitals of the North.

After the war, Dix returned to working for mental health improvements. At 80, she retired and lived in an apartment at the New Jersey State Hospital she had created. Even when invalided in her late years, she maintained an active correspondence from her bed. She died there in 1887 and was buried at Mount Auburn Cemetery in Cambridge, Massachusetts. Her gravestone is marked with a predictable lack of sentimentality: "Dorothea L. Dix."

Historian Jane Conner also provides details on **Princess Agnes Salm-Salm**, who was in Stafford County during the Union "Valley Forge" period as an army wife. An American, her original

19 Ibid.

name was probably Agnes Elizabeth Winona LeClercq Joy. She married a German, Col. Prince Felix Salm-Salm, in August 1862 in Washington, D. C. He was the commander of the 8th New York Infantry and left her in Washington while he went to serve with his regiment in western Virginia. The regiment became part of XII Army Corps and moved into Stafford after the battle of Fredericksburg. Agnes joined him in their camp near Aquia Landing in late December 1862, and in January 1863 they moved their camp to another place along Aquia Creek.[20]

Princess Salm-Salm according to her own memoir, spent her time looking after her husband and his regiment, and she was not known to have engaged in nursing activities during the army's "Valley Forge" period. Her activities, however, do provide some insight into the social life of the regimental and more senior officers. They were, especially during the Christmas and New Year periods, extremely active in lavish affairs. At the extreme end, she and her husband participated in a dinner given by Gen. Dan Sickles that was catered by Delmonico's famous New York City restaurant.

Salm-Salm was prominently involved in an incident during President and Mrs. Lincoln's week-long visit to the army in April 1863. General Sickles, while entertaining the first family at his "Boscobel" headquarters, noticed the president's melancholy demeanor, brought on from hospital visits to the wounded and sick. Sickles persuaded the petite Agnes to go over and kiss Mr. Lincoln to enliven the proceedings. She crossed the room and quietly asked the tall man to bend over so that she could whisper something in his ear. He did so, and she bestowed the kiss, which drew immediate cheery responses from the observers. The president's mood lightened and, other than the First Lady, all were suddenly happy and festive. "People said his face was ugly," Salm-Salm recalled in her memoir, "but he never appeared ugly to me, for his face, beaming with boundless kindness and benevolence towards mankind, had the stamp of intellectual beauty."

After Chancellorsville, Col. Salm-Salm's 8th New York was mustered-out, and he became the colonel of the new 68th New York Infantry, slated for duty in the West. Agnes traveled with them to Tennessee, and while there—conceivably inspired by the women she had seen in Stafford—engaged with the Christian and Sanitary Commissions in hospital work.

After the war, she followed Salm to Mexico, where he served the ill-starred Maximilian von Hapsburg—and would have suffered the same fate as the emperor had his wife not famously fallen at the feet of President Benito Juarez to beg mercy.

Returning to Germany, Colonel Salm-Salm was killed during the battle of Gravelotte in 1870, and Agnes became a young widow. She continued her hospital work and nursing throughout the Franco-Prussian War and afterwards became a socialite and celebrity in the best circles (including a friendship with Clara Barton which stretched into the twentieth-century).

During an 1899 American visit, Princess Salm-Salm participated in a reunion with 21 veterans of the old 8th New York Infantry Regiment—a regiment that had begun its Civil War service with 1,040 men. In a touching scene, she presented them with the flag of the 8th, which she had brought from Germany. She asked them to pass it from one to another until they were all gone, and then asked that it be turned over to the state of New York for perpetual safe-keeping. "This is my only request," she ended.

---

20 Conner, *Sinners, Saints and Soldiers in Civil War Stafford.*

Salm-Salm returned to Germany and lived quietly in Karlsruhe, finally dying in December 1912 (coincidentally, Clara Barton had died that April). The princess from America was buried in Bonn.[21]

Finally, Jane Conner also describes the Stafford activities of **Dr. Mary Edwards Walker**, one of the more remarkable of the many remarkable Union women of "Valley Forge." Born in 1832 on a farm in Oswego, New York, Mary Walker defied conventions most of her life. She married and soon divorced, became a physician after graduating from Syracuse Medical School, struggled to practice medicine, and became a member of the "bloomerite" movement to free women from the constricting clothing of that day.

When the war began, she closed her Rome, New York, practice and traveled to Washington to apply for a surgeon's commission. Her application was rebuffed despite a dire need for medical personnel. She would struggle through the entire war seeking a commission and/or contracts, and was occasionally successful in gaining the latter.

She began at a Washington hospital at the Patent Office under Dr. J. N. Green, who recommended her for a commission to no avail and even offered to compensate her from his own salary (she refused). She labored, basically for room and board and moved on to another hospital near the Forest Hall Prison in Georgetown. In January 1862, she returned to New York City and took some classes at the Hygeia Therapeutic College, which emphasized "natural cures," water therapies, and loose clothing rather than more traditional medicine. She returned to Washington and then to the army near Warrenton in October or November 1862, where she helped convey sick and wounded soldiers by train to the capital.

She also at that time began wearing a self-designed uniform of sorts—really more of a costume—that combined a dress with trousers and some unique decoration and trim. Perhaps she thought this might endear her to the proverbial powers-that-be and communicate some seriousness in seeking official status. Perceived as just "another lady" helping with the sick and wounded—and, effectively, she was doing little more than they had done and were doing—she persevered.

Walker's time in Stafford is gleaned exclusively from her later accounts and an article in the *New York Tribune.* "[A]t one time, when I was down at the Lacy House at Fredericksburg, after the famous battle there ." she wrote, "I was directed by the managing surgeons to take any cases I chose and dress them preparatory to sending them to Washington." This suggests she worked in the 200-bed tent hospital behind Lacy House, where patients were prepared for evacuation and not in the surgery, although the *New York Tribune* article stated, "She can amputate a limb with the skill of an old surgeon, and administer medicine equally as well." No other reference to her performing surgery of any sort has been found.

Walker also ordered hospital stewards to cease carrying patients head-down onto the steamboats' gangways. This suggests she was at Aquia Landing or conceivably at Belle Plain. Together, both accounts suggest that Mary was involved in transporting the wounded.[22]

After her Stafford service, Walker worked again in Washington, continually rebuffed in her efforts seeking a commission. In the fall of 1863, she was in Tennessee, where she was slightly more successful in finding duties. She received a contract position and was assigned to unofficially attached

21 Ibid.

22 Ibid.

duty as assistant surgeon of the 52nd Ohio Infantry in the Army of the Cumberland. However, Walker is not found on any official roster of the 52nd Ohio or of the Union Army, for that matter. The best possible accounting of her service relates she was a "Contract Acting Assistant Surgeon (civilian), U. S. Army." Her places and dates of service include the battle of First Manassas, July 21, 1861; Patent Office Hospital, Washington, D.C., October 1861; Chattanooga, Tenn., following battle of Chickamauga, September 1863; Prisoner of War, April 10, 1864-August 12, 1864, Castle Thunder Prison, Richmond, Va.; Battle of Atlanta, September 1864. Entered service at: Louisville, Ky."[23]

The Army of the Cumberland's medical director, Surgeon Glover Perin, seemed leery of Walker's service, and he had her examined by a five-member board of surgeons, which found her unfit. Despite the rejection, Walker managed the approbation of Col. (later Brig. Gen.) Daniel McCook, Jr., commander of the 52nd Ohio Infantry; Maj. Gen. Alexander McDowell McCook; Maj. Gen. George Henry Thomas; and Maj. Gen. (later Gen.) William T. Sherman; therefore, she was continued in her duties.[24]

It does not appear that Walker was in any active combat during her medical service. However, in an effort to assist civilians in the spring of 1864, she was captured as a spy by Rebel troops and sent as a prisoner-of-war to Castle Thunder, one of Richmond's military prisons. Her four-month incarceration certainly caused a stir in Richmond, and probably prompted her exchange (to her joy, for a Confederate surgeon). She again submitted a request for commission, this time directly to President Lincoln—unsuccessfully.

Returning to the West in September 1864, she was hired as a contract surgeon and assigned as surgeon-in-charge of the Louisville, Kentucky, Female Military Prison. She was again compensated as a civilian. After the war, she returned to Washington and continued her efforts to gain some kind of official status—now working on a second president, Andrew Johnson, although to no greater effect.

One amazing side-effect was that, since the government was unable to commission her, Generals Sherman and Thomas requested Secretary of War Stanton to award Walker the Medal of Honor, a military outrage at that late stage of the war, when medals went for valorous acts exclusively. In November 1865, she was awarded the medal, becoming the first and only woman to receive it. "[S]he was assigned to duty and served as an assistant surgeon in charge of female prisoners at Louisville," her citation read, noting that she:

> devoted herself with much patriotic zeal to the sick and wounded soldiers, both in the field and hospitals, to the detriment of her own health, and has also endured hardships as a prisoner of war four months in a Southern prison while acting as contract surgeon; and Whereas by reason of her not being a commissioned officer in the military service, a brevet or honorary rank cannot, under existing laws, be conferred upon her; and Whereas in the opinion of the President [Johnson] an honorable recognition of her services and sufferings should be made. It is ordered, That a testimonial thereof shall be hereby made and given to the said Dr. [Walker] and that the usual medal of honor for meritorious services be given.[25]

23 NPS/CWSSS.

24 Conner, *Sinners, Saints and Soldiers in Civil War Stafford.*

25 U. S. Army, Center for Military History, Medal of Honor Citations Archives.

Walker's service with the 52nd Ohio was not even alluded to in the citation. Although this appears a lapse of official sanity after 150 years, by way of explanation, it must be recalled that the Medal of Honor was the only official U. S. decoration and had not been exclusively awarded for extreme valor. Early in the way, many similar awards were made—such as awarding the medal to large numbers of men who had enlisted "for the war" at an early, critical stage of personnel shortages and need. The Medal of Honor must have seemed like vindication; she proudly wore her prized decoration for the remainder of her life. That life would certainly see ups and downs.

Walker's wartime notoriety resulted in postwar opportunities: she was president of the National Dress Reform Association, a delegate to the Women's Social Science Convention in Great Britain in 1866, a celebrity in Paris in 1867, and a member of the Women's Suffrage Association in Ohio in 1868. She wrote the book *Hit* (1871). She also continued to petition Congress—25 times—finally gaining a disability pension in 1874 at $8.50 per month.

In 1878, Walker wrote *The Science of Immorality*, and continued lecturing on her Civil War experiences and women's suffrage. An interesting diversion in 1881 was her unsuccessful run for a seat in the U. S. Senate. She did manage to secure a clerkship in the mailroom of the Pensions Office, however, yet due to excessive sick leave, she lost that job in a year. She then began a career of sub-prime lecturing—little more dignified than freak-show work. At the same time, she continued beseeching governments at all levels for funding and subsidies.

Arguably, her low point came in 1917. The War Department had labored since the end of the Civil War to sort and publish the Official Records and, along with those efforts, to recognize the valor of those who had contributed to the victory of Union arms. Many distinguished officers—men such as Joshua L. Chamberlain, Thomas O. Seaver, Daniel Butterfield, and Oliver O. Howard—received their awards of the Medal of Honor in those later years. At the same time, efforts were made to invalidate awards of the medal that had, in retrospect, not been awarded for valor. Nine hundred and ten such undeserving or less-deserving awards were rescinded in 1917—an action unarguable to anyone with a respect for the nature battlefield bravery and the intent to recognize it. Yet Mary Walker steadfastly refused to return her medal and continued to wear it at all times.

While taking her case directly to the Congress, the 85-year old experienced a severe fall and health, never robust, failed steadily thereafter except for a brief turnaround at Fort Ontario hospital. She died in 1919 and was buried in Rural Cemetery, Oswego, New York.

Mary's fame certainly didn't die with her. In World War II, where women served prominently in all branches of service, the Liberty ship SS *Mary Walker* was named in her honor. Later, an Army reserve center and several medical facilities were named for her. In 1982, a 20-cent U. S. postage stamp was issued in her honor.

The most interesting—and controversial—footnote, though, came in June, 1977. Responding to repeated requests by a great-grand-niece, President Jimmy Carter reinstated Dr. Mary Walker's Medal of Honor with no additional documentation than that used to award it in 1865. Dr. Mary Edwards Walker remains the first and only woman to receive our nation's highest award.[26]

---

26 Conner, *Sinners, Saints and Soldiers in Civil War Stafford*.

Appendix 3

Order of Battle:
Army of the Potomac, May 1-6, 1863

(Changes from December 31, 1862, to May 1863, are in boldface)

General Headquarters
**Maj. Gen. Joseph Hooker,
Commanding General**
Maj. Gen. Daniel Butterfield, Chief of Staff

Command of the Provost-Marshal:
General: Brig. Gen. Marsena R. Patrick
93rd New York Infantry, Col. J. S. Crocker
**6th Pennsylvania Cavalry, Cos. E and I,
Capt. James Starr**
8th U.S. Infantry, Cos. A, B, C, D, F, and G, Capt.
E. W. H. Read
**Detachment of Regular U.S. Cavalry,
Lt. Tattnall Paulding**

Patrick's Brigade: Col. William F. Rogers
**Maryland Light Artillery, Battery B,
Capt. Alonzo Snow**
21st New York Infantry,
Lt. Col. Chester W. Sternberg
23rd New York Infantry, Col. H. C. Hoffman
35th New York Infantry, Lt. Col. John G. Todd
80th New York Infantry (20th Militia), Col.
Theodore B. Gates
**Ohio Light Artillery, 12th Battery,
Capt. Aaron C. Johnson**

Engineer Brigade: Brig. Gen. Henry W. Benham
15th New York Engineers, Col. C. G. Colgate
50th New York Engineers, Col. C. B. Stuart
**U.S. Engineer Battalion:
Capt. Chauncey B. Reese**

Signal Corps: Capt. Samuel T. Cushing
Ordnance Detachment: Lt. John R. Edie
**Guards and Orderlies:
Oneida (New York) Cavalry,
Capt. Daniel P. Mann**

Artillery
Brig. General Henry J. Hunt, Chief of Artillery

Artillery Reserve: Capt. William M. Graham; Brig.
Gen. Robert O. Tyler
(assigned May 2, 1863)

1st Connecticut Heavy Artillery, Company B,
Lt. Albert F. Brooker
(previously reported as Capt. A. F. Brooke)
1st Connecticut Heavy Artillery, Company M,
Capt. Franklin A. Pratt
New York Light Artillery, 5th Battery,
Capt. E. D. Taft
New York Light Artillery, 15th Battery,
Capt. Patrick Hart
**New York Light Artillery, 29th Battery,
Lt. Gustav von Blucher**
**New York Light Artillery, 30th Battery,
Capt. Adolph Voegelee**
**New York Light Artillery, 32nd Battery,
Lt. George Gaston**
1st U.S. Artillery, Battery K,
Lt. Lorenzo Thomas, Jr.
3rd U.S. Artillery, Battery C, Lt. H. Meinell
4th U.S. Artillery, Battery G, Lt. Marcus P. Miller
5th U.S. Artillery, Battery K, **Lt. D. H. Kinzie**
32nd Massachusetts Infantry, Company C,
Capt. Josiah C. Fuller

**Train Guard
4th New Jersey (seven Cos.):
Col. William Birney; Capt. R. S. Johnston**

I Corps
Maj. Gen. John F. Reynolds
Escort
1st Maine Cavalry, Company L,
Capt. Constantine Taylor

1st Division, Brig. Gen. James S. Wadsworth

1st Brigade: Col. Walter Phelps, Jr.
22nd New York, **Maj. Thomas J. Strong**
24th New York, Lt. Col. Samuel R. Beardsley
30th New York, Col. William M. Searing
84th New York (14th Militia), Col. E. B. Fowler

2nd Brigade: **Brig. Gen. Lysander Cutler**
7th Indiana, **Lt. Col. Ira G. Grover**
76th New York, Col. William P. Wainwright
95th New York, Col. George H. Biddle
147th New York, **Col. John G. Butler**
56th Pennsylvania, Col. J. William Hoffmann

3rd Brigade: Brig. Gen. Gabriel R. Paul
22nd New Jersey, **Col.** Abraham G. Demarest
29th New Jersey, **Col.** William R. Taylor
30th New Jersey, **Col.** John J. Cladek
31st New Jersey, **Lt. Col. Robert R. Honeyman**
137th Pennsylvania, Col. Joseph B. Kiddoo

4th Brigade: Col. S. Meredith
19th Indiana, **Col.** Samuel J. Williams
24th Michigan, Col. Henry A. Morrow
2nd Wisconsin, Col. Lucius Fairchild
6th Wisconsin, **Col. Edward S. Bragg**
7th Wisconsin, Col. William W. Robinson

Division Artillery: **Capt. John A. Reynolds**
New Hampshire Light Artillery, 1st Battery,
Capt. Frederick M. Edgell
1st New York Artillery, Battery L,
Capt. John A. Reynolds
4th U.S. Artillery, Battery B, Lt. James Stewart

2nd Division: Gen. John C. Robinson

1st Brigade: **Col. Adrian R. Root**
16th Maine, **Col.** Charles W. Tilden
94th New York, **Capt. Samuel A. Moffett**
104th New York, Col. Gilbert G. Prey
107th Pennsylvania, **Col. Thomas F. McCoy**

2nd Brigade: **Brig. Gen. Henry Baxter**
12th Massachusetts, Col. James L. Bates
26th New York, **Lt. Col. Gilbert S. Jennings**
90th Pennsylvania, **Col. Peter Lyle**
136th Pennsylvania, **Col. Thomas M. Bayne**
3rd Brigade: Col. Samuel H. Leonard
13th Massachusetts, **Lt. Col. N. W. Batchelder**
83rd New York (9th Militia), **Lt. Col. J. A. Moesch**
97th New York, Col. Charles Wheelock
11th Pennsylvania, **Col. Richard Coulter**
88th Pennsylvania, **Lt. Col. Louis Wagner**

Division Artillery: Capt. Dunbar R. Ransom
Maine Light Artillery, 2nd Battery (B),
Capt. James A. Hall
Maine Light Artillery, 5th Battery (K),
Capt. George F. Leppien; Lt. Edmund Kirby;
Lt. Greenleaf Stevens

Pennsylvania Light Artillery, Battery C,
Capt. James Thompson
5th U.S. Artillery, Battery C,
Capt. Dunbar R. Ransom

3rd Division: **Maj. Gen. Abner Doubleday**
1st Brigade, **Brig. Gen. Thomas A. Rowley**
121st Pennsylvania, Col. Chapman Biddle
135th Pennsylvania, Col. James R. Porter
142nd Pennsylvania, Col. Robert P. Cummins
151st Pennsylvania, Col. Harrison Allen

2nd Brigade: **Brig. Gen. Roy Stone**
143rd Pennsylvania, Col. Edmund L. Dana
149th Pennsylvania, Lt. Col. Walton Dwight
150th Pennsylvania, Col. Langhorne Wister

Division Artillery: **Maj. Ezra M. Matthews**
1st Pennsylvania Artillery, Battery B,
Capt. James H. Cooper
1st Pennsylvania Artillery, Battery F,
Lt. R. Bruce Ricketts
1st Pennsylvania Artillery, Battery G,
Capt. Frank P. Amsden

II Army Corps
Maj. Gen. Darius N. Couch

Escort
6th New York Cavalry, Cos. D and K,
Capt. Riley Johnson

1st Division: Maj. Gen. Winfield Scott Hancock

1st Brigade: **Brig. Gen. John C. Caldwell**
5th New Hampshire, **Col. Edward E. Cross;**
Lt. Col. Charles Hapgood
61st New York, **Col. Nelson A. Miles;**
Lt. Col. K. Oscar Broady
81st Pennsylvania, **Col. H. Boyd McKeen**
148th Pennsylvania, Col. James A. Beaver;
Maj. George A. Fairlamb

2nd Brigade: **Brig. Gen. Thomas F. Meagher**
28th Massachusetts, **Col. Richard Byrnes**
63rd New York, Lt. Col. Richard C. Bentley
69th New York, **Capt. James E. McGee**
88th New York, **Col. Patrick Kelly**
116th Pennsylvania (**Battalion**),
Maj. St. Clair A. Mulholland

3rd Brigade: Brig. **Gen. Samuel A. Zook**
52nd New York, **Col. Paul Frank;**
Lt. Col. Charles G. Freudenberg

57th New York, **Lt. Col. Alford B. Chapman**
66th New York, Col. Orlando H. Morris
140th Pennsylvania, Col. Richard P. Roberts

4th Brigade: Col. John R. Brooke
27th Connecticut, Col. Richard S. Bostwick
2nd Delaware, Lt. Col. David L. Stricker
64th New York, Col. David G. Bingham
53rd Pennsylvania, Lt. Col. R. McMichael
145th Pennsylvania, Col. Hiram L. Brown

Division Artillery: **Capt. Rufus D. Pettit**
1st New York Light, Battery B,
Capt. Rufus D. Pettit
4th U.S. Artillery, Battery C, Lt. Evan Thomas

2nd Division: **Brig. Gen. John Gibbon**

1st Brigade: **Brig. Gen. Alfred Sully;**
Col. Henry W. Hudson; Col. Byron Laflin
19th Maine, Col. Francis E. Heath
15th Massachusetts, **Maj. George C. Joslin**
1st Minnesota, Lt. Col. William Colvill, Jr.
34th New York, **Col. Byron Laflin;**
Lt. Col. John Beverly
82nd New York (2nd Militia), **Col. Henry W.**
Hudson; Lt. Col. James Huston

2nd Brigade: **Brig. Gen Joshua T. Owen**
69th Pennsylvania, **Col. Dennis O'Kane**
71st Pennsylvania, Col. Richard P. Smith
72nd Pennsylvania, Col. DeWitt Baxter
106th Pennsylvania, Col. Turner G. Morehead

3rd Brigade: **Col. Norman J. Hall**
19th Massachusetts, Lt. Col. Arthur F. Devereux
20th Massachusetts, **Lt. Col.** George N. Macy
7th Michigan, Capt. Amos E. Steele, Jr.
42nd New York, **Col. James E. Mallon**
59th New York, **Lt. Col. Max A. Thoman**
127th Pennsylvania, Col. William W. Jennings

Division Artillery
1st Rhode Island Artillery, Battery A,
Capt. William A. Arnold
1st Rhode Island Artillery, Battery B,
Lt. T. Fred. Brown

Sharpshooters
1st Company Massachusetts, Capt. W. Plumer

3rd Division: Brig. Gen. William H. French
1st Brigade: **Col. Samuel S. Carroll**

14th Indiana, **Col. John Coons**
24th New Jersey, **Col. William B. Robertson**
28th New Jersey, **Lt. Col. John A. Wildrick;**
Maj. Samuel K. Wilson
4th Ohio, **Lt. Col.** Leonard W. Carpenter
8th Ohio, Lt. Col. Franklin Sawyer
7th West Virginia, **Col. Joseph Snider;**
Lt. Col. Jonathan H. Lockwood

2nd Brigade: Brig. **Gen. William Hays;**
Col. Charles J. Powers
14th Connecticut, **Maj. Theodore G. Ellis**
12th New Jersey, **Col. J. Howard Willets;**
Maj. John T. Hall
108th New York, **Col. Charles J. Powers;**
Lt. Col.. Francis E. Pierce
130th Pennsylvania, **Col. Levi Maish;**
Maj. Joseph S. Jenkins

3rd Brigade: Col. John D. MacGregor;
Col. Charles Albright
1st Delaware, **Col. Thomas A. Smyth**
4th New York, **Lt. Col. William Jameson**
132nd Pennsylvania, Col. Charles Albright;
Lt. Col. Joseph E. Shreve

Division Artillery: ——
1st New York, Battery G, Lt. Nelson Ames
1st Rhode Island Artillery, Battery G,
Capt. George W. Adams

Corps Artillery Reserve: ——
1st U.S. Artillery, Battery I, **Lt. Edmund Kirby**
4th U.S. Artillery, Battery A,
Lt. Alonzo H. Cushing

III Army Corps
Maj. Gen. Daniel E. Sickles

1st Division: Brig. Gen. David B. Birney

1st Brigade: **Brig. Gen. Charles G. Graham;**
Col. Thomas W. Egan
57th Pennsylvania, Col. Peter Sides
63rd Pennsylvania, Lt. Col. William S. Kirkwood; **Capt.**
James F. Ryan
68th Pennsylvania, Col. Andrew H. Tippin
105th Pennsylvania, Col. Amor A. McKnight;
Lt. Col. Calvin A. Craig
114th Pennsylvania, **Col. Charles H. T. Collis;**
Lt. Col. Frederick F. Cavada
141st Pennsylvania, Col. Henry J. Madill

2nd Brigade: **Brig. Gen. J. H. Hobart Ward**
20th Indiana, **Col. John Wheeler**
3rd Maine, Col. Moses B. Lakeman
4th Maine, Col. Elijah Walker
38th New York, **Col. P. Regis de Trobriand**
40th New York, Col. Thomas W. Egan
99th Pennsylvania, **Col. Asher S. Leidy**

3rd Brigade: **Col. Samuel B. Hayman**
17th Maine, Lt. Col. C. B. Merrill;
Col. Thomas A. Roberts
3rd Michigan, Col. Byron R. Pierce;
Lt. Col. Edwin S. Pierce
5th Michigan, **Lt. Col. Edward T. Sherlock;**
Maj. John Pulford
1st New York, **Lt. Col. Francis L. Leland**
37th New York, Lt. Col. Gilbert Riordan

Division ArtilleryL: **Capt. A. Judson Clark**
1st Rhode Island Artillery, Battery E,
Lt. Pardon S. Jastram
3rd U.S. Artillery, Batteries F and K,
Lt. John G. Turnbull

2nd Division: **Maj. Gen. Hiram G. Berry;**
Brig. Gen. Joseph B. Carr

1st Brigade: **Brig. Gen. Joseph B. Carr;**
Col. William Blaisdell
1st Massachusetts, **Col. N. B. McLaughlen**
11th Massachusetts, **Col. William Blaisdell;**
Lt. Col. Porter D. Tripp
16th Massachusetts, Lt. Col. Waldo Merriam
11th New Jersey, **Col. Robert McAllister**
26th Pennsylvania, **Col. Benjamin C. Tilghman;**
Maj. Robert L. Bodine

2nd Brigade: Brig. Gen. Joseph W. Revere;
Col. J. Egbert Farnum
70st New York, Col. J. Egbert Farnum;
Lt. Col. Thomas Holt
71st New York, **Col.** Henry L. Potter
72nd New York, Col. William O. Stephens;
Maj. John Leonard
73rd New York, **Maj. Michael W. Burns**
74th New York, **Lt. Col. William H. Lounsbury;**
Capt. Henry M. Allen; Capt. Francis E. Tyler
120th New York, **Lt. Col. C. D. Westbrooke**

3rd Brigade: Brig. Gen. Gershom Mott;
Col. William J. Sewell
5th New Jersey, **Col. William J. Sewell;**
Maj. Ashbel W. Angel; Capt. Virgil M. Healy

6th New Jersey, Col. George C. Burling;
Lt. Col. Stephen R. Gilkyson
7th New Jersey, Col. Louis R. Francine;
Lt. Col. Francis Price
8th New Jersey, **Col. John Ramsey;**
Capt. John G. Langston
2nd New York, Col. Sidney W. Park;
Lt. Col. William A. Olmstead
115th Pennsylvania, Col. Francis A. Lancaster;
Maj. John P. Dunne

Division Artillery: **Capt. Thomas W. Osborn**
1st New Jersey Light Artillery, Battery D,
Lt. George B. Winslow
New York Light Artillery, 4th Battery,
Lt. George F. Barstow; Lt. William T. McLean
1st U.S. Artillery, Battery H, **Lt. Justin E. Dimick;**
Lt. James A. Sanderson
4th U.S. Artillery, Battery K, Lt. Francis W. Seeley

3rd Division: **Maj. Gen.** Amiel W. Whipple;
Brig, Gen. Charles K. Graham

1st Brigade: **Col. Emlen Franklin**
86th New York, **Lt. Col. Barna J. Chapin;**
Capt. Jacob H. Lansing
124th New York, **Col. A. Van Horn Ellis**
122nd Pennsylvania, **Lt. Col. Edward McGovern**

2nd Brigade: **Col. Samuel M. Bowman**
12th New Hampshire, **Col. Joseph H. Potter**
84th Pennsylvania, Lt. Col. Milton Opp
110th Pennsylvania, **Col. James Crowther;**
Maj. David M. Jones

3rd Brigade: Col. Hiram Berdan
1st U.S. (Vol.) Sharpshooters,
Lt. Col. Casper Trepp
2nd U.S. (Vol.) Sharpshooters,
Maj. Homer R. Stoughton

Division Artillery: **Capt. A. A. von Puttkammer**
New York Light Artillery, 10th Battery,
Lt. Samuel Lewis
New York Light Artillery, 11th Battery,
Lt. John E. Burton
1st Ohio Artillery. Battery H,
Capt. James F. Huntington

V Army Corps
Maj. Gen. George Gordon Meade

1st Division: Brig. Gen. Charles Griffin

1st Brigade: Col. James Barnes
2nd Maine, **Col.** George Varney
18th Massachusetts, **Col.** Joseph Hayes
22nd Massachusetts, Col. William S. Tilton
2nd Company Massachusetts Sharpshooters,
Lt. Robert Smith
1st Michigan, Col. Ira C. Abbott
13th New York **(Battalion)**, **Capt. W. Downey**
25th New York, Col. Charles A. Johnson
118th Pennsylvania, **Col. Charles M. Prevost**

2nd Brigade: **Col. James McQuade;**
Col. Jacob B. Sweitzer
9th Massachusetts, **Col. Patrick R. Gurney**
32nd Massachusetts, **Lt. Col. Luther Stephenson**
4th Michigan, **Col. Harrison H. Jeffords**
14th New York, Lt. Col. Thomas M. Davies
62nd Pennsylvania, **Col. Jacob B. Sweitzer;**
Lt. Col. J. C. Hull

3rd Brigade: Col. Thomas B. W. Stockton
20th Maine, **Lt. Col. Joshua L. Chamberlain**
Michigan Sharpshooters, Brady's Company,
16th Michigan, Lt. Col. Norval E. Welch
12th New York, **Capt William Huson**
17th New York, Lt. Col. Nelson B. Bartram.
44th New York, Col. James C. Rice
83rd Pennsylvania, Col. Strong Vincent
Division Artillery: Capt. Augustus P. Martin
Massachusetts Light Artillery, 3rd Battery C,
Capt. Augustus P. Martin
Massachusetts Light Artillery, 5th Battery,
Capt. Charles A. Phillips
1st Rhode Island Light Artillery, Battery C,
Capt. Richard Waterman
5th U.S. Artillery, Battery D, Lt. Charles E. Hazlett

2nd Division: Maj. Gen. George Sykes

1st Brigade: **Brig. Gen. Romeyn B. Ayres**
3rd U.S. (**Cos. B, C, F, G, I and K**),
Capt. John D. Wilkins
4th U.S. (**Cos. C, F, H, and K**),
Capt. Hiram Dryer
12th U.S., 1st Battalion (Cos. A, B, C, D and G),
and 2nd Battalion (Cos. A, C and D), Maj. R. S.
Smith
14th U.S., 1st Battalion (Cos. A, B, D, E, F and
G), and 2nd Battalion (Cos. F and G), Capt. J.
B. Hager

2nd Brigade: **Col. Sidney Burbank**

2nd U.S. (Cos. B, C, F, I and K),
Capt. Salem S. Marsh; Capt. Samuel A. McKee
6th U.S. (Cos. D, F, H and I),
Capt. Levi C. Bootes
7th U.S. (Cos. A, B, E and I),
Capt. David P. Hancock
11th U.S., 1st Battalion (Cos. B, C, D, E, F and G),
and 2nd Battalion (Cos. C and D),
Maj. DeL. Floyd-James
17th U.S., 1st Battalion (Cos. A, C, D, G and H), and
2nd Battalion (Cos. A and B),
Maj. George L. Andrews

3rd Brigade: **Col. Patrick H. O'Rorke**
5th New York, **Col. Cleveland Winslow**
140th New York, **Lt. Col. Louis Ernst**
146th New York, Col. Kenner Garrard

Division Artillery: **Capt. Stephen H. Weed**
1st Ohio Light Artillery, Battery L,
Capt. Frank C. Gibbs
5th U.S. Artillery, Battery I, **Lt. M. F. Watson**

3rd Division: Brig. Gen. A. A. Humphreys

1st Brigade: **Brig. Gen. Erastur B. Tyler**
91st Pennsylvania, **Col. Edgar M. Gregory;**
Lt. Col. Joseph H. Sinex
126th Pennsylvania, **Lt. Col. David W. Rowe**
129th Pennsylvania, **Col. Jacob G. Frick**
134th Pennsylvania, Col. Edward O'Brien
2nd Brigade: Col. Peter H. Allabach
123rd Pennsylvania, Col. John B. Clark
131st Pennsylvania, **Maj. Robert W. Patton**
133rd Pennsylvania, **Col. Franklin B. Speakman**
155th Pennsylvania, Lt. Col. John H. Cain
Division Artillery: Capt. Alanson M. Randal
1st New York Light Artillery, Battery C,
Capt. Almont Barnes
1st U.S. Artillery, Battery E and G,
Capt. Alanson M. Randol

VI Army Corps
Maj. Gen. John Sedgwick

Escort: Maj. Hugh H. Janeway
1st New Jersey Cavalry, Company L,
Lt. Vorhees Dye
1st Pennsylvania Cavalry, Company H
Capt. William S. Craft

1st Division: Brig. Gen. William T. H. Brooks
Provost Guard:

4th New Jersey, Cos. A, C and H,
Capt. Charles Ewing

1st Brigade: **Col. Henry W. Brown;**
Col. William H. Penrose; Col. Samuel L. Buck;
Col. William H. Penrose
1st New Jersey, **Col. Mark W. Collet;**
Maj. William Henry, Jr.
2nd New Jersey, **Col. Samuel L. Buck;**
Lt. Col. Charles Wiebecke
3rd New Jersey, **Maj. J. W. H. Stickney**
15th New Jersey, **Col. William H. Penrose;**
Lt. Col. Edward L. Campbell
23rd New Jersey, **Col.** E. Burd Grubb

2nd Brigade: Brig. Gen. Joseph J. Bartlett
5th Maine, **Col.** Clark S. Edwards
16th New York, Col. Joel J. Seaver
27th New York, Col. Alexander D. Adams
121st New York, Col. Emory Upton
96th Pennsylvania, **Maj.** William H. Lessig

3rd Brigade: Brig. Gen. David A. Russell
18th New York, Col. George R. Myers
32nd New York, Col. Francis E. Pinto
49th Pennsylvania, Lt. Col. Thomas M. Hulings
95th Pennsylvania, **Col. Gustavus W. Town;**
Lt. Col. Elisha Hall; Capt. Theo H. McCalla
119th Pennsylvania, Col. Peter C. Ellmaker
Division Artillery: **Maj. John A. Tompkins**
Massachusetts Light Artillery, 1st Battery (A),
Capt. William H. McCartney
New Jersey Light Artillery, Battery A,
Lt. Augustin N. Parsons
Maryland Light Artillery, Battery A,
Capt. James H. Rigby
2nd U.S. Artillery, Battery D,
Lt. Edward B. Williston

2nd Division: Brig. Gen. Albion P. Howe

2nd Brigade: **Col. Lewis A. Grant**
26th New Jersey, **Col. Andrew J. Morrison;**
Lt. Col. Edward Martindale
2nd Vermont, **Col.** James H. Walbridge
3rd Vermont, **Col. Thomas O. Seaver;**
Lt. Col. Samuel N. Pingree
4th Vermont, Col. Charles B. Stoughton
5th Vermont, **Lt. Col. John R. Lewis**
6th Vermont, **Col. Elisha L. Barney**

3rd Brigade: Brig. Gen. Thomas H. Neill
7th Maine, **Lt. Col. Selden Connor**

21st New Jersey, **Col. Gilliam Van Houten;**
Lt. Col. Isaac S. Mettler
20th New York, Col. Ernst von Vegesack
33rd New York, Col. Robert F. Taylor
49th New York, Col. Daniel B. Bidwell
77th New York, **Lt. Col. Winsor B. French**

Division Artillery: **Maj. J. Watts de Peyster**
New York Light Artillery, 1st Battery,
Capt. Andrew Cowan
5th U.S. Artillery, Battery F, **Lt. Leonard Martin**

3rd Division: **Maj. Gen. John Newton**

1st Brigade: **Col. Alexander Shaler**
65th New York, Lt. Col. Joseph E. Hamblin
67th New York, Col. Nelson Cross
122nd New York, Col. Silas Titus
23rd Pennsylvania, Col. John Ely
82nd Pennsylvania, **Maj. Isaac C. Bassett**

2nd Brigade: **Col. William H. Browne;**
Col. Henry L. Eustis
7th Massachusetts, **Col. Thomas D. Johns;**
Lt. Col. Franklin P. Harlow
10th Massachusetts, **Lt. Col. Joseph B. Parsons**
37th Massachusetts, Col. Oliver Edwards
36th New York, **Lt. Col. James J. Walsh**
2nd Rhode Island, **Col. Horatio Rogers, Jr.**

3rd Brigade: **Brig. Gen. Frank Wheaton**
62nd New York, Lt. Col. Theodore B. Hamilton
93rd Pennsylvania, **Capt. John S. Long**
98th Pennsylvania, **Col. John F. Ballier;**
Lt. Col. George Wynkoop
102nd Pennsylvania, **Col.** Joseph M. Kinkead
139th Pennsylvania, **Col. Frederick H. Collier**

Division Artillery: **Capt. Jeremiah McCarthy**
1st Pennsylvania Light Artillery, Batteries C and D, Capt.
J. McCarthy
2nd U.S. Artillery, Battery G, Lt. John H. Butler

Light Division: Col. Hiram Burnham
6th Maine, Lt. Col. Benjamin F. Harris
31st New York, Col. Frank Jones
43rd New York, Col. Benjamin F. Baker
61st Pennsylvania, Col. George C. Spear;
Maj. George W. Dawson
5th Wisconsin, Col. Thomas S. Allen
New York Light Artillery, 3rd Battery,
Lt. William A. Harn

XI Army Corps
Maj. Gen. Oliver Otis Howard

Escort
1st Indiana Cavalry, Cos. I and K,
Capt. Abram Sharra

1st Division: Brig. Gen. Charles Devens, Jr.;
Brig. Gen. N. C. McLean

1st Brigade: Col. Leopold von Gilsa
41st New York, Maj. Detleo von Einsiedel
45th New York, Col. George von Amsberg
54th New York, Lt. Col. Charles Ashby;
Maj. Stephen Kovacs
153rd Pennsylvania, Col. Charles Glanz;
Lt. Col. Jacob Dachrodt

2nd Brigade: Brig. Gen. N. C. McLean;
Col. John C. Lee
17th Connecticut, Col. W. H. Noble;
Maj. Allen G. Brady
25th Ohio, Col. William P. Richardson;
Maj. Jeremiah Williams
55th Ohio, Col. J. C. Lee; Lt. Col. C. B. Gambee
75th Ohio, Col. Robert Reily; Capt. Ben Morgan
107th Ohio, Col. Seraphim Meyer;
Lt. Col. Charles Mueller

Unattached Artillery: 8th New York Battery,
Lt. Herman Rosenkranz

Division Artillery: 13th New York Battery,
Capt. Julius Dieckmann

2nd Division: Brig. Gen. Adolph von Steinwehr

1st Brigade: Col. Adolphus Buschbeck
29th New York, Lt. Col. Louis Hartmann;
Maj. Alex. von Schluembach
154th New York, Col. Patrick H. Jones;
Lt. Col. Henry C. Loomis
27th Pennsylvania, Lt. Col. Lorenz Contador
73rd Pennsylvania, Lt. Col. William Moore

2nd Brigade: Brig. Gen. Francis C. Barlow
33rd Massachusetts, Lt. Col. Adin B. Underwood
134th New York, Col. Charles R. Coster
136th New York, Col. James Wood, Jr.
73rd Ohio, Col. Orland Smith

Division Artillery: ——

1st New York Artillery, Battery I,
Capt. M. Wiedrich

3rd Division: Maj. Gen. Carl Schurz

1st Brigade: Brig. Gen. Alexander Schimmelfennig
82nd Illinois, Col. Frederick Hecker;
Maj. F. Rolshausen; Capt. Jacob Lasalle
68th New York, Col. Gotthilf Bourry
157th New York, Col. Philip P. Brown, Jr.
61st Ohio, Col. Stephen J. McGroarty
74th Pennsylvania, Lt. Col. Adolph von Hartung

2nd Brigade: Col. Wladimir Krzyzanowski
58th New York, Capt. Frederick Braun
119th New York, Col. E. Peissner
75th Pennsylvania, Col. F. Mahler
26th Wisconsin, Col. W. H. Jacobs

Unattached: 82nd Ohio, Col. J. S. Robinson

Division Artillery: ——
1st Ohio Artillery, Battery I, Capt. H. Dilger
Reserve Artillery, XI AC: Lt. Col. L. Schirmer
New York Light Artillery, 2nd Battery,
Capt. Hermann Jahn
1st Ohio Light Artillery, Battery K,
Capt. William L. DeBeck
1st West Virginia Light Artillery, Battery C,
Capt. Wallace Hill

XII Army Corps
Maj. General Henry W. Slocum

Provost Guard
10th Maine (Battalion): Capt. J. D. Beardsley

1st Division: Brig. Gen. Alpheus S. Williams

1st Brigade: Brig. Gen. Joseph F. Knipe
5th Connecticut, Col. Warren W. Packer;
Lt. Col. James A. Betts; Maj. David F. Lane
28th New York, Lt. Col. Elliott W. Cook;
Maj. Theophilus Fitzgerald
46th Pennsylvania, Maj. Cyrus Strous;
Capt. Edward L. Witman
128th Pennsylvania, Col. Joseph A. Mathews;
Maj. Cephus W. Dyer

2nd Brigade: Col. Samuel Ross
20th Connecticut, Lt. Col. William B. Wooster;
Maj. Philo. B. Buckingham
3rd Maryland, Lt. Col. Gilbert P. Robinson

123rd New York, Col. Archibald L. McDougall
145th New York, **Col. E. Livingston Price;**
Capt. George W. Reid

3rd Brigade: **Brig. Gen. Thomas H. Ruger**
27th Indiana, **Col. Silas Colgrove**
2nd Massachusetts, **Col. Samuel M. Quincy**
13th New Jersey, **Col. Ezra A. Carman;**
Maj. John Grimes; Capt. George A. Beardsley
107th New York, **Col. Alexander S. Diven**
3rd Wisconsin, **Col. William Hawley**

Division Artillery: **Capt. Robert H. Fitzhugh**
1st New York Light Artillery, Battery K,
Lt. Edward L. Bailey
1st New York Light Artillery, Battery M,
Lt. Charles Wineger; Lt. John D. Woodbury
4th U.S. Artillery, Battery F, Lt. Franklin B. Crosby;
Lt. Edward D. Muehlenberg

2nd Division: Brig. Gen. John W. Geary
1st Brigade: Col. Charles Candy
5th Ohio, **Lt. Col. Robert L. Kilpatrick;**
Maj. Henry E. Symmes
7th Ohio, Col. William R. Creighton
29th Ohio, **Lt. Col. Thomas Clark**
66th Ohio, Lt. Col. Eugene Powell
28th Pennsylvania, **Maj.** Lansford F. Chapman;
Capt. Conrad U. Meyer
147th Pennsylvania, Lt. Col. Ario Pardee, Jr.
2nd Brigade: **Brig. Gen. Thomas L. Kane**
29th Pennsylvania, **Lt. Col. William Rickards, Jr.**
109th Pennsylvania, Col. H. J. Stainrook;
Capt. John Young, Jr.
111th Pennsylvania, Col. G. A. Cobham, Jr.
124th Pennsylvania, Col. Simon Litzenberg
125th Pennsylvania, Col. Jacob Higgins

3rd Brigade: Brig. Gen. George S. Greene
60th New York, Col. J. C. O. Redington
78th New York, **Maj. Henry R. Stagg;**
Capt. William H. Randall
102nd New York, Col. J. C. Lane
137th New York, Col. David Ireland
149th New York, **Maj. Abel G. Cook;**
Capt. Oliver T. May; Lt. Col. Koert Van Voorhis

Division Artillery: Capt. Joseph M. Knap
Pennsylvania Artillery, Battery E,
Lt. Charles A. Atwell; **Lt. James D. McGill**
Pennsylvania Artillery, Battery F,
Capt. Robert B. Hampton; **Lt. James P. Fleming**

Cavalry Corps
Brig. Gen. George Stoneman

1st Cavalry Division: Brig. Gen. Alfred Pleasonton

1st Brigade: Col. Benjamin F. Davis
8th Illinois Cavalry, Lt. Col. D. R. Clendenin
3rd Indiana Cavalry, Col. George H. Chapman
8th New York Cavalry: ——
9th New York Cavalry, Col. William Sackett

2nd Brigade: Col. Thomas C. Devin
1st Michigan Cavalry, Company L, Lt. J. Truax
6th New York Cavalry, Lt. Col. Duncan McVicar;
Capt. William E. Beardsley
8th Pennsylvania Cavalry, Maj. Pennock Huey
17th Pennsylvania Cavalry, Col. J. H. Kellogg

Division Artillery: ——
New York Light Artillery, 6th Battery,
Lt. Joseph W. Martin

2nd Cavalry Division: Brig. William W. Averell

1st Brigade: ——
1st Massachusetts Cavalry, Lt. Col. G. S. Curtis
4th New York Cavalry, Col. L. P. Di Cesnola
6th Ohio Cavalry, Maj. Benjamin C. Stanhope
1st Rhode Island Cavalry,
Lt. Col. John L. Thompson

2nd Brigade: Col. John B. McIntosh
3rd Pennsylvania Cavalry, Lt. Col. E. S. Jones
4th Pennsylvania Cavalry,
Lt. Col. William E. Doster
16th Pennsylvania Cavalry,
Lt. Col. Lorenzo D. Rogers

Division Artillery:——
2nd U. S. Artillery, Battery A, Capt. J. C. Tidball

3rd Cavalry Division:
Brig. Gen. David McM. Gregg

1st Brigade: Col. Judson Kilpatrick
1st Maine Cavalry, Col. Calvin S. Douty
2nd New York Cavalry, Lt. Col. H. E. Davies
10th New York Cavalry, Lt. Col. William Irvine

2nd Brigade: Col. Percy Wyndham
1st Maryland Cavalry, Lt. Col. James M. Deems
1st New Jersey Cavalry, Lt. Col. Virgil Brodrick
1st Pennsylvania Cavalry, Col. John P. Taylor

Regular Reserve Brigade:
Brig. Gen. John Buford
6th Pennsylvania Cavalry, Maj. R. Morris, Jr.
1st U.S. Cavalry, Capt. R. S. C. Lord
2nd U.S. Cavalry, Maj. Charles J. Whiting
5th U.S. Cavalry, Capt. James E. Harrison
6th U.S. Cavalry, Capt. George C. Cram

Corps Artillery: Capt. James M. Robertson
2nd U.S. Artillery, Batteries B and L,
Lt. Albert O. Vincent
2nd U.S. Artillery, Battery M, Lt. Robert Clarke
4th U.S. Artillery, Battery E, Lt. Sam S. Elder

Bibliography

Manuscripts

Fredericksburg and Spotsylvania National Military Park (FSNMP), "Chatham" ("Lacy House"), Stafford, VA

> Bound Volume Collection, FSNMP Library, "Chatham." Over 500 of these volumes containing primary and secondary source materials and collected over an extended period exist in the library. Those used are listed in the footnotes, and cited, for example, "BV 428, part 1, FSNMP. Rev. James W. Hunnicutt, *The Conspiracy Unveiled. The South Sacrificed; or The Horrors of Secession*. Philadelphia, PA: J. B. Lippincott and Company, 1863. Hunnicutt, a Southern unionist, was editor of the *Fredericksburg Christian Banner*."

Private Collections

John Hennessy, Stafford, VA

> Card Files, a unique collection of primary and secondary materials especially strong in New York, Connecticut, and other New England sources. They are arranged topically, listed in the notes, and cited, for example, "CHJHCF. Cites: 'Letters of Col. John S. Crocker to his wife, 93rd NY, NYSL' [NY State Library]."

White Oak Civil War Museum and Research Center, Stafford, VA

> Various primary source materials related to Civil War activities in Stafford County. Arranged by army corps, for example, "I Corps." This collection also contains a large number of field maps and sketches and related notes. D. P. Newton, owner, has been recognized by the Virginia Historical Society and the Civil War Trust.

Albert Z. Conner, Stafford, VA

> Various primary source materials related to Civil War activities in Stafford County. They consist of primary and secondary source materials, for example, "Field-printed order, as specified, from the author's collection."

Official Records

The War of the Rebellion: A Compilation of the Official Records of the Union and Confederate Armies. Washington, D.C.: Government Printing Office, 1881-1889.

Official Records of the Union and Confederate Navies in the War of the Rebellion. Washington, D.C.: Government Printing Office, 1897.

Register of Officers and Agents, Civil, Military, and Naval, in the Service of the United States on the Thirteenth September 1863. Washington, D.C., Government Printing Office, 1864.

Newspapers and Periodicals

Albany (NY) *Evening Journal*
Flemington (NJ) *The Republican*
Fredericksburg (VA) *Christian Banner*
Fredericksburg (VA) *The Free Lance*
Hamburg (PA.) *Item*
Hartford(CT) *Daily Courant*

Hunterdon (NJ) *Republican* [may be the same as the Flemington citation above]
Indianapolis (IN) *Journal*
Lancaster (PA) *Daily Express*
Lewiston (ME) *Daily Evening Journal*
Milwaukee (WI) *Sentinel*
Mount Vernon (NY) *Argus*
Newark (NJ) *Daily Advertiser*
New Haven (CT) *Daily Morning Journal*
New York (NY) *Harper's Weekly*
New York (NY) *Herald*
New York (NY) *Sunday Mercury*
New York (NY) *Times*
Philadelphia (PA) *The Press*
Rochester (NY) *Daily Union and Advertiser*
Trenton (NJ) *Daily State Gazette*
Vermont *Watchman and State Journal*
Waterbury (CT) *American*

Published Primary Sources

Adams, John G. B., *Reminiscences of the Nineteenth Massachusetts Regiment*. Boston, MA: 1899.

Adams, John R., *Memorial and Letters of Rev. John R. Adams, D.D., Chaplain of the Fifth Maine and the One Hundred Twenty-first New York Regiments During the War of the Rebellion, Serving from the Beginning to its Close*. Privately Printed, 1890.

Blight, David W., ed., *When This Cruel War is Over: The Civil War Letters of Charles Harvey Brewster*. Amherst, MA: University of Massachusetts Press, 1992.

Brady, James P., comp., *Hurrah for the Artillery! Knap's Independent Battery E, Pennsylvania Light Artillery*. Gettysburg, PA: Thomas Publications, 1992

Brooks, Noah, *Washington in Lincoln's Time*. New York, NY: The Century Company, 1895.

Chesson, Michael B., ed., *J. Franklin Dyer, Journal of a Civil War Surgeon*. Lincoln, NE, and London, UK: University of Nebraska Press, 2003.

Cooney, Charles F., ed., *Sidney Morris Davis: Common Soldier, Uncommon War: Life as a Cavalryman in the Civil War*. Bethesda, MD: John H. Davis Jr., publisher, 1994.

Conway, Moncure Daniel, *Testimonies Concerning Slavery*. London, UK: Chapman and Hall, 1864.

Couch, Darius N., "Sumner's 'Right Grand Division'," in Clarence C. Buel and Robert U. Johnson, ed., *Battles and Leaders of the Civil War*. New York, NY: The Century Company, 1888; four volumes.

Curtis, Orson Blair, *The History of the Twenty-fourth Michigan of the Iron Brigade (Known as the Detroit and Wayne County Regiment)*. Detroit, MI: Winn and Hammond, 1891.

Davis, Oliver Wilson, *Life of David Bell Birney, Major General United States Volunteers*. Philadelphia, PA: King and Baird, 1867.

Dawes, Rufus Robinson, *Service With The Sixth Wisconsin Volunteers*. Marietta, OH: E. R. Alderman and Sons, 1890.

Duncan, Russell, ed., *Blue-Eyed Child of Fortune: The Civil War Letters of Colonel Robert Gould Shaw*. Athens, GA and London, UK: University of Georgia Press, 1999.

Eckert, Edward K. and Nicholas J. Amato, ed., *Ten Years in the Saddle: The Memoir of William Woods Averell, 1851-1862*. (San Rafael, CA: Presidio Press, 1978).

Favill, Josiah Marshall, *The Diary of a Young Officer Serving with the Armies of the United States During the War of the Rebellion*. Chicago, IL: R. R. Donnelley & Sons, 1909.

Fatout, Paul, ed., *Letters of a Civil War Surgeon*. West Lafayette, IN: Purdue University Press, 1996.

Ford, Worthington C., ed., *A Cycle of Adams Letters, 1861-1865*. Houghton Mifflin, 1920.

Fornieri, Joseph R., ed., *The Language of Liberty: The Political Speeches and Writings of Abraham Lincoln*. Washington, DC: Regnery Publishing, 2003.

Goss, Warren Lee, "Carrier of Victory? The Army Mule," in *Civil War Times Illustrated*, Vol. 1, No. 4, July 1962. From *Recollections of a Private*, an 1890 memoir by Goss, a Union Veteran, published by Thomas Y. Crowell and Company.

Greiner, James M., Janet L. Coryell, and James R. Smither, ed., *A Surgeon's Civil War: The Letters of Daniel M. Holt, M.D.* Kent, OH: Kent State University Press, 1994.

Griffin, Richard N., ed. *Three Years a Soldier: The Diary and Newspaper Correspondence of Private George Perkins, Sixth New York Independent Battery, 1861-1864*. The University of Tennessee Press, 2006.

Haupt, Herman, *Reminiscences of General Herman Haupt*. North Stratford, NH: Ayer Company, 2000.

Hays, Gilbert Adams, comp., *Under the Red Patch: Story of the Sixty-third Regiment Pennsylvania Volunteers*. Pittsburgh, PA: 63rd Pennsylvania Volunteer Regiment Association, 1908.

Holy Bible. New York, NY: American Bible Society, 1857.

Howard, Oliver Otis, *Autobiography of Oliver Otis Howard, Major General, United States Army*. New York, NY: The Baker & Taylor Company, 1907.

Hunnicutt, Rev. James W., *The Conspiracy Unveiled. The South Sacrificed; or The Horrors of Secession*. Philadelphia, PA: J. B. Lippincott and Company, 1863.

Markle, Donald E. Markle, ed., *The Telegraph Goes to War: The Personnel Diary of David Homer Bates, Lincoln's Telegraph Operator*. Hamilton, NY: Edmonston Publishing, 2003.

Merritt, Wesley, "Personal Recollections—Beverly's Ford to Mitchell's Station, 1863," in Theophilus F. Rodenbough, editor, *From Everglade to Canon with the Second Dragoons*. New York, NY: D. Van Nostrand, 1875.

Messent, Peter and Steve Courtney, ed., *The Civil War Letters of Joseph Hopkins Twichell: A Chaplain's Story*. Athens, GA and London, UK: The University of Georgia Press, 2006.

Milano, Anthony J., *Copperhead defiance from a Yankee officer: private letters of Major Henry Livermore Abbott, Harvard College, class of 1860, Twentieth Regiment, Massachusetts Volunteer Infantry, 1861-186*. Harvard University Thesis, 1987.

Ministry of Defense, USSR, *Dictionary of Basic Military Terms*. Moscow: Military Press of the Ministry of Defense, USSR, 1965.

Moore, Frank, *Women of the War: Heroism and Self-sacrifice*. Hartford, CT: S. S. Scranton, 1867.

Morhaus, Sergeant Henry C., *Reminiscences of the 123d Regiment, N. Y. S. V.* Greenwich, NY: People's Journal Book and Job Office, 1879.

Mulholland, St. Clair, *A Story of the 116th Regiment of Pennsylvania Volunteers in the War of the Rebellion*. Philadelphia, PA: McManus Jr., 1903.

Nevins, Allan, ed., *A Diary of Battle: The Personal Journals of Colonel Charles S. Wainwright, 1861-1865*. Gettysburg, PA: Stan Clark Military Books, 1996.

New York (State), *Third Annual Report of the Bureau of Military Statistics*. Albany, NY: The Bureau of Military Statistics, 1866.

Plumb, R. G., ed., "Letters of a Fifth Wisconsin Volunteer" (Lt. James H. Leonard [1843-1901], 5th Wisconsin Infantry), in *Wisconsin Magazine of History*, Volume 3, September 1919-June 1920.

Posner, Richard A., ed., *The Essential Holmes: Selections From the Letters, Speeches, Judicial Opinions, and Other Writings of Oliver Wendell Holmes, Jr.* Chicago, IL: University of Chicago Press, 1992.

Richardson, Albert D., *The Secret Service: The Field, the Dungeon, and the Escape*. Hartford, CT: 1865.

Rhodes, Robert Hunt, ed., *All For the Union: The Civil War Diary and Letters of Elisha Hunt Rhodes*. New York, NY: Vintage Books, Random House, 1992.

Scott, Robert Garth, ed., *Fallen Leaves: The Civil War Letters of Major Henry Livermore Abbott*. Kent, OH: Kent University Press, 1991.

Shoaf, Dana B., ed., "'On the March Again at Daybreak': The Gettysburg Diary of Major John I. Nevin, 93rd Pennsylvania Infantry," in *Civil War Regiments: A Journal of the American Civil War*, (Mason City, IA: 1999), Volume Six, Number 3.

Smith, Russell P., ed., "Cyrus Forwood and the Crazy Delawares at Fredericksburg," *Fredericksburg History and Biography*, Volume IV, 2005.

Sparks, David S., ed., *Inside Lincoln's Army: The Diary of Marsena Rudolph Patrick, Provost Marshal General, Army of the Potomac*. New York, NY: Thomas Yoseloff, 1964.

Staudenraus, J., ed., *Mr. Lincoln's Washington: Selections from the Writings of Noah Brooks, Civil War Correspondent*. New York, NY: Thomas Yoseloff, 1967.

Stuart, Gladys S. and Adelbert M. Jakeman Jr., *John H. Stevens, Civil War Diary*. Miller Books, 1997.

Styple, William B., ed., *Writing and Fighting in the Civil War: Soldier Correspondence to the New York Sunday Mercury*. Kearny, NJ: Belle Grove Publishing Company, 2000.

——. *With a Flash of His Sword: The Writings of Major Holman S. Melcher, 20th Maine Infantry*. Kearny, NJ: Belle Grove Publishing, 1994.

——. *Generals in Bronze*. Kearny, NJ: Belle Grove Publishing, 2005.

Swinton, William, *Campaigns of the Army of the Potomac: A Critical History of Operations in Virginia, Maryland and Pennsylvania from the Commencement to the Close of the War*. New York, NY: Charles B. Richardson, 1866.

Thompson, S. Millett, *History of the Thirteenth Regiment, New Hampshire Volunteer Infantry, in the War of the Rebellion, 1861-1865*. Boston, MA: Houghton Mifflin, 1888.

Walker, Francis A., *History of the Second Corps in the Army of the Potomac*. New York, NY: Charles Scribner's Sons, 1886.

Secondary Works

Barton, Michael and Larry M. Logue, ed., *The Civil War Soldier: A Historical Reader*. New York, NY: New York University Press, 2002.

Barton, John V., "The Procurement of Horses," *Civil War Times Illustrated*, Volume VI, No. 8, December 1967, 16-24.

Bates, Samuel P., *The Battle of Chancellorsville*. Meadville, PA: Edward T. Bates, 1882.

Beatie, Russel H., *The Army of the Potomac*. New York and California: Savas Beatie, -2007; three volumes covering November 1860-September 1861, September 1861-February 1862, and March 1862-May 1862.

Blight, David W., *Race and Reunion: The Civil War in American Memory*. Cambridge, MA, and London, UK: The Belknap Press of Harvard University Press, 2001.

Boritt, Gabor, *The Gettysburg Gospel: The Lincoln Speech That Nobody Knows*. New York, NY: Simon and Schuster, 2006.

Bowen, Catherine Drinker, *Yankee from Olympus: Justice Holmes and His Family*. Boston, MA: Little, Brown and Company, 1945.

Carwardine, Richard, *Lincoln: A Life of Purpose and Power*. New York, NY: Alfred A. Knopf, 2006.

Catton, Bruce, *The Army of the Potomac: Glory Road*. New York, NY: Doubleday and Company, 1952.

Coggins, Jack, *Arms and Equipment of the Civil War*. New York, NY: Barnes and Noble Books, 1990.

Commager, Henry Steele, ed., *Documents of American History*. New York, NY: F. S. Crofts and Company, 1945, third edition.

Conner, Albert Z. Jr., *A History of Our Own: Stafford County, Virginia*. Virginia Beach, VA: Donning Company Publishers, 2003.

Conner, Jane Hollenbeck, *Lincoln in Stafford*. Stafford, VA: Parker Publishing, LLC, 2006.

———. *Sinners, Saints and Soldiers in Civil War Stafford*. Stafford, VA: Parker Publishing LLC, 2009.

Davis, Burke, *J.E.B. Stuart: The Last Cavalier*. New York, NY: Rinehart & Company, 1957.

Davis, William C., *Lincoln's Men: How President Lincoln Became the Father to an Army and a Nation*. New York, NY: The Free Press, 1999.

Driver Jr., Robert J. and H. E. Howard, *2nd Virginia Cavalry*. (Lynchburg, VA: H. E. Howard, 1995).

Eby, Jerrilynn, *They Called Stafford Home: The Development of Stafford County, Virginia, from 1600 until 1865*. Bowie, MD: Heritage Books, Inc., 1997.

Esposito, Brigadier General Vincent J., USA (Ret.), chief ed., *The West Pont Atlas of the American Wars*, 2 vols. New York, NY: Frederick A. Praeger, Publishers, 1959.

Evans, Charles M., *War of the Aeronauts: A History of Military Ballooning in the Civil War*. Mechanicsburg, PA: Stackpole Books, 2002.

Fishel, Edwin C., *The Secret War for the Union: The Untold Story of Military Intelligence in the Civil War*. Boston and New York, NY: Houghton Mifflin Company, 1996.

Fitzgerald, Ruth Coder, *A Different Story: A Black History of Fredericksburg, Stafford, and Spotsylvania, Virginia*. Fredericksburg, VA: Unicorn, 1979.

Fleming, Thomas, *Washington's Secret War: The Hidden History of Valley Forge*. New York, NY: Smithsonian Books, an Imprint of HarperCollins Publishers, 2005.

Fletcher, George P., *Our Secret Constitution: How Lincoln Redefined American Democracy*. Oxford, UK, and New York, NY: Oxford University Press, 2001.

Foner, Eric, *Reconstruction: America's Unfinished Revolution: 1863-1877*. New York, NY: Harper & Row, Publishers, 1988.

Goolrick, John T., *The Story of Stafford: A Narrative History of Stafford County, Virginia*. Stafford County, VA: Board of Supervisors and Bicentennial Commission, 1976.

Goolrick, William K., *Rebels Resurgent: Fredericksburg to Chancellorsville*. Alexandria, VA: Time-Life Books, 1985.

Hagerman, Edward, *The American Civil War and the Origins of Modern Warfare: Ideas, Organization, and Field Command*. Bloomington and Indianapolis, IN: Indiana University Press, 1992.

Hanson, Raus McDill, *Virginia Place Names: Derivations and Historical Uses*. Verona, VA: McClure Press, 1969.

Harrison, Noel G., "In the Wake of December's Disaster: Photography after the First Battle of Fredericksburg," in *Fredericksburg History and Biography*. Fredericksburg, VA: Central Virginia Battlefields Trust, Volume No. 8, 2009.

Haydon, F. Stansbury, *Military Ballooning during the Early Civil War*. Baltimore, MD: Johns Hopkins University Press, 2000.

Hebert, Walter H., *Fighting Joe Hooker*. Indianapolis, IN, and New York, NY: The Bobbs-Merrill Company, Publishers, 1944.

Hennessy, John J., "We Shall Make Richmond Howl: The Army of the Potomac on the Eve of Chancellorsville," in Gary W. Gallagher, ed., *Chancellorsville: The Battle and Its Aftermath*. Chapel Hill, NC, and London, UK: The University of North Carolina Press, 1996.

Holzer, Harold, "A Promise Fulfilled," in *Civil War Times Illustrated*, December 2009, 28-35.

Jordan Jr., Ervin L., *Black Confederates and Afro-Yankees in Civil War Virginia*. Charlottesville, VA: University Press of Virginia, 1995.

Kunhardt III, Philip B., Peter W. Kunhardt, and Peter W. Kunhardt Jr, *Looking For Lincoln: The Making of an American Icon*. New York, NY: Alfred A. Knopf, 2008.

Longacre, Edward G., *Fitz Lee: A Military Biography of Major General Fitzhugh Lee, C.S.A.* Cambridge, MA: DeCapo Press, 2005.

Lonn, Ella, *Desertion During the Civil War*. Lincoln, NE, and London, UK: University of Nebraska Press, 1998.

Lowry, Thomas P., M. D., *Sex in the Civil War: The Story the Soldiers Wouldn't Tell*. Mechanicsburg, PA: Stackpole Books, 1994.

Manning, Chandra, *What This Cruel War Was Over: Soldiers, Slavery and the Civil War*. New York, NY: Alfred A. Knopf, 2007.

Marszalek, John F., *Commander of All Lincoln's Armies: a Life of General Henry W. Halleck*. Cambridge, MA, and London, UK: The Belknap Press of Harvard University Press, 2004.

McCaslin, Richard B., *Lee in the Shadow of Washington*. Baton Rouge, LA: Louisiana State University Press, 2001.

McPherson, James M., *Tried By War: Abraham Lincoln as Commander in Chief*. New York, NY: The Penguin Press, 2008.

———. *For Cause and Comrades: Why Men Fought in the Civil War*. Oxford, UK, and New York, NY: Oxford University Press, 1997.

———. *This Mighty Scourge: Perspectives on the Civil War*. Oxford, UK, and New York, NY: Oxford University Press, 2007,

Miller, Richard F., *Harvard's Civil War: A History of the Twentieth Massachusetts Volunteer Infantry*. Hanover and London, NY: University Press of New England, 2005.

Musselman, Homer D., *Stafford County in the Civil War*. Lynchburg, VA: H. E. Howard, 1995.

———. comp., *Stafford County, Virginia: Veterans and Cemeteries*. Fredericksburg, VA: Bookcrafters, 1994.

Nevins, Allan, *The War for the Union: War Becomes Revolution 1862-1863*. New York, NY: Charles Scribner's Sons, 1960, Volume II.

Newman, Ralph and E. B. Long, *The Civil War*. New York, NY: Grosset & Dunlap, 1956.

Nolan, Alan T., *The Iron Brigade: A Military History*. Bloomington, IN: Indiana University Press, 1994.

O'Reilly, Francis A., *The Fredericksburg Campaign, Winter War of the Rappahannock*. Baton Rouge, LA: Louisiana University Press, 2003.

Palmer, Brigadier General John McAuley Palmer, U. S. A. (Retired), *America in Arms*. New Haven, CT: Yale University Press, 1941.

Phisterer, Frederick, *Statistical Record of the Armies of the United States*. Edison, NJ: Castle Books, 2002.

———. *New York in the War of the Rebellion*. Albany, NY: J. B. Lyon Company, 1912, third edition.

Poirier, Robert G., *By the Blood of Our Alumni: Norwich University Citizen Soldiers in the Army of the Potomac*. Mason City, IA: Savas Publishing, 1999.

———. *They Could Not Have Done Better: Thomas O. Seaver and the 3rd Vermont Infantry in the War for the Union*. Newport, VT: Tony O'Conner Civil War Enterprises, 2005.

Rable, George C., *Fredericksburg! Fredericksburg!* Chapel Hill, NC, and London, UK: The University of North Carolina Press, 2002.

Randall, N. J. G. and David Donald, *The Civil War and Reconstruction*. Boston, MA: D. C. Heath and Company, 1961.

Rhodes, Captain Charles D., General Staff, U. S. A., "The Mounting and Remounting of the Federal Cavalry," in Francis Trevelyan Miller, ed.-in-chief, *The Photographic History of the Civil War*, Part Four: "The Cavalry," 1911.

Sandburg, Carl, *Abraham Lincoln: The War Years*. New York, NY: Harcourt, Brace and World, 1939.

Shannon, Fred A., "The Life of the Common Soldier in the Union Army, 1861-1865," in Michael Barton and Larry M. Logue, ed., *The Civil War Soldier: A Historical Reader*. New York, NY: New York University Press, 2002; original article published in March 1927 in the *Mississippi Valley Historical Review* 13, No. 4; pp 465-482.

Smith, Stuart W., ed., *Douglas Southall Freeman on Leadership*. Newport, RI: Naval War College Press, 1990.

Stanco, William, "President Lincoln & Congress during the Civil War," in *The Capitol Dome, Newsletter of the United States Capitol Historical Society*, Volume 46, No. 1 Spring 2009, 25-30.

Strauss, William and Neil Howe, *Generations: The History of America's Future*. New York, NY: William Morrow and Company, 1991.

Taaffe, Stephen A., *Commanding the Army of the Potomac*. Lawrence, KS: University Press of Kansas, 2006.

Tidwell, William A., James O. Hall, and David W. Gaddy, *Come Retribution: The Confederate Secret Service and the Assassination of Abraham Lincoln*. Baton Rouge, LA: Louisiana State University Press, 1988.

Tidwell, William A., *April '65: Confederate Covert Action in the American Civil War*. Kent, OH: Kent State University Press, 1995.

Time-Life Editors, *Spies Scouts and Raiders: Irregular Operations*. Alexandria, VA: Time-Life Books' *The Civil War* Series, 1985.

Wagner, Margaret E., Gary W. Gallagher, and Paul Finkelman, ed., *Library of Congress Civil War Desk Reference*. New York, NY: Simon and Schuster, 2002.

Warner, Ezra J., *Generals in Blue: Lives of the Union Commanders*. Baton Rouge, LA: Louisiana State University Press, 1992.

Weber, Jennifer L., *Copperheads: The Rise and Fall of Lincoln's Opponents in the North*. Oxford, UK, and New York, NY: Oxford University Press, 2006.

Wert, Jeffry D., *The Sword of Lincoln: The Army of the Potomac*. New York, NY, and London, UK: Simon and Schuster, 2005.

Wheeler, Richard, *Voices of the Civil War*. New York, NY: Penguin Books, 1976.

Williams, T. Harry, *Lincoln and His Generals*. New York, NY: Alfred A. Knopf, 1952.

Wittenberg, Eric J., *Rush's Lancers: The Sixth Pennsylvania Cavalry in the Civil War*. Yardley, PA: Westholme Publishing, 2007.

———. *The Union Cavalry Comes of Age: Hartwood Church to Brandy Station, 1863*. Washington DC: Potomac Books, Inc., 2003.

Woodward, C. Vann, *The Strange Career of Jim Crow*. Oxford, UK and New York, NY: Oxford University Press, 2002.

Woodworth, Steven E., *While God Is Marching On: The Religious World of Civil War Soldiers*. Lawrence, KS: University Press of Kansas, 2001.

Automated Data Base

National Park Service, Civil War Soldiers and Sailors System, which can be found at http://www.civilwar.nps.gov/cwss/soldiers.cfm

Index

Albert Z. Conner Jr., a graduate of the Virginia Military Institute (VMI) and Georgetown University, is a Vietnam infantry combat veteran and career intelligence officer. He has worked as a military historian since 1995. Al developed his unique knowledge and analytical skills by studying the armed forces of several nations (including our own). He has widely published on many aspects of military history.

Al is a former president of the Fredericksburg Civil War Roundtable and Stafford County Historical Society, advisory board member of the Adams '71 Center for Military History and Strategic Analysis at VMI, and a volunteer with the Fredericksburg and Spotsylvania National Military Park. He lives in Stafford, VA, the scene of this remarkable story.

Chris Mackowski, Ph.D., is a professor in the School of Journalism and Mass Communication at St. Bonaventure University in Allegany, NY, and worked as a historian with the National Park Service at Fredericksburg and Spotsylvania National Military Park, where he leads tours of the major Civil War battlefields there. He is the author of many books, including (with Kris White) *Chancellorsville's Forgotten Front: The Battles of Second Fredericksburg and Salem Church, May 3, 1863* (Savas Beatie, 2013) and *Grant's Last Battle: The Story Behind the Personal Memoirs of Ulysses S. Grant* (Savas Beatie, 2015).

Chris is the co-founder (with Kris White) of the popular Emerging Civil War blog, and the Emerging Civil War series of books, in conjunction with Savas Beatie. Chris lives with his wife in Fredericksburg.